THE LIBRARY
NATIONAL FOUNDATION FOR
EDUCATIONAL RESEARCH

DATE:
18-8-98

CLASS:
WAK     OLS

ACCN. NO:
30699

AUTHOR:
OLSON, D.R.

# LITERACY AND ORALITY

# LITERACY AND ORALITY

*Edited by*
David R. Olson
and
Nancy Torrance

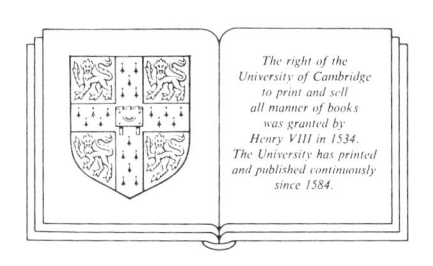

CAMBRIDGE UNIVERSITY PRESS
CAMBRIDGE
NEW YORK   PORT CHESTER   MELBOURNE   SYDNEY

Published by the Press Syndicate of the University of Cambridge
The Pitt Building, Trumpington Street, Cambridge, CB2 1RP
40 West 20th Street, New York, NY 10011, USA
10 Stamford Road, Oakleigh, Melbourne, 3166, Australia

© Cambridge University Press 1991

First published 1991

Printed in the United States of America

*Library of Congress Cataloging-in-Publication Data*
Literacy and orality / David R. Olson and Nancy Torrance (eds.).
p. cm.
Papers presented at a conference held June 1987.
ISBN 0-521-39217-9. – ISBN 0-521-39850-9 (pbk.)
1. Written communication – Congresses.  2. Literacy – Congresses.
3. Oral communication – Congresses.  4. Cognition – Congresses.
I. Olson, David R.  II. Torrance, Nancy.
P211.L725    1991                                          90-1692
302.2'244 – dc20                                              CIP

*British Library Cataloging in Publication Data*
Literacy and orality.
1. Written communication compared with oral communicaton
I. Olson, David R.  II. Torrance, Nancy
302.224

ISBN 0-521-39217-9 hardback
ISBN 0-521-39850-9 paperback

This volume is dedicated to the memory
of Eric Havelock,
1903–1988

# Contents

| | |
|---|---|
| *Contributors* | *page* ix |
| *Preface* | xi |
| Introduction<br>DAVID R. OLSON AND NANCY TORRANCE | 1 |

### Part I  Oral and literate aspects of culture and cognition

| | | |
|---|---|---|
| 1 | The oral–literature equation: a formula for the modern mind<br>ERIC HAVELOCK | 11 |
| 2 | A plea for research on lay literacy<br>IVAN ILLICH | 28 |
| 3 | Oral metalanguage<br>CAROL FLEISCHER FELDMAN | 47 |
| 4 | Rational thought in oral culture and literate decontextualization<br>J. PETER DENNY | 66 |
| 5 | Cree literacy in the syllabic script<br>JO ANNE BENNETT AND JOHN W. BERRY | 90 |
| 6 | Literacy: an instrument of oppression<br>D. P. PATTANAYAK | 105 |

### Part II  Oral and literate forms of discourse

| | | |
|---|---|---|
| 7 | Lie it as it plays: Chaucer becomes an author<br>BARRY SANDERS | 111 |
| 8 | The invention of self: autobiography and its forms<br>JEROME BRUNER AND SUSAN WEISSER | 129 |
| 9 | Literacy and objectivity: the rise of modern science<br>DAVID R. OLSON | 149 |

10  Thinking through literacies                                    165
    JEFFREY KITTAY

### III  Oral and literate aspects of cognition

11  Literacy: its characterization and implications                177
    R. NARASIMHAN
12  The separation of words and the physiology of reading          198
    PAUL SAENGER
13  Linguists, literacy, and the intensionality of Marshall
    McLuhan's Western man                                          215
    ROBERT J. SCHOLES AND BRENDA J. WILLIS
14  A neurological point of view on social alexia                  236
    ANDRÉ ROCH LECOURS AND MARIA ALICE PARENTE
15  Literacy as metalinguistic activity                            251
    DAVID R. OLSON

*Author index*                                                     271
*Subject index*                                                    276

# Contributors

JO ANNE BENNETT, Department of Psychology, Queen's University, Kingston

JOHN W. BERRY, Department of Psychology, Queen's University, Kingston

JEROME BRUNER, New York University, New York

J. PETER DENNY, Department of Psychology, University of Western Ontario, London, Ontario

CAROL FLEISHER FELDMAN, Department of Psychology, New York University, New York

ERIC HAVELOCK, Sterling Professor Emeritus at Yale University until his death in 1988

IVAN ILLICH, Technology and Society Program, University of Pennsylvania, Philadelphia

JEFFREY KITTAY, Visiting Scholar, Department of French, New York University, New York, and publisher of *Lingua Franca, the Review of Academic Life*

ANDRÉ ROCH LECOURS, Faculté de Médecine, Université de Montréal, and Directeur, Laboratoire Théophile-Alajouanine, Centre de recherche du Centre Hospitalier Côte-des-Neiges, Montreal

R. NARASIMHAN, Tata Institute of Fundamental Research, Bombay

DAVID R. OLSON, Centre for Applied Cognitive Science, Ontario Institute for Studies in Education, Toronto

MARIA ALICE PARENTE, Department of Speech Pathology, Faculty of Medicine, University of São Paulo, Brazil, and Laboratoire Théophile-Alajouanine, Centre de recherche du Centre Hospitalier Côte-des-Neiges, Montreal

D. P. PATTANAYAK, Central Institute of Indian Languages, Ministry of Education and Culture, India

PAUL SAENGER, Newberry Library, Chicago

BARRY SANDERS, Peter and Gloria Gold Professor of English and the History of Ideas, Pitzer College, Claremont, California

ROBERT J. SCHOLES, Institute for the Advanced Study of Communication Processes, Department of Speech and Program in Linguistics, University of Florida, Gainesville

NANCY TORRANCE, Centre for Applied Cognitive Science, Ontario Institute for Studies in Education, Toronto

SUSAN WEISSER, Department of English, Adelphi University, New York

BRENDA J. WILLIS, Division of Communication, Central Florida Community College

# Preface

This volume grew out of a conference held in June 1987 under the joint auspices of the McLuhan Program at the University of Toronto and the International Institute for Semiotics and Structural Studies and was sponsored by a grant from the Social Science and Humanities Research Council of Canada. The conference was extremely well attended, with some two hundred people participating in the sessions over a three-day period.

We regret that three of the papers presented at the conference do not appear in this volume, nor do any of the discussion papers. Brian Stock of the Pontifical Institute of Medieval Studies, St. Michael's College, discussed the ways in which the written word came during the Middle Ages to provide abstract, intellectualized models in terms of which any event, including one's own internal experiences, could be interpreted and judged. Jacques Derrida, Ecole normale de France, contrasted two views of interpretation that continue to be central to our modern understanding of texts: that of Spinoza, who claimed that meaning was independent of outward verbal form and could, therefore, be translated from one language to another without loss of meaning, and that of Gershom Scholem, a modern Jewish mystic who claimed that meaning or content is tied to verbal form such that any change in that form involves a change in meaning. Manfred Bierwisch, Max-Planck Institute for Psycholinguistics, discussed the basic structural similarities between speech and writing, similarities that led him to conclude, with Saussure, that writing is simply a record of speech and of minor linguistic or cognitive significance, a view that conflicted with, but also helped to clarify, the views of many other participants.

During the conference, tape recordings of interviews with the conference participants were made and edited by David Cayley of the Canadian Broadcasting Corporation for public broadcast. The transcripts from these interviews are available for seven dollars from CBC Transcripts, Box 6400, Station "A," Montreal, Quebec H3C 3L4, Canada.

No matter how brilliant the contributors to a volume such as this, an incredible amount of hard work is required for its production. We would like to express our sincere thanks to Marie McMullin for her supervision of these activities and to Susan Milmoe, Helen Wheeler, and Laura Dobbins of Cambridge University Press for their help and advice.

While we were editing his chapter for this volume, news of the death of Eric Havelock reached us. He was among the first to recognize that writing contributed to changing patterns of social organization, to a new awareness of language and mind, and to the kind of introspective reflectiveness that we "moderns" take for granted. He was an original thinker and a founding figure in the study of orality and literacy, and we are pleased to dedicate this volume to his memory.

# Introduction

DAVID R. OLSON and NANCY TORRANCE

This volume is a continuation of the line of research and thinking that we set out in our earlier book, *Literacy, Language and Learning,* as follows:

The effects of literacy on intellectual and social change are not straightforward. . . . it is misleading to think of literacy in terms of consequences. What matters is what people do with literacy, not what literacy does to people. Literacy does not cause a new mode of thought, but having a written record may permit people to do something they could not do before – such as look back, study, re-interpret, and so on. Similarly, literacy does not cause social change, modernization, or industrialization. But being able to read and write may be vital to playing certain roles in an industrial society and completely irrelevant to other roles in a traditional society. Literacy is important for what it permits people to do – to achieve their goals or to bring new goals into view. (Olson, Hildyard, & Torrance, 1985, p. 14)

While the earlier volume showed some of the ways that literacy came to serve a variety of functions in a literate society, the present one shows how those functions are related to those served by orality in traditional cultures and how, in literate societies, oral discourse surrounds and conditions the uses of written texts. Oral discourse is often about archival written texts, about how to go about consulting them, interpreting them, criticizing them, paraphrasing them, and finally, creating them, always for some purpose. It is this oral discourse about written texts that provides such fertile ground for modern, skeptical, interpretive thought.

In Part I, Eric Havelock, Ivan Illich, Carol Feldman, Peter Denny, Jo Anne Bennett and John Berry, and D. P. Pattanayak examine from a cultural-historical perspective the rise of literacy, its uses and its consequences for modern society. The chapters show that the functions sometimes assigned to literacy are often served, in nonliterate societies, by oral forms of great subtlety and power. Literacy plays into and alters these forms particularly by extending the set of devices for turning texts into objects of discourse. In the process, the attitudes to self, knowledge, and society that we in modern times take to be universals in human nature may be seen as products of an evolving literate tradition.

Beginning this section, Eric Havelock traces the history of the orality–literacy hypothesis beginning with the work of Parry and Lord and through the simultaneous developments in the writings of McLuhan, Ong, Goody and Watt, and himself working in the late 1950s and early 1960s. He discusses the pivotal insight that verse is a product of orality, which in order to be preserved, exploits the resources of the ear, while prose is a product of literacy "freed from the constraints of memorization." It is the evolution of the form of discourse we know as written prose that is critical for the development of modern, Western forms of thought including science, philosophy, and justice. He traces these linguistic and conceptual changes to the invention of an unambiguous writing system, the Greek alphabet, and examines the significance of the two resulting forms of thought, orality and literacy, in contemporary life.

Ivan Illich differentiates "scribal literacy," the ability to read and write, from "lay literacy," the set of pervasive competencies and the knowledge that is required to participate in a literate society. Not only are these pervasive attitudes and beliefs essentially part of the "oral culture," they are so pervasive in a literate society that they are sometimes mistaken for universals of human culture. Illich traces in detail the invention of literate practices in the early Middle Ages and their role in the evolution of our contemporary notions of self and society, and he urges renewed attempts to uncover and, where necessary, debunk our "certainties" about literacy and modernity.

Carol Feldman argues against the "general claim" that writing and the spread of literacy have given rise to the particular forms of consciousness found in modern Western thought. Like Bruner, she argues that the say–mean or text–interpretation distinction cannot be unique to literate cultures, but is rather a universal aspect of language. As evidence, she notes the distinctive registers or genres found in oral discourse in "traditional" societies in which speakers use special types of discourse and particular interpretive assumptions for dealing with different kinds of discourse, such as oratory and ritualized speech. Using examples from the Wana of Indonesia, she argues that many oral cultures do have oral genres of text and interpretation and, moreover, that those cultures show the same preoccupation with the nature of interpretation as does Western philosophy.

Peter Denny considers the evidence on the effects of literacy on human cognition and discusses the various claims made to account for differences between literate and oral societies, such as that literate Western thought is more reflective, more abstract, more complex, and more logical than thought in preliterate societies. He then describes current research that shows that for the most part, these claims are wrong. He finds, however, that Western thought has one distinctive property absent in preliterate hunter-gatherer societies and nearly absent in agriculturalist societies, namely the greater tendency for decontextualization. He shows that this is the case by systematizing the cross-cultural and historical evidence along two dimensions, contextualization and differentiation. He finds that as societies evolved from hunter-gatherer through agriculturist to industrialist, there is a steady decrease in the tendency to make connections *between* thought units, whereas the tendency to make distinctions *within* a thought unit is high initially, decreases with the rise of agriculturalist societies, and then increases again with industrialization. While he sees these changes as a result of increasing population within a cultural group, he supports the notion of literacy as amplifying the contextualization that began in classical Greece.

Jo Anne Bennett and John Berry describe the rapid and nearly universal spread of a syllabic writing system among the previously nonliterate Cree. They suggest that the spread of Cree writing was due to a number of factors, particularly the simplicity of the writing system itself, which involves fewer than a dozen symbols, and the importance of the social functions served by letter writing in Cree society. They note that as those functions, largely to do with interpersonal communication, are taken over by the telephone, the indigenous Cree literacy tends to wane. English literacy, perpetuated by the schools and serving a variety of social and institutional functions, tends to persist and becomes even more pervasive.

D. P. Pattanayak has pointed out that four features may in different ways be used to characterize an oral culture. In oral societies, there are texts fixed through memorization, there are institutions such as ritual and oratorical contexts in which those texts are used, there are procedures for inculcating members into the use of those texts, and there are ways for talking about, explaining, and referring to those texts.

Part II of the book includes chapters by Barry Sanders, Jerome Bruner and Susan Weisser, David Olson, and Jeffrey Kittay and is concerned with the evolution of specialized forms of discourse functioning as modes of reflection in the Early Modern period.

Barry Sanders describes Chaucer's *Canterbury Tales* as the first true fiction, tracing the development of the joke in "The Miller's Tale" to an elaborate interplay between orality and literacy. Chaucer has created a fictional world that, to be fully appreciated, must be read as if it were an oral joke. Sanders argues that Chaucer has taken an oral form, the joke, and analyzed and reshaped that form in literacy to produce the first piece of true fiction. To understand the intricacies of "The Miller's Tale" fully, it must be *read,* and to appreciate its spirit fully, the storyteller's joke must also be *heard.* Hence the reader becomes the author's audience for the first time in history. For Sanders, the invention of fiction and the notion of author are part of the development of a literate tradition.

Jerome Bruner and Susan Weisser examine the development of techniques for self-report, noting how the adult autobiographical style emerges as the functions and conventions of self-report change. While acknowledging literacy as an instrument of change toward modernity, they argue that the primary determinant of the modern mind is nevertheless the historical transformation of self-consciousness. This emerging style of self-report enables individuals to textualize their own lives, and thereby subject them to interpretation and reinterpretation. The authors conclude that the impact of literacy was to hasten the change to a more self-conscious form of self-accounting as did other historical factors marking the end of the Middle Ages. The primary determinant of modern thought, however, is to be found in the inherent universal structures of thought and language, including those devices for distinguishing one from the other. It is the rise of genres for autobiography that enable the individual to formulate and reformulate the earliest and most elementary of theories, those regarding the self. Not only do such autobiographies report a self, they construct a self; one may "represent" oneself in a particular way and then attempt to live up to it, a practice Brian Stock (1983) informs us began with the monastic tradition.

David Olson considers two views as to how literacy contributed to the rise of early modern science. The instrumental view, which he credits to Eisenstein, suggests that the printing press was a decisive factor in that it made possible an "archival research tradition" and placed an "original" copy of texts, free of copyist errors, in the hands of every scholar. The conceptual-change view, a view Olson shares with Scholes and Willis (Chapter 13, this volume), suggests that literacy was responsible for a new understanding of the distinction between the objectively "given," whether in texts or in nature, and the subjective perceptions and interpretations of the reader. It was this conceptual distinction, he argues, that was basic to the rise of early modern science.

In the final chapter of Part II, Jeffrey Kittay advocates a consideration of literacy within a broader description of communication than is typically assumed in the literature. Accordingly, he takes a view of literacy as much more than the encoding and decoding of oral language. Rather, literacy is, as he says, a "signifying practice," more general than a genre and containing various forms of communication. As a signifying practice, literacy may be contrasted with orality. He discusses two major issues that arise from the literacy hypothesis. First is the issue of writing as *decontextualized,* the problem not only of whether in writing one can make all aspects of the communication explicit, but also of whether it is appropriate to make every aspect explicit. Second is the issue of *universality* of effect, the problem of whether all cultures with writing would be cognitively similar or, as he suggests, cognitively innovative in different ways depending on other cultural aspects, such as a relative openness to new ways of communicating and/or physical aspects of the materials and orthography under investigation.

In Part III of this volume, R. Narasimhan, Paul Saenger, Robert Scholes and Brenda Willis, Roch Lecours and Maria Parente, and David Olson examine the issue of literacy and language from a psychological perspective. The authors here consider the psychology of literacy and its acquisition.

Narasimhan criticizes aspects of the literacy hypothesis that emphasize the consequences of alphabetic literacy in post-Homeric Greece, of script literacy in Western European culture, and of textual literacy in triggering the growth of empirical scientific culture in postmedieval Europe. He proposes a broader framework for understanding literacy by relating it to reflective behavior based on the use of natural language and underpinned by various technologies, and then considers the cognitive implications of such a framework. The Western European experience is contrasted with the oral tradition in India, and the relationships between the specific and more general consequences of literacy are discussed in terms of institutional and technological feedbacks.

Paul Saenger examines the ways in which the form of the writing system determines the mental skills relevant to reading. He points out that while syllabic scripts such as Hebrew have used word separation since antiquity, alphabetic scripts (Greek and Latin) abandoned the use of word spaces in the early centuries A.D. only to reintroduce them beginning in the eighth century. He suggests that the abandonment of word spaces was a consequence of the fact that there was no need for rapid word identification as (1) texts were read aloud, (2) reading was from a limited corpus of texts, and (3) reading was done by only a restricted class, often professional readers. When these factors no longer held, word spacing was reimposed and spread from the British Isles through all alphabetic scripts. Silent reading, he suggests, constitutes the great divide in the history of reading, separating antiquity from modern cultures. It offered a number of intellectual advantages, including rapid reading and scanning of text, activities that subordinate the text to the goals, intentions, and interpretations of the reader. Some of these advantages are examined in the chapters by Kittay and Illich.

Robert Scholes and Brenda Willis argue that linguists have for the most part failed to consider the effects of becoming literate on a speaker's knowledge of the language. They present research on the metalinguistic performance of literate and nonliterate adults that indicates that some phonological, morphological, and syntactic elements ascribed to the grammar of all native-language speakers are available consciously only to those who also read the language. As a result of this research, they posit two levels of linguistic knowledge, reflecting an intensional–extensional dichotomy. Whereas the linguistic knowledge of nonliterate adults is predominantly extensional in nature, that is, the features in consciousness are those that are related to nonlinguistic properties of objects and features of objects in the world, the linguistic knowledge of literate adults also includes consciousness of purely linguistic features. Their extensional–intensional hypothesis is somewhat similar to Olson's metalinguistic hypothesis as an explanation for the implications of literacy.

Roch Lecours and Maria Parente present and discuss research on the cerebral representation of language in nonliterate adults. They consider the notion that some influence is exerted by written language learning on the functional lateralization of language to the left hemisphere of the brain for the majority of people. They present research in which literate and nonliterate, healthy and brain-damaged subjects are compared on their performances on matching, repetition, and naming tests for aphasiology. Finding no differences in the incidence of aphasia between nonliterate and literate subjects with left-brain damage, they confirm the previously held view that left cerebral dominance for language does not depend primarily on literacy. However, their finding of differences in naming ability between right-brain-damaged nonliterates and neurologically healthy nonliterates, a difference that does not occur in literates, leads them to conclude that left cerebral dominance for language may be less exclusive among nonliterates than among schooled individuals.

David Olson examines some of the possible ways in which the availability of a writing system could alter cognitive processes. He considers four possibilities, which he refers to as the modality, the medium, the mental skills, and the metalinguistic hypotheses. Of these, the metalinguistic hypothesis is not only the most promising avenue toward explaining the intellectual advantages of literacy but, in addition, can incorporate the insights offered by the first three hypotheses. The metalinguistic hypothesis he offers is that writing per se is a metalinguistic activity. Just as speech represents the world and thereby makes the world an object of reflection, so writing represents speech and thereby makes speech an object of reflection. Writing has its advantage through exploiting the relations between these two levels of awareness, a point made by Saenger.

In the attempt to chart the relations between literacy and orality, we contrast two perspectives. On the one hand, the "continuity theory" argues that orality and literacy are essentially equivalent linguistic means for carrying out similar functions. Psychologically their differences are not important, and yet because of their material differences, they may be put to somewhat different ends. Writing is readily preserved through time and space and hence is instrumental to such activities as constructing an "accumulative archival tradition" and to private and silent Bible study (Eisenstein, 1979). The role of literacy is more social and institutional than it is psychological or linguistic.

The "great-divide theory," on the other hand, argues that orality and literacy, while importantly interactive, really do, after all, allow old functions to be served in new ways and to bring new functions into view. In so doing, they realign psychological processes and social organization. On this view, literacy in Western societies has been an engine of social and psychological change.

Both views, however, have shed the ethnocentrism implicit in earlier views that have seen literacy as the "royal road" to enlightenment and modernity. Even if literacy plays an important role in carrying out a set of functions such as those of government, justice, theology, philosophy, and literature, it is a means that is embedded in rich oral practice and oral culture. While the competencies involved are inevitably specializations of those that are part of the mental and linguistic resources of every individual, it is the responsibility of education to build upon and expand those resources both through literacy and through oral discourse about written texts.

### REFERENCES

Eisenstein, E. (1979). *The printing press as an agent of change.* Cambridge University Press.
Olson, D. R., Hildyard, A., & Torrance, N. (1985). *Literacy, language, and learning: The nature and consequences of reading and writing.* Cambridge University Press.

# PART I
Oral and literate aspects of culture and cognition

# 1

## The oral–literate equation: a formula for the modern mind

ERIC HAVELOCK

Going back twenty years, or even less, I do not think that the program of a colloquium of distinguished scholars from five countries would have carried the title "Orality and Literacy." To be sure, phrases like "oral formula" and "oral composition" in connection with Homer had come into currency at Harvard about the time, just after the Second World War, when I joined the faculty. This was because of the close connection of Milman Parry and Albert Lord with that university. Even then, as I recollect, the application of these terms was still met with strong resistance from conservative scholars. Today, the nouns *orality* and *oralism* are on a different footing, symbolizing conceptions that have extended far beyond Homer and the Greeks. They characterize whole societies that have relied on oral communication without the use of writing. They also seek to identify a given type of language used in oral communication. And finally, they are used to identify a given type of consciousness, which is supposed to be created by orality or expressible in orality.

These conceptions take shape as they are focused against literacy, considered also as both a social condition and a state of mind, with its own levels of language and cognition expressible in writing. The two, orality and literacy, are sharpened and focused against each other, yet can be seen as still interwoven in our own society. It is of course, a mistake to polarize these as mutually exclusive. Their relationship is one of mutual, creative tension, one that has both a historical dimension – as literate societies have emerged out of oralist ones – and a contemporary one – as we seek a deeper understanding of what literacy may mean to us as it is superimposed on an orality into which we were born and which governs so much of the normal give and take of daily life. The tension can sometimes be perceived as pulling one way in favor of a restored orality and then the other way in favor of replacing it altogether by a sophisticated literacy.

## The breakthrough: 1962-3

Twenty-five years ago, within the space of less than twelve months there appeared four publications that, in retrospect, can be said to have made a joint announcement: that orality (or oralism) had to be put on the map. As a subject of intellectual interest, its time was arriving. These works were *The Gutenberg Galaxy* by McLuhan (1962), *La pensée sauvage* by Lévi-Strauss (1962), an article by Jack Goody and Ian Watt entitled "The Consequences of Literacy" (1963), and finally *Preface to Plato*, by myself (1963). No one of these writers so far as I know was in communication with any of the others (though Watt and I had shared some oral communication in this connection many years before). Was this grouping as it occurred a pure accident or did it reflect a common and widespread response, even if an unconscious one, in France, England, the United States, and Canada, to a shared experience of a technological revolution in the means of human communication? Radio, not to mention its immediate predecessor, the telephone, and its successor, television, was transforming the reach of the spoken, that is, of the oral, word. For McLuhan, the revolution was a fact of life, now fully acknowledged. It is fitting that we remember him today. He made orality the subject of ongoing investigation in scores of institutes and departments of universities devoted to the study of communications technology.

For Lévi-Strauss, the focus was on myths of the past, not technologies of the present, and he often tended to use textual terms, not oral ones, to describe the bipolar structures that he perceived in tribal myths, tempting his reader to see an almost literate consciousness at work under purely oralist conditions. But the word *"sauvage"* in his title gives the case away. It betrays his deep conviction that the thought patterns as perceived in these mythologies were primitive, that is, preliterate. The implication is there, though it is not a factor that he stresses. As for *Preface to Plato*, as the title indicates, the oralist issue was raised solely in connection with the ancient Greeks, though the track being followed here was quickly perceived by McLuhan as relevant to his own work and generously acknowledged.

I select for mention the concurrent appearance of these four works only because they seem to mark a watershed that had been reached, or perhaps more accurately they point to a dam starting to burst, releasing a flood of intellectual activity devoted to the explanation of what I have called the oral–literate equation. Readers of Walter Ong's *Orality and Literacy* (1982) who consult the extensive bibliography of that work will notice the meager list of relevant publications in this field preceding 1962 and the flood that then sets in in the years following.

## The precedents

But first it is fitting to cast a backward glance at some things that happened before 1962. There were pioneers before McLuhan who scarcely knew at the time that they were, or might have been, so regarded. Let me select five. I have already mentioned Milman Parry. His doctoral thesis, *L'Epithète traditionelle dans Homère,* was the founding document of the modern Homeric oralist theory of composition. It was published in Paris in 1928 (Parry, 1971). After Parry, the oral–literate question (as it was later to become) received impetus from a very unexpected quarter when Harold Innis published *The Bias of Communication* (1951). It was perhaps characteristic of the times that France, the country of Meillet, and that body of linguistic theory associated with his name should have been the one that drew Parry to study there and proved hospitable to him, many years before Parry's view of the Homeric language gained any currency either in his native country or in Great Britain. One may add a footnote: Those who study the bibliography of the scholarship that has either explored or alluded to the relationship between the spoken and the written word – to the book text and the word behind the text – will be struck by the central role played in this area by French scholars. As I have said, by the years 1946–7, Parry's thesis, reinforced by articles subsequently published in the Harvard Studies in Classical Philology, was gaining notice at Harvard, and his pupil Albert Lord was able to begin giving recordings of performances of the Balkan material Parry had collected, some of which I heard myself. If we are guided by the chronology of published books, the comparative conclusions to be drawn – as between Homer and surviving modes of oral composition – were finally put together in Lord's *The Singer of Tales* (1960). Lord's work extended these studies to cover thematic as well as formulaic patterns in epic composition.

Innis was an economist of conservative leanings, known for his exhaustive studies of the nature and structure of the Canadian transportation system, which, as I understand it, remain classics in their field. What, we may ask, induced him in a few short years at the close of his life to transfer his attention to the history of communication technologies and their social and cultural effects, ranging all the way from the ancient kingdoms of Mesopotamia to the present day? Surely for one whose professional career had been spent upon the niceties of economic measurement and management, this intrusion late in life of a quite different preoccupation will seem unusual. Yet it had roots that are understandable when it is recalled that Innis had also turned his attention to the economics of the pulp and paper industry, observing its function of turning trees into newsprint, feeding the voracity of the modern press. That voracity had been rendered possible by an advance in the technology of printing: The flatbed press was superseded by the roller press, resulting in a quantitative jump in the production of the means of mass communication. He saw the forests of his native land converted into a moment's reading on a New York subway.

Recalling his own upbringing in a small town, where communication besides being personal was economical, unhurried, and to a degree reflective, he leapt to the conclusion that the mass media of modernity did not give modern man time to think. Instant news robbed him of historical sense, to look backward, and of the power to look forward, to envisage a probable future of consequences that follow from present decisions. This was the bias of modern mass communication. The technology itself encouraged a state of mind that he regretted.

He set himself the historical task of pursuing the ways in which previous technologies of the word had worked to produce their corresponding social and cognitive effects. It was here that he linked up with the issue of oralism as opposed to literacy although he avoided any simple dichotomy between them. One detects in his work a thread of preference – I will call it romantic – for certain advantages that the oral word might have over the written, certainly as printed.

He drew some support from the Homeric model provided by Parry, which tempts me to add a brief personal note. Innis and I had known each other for some years, not intimately, but with mutual regard. During the summer of 1943 I read Parry's work – I should have read it earlier – and later gave one or two public lectures on Homer and oral composition at the University of Toronto. Innis came to hear them and at once connected what I was saying with what he had been contemplating in a different context.

A year later there appeared a work of a different order, equally destined to exert future influence upon the understanding of the oral–literate equation. This was I. J. Gelb's *A Study of Writing*, with the subtitle *The Foundations of Grammatology* (1952). One notices an anticipation, fourteen years later, of the title of Jacques Derrida's deservedly famous work *De la grammatologie* (1976). The importance of Gelb's work in the context of the oral–literate question is perhaps not yet fully appreciated. While it avoided making those unique claims for the Greek alphabet that I have myself put forward, it effectively disposed of any claims to adequacy put forward on behalf of previous writing systems. In particular, the Phoenician system from which the Greeks demonstrably borrowed many letters and phonetic values was nevertheless exposed as what Gelb called an "unvocalized syllabary" that did not permit precise phonetic identification by the reader of what the writing system was trying to say. The ambiguities in reading and interpretation were formidable – so much so it appears as to preclude the formation of any body of Phoenician literature in our sense or in the Greek sense, for none is known to exist. The system was a commercial shorthand, but that was all.

Six years later, in 1958, Walter Ong published his *Ramus: Method and Decay of Dialogue*. Here was another anticipation of the future, again perhaps not at first fully realized, a preliminary exposure of a problem that was to bear directly upon the oral–literate equation but coming this time from the study and practice of rhetoric. This essentially oralist discipline had from antiquity played a central role in the education of society's elites. It retained some influence even in the days of our forefathers and has always occupied a favored place in the educational institutions of Catholicism.

What Ong perceived was the drastic limitations placed upon the vitality, the very language of rhetoric, when its rules become textualized, formalized, fossilized in a written system – in, one can say, a literate discourse. The "oral dialogue," in his own words, when tabulated in this form for purposes of instruction simply "decays." Ong's insight has led to the fruitful production of many subsequent meditations, establishing him as a leading figure in the oral–literate enterprise.

Since 1963, as I have said, publications bearing on the equation have proliferated, and I will not attempt a further bibliography. What remains is to outline the various scholarly disciplines, each of them distinct from the other, that in these years have either become involved in the oral–literate equation or touched closely upon it, sometimes unawares. As one considers them, an emerging pattern becomes discernible, one not yet fully formulated or realized but becoming a latent and powerful force in the advancement of understanding of society and the human mind.

As noted already, a division falls between studies that stress the oralist half of the equation and those committed to the literate half. Among the former, the anthropologists take pride of place, more specifically the cultural anthropologists. Names that occur are Goody (1987) and Finnegan (1977), among others (see Feldman, Chapter 3, and Denny, Chapter 4, this volume). In the context of cultural anthropology, one should not forget such founding fathers as Malinowski (1979) and Jousse (1925), who respectively brought Polynesia and the Near East into the picture. Lévi-Strauss's own researches in the Amazon Basin also predated the outbreak of the Second World War. And of course there was Parry and Lord in the field of classical learning supplemented by contemporary studies in the Balkans. Armed with recording tape and disk – another technological addition to media equipment – scholars have been able to penetrate into parts of the world where the vestiges of what Ong and myself have styled a condition of "primary orality" could be brought back for replay and study. These were the songs, chants, epics, dances, performances, and music, still orally preserved and communicated in surviving tribal societies on the fringes of what we are pleased to call the civilized world. Africa and Polynesia in particular have been used as sources for such material, supplying some prototypes of the kind of language that held a nonliterate society together even though the material now available is usually compromised by literacy. These have been McLuhan's inheritors insofar as what he claimed to find resurrected in the present, at least in spirit, they further explored as a remnant of the historical past. Concurrently, but coming from the other side of the world, there appeared in 1976 a work entitled *Cognitive Development: Its Cultural and Social Foundations*, an English translation of the researches of Alexander Luria conducted forty-five years earlier in the Soviet Republics of Uzbekistan and Kirghizia. No later investigator has quite approached in depth the conclusions he was able to draw, particularly since he took care to make comparison with literates in the same community.

On a different plane, one should include in the oral–literate context the modern science of linguistics. Whereas comparative philology, as it used to be called, based itself upon a comparison of texts to discover, for example, the Indo-European roots of our own language, linguistics as now understood seeks to penetrate to the phonetics that lie behind the letters, proposing what in effect is a science of oralist sound mechanisms. The elements to be analyzed are phonemes, not written words – acoustic phenomena requiring pronunciation, not silent reading. Indeed, the written word can disguise the phoneme, which has to be discovered behind the alphabetic representation and will require its own type of notation. The oral word is being sought behind its literate representation even though one may detect, in historical studies in the linguistics field, a recurrent temptation to reconstruct a symbolism of written signs at the expense of the oral original. One detects a tendency to work and think on the basis of the text as it is visible rather more than as it is heard (see Olson, Chapter 9, Scholes & Willis, Chapter 13, and Lecours & Parente, Chapter 14, this volume).

The roots of orality as identifying a condition of social communication and perhaps personal cognition are as obvious in our present as in our past. The historical dimension is primary even though there may be a valid case to be made for the continuing presence and validity for what is being called an oral consciousness in our midst to this day. The Parry–Lord methodology united a Greek past with a Balkan present, that is, they united Homer with a peasant poetry as still practiced in Yugoslavia.

### The inheritors

Quite recently, another historical perspective has opened up in addition to the Greek, focusing on Palestine in the time of Jesus. Werner Kelber's *The Oral and the Written Gospel* (1983) draws the conclusion that the story as recorded in the three synoptic Gospels combines material composed according to the rules of oral memorization with contrasting materials that can be called literate designed for readers who would nonetheless presumably have it read aloud to them. The sayings and parables of Jesus on the one hand and the narrative of the Passion on the other exhibit the contrast.

As a footnote to Kelber, one may note that the Old Testament, particularly as written in the form familiar to the Judaic culture, in fact records the operation of an oral–literate equation, in which oral originals have been codified in script, first Phoenician, then Aramaic, and finally Hebrew. The light that may be shed on the forms of Hebrew composition required for oral commemoration still awaits fuller exploration (see Jaynes [1976] for an interesting attack on this question).

I have a perception – it is only that, and I may be wrong – that the problem of interpreting the sacred writings of Judaism, which has proven to be a continuous enterprise to the present day, is one that would not have arisen in quite its present form had the original writings had the advantage of transcription into the Greek alphabet.

There may be a connection between Talmudic scholarship centered as it is upon a whole group of sacred texts considered as texts and that contemporary enterprise in the field of comparative literature and literary criticism that goes by the name of deconstructionism, as expounded in France by Jacques Derrida, before migrating to the English Department of Yale University. What one notices in the movement is a reaction of distrust to the written word as such. To be sure, the attention is on texts, but on the deconstruction thereof. And what remains when you carry this out, if not the looming presence of the spoken word, is the oralist mode of communication for which the text is only a sign and perhaps an ambiguous or misleading one. I will not venture further into a field that lies beyond my own knowledge except to note once more that the rediscovery of the rules of orality may be part of the answer, perhaps not the whole one, to the dilemmas posed by the deconstructionist methods of interpretation.

McLuhan placed a negative evaluation on the printing press, viewing it as the creator of typographical or linear thinking, as opposed to the richer, more complex and multifaceted levels of consciousness and communication that he saw emerging in the use of the electronic media. Those disciplines so far reviewed that have grappled with oralism since his day can be said to be his inheritors in that their effort has been directed toward getting behind what is written in order to recapture what is said or performed.

But the same revived interest in the spoken word has provoked closer attention to its counterpart, the book, the printed text, the written word. Rather than being a negative force in cultural evolution, the printed book and its growing readership can be viewed as a potent force for change, both cognitive and social. Print becomes an instrument for enlarged reflection of philosophy, of science on the one hand and a growing democratization and affluence within European society on the other. Far from going back to orality, what we can be invited to explore in depth are the new possibilities of literacy, a literacy of readers of communication by print, rather than literacy by voice. That something new had come to pass in the production of the printed book was noted forty years ago by Chaytor (1945) in England and later by Febvre and Martin (1976) in France. More recently, Gutenberg's printing press has received its due as expressed in the title of Elizabeth Eisenstein's (1979) groundbreaking work, *The Printing Press as an Agent of Change: Communication and Cultural Transformations in Early Modern Europe*.

From Homer in antiquity to the New Testament, to rhetoric, to modernist deconstructionism; from the African tom-tom to the Polynesian song, to the myths of the American Indian, to the illiterates of Soviet Russia; from the typography of Gutenberg to that of the roller press, and finally to the radio and television of the present – there are contacts between all these varieties of human knowledge arising within the context of the oral–literate equation, yet it will be realized how diverse, pluralistic, and distinct are these various avenues of exploration, pursuing as they do specific objectives.

Nor have I included as I might the ways in which modern philosophers in their speculations have also occasionally brushed against the oralists' question, having viewed, perhaps reluctantly, the presence of oralism in the modern mind. On the one hand, the philosophers of hermeneutics (one thinks here of Heidegger), searching for hidden and deeper meanings concealed in textualized statements, have come near to suggesting that buried behind the text may be realities expressible in oral language rather than written even though the hidden reality is described as a being in metaphysical, not oral, terms. On the other hand, one observes the remarkable conversion (if that is the word) of Wittgenstein from a view or perspective of language as the instrument of logical clarity withdrawn from the popular consciousness to one that prefers to recognize language as the nurse of ordinary human communication, and presumably of human cognition – a language formed as it responds to the conventions observed in any given linguistic group. What are these conventions if not oral ones, performed or commemorated on the lips of the people without benefit of reading or writing?

In a parallel direction, the observations of J. L. Austin (1962) at Oxford began to focus on the exploration of the syntax of performative speech: the language that says go and he goeth, come and he cometh. In this, too, we recognize the oral accents of the child who is not interested in defining the quality of an object but wants something done to it or by it.

The competition between orality and literacy continues to flourish: It is announced in a growing chorus of publications. But has the chorus any concordance? Is there not a need to construct some overall pattern into which these various perceptions can fit – some overarching body of theory covering the oral–literate equation both as it has operated historically and as it may still operate in the present; a theory that will state certain fundamentals of the situation to which all investigations can relate themselves?

### The causes

So far in my summarization, the one missing contribution has been my own. Of those partaking in this project, I suppose I am the only one professionally committed to the study of two classical languages, Greek and Latin. The claims of classical antiquity to supply the basis of our own culture have often been overworked and overstated. The gifts of Greece on which I have sought to place an accent concern technology and the social and political sciences rather than the realm of metaphysical and moral values – not on beauty, truth, and goodness of the Platonic model but on the nuts and bolts of linguistic communication.

From this perspective I conclude that some theoretic order can be placed upon the oralist–literate equation only as it relates to the invention of the Greek alphabet. By an understandable paradox, this instrument of future literacy first functioned as a complete recording of preliteracy.

But before considering the Greeks, let me go back to the cultures that had employed writing systems prior to them as far back as seven thousand years in Egypt, Sumer, Babylon, Assyria, Hebrew Palestine, and perhaps elsewhere. These had all been cultures that had experimented with the use of writing, and they have always been seen as elevating themselves to the status of literacy – a conclusion that in my view is profoundly mistaken. I ask you now before coming to the Greeks to go back a million years or more in the history of our species.

Evolution properly understood is a biological process, not a cultural one. It seems to be established that humans represent a species in which the brain increased in cubic capacity at a phenomenal rate during perhaps a million years. Natural selection gave an advantage to those with this enlarged capacity, because it provided the means to pronounce articulate language. The difference between our brains and those of the hominids represents in the main this capacity. The use of tools so often identified in popular accounts as the clue to our superiority is not relevant to the main issue since both hominids and other animal species can manipulate tools.

The specialization of the brain had to be accompanied by a parallel specialization of the organs that articulate speech sounds. Nothing remotely resembling it is to be found in the entire animal kingdom. This apparatus works to produce language by initially using the lungs to expel a column of air, which is then exposed to the most extraordinary range of vibrations, of closures, openings, and stops imposed on it by the throat, tongue, lips, teeth, and nose. Experiment with them yourselves to discover the combinations necessary for the pronunciation of simple English. Like brain size, this was a necessary component of our human evolution. The evolution that brought the simple capacity for upright posture seems simple by comparison. The product of this million years of specialization that identifies our species as human is language.

Over a span of perhaps seven thousand years or less, the human species learned the trick whereby hand and eye, supplementing the ear and the mouth, can draw small visible shapes that will trigger a memory of language as previously pronounced and heard. What a mere moment in evolutionary time has this epigraphic accomplishment occupied! The natural human being is not a writer or a reader but a speaker and a listener. This must be as true of us today as it was seven thousand years ago. Literacy at any stage of its development is in terms of evolutionary time a mere upstart, an artificial exercise, a work of culture, not nature, imposed upon the natural man.

Two conclusions seem to follow that concern the history of orality in its remote past. First, it is accepted that prehistoric human societies formed on the basis of intercommunication through language, whether the members were hunter-gatherers, farmers, or something in between (see Denny, Chapter 4, this volume). For uncounted millennia, they managed their affairs – the common agreements, customs, and properties that render any society operable by the use of oral language alone. They behaved, thought, and reacted orally. That is our inheritance, and as such we deny it at our peril. It is surely false to dismiss the inheritance by using such labels as primitive, savage, or illiterate. What Lévi-Strauss was investigating was not La pensée sauvage, but La pensée oraliste.

Second, because our oral inheritance is as much a part of us as the ability to walk upright or use our hands, is it likely that such an inheritance would allow itself to be quickly superseded by what we call literacy? This question particularly is pertinent when one considers the sheer clumsiness, ambiguity, and difficulty of interpretation that beset all writing systems before the Greek. Leaving aside the uncounted millennia when human societies were exclusively oral, one is entitled to conclude that from the Egyptians and Sumerians to the Phoenicians and Hebrews (not to mention the Indians and Chinese), writing in the societies where it was practiced was restricted to priestly or commercial elites who took the trouble to learn it. The affairs of law, government, and daily life were still managed by oral communication as they are largely to this day in Islam no less than in China.

One further conclusion concerns us. The mechanisms of modern education place primary emphasis on the speedy mastery of reading and writing as a preparation for the curriculum of secondary schools and adult life. Should we not be prepared to consider the possible conditions imposed upon the management of our educational systems by our oral inheritance? Are the clues to our developed adult condition still to be found in the primary school and what goes on there rather than in the high school where, supposedly, literacy is achieved?

The proposition I would offer is that the developing child should be expected in some sense to relive the conditions of this inheritance – that the teaching of literacy be conducted on the supposition that it is to be preceded by a curriculum of song, dance, and recitation and that it be accompanied by continual instruction in these oral arts.

Good readers, I suggest, grow out of good speakers and reciters. The recitation that comes most naturally to children is one that fulfills oral conditions: It is narrative and to a large extent rhythmic. If our forefathers were more literate than we are, was it because they learned to speak well even as they learned to read well, acquiring an increased vocabulary by rhetorical practice? Premature pressure on the child's eye to read a text in preference to training the ear to listen carefully and repeat orally may well inhibit full literate development by omitting a necessary stage in the developmental process in which oral practice becomes the close companion of the word visually read. If we follow the contrary instruction of some education theorists – Jean Piaget (1926), among others – we hasten to advance in children the power to conceptualize, to gain a sophisticated grasp of relations of time and space. Should not our perception of the educational process, at least to perhaps the tenth year, be guided equally by John Dewey's (1933) conception of persons "as being in the first instance not a thinker, but rather agents, patients, doers, sufferers, and enjoyers"? So now I come to the Greeks, through whose experience, as I have proposed, we may discover a few more fundamentals that will guide our understanding of what orality is, what literacy is, and what is the relationship between them.

Parry's perception of the rules governing Homeric composition were made when he was still a graduate student at Berkeley, without benefit of comparative studies. He confronted the Homeric text as we all have it. His concentration on the standardized epithets attached to proper names led him to conclude that these and other formulas were aids to improvising the tale as it unfolded. They were placed in the bard's memory, ready to be drawn on when a follow-through was required. The study subsequently extended itself to other formulaic phrases more germane to the narrative. Their function was perceived to aid improvisation, filling in metrical gaps to allow the singer to maintain the flow. It should, however, be noted that his work introduced the concept of the storage of material in oral memory, even if, semantically speaking, the material so stored was of limited significance. Such conclusions were later confirmed empirically by the practice of Yugoslav singers as they too, in part, improvised their recitations, telling a tale that included repeated phraseology already used in previous versions (Lord, 1960).

My own tentative approach to realizing what afterward grew into the oral–literate equation was prompted by inspection of a quite different area of Greek literature, namely the remains of the pre-Socratic philosophers. I asked myself why some of these thinkers, while engaged in serious speculation, still chose to compose it in verse, and Homeric verse at that. Alternatively, why did one of them, Heraclitus, choose to publish his thought in self-contained aphorisms, that is, oral sayings on the model that can still be read in the New Testament Gospels rather than in the connected language of prose exposition? After encountering Parry's thesis, I put two and two together and concluded that down to the early fifth century in Greece, oralist rules of composition were still required in expounding even serious philosophic thought and some scientific thought. Platonic prose marked a decisive turn away from these rules; it was the first body of such prose of an extended character written out in any culture known to us.

Observing further that Plato's text contained an explicit rejection of both Homer and Greek drama as unsuitable for the curriculum of higher education that his academy was designed to offer, I concluded that a great divide in Greek culture had begun to occur, perhaps at the time when Plato was born or a little earlier, which separated an oralist society relying mainly on metrical and recited literature for the content of its cultural knowledge to a literate society that was to rely in the future on prose as the vehicle of serious reflection, research, and record.

This meant that the Greek tongue before Plato, even when written, was composed according to the rules of oral composition and had to carry the burden of personal instruction and social guidance that Plato now proposed to supply in his dialogues.

I turned back to reread Homer in the light of this conclusion and observed how much of his tale is told through the narration of typical situations as they arise from day to day in the backdrop of society. A high proportion of the rhetoric is made up of proverbial wisdom and common sentiments of the community. Parry's view of the formula stored in memory as an aid to improvisation could be enlarged. Both Homeric poems could be viewed as massive repositories of cultural information, covering custom, law, and social propriety, which had also been placed in storage. The notion of memorization replacing improvisation was confirmed by the role that the earlier Greeks assigned to memory in their divine hierarchy.

I earlier proposed for Homer the concept of the tribal encyclopedia, one rightly criticized later for its textual overtone applied to what was supposed to be an oral process. A remedy for this was later supplied when I turned back to the Darwinian evolutionists. In that crucial twelve months between 1962 and 1963, there also appeared a book with the title *Animal Species and Evolution* (1963), the magisterial work of Ernst Mayr, professor of zoology at Harvard. In the concluding chapters, Mayr turned from the genetics of the evolutionary process to consider that cultural development superimposed upon the biological by man. Borrowing from the conception of information stored in our genes, he applied it to cultural information put in storage in language, so that it can be reused as the child is taught by the parent or its society. The child absorbs what we call the tradition of the society. The tradition I concluded could be stored only in a language that is memorized and transmissible between the generations.

Turning back to Homer, the Greek epics could then be perceived as massive storage repositories of cultural information. We possess them now because they were written down, but the content is that appropriate to a preliterate society.

The language used for this purpose, while Greek, is a special kind of Greek, not that of Xenophon or Demosthenes, but a metrical chant repeatable for hundreds and indeed thousands of lines, memorizable because metrical, as the repeated beat of the line becomes inevitable in a way that is not typical of prose. Further, the vocabulary appears to be somewhat artificial when compared with the vernacular dialects of the time in Greece; it has a slightly archaic flavor reminiscent of the archaisms of the Old Testament.

One purpose of the epic was informational storage. The other, obvious one was entertainment. It has to tell a tale in which the actors were persons doing things or suffering them, with a notable absence of abstract statement. One could reflect, but always as a human being, never as a philosopher, an intellectual, a theorist.

The secrets of orality, then, lie not in the behavior of language as it is exchanged in the give and take of conversation but in the language used for information storage in the memory. This language has to fulfill two requirements: It must be rhythmic and it must be narrativized. Its syntax must always be one that describes an action or a passion, but not principles or concepts. To give a simple example, it will never say that honesty is the best policy but that "the honest man always prospers."

These oral linguistic habits form part of our biological inheritance, which can be supplemented through literacy but never wholly superseded. If we seek to suppress them, we do so at our peril.

Yet there is another side to the coin. Without modern literacy, which means Greek literacy, we would not have science, philosophy, written law, or literature, nor the automobile or the airplane. Something happened to make these possible. A slow revolution was occuring when Plato wrote, and the secret of that success lay in the superior technology of the Greek alphabet.

What was achieved was a combined operation of astonishing complexity. A limited set of shapes small enough to be outlined quickly by the hand was devised that could be manipulated to form groups of shapes, combinations of two, three, or four, running to the thousands of such groupings that could correspond to the thousands of linguistic noises produced by the specialized organs of the throat and mouth. A given language restricted itself to a given number. The row of letters on a page became the automatic prompters of corresponding speech that the brain recites to itself. For centuries after the invention, the oral original still had to be pronounced by the lips of the reader as he read (see Saenger, Chapter 12, this volume).

For the first time in history, the person who could learn to read in this way was the child. It was slowly discovered that if this Greek trick was taught to the child at the time when his oral mastery of language was still incomplete, the two habits, the oral and the visual, could be taught side by side in combination, with the result that recognition of the acoustic values triggered by the visual shapes could become an automatic reflex. The capacity for the reflex depended first on limiting the number of shapes to under thirty so that they could be easily memorized, then on giving the shapes the power to register linguistic sounds comprehensively and exhaustively, leaving no room for guesswork as to what the right oralist values were. The Greek alphabet provided an exhaustive table of atomic elements of acoustic sound that by diverse combinations could represent the molecules, so to speak, of linguistic speech. The basic structural principle remains, whether exploited in Greek, Roman, or Cyrillic writing. This was the Greek breakthrough. Previous systems had never been able to register the full range of language as orally employed.

At first the alphabet was used to record oral language as previously composed for memorization in Greek epics, lyrics, and drama. The conceptual revolution began when it was realized that the full register of linguistic sound could be placed in a new kind of storage no longer dependent on the rhythms used in oral memory recall. It could become a document, a permanent set of visible shapes, no longer a fleeting vibration in the air but shapes that could be laid aside until rescanned for some purpose and indeed forgotten. The mechanisms of the oral memory could then be slowly superseded in favor of documented prose, the first histories, the first philosophies, the first bodies of prosaic law, the first bodies of prosaic rhetoric. Still more, the narrative requirement, the activist syntax, and the living agents required for all oral speech held in the memory could also be laid aside, replaced by a reflective syntax of definition, description, and analysis. Such was the prose of Plato and all his successors, whether philosophic, scientific, historical, descriptive, legal, or moral. European culture slowly moved over into the ambience of analytic, reflective, interpretative, conceptual prose discourse.

The rhythmic word as a storage vehicle for information slowly became obsolete. It lost its functional relationship to society. In retrospect we can see that such changes never occur as rapidly as historical logic might require. The poetic word long retained a functional, that is, a didactic, role in European society. The *Aeneid*, *The Divine Comedy*, *Paradise Lost* all remind us of this fact. Only in the twentieth century, one may say, has the logic of the transfer from memory to document been completely fulfilled. Ours is indeed a prosaic culture.

The burden of my argument, however, has been that the oralist inheritance must still be allowed to function. However limited may be its forms of expression and cognition – rhythmic, narrativized, action oriented – these are a necessary supplement to our abstract literate consciousness.

**Summary**

First, there is the historical priority of orality over literacy in human experience; second, the priority of the storage function of language over the casual use thereof; third, the priority of the poetic experience over the prosaic in our psychological makeup; and fourth, the priority of memory and the act of memorization over invention or what we loosely call creativity. There is the priority of the act over the concept, of concrete perception over abstract definition, and finally, priority of the Greek alphabet over all previous types of writing, providing the sole instrument of full literacy to the present day.

With such assumptions at the back of his mind, the anthropologist recording tribal myth and story will look for a distinction between functional material memorized for its social usefulness and stories and songs now improvised for mere entertainment. The educator will seek to retain and develop through the grade school and the high school many oral elements of the curriculum and of the kindergarten. The psychologist will realize that the language he is using to classify the operations of the human mind is a literate language superimposed upon primary modes of thinking that are not conceptual at all but that still remain stubbornly effective at the back of our minds.

REFERENCES

Austin, J. L. (1962). *How to do things with words* (J. O. Urmson, ed.). New York: Oxford University Press.
Chaytor, H. J. (1945). *From script to print.* Cambridge University Press.
Derrida, J. (1976). *Of Grammatology* (G. C. Spivak., trans.). Baltimore: Johns Hopkins University Press.
Dewey, J. (1933). *How we think.* New York: Heath.
Eisenstein, E. (1979). *The printing press as an agent of change: Communication and cultural transformation in early modern Europe.* Cambridge University Press.
Febvre, L., & Martin. H.-J. (1976). *The coming of the book: The impact of printing 1450–1800* (G. Nowell-Smith & D. Wootton, eds., D. Gerard, trans.). London: N.L.B. Foundations of History Library.
Finnegan, R. (1977). *Oral poetry.* Cambridge University Press.

Gelb, I. J. (1963). *A study of writing: The foundations of grammatology.* Chicago: University of Chicago Press.
Goody, J. (1987). *The interface between the written and the oral.* Cambridge University Press.
Goody, J., & Watt, I. (1963). The consequences of literacy. *Contemporary Studies in society and history* 5:304–45. Republished in J. Goody, (ed.) (1968). *Literacy in traditional societies.* Cambridge University Press.
Havelock, E. (1963). *Preface to Plato.* Cambridge, Mass.: Harvard University Press.
  (1982). *The literate revolution in Greece and its cultural consequences.* Princeton, N.J.: Princeton University Press.
Innis, H. (1951). *The bias of communication.* Toronto: Toronto University Press.
Jaynes, J. (1976). *The origin of consciousness in the breakdown of bicameral mind.* Boston: Houghton-Mifflin.
Jousse, M. (1925). *Etudes de psychologie linguistique.* Paris: Beauchesne.
Kelber, W. (1983). *The oral and the written gospel: The hermeneutics of speaking and writing.* Philadelphia: Fortress.
Lévi-Strauss, C. (1962). *La pensée sauvage.* Paris: Plon.
Lord, A. (1960). *The singer of tales.* Havard Studies in Comparative Literature, 24. Cambridge, Mass.: Harvard University Press.
Luria, A. R. (1976). *Cognitive development: Its cultural and social foundations.*(M. Cole, ed., M. Lopez-Morillas & L. Solotaroff, trans.) Cambridge, Mass.: Harvard University Press.
Malinowski, B. (1979). *The ethnography of Malinowski: The Trobriand Islands 1915–1918.* London: Routledge & Kegan Paul.
Mayr, E. (1963). *Animal species and evolution.* Cambridge, Mass.: Harvard University Press.
McLuhan, M. (1962). *The Gutenberg galaxy.* Toronto: University of Toronto.
Ong, W. (1958). *Ramus: Method, and decay of dialogue.* Cambridge, Mass.: Harvard University Press.
Ong, W. (1982). *Orality and literacy: The technologizing of the word.* London: Methuen.
Parry, M. (1971). *The collected papers of Milman Parry* (A. Parry, ed.). Oxford: Oxford University Press (Clarendon Press).
Piaget, J. (1926). *The child's conception of the world.* New York: Harcourt Brace.

# 2
# A plea for research on lay literacy
IVAN ILLICH

By "lay literacy," I mean a symbolic fallout from the use of the alphabet in Western cultures. I mean something quite different from clerical literacy, which consists in the ability to read and write. By lay literacy, I mean a distinct mode of perception in which the book has become the decisive metaphor through which we conceive of the self and its place. By lay literacy, I do not mean the spread of written contents, beyond the pale of the clerics, to others who can only listen to what is being read to them. I use the term lay literacy to speak of a mind frame defined by a set of certainties that has spread within the realm of the alphabet since late medieval times. The lay literate is certain that speech can be frozen, that memories can be stored and retrieved, that secrets can be engraved in conscience – and therefore examined – and that experience can be described. By lay literacy, I mean, therefore, a weave of categories that – since the twelfth century – has shaped the mental space of the illiterate laity just as much as that of the literate clergy. Lay literacy constitutes a new type of space in which social reality is reconstructed, a new kind of network of fundamental assumptions about all that can be seen or known. In what follows, I have tried to trace the evolution of this mind-set and the transformation of a number of certainties that can exist only within it. I have tried to illustrate how such a transformation happens by telling the story of "the text."

### The history of lay literacy

Two reasons commend the history of lay literacy to the attention of people who pursue research on (and not only in) education. The first is the new level of concern within the educational enterprise, with universal clerical literacy as a goal to be reached before the year 2000. The second is the widespread tendency to replace the book with the computer as the fundamental metaphor of self-perception.

As to the first, we are all aware that new psychological, managerial, and electronic techniques are being used to spread the clerical skills of reading and writing. Whether, and if so how, these literacy campaigns interact with lay literacy ought to be better understood. Fifty years ago, Luria (1976) studied the major shifts that occur in mental activity as people acquire clerical literacy. Their cognitive processes cease to be mainly concrete and situational. They begin to draw inferences not only on the basis of their own practical experience, but also on assumptions formulated in language. Since Luria did these studies in Stalinist Russia, much has been learned about the change that clerical literacy induces in perception, representation, reasoning, imagination, and self-awareness. But in most of these studies, a causal link is assumed to exist between the individual's writing skill and the new mind frame he or she acquires. As I will show, in the light of the history of lay literacy, this assumption is largely false. Since the Middle Ages, the certainties that characterize the literate mind have spread, overwhelmingly, by means other than instruction in the skill of reading and writing. This is a point that should be kept present in the current discussions on illiteracy, semiliteracy, and postliteracy. The approach currently used in spreading the skill of "written communication" might actually be subversive to the literate mind.

While I do want to call your attention to the just-mentioned independence of the literate mind from personal writing skills, my main argument centers on the current transmogrification of the literate mind itself. During the last decade, the computer has rapidly been replacing the book as the prime metaphor used to visualize the self, its activities, and its relatedness to the environment. Words have been reduced to "message units," speech to the "use of language," conversation to something called "oral communication," and the sound symbols of the text to (binary) "bits." I want to argue that the mental space into which literacy certainties fit and that other mental space that is engendered by certainties about the *Turing Machine* are heteronomous. The study of the mental space that has been generated by lay literacy seems to me a necessary step if we are to grasp the nature of that entirely different mental space that is becoming dominant in our time. And just as lay literacy is largely independent of the individual's clerical skills, so is the cybernetic mind largely independent of the individual's technical proficiency on a computer.

Solid foundations for research on the literate mind have been laid; I only plead that the result of this research be applied in education, to recognize unacknowledged postulates that are implied in the axioms from which educational theories flow. The first to observe the depth of the epistemological break between oral and literate existence was Milman Parry, some sixty years ago (1971). Through him we come to recognize the Island of Literacy that rises out of the magma of epic orality as a potter-scribe takes down the song of a bard that we call the *Iliad*. Parry's pupil Albert Lord (1960) convinced us that the steps by which one becomes a bard cannot be grasped with the same concepts as those by which one becomes a literate poet. Eric Havelock (1963) argued convincingly that the profound changes in the style of reasoning, in the mode of perceiving the universe, and the appearance of "literature" and science in Greece of the sixth and fifth century B.C. can be understood only in connection with a transition from the oral to the literate mind. Others have explored how the unique and once-and-for-all invention of the alphabet spread to Brahman India and thence to the Orient. Elisabeth Eisenstein (1979), in her monumental study on the impact of the printing press on Renaissance culture, has dealt with another major transformation within the literate mind in yet another epoch. Jack Goody (1980), the anthropologist, turned our attention to the ever ongoing "alphabetization of the savage mind." And Walter Ong (1982) over the last two decades has pulled together the research of psychologists, anthropologists, and students of epics to argue that alphabetization is equivalent to the "technologization" of the word. So far, however, no one has attempted a history of the literate mind as distinct from clerical literacy. And it is a discouraging task. The literate mind is a phenomenon both brilliantly clear and as slippery as a jellyfish whose features can be discerned only so long as it is observed within its own milieu.

*The liturgy of schooling*

To make my plea for this novel research plausible, I will explain the steps that led me to my present position. This I will do by criticizing my own *De-schooling Society* (1973) for its näive views. My travelogue began sixteen years ago, at a point when that book was about to appear. During the nine months the manuscript was at the publisher's, I grew more and more dissatisfied with its text, which did not, by the way, argue for the elimination of schools. This misapprehension I owe to Cass Canfield, Harper's owner, who named my baby and, in doing so, misrepresented my thoughts. The book, instead, advocates the disestablishment of schools in the sense in which the church in the United States has been disestablished. But what I called for was the "disestablishment of schools" for the sake of education, and here – I noticed – lay my mistake. I saw then that much more important than the disestablishment of schools was the reversal of those trends that make of education a pressing need rather than a gift of gratuitous leisure. I had begun to fear that the disestablishment of educational church would lead to a fanatic revival of many forms of degraded education. Norman Cousins published my recantation in the *Saturday Review* during the very week my book came out. In it, I argued that the alternative to schooling is not some other type of educational agency, or the design of educational opportunities injected into every aspect of life, but a society that fosters a different attitude to tools. Since then, my curiosity and my reflections have focused on the historical circumstances under which the very idea of educational needs can arise.

To make it easier to follow my route, let me recall for you how I came to the study of education. I came from theology. As a theologian, I specialize in ecclesiology, which constitutes the only old learned tradition that – in social analysis – distinguishes fundamentally between two entities: the visible community in which the spirit is embodied and the quite different community that is the city or the state. This dualism is of its essence. Emboldened by fifteen hundred years of ecclesiology, I saw the church as more than a metaphor for the new alma mater. I intended, increasingly, to stress the fundamental continuity between the two seemingly opposed agencies, at least insofar as they define the meaning of education in successive centuries.

Within ecclesiology, the study of liturgy has always been my favorite topic. This branch of learning deals with the role of the cult in bringing about the phenomenon of "church." Liturgy studies how solemn gestures and chants, hierarchies and ritual objects create not only faith but also the reality of the community-as-church, which is the object of this faith. Comparative liturgy sharpens the eye to distinguish the essential mythopoetic (myth-making) rituals from the accidents of style. So sensitized, I began to look on those things that go on within schools as parts of the liturgy. Accustomed to the great beauty of Christian liturgy, I was of course put off by the abject style so common in schools.

I then began to study the place that the liturgy of schooling holds in the social construction of modern reality and the degree to which it has created the need for education. I began to discern the traces that schooling leaves in the mind-set of its participants. I focused my attention on the form of the scholastic liturgy by putting into parentheses not only learning theory but also research that measures the achievement of learning goals. In the articles published in *De-schooling Society*, I gave a phenomenology of schooling: From Brooklyn to Bolivia, it consists of age-specific assemblies around a so-called teacher, for three to six hours on two hundred days of the year; yearly promotions that celebrate the exclusion of those who fail or are banned into a lower stream; and subject matter more detailed and carefully chosen than any monastic liturgy ever known. Everywhere, attendance varies from twelve to forty-eight pupils, and teachers may only be those who have absorbed several years of this mumbo jumbo in excess of their pupils. Everywhere, pupils were deemed to acquire some "education" – which the school was deemed to monopolize – and which was deemed necessary to make pupils into valuable citizens, each knowing at which class level he has dropped out from this "preparation for life." I saw then how the liturgy of schooling creates the social reality in which education is perceived as a necessary good. I was even aware then that enveloping, lifelong education could, in the last two decades of the twentieth century, replace schooling in its myth-making function. I did, however, not then suspect what I now propose as a subject for research: the waning of the traditional key concepts of *literate* education, since the terms for them are used in metaphors that fit the computer. I did not then conceive of schooling as one of the masks behind which this transmogrification could take place.

At the time I was engaged in these reflections, we were at the height of the international development effort. School appeared as the worldwide stage on which the hidden assumptions of economic progress were being acted out. The school system demonstrated where development could not but lead: to international standardized stratification, to universal dependence on service, to counterproductive specialization, to the degradation of the many for the sake of the few. As I wrote *De-schooling*, the social effect, and not the historical substance, of education was still at the core of my interest. I still accepted that, fundamentally, educational needs of some kind were an historical predicament of human nature.

### *Constitution and evolution of a mental space*

My belief in my own unexamined assumption that by nature human beings belong to the species of *homo educandus* started to dim as I studied the history of economic concepts from Mandeville to Marx (with Rene Dumont) and from Bentham to Walras (with Elie Halévy) and also as I became aware (with Karl Polanyi) of the historical nature of my own certainties regarding scarcity. I recognized that in economics, there exists an important critical tradition that analyzes as historical constructs the assumptions that economists of all colors make. I became aware that *homo economicus*, with whom we emotionally and intellectually identify, is of quite recent creation. And thus I learned to understand "education" as learning *when it takes place under the assumption of scarcity in the means that produce it*. The need for "education" in this perspective appears as the result of societal beliefs and arrangements that make the means for so-called socialization scarce. And, in this same perspective, I began to notice that educational rituals reflected, reinforced, and actually created belief in the value of learning pursued under conditions of scarcity. With so far limited success, I tried to encourage my students to do for the field of pedagogics what others have done in the field of economics.

Polanyi has shown that the exchange of goods predates, by many centuries if not millennia, the economic marketing of commodities. This preeconomic exchange is performed by status traders who act more like diplomats than businessmen. By commenting on the *Politics* of Aristotle, Polanyi (1944) shows that the technique of marketing, in which the value of a good is made to depend on demand and supply and provides a profit for the merchant, is a Greek invention of the early fourth century B.C. I found increasing evidence that the conceptual space within which *paideia* acquired a meaning comparable to what we call "education" defined itself at about the same time. The "dis-embedding," to use Polanyi's term, of a formal economic sphere within society happens during the same decade as the disembedding of a formal educational sphere.

During that same century, also, "Euclidean space" came into formal existence. Its creation and destiny provide a useful analogy to illustrate what I mean by a "mental space." Euclid was careful to state the axioms on which he built his geometry. He wanted them remembered as stipulations. However, as we moderns are now acutely aware, in one instance he stated as a "self-evident" axiom something that, in fact, required a postulate. When Euclid stated as axiomatic that two parallel lines never intersect, he unknowingly implied the existence of one space, namely that particular "space" that is now named after him. He made an assumption that, remaining unexamined, turned into a certainty. And, for two thousand years, the Western learned tradition took it as a natural fact. Not until the turn of our century did Riemann (see Cassirer, 1957, p. 418n) demonstrate that a space in which two parallel lines never intersect is, for the mathematician, only a special case. Soon after Riemann had laid the mathematical foundation for relativity, anthropologists noticed that the members of many cultures do not see with Euclidian eyes. Ethnolinguists then confirmed that, for instance, Hopis or Dogons speak about space and directions in ways that can more easily be translated into the terms of mathematical tensors than into any Indo-Germanic language. On the other hand, historians found that ancient literatures describe space much more thoroughly by reference to smells, sounds, and the experience of moving through an atmosphere than by evoking visual experience.

Art historians, like Panofsky (1924), and philosophers, like Susan Langer (1942), have made plausible that most artists paint the space that they and their epoch see. They do not organize their perception in the perspective created by Dürer, or within the coordinates of Descartes. Perspective, so the argument goes, was introduced into painting to express the newfound ability to see the world predominantly in a self-centered way. Parallel to Kuhn's (1962) chain of descriptive paradigms succeeding each other in the sciences, art historians speak of successive depictive paradigms that correspond to distinct ways of perceiving visual space.

No attempt that can be compared with the historiography of economic or visual space has so far been made to explore the constitution and evolution of the mental space within which pedagogical ideas take their shape. This does not mean that all academic disciplines have remained prisoners to this "space"; it only means that the principal challenge to this mental confinement has been by noneducators and, so far, has not been accepted within the educational profession. Milman Parry's (1971) discovery of the heteronomy between oral and alphabetic existence could have made educators recognize the postulates that they unknowingly imply in the axioms of their field. But the relevance of Parry's discovery for an historical theory of education has so far gone unnoticed.

In his doctoral thesis on Homeric epithets, Parry was the first (in 1926) to notice that the transition from epic orality to written poetry in archaic Greece marks an epistemic break. He argued that for the literate mind, it is nearly impossible to reexperience the context within which the preliterate bard composes his songs. No bridge, built out of the certainties inherent in the literate mind, can lead back into the oral magma. I cannot here sum up the conclusions and insights reached during the last 50 years by Notopoulos (1938), Lord (1960), Havelock (1963), Peabody (1975), and Ong (1982) – the works that convinced me. But, for those who have not followed their writings on the heteronomy of epic orality and literate poetry, let me hint at some of the firm conclusions I have drawn. In an oral culture, there can be no "word" such as we are accustomed to look up in the dictionary. In that kind of culture, what silence brackets may be a syllable or a sentence, but not our atom, the word. All utterances are winged, forever gone before they are fully pronounced. The idea of fixing these events into a line, of mummifying them for later resurrection, cannot even occur. Therefore, memory, in an oral culture, cannot be conceived as a storage room or a wax tablet. Urged on by the lyre, the bard does not "look up" the right word; one fitting utterance from the grab bag of traditional phrases moves his tongue at the appropriate beat. Homer, the bard, never tried and rejected "*le mot juste.*" Virgil changed and corrected the *Aeneid* up to the hour of his death; he already was the prototype of the literate poet, the genial "Schrift-Steller."

Appropriately, the equivalent of our "curriculum" was called *Mousike* in the fifth-century B.C. schools of Athens. Students learned to compose; writing remained a servile skill exercised mostly by potters until around the year 400 B.C. when Plato went to school. Only then does true "subject matter" come into being; only then can the wisdom of previous generations be transmitted in that generation's words, to be commented upon, in distinct and new words, by the teacher. Alphabetic recording is as much a condition for what we call science and literature as it is necessary for the distinctions between "thought" and "speech." Plato, one of the few giants who struggled over the divide between orality and literacy, made this transition from ever new recall experience to literate memory the subject of his *Phaedrus*. He was acutely aware that with the teacher who sows (written) words, which can neither speak for themselves nor teach the "truth" adequately to others (1952, 276a), an entirely new epoch had opened and that the use of the alphabet would bar the return to the oral past.

With more clarity than the moderns, Plato seems to have been aware that with literacy, a new mental space had come into existence, and within it, previously unimagined concepts that would give an entirely new meaning to the upbringing of Lysias. Two things therefore can be distinguished in the history of educational assumptions: the beginning of pedagogical space, which might now be threatened, and the transformations of the web of pedagogical concepts that take substance within this space.

### The story of the text

To demonstrate how one such axiom fitting the literate space has expanded and acquired a certain dominance, I will choose as my example the "text." The word is classical: In Latin it means textured and – only rarely – the composition of well-arranged sentences. At the time of the Lindisfarne Bible, the word is first used as an equivalent for Holy Scripture. Then, in the fourteenth century, it is actually used for the concept that we now take for granted, a concept that – as I will immediately show – had appeared under different designations already two hundred years earlier. I want to speak about the emergence of this idea or concept, not about the use of the term.

I choose the idea of the text as my example for two reasons: The idea is important in educational theory, and – thoroughly transmogrified – it is central to communication theory. From the mid-twelfth century onward, the text is past speech, so encoded that the eye can pick it up from the page; in communication theory, the term stands for any binary sequence. The text, as a hinge element within the literate mind, has a beginning and an end.

By definition, the alphabet is a technique to record speech sounds in visible form. In this sense, it is much more than any other notational system. The reader who is faced by ideograms, hieroglyphs, or even the nonvocalized Semitic beta-bet must understand the sense of the line before he can pronounce it. Only the alphabet makes it possible to read correctly without any understanding. And, in fact, for well over two thousand years, the decoding of the alphabetic record could not be performed by the eye alone. "Reading" meant loud and mumbled recitation. Augustine, the champion orator of his time, was surprised when he discovered that it was possible to engage in silent reading. In the *Confessions* (1942), he tells about his discovery of learning to read without making noise and without waking his brethren.

While occasionally practiced, silent reading would have been normally impossible until into the seventh century: The break or empty space between words was unknown. Only a few monumental inscriptions spoke to the eye by separating word from word. On wax tablets, papyrus, and parchment, each line was an uninterrupted sequence of letters. There was almost no other way of reading than rehearsing the sentences aloud and listening to hear whether they made sense. Mere "dicta" – speech fragments out of context – were practically unreadable. A sentence meant for the record was "dictate": It was spoken in *cursus*, the classical prose rhythm that we have now lost. By getting the hang of the *cursus* that the *dictator* had chosen, reading at sight became possible. The sense remained buried in the page until it was voiced.

Word breaks were introduced in the eighth century, in Bede's time, as a didactic device. They were meant to facilitate the acquisition of Latin vocabulary by "thickheaded Scottish novices" (see Saenger, 1982). As a side effect, the procedure of copying manuscripts changed. Thus far, either the original had to be dictated by one monk to several scribes or each scribe had to read aloud as many words as he could keep in his auditory memory and then write them down while "dictating to himself." Space between words made silent copying possible; the copyist could then transcribe word for word. The previous line made up of an uninterrupted sequence of thirty to fifty minuscules just could not have been copied at sight.

Even though the codex of the Middle Ages contained visibly separated words, rather than the unbroken Indian line of letters, it still did not make the text visible. This new reality took shape only after the time of Bernhard and Abelard. It was brought forth by the convergence of two dozen techniques, some with Arabic, others with Classical antecedents, and some entirely new. These new techniques conspired to support and shape a substantially new idea: that of a text which is distinct both from the book and from its readings.

Chapters could get titles and be divided by subtitles. Chapter and verse could be numbered; quotations marked by underlining in a different color of ink; paragraphs introduced and, occasionally, marginal glosses could summarize their subject; miniatures become less ornamental and more illustrative. Thanks to these new devices, a table of contents and an alphabetical subject index could now be prepared, and references from one part to the other could be made within chapters. The book that formerly could only be read through could be made accessible at random: The idea of consultation could acquire a new meaning, thanks to these devices. Books could be chosen and picked up in a new mode. At the beginning of the twelfth century, it was still the custom that on certain feast days of each season, the abbot would solemnly take the books from the treasury, where they were kept with jewels and relics of saints, and lay them out in the chapter room. Each monk then picked one for his *lectio* during the following months. By the end of this same century, books had been moved out of the ark in the sacristy, and they began to be stored in a separate library, well titled, on shelves. The first catalogues were made of monastery holdings, and by the end of the next century, Paris and Oxford each boasted a union catalogue. Thanks to these technical changes, consultation, the checking of quotations, and silent reading became common, and *scriptoria* ceased to be places where each one tried to hear his own voice. Neither the teacher nor the neighbor could now hear what was being read and – partly as a result – both bawdy and heretical books multiplied. As the old habit of quoting from a well-trained memory palace was replaced by the new skill of citing right out of the book, the idea of a "text" that is independent from this or that manuscript became visible. Many of the social effects that have often been attributed to the printing press were in fact already the result of a text that could be looked up. The old clerical skill of taking dictation and reading out lines was now complemented by the skills of contemplating and searching the text with the eyes. And, in a complex way, the new reality of text and the new clerical skill affected the literate mind common to clerisy and laity alike.

For most practical purposes, penmanship and clerical status coincided until well into the fourteenth century. The mere ability to sign and to spell were taken as proof for clerical privilege, and anyone who could prove such capacity could escape capital punishment. But while the majority of clerics were much too unskilled to "look up" the text of a book, during the thirteenth century, for a vast lay population, the text became a constitutive metaphor for the entire mode of existence.

For those of you who are not medievalists and who still desire a solid introduction to what is known to historians about the growing lay literacy of the West at that time, I recommend a book by Michael Clanchy (1979), *From Memory to Written Record, England, 1066–1307*. He stresses not what clerical literacy contributed to literature and science, but how the spread of letters changed the self-perception of the age and ideas about society. In England, for instance, the number of charters used in the transfer of properties increased by a factor of 100 or more between the early twelfth and the late thirteenth century. Further, the written charter replaced the oath, which was oral by its very nature. The "testament" replaced the clod of soil that the father had formerly put into the hand of the son whom he had chosen as heir to his lands. In court, a writ got the last word! Possessing, an activity exercised by "sitting upon," *sedere*, was overshadowed in importance by "holding" (tenancy, maintenance) a title, something one does with the hand. Formerly, you solemnly walked with the buyer around the property that you wanted to sell: Now you learned to point it out with your finger and had the notary describe it. Even the illiterate acquired the certainty that the world is owned by description: "thirty steps from the rock shaped like a dog, and then to the brook in a straight line. . . ." Everyone now tended to become a *dictator*, even though scribes remained few. Surprisingly, even serfs carried seals, to put beneath their *dictation*.

Everyone now kept records, even the devil. Under the new guise of a hellish scribe, portrayed as the "writing devil," he appeared in late Romanesque sculpture. He squatted on his coiled tail and prepared the record of every deed, word, and thought of his clients for the final reckoning. Simultaneously, a representation of the Final Judgment appeared in the tympanum above the main entrance of the parish church. It represented Christ, enthroned as a judge, between the gate of heaven and the jaws of hell, with an angel holding the book of life opened at the page corresponding to the individual poor soul. Even the rudest peasant and humblest charwoman could no more enter the church portal without learning that their names and their deeds appear in the text of the heavenly book. God, like the landlord, refers to the written account of a past, which, in the community, had been mercifully forgotten.

In 1215, the Fourth Lateran Council made auricular confession obligatory: The conciliar text was the first canonical document that explicitly stated that an obligation was binding on all Christians, *both* men and women. And confession interiorized the sense of the "text" in two distinct ways: it fostered the sense of "memory" and of "confession." For a millennium, Christians recited their prayers as they picked them up within the community, with great local and generational variants. Sentences were often so corrupted that they might foster piety, but certainly did not make sense. The twelfth-century church synods tried to remedy this state of affairs. Their canons imposed on the clergy the duty of training the laity's memory by having them repeat the words of the *Pater* and *Credo,* word for word, as they are in the Book. When the penitent went to confession, he had to prove to the priest that he knew his prayers by heart, that he had acquired the kind of memory on which words could be engraved. Only after this memory test could he proceed to the examination of another spot of his heart, henceforth called his conscience, in which the account of his evil deeds, words, and thoughts had been kept. Even the illiterate "I" that speaks in confession now perceived through new, literate, eyes, its own "self" in the image of a text.

### *Lay self, lay conscience, lay memory*

The new kind of past, frozen in letters, was cemented as much in the self as in society, in memory and conscience as much as in charters and account books, descriptions and signed confessions. And the experience of an individual self corresponded to a new kind of subject of the law that took shape in the law schools of Bologna and Paris and became normative over the centuries for the conception of person, whenever Western society extended its influence. This new self and this new society were realities that arose only within the literate mind.

In an oral society, a past statement can only be recalled by a similar one. Even in societies in which nonalphabetic notations are kept, speech does not lose its wings: When pronounced, it is gone forever. Pictographic or ideographic notation suggests to the reader an idea for which he must, anew, find a word. The alphabetic text fixes the sound. When it is read, the past *dictator's* sentences become present. A new kind of building material for the present has come into being: It is made up of the actual words of speakers long dead. And, in the late Middle Ages, the constitution of the visible text brought whole constructions from the past, in a new way, into the present.

In an oral society, a man had to stand by his word. He confirmed his word by taking an oath, which is a conditional curse called upon himself in the event that he should become unfaithful. While swearing, he grasped at his beard or his balls, pledging his flesh as a troth. When a freedman swore, any case against him came to rest. Under the literate regime, the oath paled before the manuscript: It was no more the recall but the record that counted. And if there was no record, the judge was empowered to read the heart of the accused, so torture was introduced into the proceedings. The question was applied and pried open the heart. Confession under torture now took the place of oath and ordeal. Inquisitorial techniques taught the accused to accept the identity between the text that the court read out to him and that other text that was etched in his heart. Only in the visual comparison of two texts could the identity of the two contents, that of the original and that of the copy, be visually imagined. A miniature of 1226 preserves the first picture of the "corrector," a new official who leans over the shoulder of the scribe to certify the "identity" between two charters. It was again a clerical technique that was reflected in the new law of judicial evidence that demanded the judge to check the defendant's utterance against the truth at the bottom of his heart.

The literate mind implies a profound reconstruction of the lay self, the lay conscience, the lay memory, no less than the lay conception of the past and the lay fear of having to face the doomsday book at the hour of death. All of these new features, of course, the laity and the clergy shared, and they were effectively transmitted outside of schools and *scriptoria*. This point has, so far, been largely neglected by the historians of education. They have mainly focused on the evolution of clerical literacy and have seen in these transformations of mental space but a side effect of chancery skills. Historians have well explored the style of letters, of abbreviation, of integration between text and ornament: They have enlarged our knowledge of the impact that papermaking and the new smooth writing surface in the thirteenth century had on the evolution of the cursive script, which enabled scholastic masters to lecture from notes written by their own hand rather than those dictated; they have observed the enormous increase in sealing wax used in chanceries; they can tell us that for a typical court session in the mid-twelfth century, barely a dozen sheep would lose their skin, while a century later several hundred hides would be needed to make into parchment. If historians have paid attention to the evolution of lay literacy, or more generally to the new configuration taken by the literate mind, they have usually observed how it takes shape among clerics: how the new self came to be explored as a new psychological domain in the autobiographies of Guibert and Abelard; how new scholastic logic and grammar presupposed the visual textualization of the page. At best, some historians have attempted to understand how the increasing frequency with which fabliau romances, travelogues, and homilies were written for reading in front of a large public affected the style in which these were composed. Yet obviously, while schools, *scriptoria,* and the new technical notions of clerical literacy were essential to the spread of the literate mind, they were of secondary importance in its actual shaping and spread for the majority who, absent these measures, acquired it with amazing speed.

The details I have given, all taken from the later twelfth century, which I know best, illustrate what I mean by the impact that one particular literate technique can have on the shape of an epoch's literate mind. They illustrate the arguable effect that the visible text had at that moment on a web of other concepts that, in their formation, are dependent on the alphabet. I point to such notions as self, conscience, memory, possessive description, and identity. It is the historian's task to see how this web is transformed in successive epochs – under the influence of late medieval *narratio,* of "fiction," Renaissance critical text editions, the printing press, vernacular grammar, the "reader," and so on. At each stage, the historian of education would get new inspiration by starting the inquiry from the evidence of new forms of lay literacy rather than from new ideals and techniques of teachers. However, my plea for research is not primarily motivated by my interest in this neglected side of educational research, in dealing with phenomena that take place within the alphabetic culture space. My main reason for pleading for this research is a concern with the exploration of that space itself. I feel my very self threatened by the waning of this space.

### Exile of the literate mind

I still remember a shock I had in Chicago in 1964. We were sitting around a seminar table; opposite to me sat a young anthropologist. At what I thought was the critical point of the conversation, he said to me, "Illich, you can't turn me on, you do not communicate with me." For the first time in my life, I became aware that I was being addressed not as a person but as a transceiver. After a moment of disarray, I began to feel outrage. A live person, to whom I thought that I had been responding, experienced our dialogue as something more general, namely, as "one form of human communication." I immediately thought of Freud's description of three instances of sickening outrage experienced in Western culture: the "Kränkungen" when the heliocentric system, evolution, and the unconscious had to be integrated into everyday certainty. It was then, twenty years ago, that I began to reflect on the depth of the epistemological break that I propose for examination. I suspect that this break is deeper than those suggested by Freud – and certainly it is more directly related to the subject with which educators deal.

Only after several years of research on the history of that conceptual space that emerged in archaic Greece did I grasp the depth at which the computer-as-metaphor is exiling anyone who accepts it from the space of the literate mind. I began to reflect on the emergence of a new mental space whose generating axioms are no longer based on the encoding of speech sounds through alphabetic notation, but instead on the power to store and manipulate "information" in binary bits.

I am not proposing that we examine the effects that the computer as a technical tool has on the keeping of and access to written records; nor how it can be used for the teaching of "the three R's." Equally, I am not proposing to study the perspective that the computer leaves on modern style and compositions. I call rather for reflection on a web of terms and ideas that connects a new set of concepts, whose common metaphor is the computer, and that does not seem to fit into the space of literacy, within which pedagogics originally took shape.

In calling for such attention, I want to avoid the temptation to assign any causal function to the electronic machine. Just as it was a major mistake to maintain that the printing press was necessary to have the Western mind moulded by "linear thought," so too it would be a mistake to believe that the computer itself threatens the survival of the literate mind. Centuries before Gutenberg cut his first font, a combination of small techniques in the *scriptoria* of twelfth-century monasteries created the visible text in which a very complex evolution of literate life-styles and imagery found its appropriate mirror. And, in a similar way, I suspect that a future historian will see the relationship between the computer and the waning of literate space. Under circumstances much too complex even to hint at, at the height of economic and educational development during the second quarter of the twentieth century, the web of literate axioms was weakened, and the new mental space or "structure" found its metaphor in the Turing Machine. It would be unwise, in this plea, to propose how this new break should be studied. But by recalling a story told by Orwell, I hope to make it plausible that the exploration of the break we are witnessing is central to the concern of any research on what "education" might be about.

It is important to remember that at the time Orwell worked on *1984*, the language of "role theory," which Mead (1934) and others had coined a decade earlier, was just being picked up by sociology. The vocabulary of "cybernetics" was still confined to the lab. Orwell, as a novelist, sensed the mood of the time and invented the parable for a mind-set whose elements were as yet unnamed. He reflected on the effects that the treatment of speech as communication would have on people before the computer was available as a model. In 1945, Western Union placed an ad in the *New York Times* seeking to employ "communications carriers," a euphemistic neologism for messenger boys. The *OED Supplement* gives this instance as the first use of the term with its current meaning.

Thus, Orwell's *Newspeak* is much more than a caricature of propaganda or a parody of Basic English, which in the thirties had fascinated him. *Newspeak,* at the end of the novel, is for him the cipher for something that then had no English equivalent. This becomes clear in the scene in which O'Brien from the Thought Police says to Smith whom he tortures, "We do not merely destroy our enemies, we change them . . . we convert, we shape them . . . we make our enemy one of ourselves before we kill him . . . we make his brain perfect before we blow it out" (1949). At this point, Smith, the novel's antihero, still believes that what O'Brien says must make sense. The next pages describe how Smith is disabused of his literate mind. He will have to accept that O'Brien's world is both senseless and selfless and that the therapy he undergoes has the purpose to make him join it.

Winston Smith works at the Ministry of Truth. He specializes in the abuse of language, propaganda, in a caricature of Basic English. He practices extreme distortions that are possible within the literate mind. O'Brien has the task of leading him into an entirely new world, a "space" that Smith must first understand and then accept. O'Brien says to him, "Tell me why we cling to power . . . speak!" Strapped, Winston answers, "You rule over us for our own good . . . you believe that human beings are not fit to govern themselves." This answer, which would have pleased Ivan's Inquisitor in Dostoyevski's novel, makes O'Brien turn the pain to "33 degrees." "We seek power entirely for its own sake." O'Brien insists that the *state is* power, and he has previously made Smith understand that his power consists in the ability to write *the* book. Winston is to be a line in that book, written or rewritten by the state. "Power is in tearing human minds to pieces," says O'Brien, "and putting them together again in new shapes of our own choosing." Torture enables Winston to abandon his belief that *Newspeak* is a degraded form of English; he understands that *Newspeak* is an exchange of meaningless know-how, without any *why* and without any *I*. When O'Brien holds up four fingers and calls them "three," Winston is to understand the message, not the speaker. At a loss for an English word for the exchange of message units between machines, Orwell calls the kind of intended relationship "*collective solipsism.*" Without knowing the appropriate word, namely, "communication," Winston has come to understand the world in which O'Brien's state operates. Orwell insists that the mere understanding of this world is not enough; it must be accepted.

To accept his existence without sense and self, Winston needs the ultimate therapy of "Room 101." Only after this betrayal does he take himself for granted as part of "a phantasy world in which things happen as they should" – namely, on screen. And to accept being just a message unit of senseless power, Winston has first to erase his own self. Neither violence nor pain could break what Orwell calls his "decency." To become selfless, like O'Brien, Winston must first betray his last love, Julia. Later, when the two former lovers meet as burned-out hulls, they know that in Room 101 they had meant what they said. Self-betrayal in face of torture was the last thing Winston *meant*. According to Orwell, only betrayal would integrate the victims into the executioner's solipsistic system of meaningless communication.

I have now told you my fable. It is the story of the state that has turned into a computer and that of educators who program people so that they come to lose the distinction between *self* and *I* that has come to flower within literate space. They learn to refer to themselves as "my system" and to input themselves as appropriate lines into the Mega-text. In the novel, Orwell speaks tongue-in-cheek. He tells more than a cautionary tale, but he does not portray something he believes ever could come to be. He creates the cipher for the state that survives society; communication between role-players that survive the literate mind; people who survive the betrayal of "decency." For Orwell *1984* is the cipher of something impossible that his journalistic genius made appear imminent.

In retrospect, Orwell appears to some of us as an optimist; he thought that the cybernetic mind would spread only as a result of intensive instruction. In fact, many people now accept the computer as the key metaphor for themselves and for their place in the world, without any need for "Room 101." Surreptitiously, they cross over from the mental domain of lay literacy to that of the computer. And they do so, often with as little competence in the use of machine as thirteenth-century laymen had in the use of pen and parchment. The cybernetic mind engulfs a new kind of layman, without assistance from educational agencies. This is the reason why, at the outset, I called attention to two rarely formulated questions: First, is there any reason to believe that the new intense concern of the educational establishment with universal *clerical* literacy can, in fact, strengthen and spread the literate mind? And, second, has schooling now become an initiation ritual introducing participants to the cybernetic mind by hiding from them the contradiction between the literate ideas they pretend to serve and the computer image they sell?

With these suggestions I hope to have clarified the subject and the urgency of the research for which I plead. This research is based on an historical phenomenology of assumptions about speech. Only the technique of the alphabet allows us to record speech and to conceive of this record – in the alphabet – as "language" that we *use* in speaking. A certain kind of viewing the past and of bringing up the young are determined by this assumption. The research I call for could set out to identify the assumptions that are characteristic and proper to "education" only within this mental space.

The research would further explore to what degree literates and illiterates alike share the special mind-set that arises in a society that uses alphabetic record. It would recognize that the literate mind constitutes an historical oddity of seventh-century origin. It would further explore this space that is uniform in its characteristics but diverse in all the distortions and transformations these permit. Finally, this research would recognize the heteronomy of the literate space in regard to three other domains: the worlds of orality, those shaped by nonalphabetic notations, and, finally, that of the cybernetic mind.

You can see that my world is that of literacy. I am at home only on the island of the alphabet. I share this island with many who can neither read nor write but whose mind-set, like mine, is fundamentally literate. And they are threatened, as I am, by the betrayal of those clerics who dissolve the words of the book into just one communication code.

## ACKNOWLEDGMENTS

A version of this chapter appeared in *Interchange* 18/1–2 © the Ontario Institute for Studies in Education, 1987.

## REFERENCES

Augustine, Saint, Bishop of Hippo. (1942). *Confessions*. New York: Sheed & Ward.
Cassirer, E. (1957). *The philosophy of symbolic forms. Vol. 3: The phenomenology of knowledge*. New Haven, Conn.: Yale University Press.
Clanchy, M. T. (1979). *From memory to written record, England, 1066–1307*. Cambridge University Press.
Eisenstein, E. (1979). *The printing press as an agent of change: Communication and cultural transformation in early modern Europe*. Cambridge University Press.

Goody, J. (1980). *The interface between the written and the oral.* Cambridge University Press.
Havelock, E. (1963). *Preface to Plato.* Cambridge, Mass.: Harvard University Press.
Illich, I. (1973). *De-schooling society.* New York: Penguin.
Kuhn, T. (1962). *The structure of scientific revolutions.* Chicago: University of Chicago Press.
Langer, S. (1942). *Philosophy in a new key.* Cambridge, Mass.: Harvard University Press.
Lord, A. (1960). *The singer of tales.* Harvard Studies in Comparative Literature, Vol. 24. Cambridge University Press.
Luria, A. R. (1976). *Cognitive development: Its cultural and social foundations.* Cambridge, Mass.: Harvard University Press.
Mead, G. H. (1934). *Mind, self and society.* Chicago: University of Chicago Press.
Notopolous, J. A. (1938). Mnemosyne in oral literature. *Translations of the American Philosophical Association* 69:465–93.
Ong, W. (1982). *Orality and literacy: The technologizing of the word.* London: Methuen.
Orwell, G. (1949). *1984.* New York: Harcourt, Brace & World.
Panofsky, E. (1924). *Idea.* Leipzig: Teubner.
Parry, M. (1971). *The collected papers of Milman Parry* (A. Parry, ed.). Oxford: Oxford University Press (Clarendon Press).
Peabody, B. (1975). *The winged word: A study in the technique of ancient Greek oral composition as seen principally through Hesiod's work and days.* Albany: State University of New York Press.
Plato (1952). *Phaedrus.* Indianapolis: Bobbs-Merrill.
Polanyi, K. (1944). *The great transformation: The political and economic origins of our times.* Boston: Beacon.
Saenger, P. (1982). Silent reading: Its impact on late medieval script and society. *Viator* 13:367–414.

# 3
# Oral metalanguage
CAROL FLEISHER FELDMAN

Olson (1986), McLuhan (1962), Goody and Watt (1968), Havelock (1982), Ong (1982), Chafe and Danielwicz (1987), and others claim, roughly, that writing is necessary for the forms of consciousness found in modern Western thought. Naturally, this summary of their shared view is much too simple, and they would rightly insist on caveats to every term. For example, for Olson (1986), it is not a matter of writing *tout court*, but rather of "some deeper involvement in a literate tradition" (p. 112). Moreover, writing may not be strictly *necessary* for consciousness but rather "provides the means for splitting [text from interpretation by] fixing part of its meaning as the text and permitting interpretations to be seen for the first time as interpretations" (p. 114). And it may not be consciousness itself that is affected but rather some special form of self-consciousness such as recognizing one's own "interpretations as merely interpretations" (p. 114). These are Olson's caveats. Other proponents of the general view have others of their own. Nevertheless, I think it is fair to say that they share the general view as stated. Where they see the remaining problem is in the lack of a specific mechanism to account for how exactly writing works its effects on mind. Let me quote Olson (1986): "Even if there was no agreed theory on the role of literacy in social and cognitive change, there was and continues to be a general agreement that literacy, printing, and the alphabet, however they did it, were fundamental to those changes" (p. 111). I shall refer to this view hereafter as the *general claim*.

On encountering this literature for the first time, I was puzzled – less by the view itself than by the feeling among its contemporary proponents that it is generally shared. I had just been reading the rather extensive modern anthropological literature on oratory and other oral forms that invite reflection or interpretation. Among the special forms of talk described in the anthropological literature are Wana poetry, Ilongot oratory, Indian myths, and other highly patterned and artful oral forms found, usually, in cultures that have no important (or any) written literature. These are artful forms in that they differ from the everyday talk used for getting on with, getting things done with, and gossiping with others; and they require self-consciousness and skill from their producer. In these two crucial respects – in their remoteness from everyday activity and in requiring skill of their makers – they are much like our artful genres of poetry, legal briefs, biblical exegesis, and the novel, to mention only a few. For these reasons, they might reasonably be conceived of as artful oral genres. Our artful genres tend today to be written. But is it the mere fact that they are written that invites reflection and interpretation or is it something about the patterns embodied in the genres themselves that does? And if it is artful genre that invites reflection, would not artful oral genres invite it too?

To me it seems that the anthropological literature on oral genre is relevant to the *general claim*, because it apparently runs counter to it, and it has not had a hearing in the emerging agreement among psychologists and educators. That is not surprising since anthropologists interested in oral genres have not, of course, organized their analyses around the terms of an emerging agreement outside their own field. Perhaps that is why the data have been overlooked. And that is what I propose to remedy here – by reexamining anthropological reports about oral genres in the terms of the *general claim,* ferreting out, where I can, a distinction between text and interpretation in oral genres that the *general claim* assigns to writing alone.

My argument hinges on the claim that there are, elsewhere, oral genres comparable to our written genres. It often seems that proponents of the *general claim* think of written, but not oral, language as having a variety of distinctive genres, for they apparently assume that oral language is limited in its form to the genre of everyday conversation. Behind this may lie a deeper unexamined assumption: that oral production takes the same form in our culture as it does in others – perhaps even that oral production *always* has the form of the conversations of everyday life. But this is not necessarily true. In fact, in some oral cultures one finds very distinctive oral forms that are thoroughly different from the talk of everyday conversation, that is, distinctive oral genres. Oral forms may be more varied and better defined in these cultures partly because there is no competing written language, although they *can* be richer in literate cultures than they are in the urban culture of North America – for example, to take one striking case, in rural parts of the southwest of the Republic of Ireland where an unusually rich legacy of oral genres has persisted despite a relatively recent and now widespread literacy.

It is perhaps because the range of genres is so much more evident in written than spoken language here that when we psychologists think of oral forms, we tend to imagine only conversation. Chafe and Danielewicz's (1987) study is an exception to this. It compares two oral and two written forms found in our culture: conversation and lecturing versus letter writing and the writing of academic papers. A very extensive empirical analysis was undertaken to count such features as hedges, contractions, and words per intonation unit, among many others. The picture that emerges is one that does not yield to a clear characterization in terms of general differences between speaking and writing. Rather, it suggests to Chafe and Danielewicz a continuum (of writing likeness) from conversation through lectures and letters to academic writing. But where they see a mixture of oral and written features varying along a single continuum, I see multiple genres.

Certain kinds of linguistic jobs, for example, dispute resolution, arise in virtually every culture. In many cultures, this takes on a ceremonial form that lies outside the ordinary events of everyday life. Even here, a central part of legal life is oral argument. Elsewhere, the entire procedure is oral. So, for example, when a culture lacks a written genre of legal briefs, one often finds there an oral genre that serves the same function, namely, of stating the case of the disputant. But one had best not be too much of a structuralist about this, for there are enormous differences across cultures in how disputes are resolved in talk. In some cultures "the brief" focuses on the facts and strives to make explicit the differences in the various disputants' versions of them in order to elicit a judgment in favor of one and against the other, while in other cultures the brief actually avoids stating the facts in order to arrive at a new consensus that everyone can live with without shame. In the same way, stories in some cultures are strictly factual recitations of events, while in others they are fanciful and inventive. Moreover, even if the *forms* are the same, the *meaning* to members of different cultures of legal briefs or even of storytelling can differ, as Geertz (1973), for example, has shown for the cultural meaning of gambling in the Balinese cockfight.

My point, then, is not that there are universal forms, or even universal meanings to common forms, but rather that there are many important events in human social life that occur, virtually universally, in *some* form – not just dispute resolution and storytelling, but the amusement and instruction of the young, marriage arrangements, the healing of the sick, the propitiation of the deities, and the like. And these events, as signal social events, not only *take place in*, but in Wittgenstein's sense are *made by*, their characteristic forms of talk, for these forms of talk are much like those other event-making forms of language that Wittgenstein (1953) called "forms of life." Wittgenstein described such activities as reporting an event, forming and testing a hypothesis, making up a story, and guessing riddles as "language games" in order "to bring into prominence the fact that the *speaking* of language is part of an activity, or of a form of life" (23:11). In nonliterate cultures, the language in which these activities are arranged, negotiated, and constructed can, and often does, have the form that I have described as artful oral genre.

In our culture, artful genres are typically written rather than spoken. Indeed, there may be something about the acquisition of general literacy in a social group, with its advantages for memory for text, that leads to a gradual transformation of oral artful genres to writing and a consequent depletion of the range of artful oral forms. For one thing, all that genres do – whether they are written or oral – is to create a text in which the words themselves, and not just their intended meaning, matter. Though the rhythm and rhyming patterns often adopted by oral cultures obviously help to "record" the words themselves, the limitations of human memory and particularly its reconstructive character (see, e.g., Bartlett, 1950) limit the broad availability of talk. Writing (or at least those forms that record the actual spoken words, as not all do) is plainly a superior tool, for it makes the words themselves even more public, more available in principle, to people much more widely distributed in place and time.

But whether genre is written or spoken, it works much the same way, by fixing a form for expression. What varies inside that form, namely the specific words uttered, is emphasized or highlighted by the fixed frame in which it occurs. To borrow a notion from Jakobson (1981) and the Russian formalists, in a sense the genre serves as the unmarked basis against which the particular words uttered within it are the marked or the new. Words occurring in any genre, then, are made more singular and memorable by it. This general characteristic of genre assists in one aspect of the *general claim:* an emphasis on locution (Austin, 1965) – the words themselves – as distinct from intended meaning (illocution) or effect (perlocution). In short, within a genre the words themselves, and not just their meaning, can acquire a certain salience.[1] And, to follow the *general claim* one step further, only when words are fixed in this way as text (and perhaps once further conditions are met) can they invite interpretation and reflection.

Many nonliterate cultures that have any oral genres have several oral genres that are distinguished by their members from the small talk of everyday life and from one another. For example, Rosaldo (1971, pp. 67–94) reports that among the Ilongot of the Philippines there are thirteen oral genres, each identified by a distinctive genre name, that are divided by the Ilongot into three main categories: straight speech (*pipiyan qupu*), crooked speech (*qambaqan*), and the language of spells (*nawnaw*). There are three genres of straight speech: news or gossip (*beita*), stories about the recent past (*tade:k*), and myths or stories about a more distant past (*tudtud*). There are five genres of crooked speech: riddles (*kinit*), children's rhymes (*qayaman*), songs (*piya*), performances – usually of daring behavior – (*dulag*), and oratory (*purung*). Finally, there are five genres of spells: boasts of headhunting prowess (*qeyap*), highly conventionalized and formalized boasts and pronouncements (*qimanu*), curses (*qayu*), invocations in the service of healing by laymen (*nawnaw*), and such invocations when known only to shamans (*qanitu*).

Except for gossip (*beita*), none of these are the language of everyday talk, and all of the genres are marked in some fashion as distinctive from everyday talk. For example, stories (*tade:k*), the nearest relative to everyday talk, are said to be marked by a technical vocabulary (kinds of weapons, locations, and strategies and details of killing), direct quotation (mostly involving commands, and other routinized speech acts), and "a tone of immediacy and involvement characterized by brief verbal phrases and the connective *san man nu*, 'and then,' which links actions in a string" (1971, p. 71).

In contrast, all of the genres of crooked speech are even more distinctively marked by (1) elaboration of the devices of word play, including rearrangement, substitution, and partials; (2) ornamentation or beauty, including an affixation to cast words into iambic rhythms and special vocabulary that usually has iambic rhythm; and (3) metaphor, including comparisons between humans and plants and similes generally framed by the phrase "be (you) like . . ." (e.g., "May we be like kissing fleas" as a metaphor for friendship at peace meetings). Moreover, they are further marked by (4) reduplication of roots and repetition of whole phrases; (5) special narrative vocabulary like a word for "to deceive" and another for "unfortunately"; and (6) a marked rhythmic pattern. Finally, they have (7) a "quality of wit, facility, and daring, which would be hard to identify in 'straight' discourse" (1971, p. 81).

Some of the genres are seen as, and are in fact, different from everyday talk in having an element of artfulness or special skill. In this sense, special, beautiful, or elegant forms of talk in oral cultures may have characteristics similar to some of our literary genres.

My answer to the *general claim* is that, in both oral and written cultures, there are genres in which the words themselves matter, which may or may not be part of a system of interpretation. One way to focus attention on words is with special oral devices as described above. Another is with writing. Now consider the second step. Fixing a text or focusing on locution is, as supposed in the *general claim*, essential for the special kind of reflection that is interpretation. But emphasis on locution is not always part of a system where it is taken as a stipulation for further interpretation. Writing is one good way to fix a locution for interpretation, provided "that it enters into a literate tradition" (Olson, 1986, p. 111). For, as Bright (1984 and personal communication) observes, writing can be part of the low culture, used only for keeping shopping lists, as he thinks it was by the ancient Greeks, used only for noninterpretive purposes as he supposes it was by the Indians whose high culture of the Vedas was entirely oral.

In the same way, some oral genres invite interpretation, others not. Thus, an oral genre may have the effect of emphasizing the words uttered without inviting interpretation of any kind. Commands, for example, may be a case where the actual words matter (e.g., "I said 'bring me my *pipe*'"), but no interpretation is invited. The language of magic spells and incantations of the shaman may provide another such case in which the exact words matter, yet they are seen as arbitrary and impenetrable by anyone but, perhaps, the shaman who utters them.

Let me rephrase the *general claim* this way: Reflection is assisted when a text is fixed in a manner that invites subsequent interpretation. What is involved in "fixing a text" is making the locution itself salient. What is involved in inviting an interpretation is the evocation of known procedures that are part of the tool kit of the culture for unpacking, explaining, or discussing the locution. The locution, then, must have meanings, implications, or explanations that can be developed not in the context of a "literate tradition" specifically, but in the context of a system of interpretation more generally.

My claim, then, is that (some) writing as we know it in our culture and certain oral genres that appear in nonliterate cultures provide two alternative means to fix a locution for subsequent interpretation. Indeed, I suggest that there may be two universals, or near universals, of human culture expressed here: first, to salivate over words or seek for elegant expression, and second, to want to interpret or make meanings of utterances, to strive to look behind the surface of what is said or merely seen to what is meant.[2] As to the first, as people everywhere have language, it should not surprise us that they find a way to formulate it into genres, and even into some artful genres; for people everywhere and in a most astonishing range of ways seek to create and invent for the sheer beauty of the thing – to move beyond adaptive necessity. And with respect to the second, people everywhere create systems for making meanings behind, beneath, or beyond the mere appearances of things. I have argued elsewhere (Feldman, 1988a) that the special genres discussed here enter into a system for making meanings and even for making the self.

If these are universals of the human condition, the *trigger* surely is not writing, but rather the universal human social and cognitive plight. And the *means* surely is not writing, but the more nearly universal tool of artful genre that occurs (largely) in writing in literate cultures and in talk in oral ones.

For some reason that is unclear to me, advocates of the *general claim* have lately been very excited by the claim that there is a people somewhere who cannot distinguish between saying and meaning, who have no notion of intention, or in another version, have no lexicon to distinguish "say" and "mean," or "is" and "seems." They like to attribute this very basic deficiency to a lack of writing. For the reasons given above, I do not believe that there are or can be any people like this: We cannot imagine what such a people would be like, what their lives would be about, in short, how they could be human. But the *general claim* cannot really be helped with negative evidence. As long as *any* oral cultures have systems of text and interpretation, writing cannot be necessary for them. I turn now to a detailed examination of two such cases: Wana *kiyori*, a form of oral poetry, and Ilongot oratory, with its enormous amount of talk about talk and a distinction between "say" and "think" that gives rise to a system of interpretation.

### Wana poetry, or *kiyori*

The discussion of the Wana that follows is based on the work of Jane Atkinson (1984 and personal communication). The Wana are a group of about five thousand people who inhabit a mountainous interior area in Indonesia. They have several oral forms that are genre-like – legal language, priestly language, and poetry. One poetic form, *tende bomba,* is the love poem. A second poetic form, *kiyori*, is usually about politics, broadly construed.

Atkinson described the form of *kiyori* as

a two-line stanza, each of which is broken into two half lines consisting of eight syllables each. The final two vowels of each line are rhymed assonantally with the final two vowels of the other three half lines. When formally delivered in kiyori style, the stanza is spoken slowly and emphatically with a fixed pitch contour. . . . A [line] is delivered on a single breath. The speaker then pauses for a second breath and delivers the second line in the same manner as the first. (p. 38)

*Kiyori* make use of special elegant vocabulary that does not appear in ordinary conversation and of metaphors. "They thus meet the requirements of specific form that Bloch used to characterize 'formal language,' requirements of meter, assonance, pitch, contour and metaphor" (p. 58). At the same time, and for the same reasons, they meet our requirements for artful oral genres.

In Atkinson's account, the metaphoric language of *kiyori*, which means "wrapped words," words that are ambiguous or have multiple meanings, is essential to them. Atkinson says, "As opposed to 'straight speech,' kiyori offers a way to disguise meaning, to say something indirectly in an elegant way" (p. 41).

*Kiyori* are delivered in a special posture and tone of voice, usually by a man to one or more other men. Often a *kiyori* is repeated several times, not just to correct false starts, but even after it is perfected. The person to whom it is delivered may also repeat it right after hearing it. These procedures, together with the fixed, brief form and the redundancies of rhyme and meter, are plainly designed to fix the locution in memory.

The replies to a *kiyori* may be in *kiyori* or in conversational style. In either case, they are often interpretations:

> If the receiver is a skilled versifier, an exchange of kiyori will follow. Often succeeding kiyori pick up a phrase or a theme from the kiyori that came before. Sometimes, exchangers of kiyori confirm the opinions expressed by their partners. Other times they disagree or change the emphasis, but through the use of the refined verse form, dissension may remain implicit rather than being drawn out in extended and explicit debate. (p. 40)

After the delivery and the reply, there may be a general conversation in which further interpretations are discussed. The following examples will serve to illustrate the genre and the kind of interpretation to which they give rise:

> My life is poor
> I hunch over weeping
> Once the promised date has passed, then
> Peace will arise. (p. 49)

An elder interpreted the verse later as meaning that "the Wana are poor, the government keeps adding to their woes, but people should expect safety after the national election [scheduled to come six months later]." Specifically, the metaphoric "promised date" is interpreted as "pending elections."

The reply to a *kiyori* can also be a second *kiyori* interpreting the first. Atkinson says of the two *kiyori* that follow: "Like many kiyori delivered in response to others, this one picks up a theme from the preceding verse, then brings out another aspect of it. The second kiyori makes explicit the issue of the royal line's return" after the world disaster anticipated in the first (p. 53).

Here is the first *kiyori:*

> Let us not be careless
> in dividing belongings among the children.
> Wait 'til it has been swept,
> The crop, survivors of the destruction.

And the reply:

> When it is safe once again,
> it will be possible to see
> if Meki remembers mother
> from over there where it has darkened.

I think it is clear that the speaker who uses *kiyori* fixes his locution in shared memory, and that once the locution is fixed, it invites interpretation. The fact that the form uses ambiguous expressions, locutions that may have many possible meanings, may further add to the invitation to interpretation, or it may merely give interpretations of *kiyori* their special character and interest. But if metaphor and ambiguity are essential to interpretation of *kiyori*, that may tell us something we did not know about the general character of texts that invite interpretation.

Wana even have a form of what might be called "joke *kiyori*." Pantenggel is a favorite character of Wana tales who always talks in *kiyori* that people love to hear him tell. In the tales, Pantenggel is frustrated in his daily chores by people who want to hear him "express his dismay in verse" (p. 41). The humor lies in the discrepancy between the weighty form and the homely themes he discusses. These joke *kiyori* constitute an ironic subgenre, a form of reflection or metainterpretation on the making of serious *kiyori* itself.[3] They are interpretations of text in a (joke *kiyori*) genre that invites further interpretation. The analogy here would be literary criticism undertaken in a form that is itself an interpretable genre, as, for example, the critical writing of Harold Bloom (1989).

To summarize, I have argued that Wana *kiyori* are a genre that fixes a text for subsequent interpretation. The argument has two parts. The first is the claim that they fix a text. Wana culture prescribes a manner of presentation – namely, repeated presentations by the producer and subsequent repetition by the recipient – and a fixed form that are both plainly designed to contribute to their memorability as text. Corrections and repairs are given until the *kiyori* is word perfect and perfectly recalled. The second is the claim that the text is fixed for the purpose of subsequent interpretation. *Kiyori* are sometimes replied to by an interlocutor who produces a *kiyori* that is an interpretation of (some aspect of) the first *kiyori; kiyori* are routinely discussed and interpreted in ordinary conversation, even some long time after their production, if the circumstances make the *kiyori* apposite; and there are joke *kiyori*.

Finally, I want to conjecture that oral *kiyori* have these essential properties of certain written language forms because the oral *kiyori* and the written forms share a similar genre-like structure: Both are marked forms, marked as different from the language of everyday conversation; both have distinctive linguistic (lexical and syntactic) patterns; and both are used for particular occasions. The genre patterns, in both cases, assist in fixing a text both by placing an emphasis on the locution and by preserving it: Writing makes it into a physical object; *kiyori* makes it memorable. In addition, both provide a mechanism for subsequent interpretation. Just as our written genres carry their systems of interpretation with them by being part of a literate tradition, so the Wana *kiyori* occur within a system of oral interpretation.

The text and interpretation system for *kiyori* is thought by the Wana to hinge on the ambiguity of the locution in relation to the intended meaning. This feature has not been thought by advocates of the *general claim* to be essential to the interpretability of written texts. But perhaps it is. In our culture, written texts come in a variety of genres. Some of them place a great premium on explicitness, on reduction of ambiguity, while others, like the Wana *kiyori*, strive to increase it. If there were any genres that had perfectly explicit locutions, it is hard to imagine what interpreting them would involve. Perhaps only written texts that make use of artful ambiguity are subject to interpretation. Or, alternatively, written text may be, by its very nature, ambiguous with respect to the intentions of the utterer.

So far, there seems to be no essential difference between the text and interpretation system found in the oral form of Wana *kiyori* and in writing. The essential matter of establishing a text and reflecting on it cannot require writing. There are nevertheless differences between written and spoken texts. These differences seem to be attributable to the limitations of memory and to be a matter of degree rather than of kind. First, *kiyori* are very short. Written texts can be much longer. Second, *kiyori* cannot exist across great swaths of time and space, for memory is short and reconstructive, and texts uttered rather than written three hundred years ago or (without electronic transmission) far away are simply unavailable exactly as uttered to an oral culture. Third, the sequence of text and interpretation stops after two to four steps for *kiyori* – no one, perhaps, interprets a *kiyori* with respect to a *kiyori* twenty steps back in its derivation. What writing makes possible, perhaps, is Rashi's commentary on the *Mishnah*, with its multilevel commentaries on commentaries on the Bible, as an ever-extendable series with no constraints of memory to limit derivational depth. This is a matter of degree rather than of kind because the important cognitive process of reflecting on a reflection (called "going meta" these days) *is* facilitated by the mechanism of oral genre. Nevertheless, greater derivational depth together with the more extended text made available by writing makes possible a variety of genres unavailable to oral culture, and this possibility may have some other cognitive consequences that I cannot explore here.

Now let me turn to another case: Ilongot oratory, or *purung*. If Wana *kiyori* resemble our poetry, *purung* more nearly resemble our prose.

## Ilongot *purung*

The Ilongot are a rural group of dry-rice farmers who live along rivers in the mountains of Northern Luzon, in the Philippines. Traditionally, and until very recently, they were headhunters. They were visited by Spanish priests in earlier centuries and by the anthropologist William Jones in about 1906. More recently they were studied by two very gifted ethnographers, Renato Rosaldo (1980, inter alia) and Michelle Rosaldo (1971, 1973, 1980, 1984), whose work gives a rich picture of the Ilongot's social and linguistic life. In the following discussion, I draw heavily on their work.

The Ilongot themselves distinguish, by names, several oral genres. Their extended list of oral genres is given above, so I will just summarize the essential points here. First, there is the language of ordinary conversation, *beita*. It is gossip or the sharing of news and is considered talk of little importance. In contrast with the next two genres, it is considered to be "straight speech," a notion associated with our ideas of reference or clarity (Rosaldo, 1971, p. 70). *Nawnaw* is the genre of magic spells. *Nawnaw* are long and rhythmical and are conducted in the language of metaphor. They are seen as neither crooked nor straight. *Purung* are formal oratory conducted with the formal code called *qambaqan*, or "crooked speech." To orate is to speak the crooked language of *qambaqan*. Oratory is "not a genre for communicating information." Nevertheless, "the idea of 'crooked' language is not . . . one of deviousness or deception. Rather it seems to be linked to the feeling that men are equal, individual, and difficult to understand" (1973, p. 221).

Before focusing on the language of *purung*, I want to anticipate a possible source of confusion, for elsewhere, and in a very well known paper, Rosaldo (1982) discussed another language form very different from *purung*, the speech act called *tuydek*, which she glosses as "commands" (p. 208). *Tuydek* have nothing to do with *purung*. *Tuydek* are orders issued to bring this or that, usually orders given to children, sometimes by a man to his wife. They serve to reconstruct hierarchical relationships that are fragile in an egalitarian society, to get the desired object, and to teach the young the language. Indeed, this form was used to teach the Rosaldos the language when they first arrived. In the context of the discussion of *tuydek*, Rosaldo disagrees with Searle (1969) about underlying intentionality: Searle's categories of speech acts, she argues, "can be criticized for an undue emphasis on the speaker's psychological state, and corresponding inattention to the social sphere" (1982, p. 227). But that, I would argue, is in the nature of that peculiar speech act, the command. *Purung* is another matter altogether. *Purung* are about mental states and underlying intentions; for as Rosaldo says, "the careful speech of purung is, thus, predicated upon a particular view of people's hearts and thoughts, a view that claims that troubled feelings can be quieted if their source, once 'hidden,' is made known. One tries to find the words that will occasion revelation" (1984, p. 150).

*Purung* has a distinctive setting, sound, and linguistic form. As to setting, *purung* is commonly scheduled and is always a public performance. Orators wear nothing except for their g-strings, stand with back arched and graceful, or sit with hands at sides, the posture tense and studied. Gestures are limited to the movement of the shoulders. The right hand may be fixed to a knife tied at the hip. As to sound, *purung* has a distinct high pitch with flat intonation.

Its form is marked with iambic stresses, phonological elaboration, repetition, special vocabulary, puns, metaphor, and hedges. Utterances are hedged by the use of qualifying words ("kind of," "just," "unfortunately," "maybe") and grammatical markers of uncertainty (e.g., reduplication as in "*sibe:sibera*," for "just, kind of, answering") that qualify their force and suggest politeness and humility (1973, pp. 216–17). In addition, *purung* are marked with opening statements as well as formal markings for the ends of turns (e.g., "Well, I am done there"), which constitute only a small part of the astonishing amount of talk about talk. A routine greeting to the assembled company at a *purung* is "So you have come here, and can you *tell* me why you came, so that our fathers and brothers may *hear* it all?" One *purung* began with the opening "Well, whatever it was you *called* me for, I came to *hear*; alas, I can't *speak* well, but I *said* to myself, 'Maybe there is some reason he *commanded* me, so I will go and *hear* its *name*'" (M. Rosaldo, 1980, p. 193, my italics).

All of this distinctive linguistic patterning is closely tied to its distinctive purpose. For though *purung* are a medium of dispute resolution, they are very different from our legal proceedings. Oratory is not a genre for conveying information, making accusations, or discovering the true facts,[4] though it is used to resolve disputes that center on conflicting versions of the facts, but rather is a genre used to arrive at a single version both parties can accept: "Oratory implies the public meeting of opposed parties, parties who, without the help of judge or arbitrator, must find their way towards an agreement" (1973, p. 218). "Oratory provides a focused context in which it is appropriate to invoke shared norms and public understandings, and explain obligations and commitments in terms of social ideals. . . . A number of the stylistic devices or conventions used in oratory reflect and support this orientation. Through them, assumptions which are rarely addressed in everyday interaction are made explicit" (1973, p. 209). Once all such assumptions are made public, it should be possible to construct a common, consensual version.

*Purung*, then, is a genre that has many specific distinguishing features that seem relevant to its distinctive purpose. It focuses attention on the actual words uttered, the locution, with its extensive talk about talk. And the locutions are part of a system of interpretation that is embodied in the *purung* itself; replies often take the form of an interpretation of a prior speaker's utterance. And there are other signs that *purung* is an interpretive system. For one thing, it is heavily marked with metaphor and pragmatic markings that create the kind of gaps or implicitness that we saw interpreted in the case of the *kiyori*. For another, there is a clear sense expressed often by the speakers in oratory that what is said is not necessarily what the (other) speaker thinks. This distinction establishes a pattern of interpretation of what the other may think made in light of what he said. Rosaldo (1973, p. 209) says that, on the one hand, there is the threat that "men may be hiding their true meaning . . . expressed in phrases like 'I hear you, but in my heart'. . . . On the other hand, oratorical conventions demand that the private itself be made public, that thoughts be exchanged" (1973, p. 209).

Interestingly, as in the case of *kiyori*, there are joke *purung*. When a confrontation nears resolution, a serious *purung* may fade into a playful and more exaggerated, parodic use of the same linguistic patterns and eventually be joined by some of the younger men who may be using the opportunity to practice their oratorical skills (1973, p. 204). Moreover, the end of a *purung* can fade into a discussion of the *purung* and interpretation of the locutions of the speakers.

Finally, *purung* is a special skill and a recognized expertise had by only a small number of members of the community who speak for any others who may need to enter a formal negotiation. Plainly, if it is any kind of genre at all, it is an artful genre.

I want to argue that *purung* has the special patterns and purposes that make a well-defined genre, and that in the respect of fixing a text and placing an emphasis on locution for subsequent interpretation, it meets the requirements for writing in the *general claim*. The emphasis on locution is apparent in the extensive use of references to the words themselves, in the extensive talk about talking. Interpretation goes on in the course of the *purung* itself as responses attempt to interpret the indirect language of prior utterances. Let me give an example (from Rosaldo, 1973, pp. 201–5) of three turns that illustrate both references to the words themselves and the effort to interpret them in oratorical responses.

Badilyu has heard a rumor ("some gossip" and "something the wind brought") that Naqmun, a kinsman of his, demands an expensive gift, a gun, as bride price. This is something that Naqmun should not do as a kinsman, and Badilyu has called a *purung*. He replies to Naqmun's opening speech as follows:

Okay, if you are finished with that, let's let our brothers, our fathers, hear it all. Don't think that I am hiding the reason, the true reason, that I called you here. Well, the reason that I called for you is that there is something the wind brought, some gossip reached my ears.

Naqmun's response is to say that he will not after all ask for the gun, for how could he as an affine ("son") of Badilyu; he interprets Badilyu's phrase "something the wind brought" as "some little bit I said . . . before":

Yes, since you are my father, and, well, uncle, as I am your child, well, it is true, there was some little bit I said, something I said before. But even if I said that, uncle, I will not continue it now. Since I said to myself, also, my heart said, "well, now, my life, how can I continue this, since I am the child of my elders; what words can I give them, as I am their son."

Badilyu continues to probe and Naqmun to deny his earlier request, and finally Badilyu replies as follows. His reply is, in a sense, an interpretation of Naqmun's rather mixed set of desires expressed in the locution "since I said to myself . . . 'now . . . how can I continue this, since I am the child of my elders.'" On the one hand, Naqmun would like payment, on the other, he recognizes that being kin it is improper to ask for it. This contradiction remains unresolved in Naqmun's speech. The resolution is the missing piece that Badilyu is talking about in his reply:

Don't speak now, okay, you my child. Now you may say I'm repeating myself, that I am weeding over and over, the same grass, the same garden. But even if we had hoed it once, you know, there are weeds which continue to grow. Think then, if you knew what I know my child; you too, then, would return, again and again, looking and searching. Is there no straight path? It is for that that I am returning, to see what I have stepped over, what words of my child I have skipped past. I return because my heart is asking, if you have not kept something reserved, some words you would yet give me – about your sister, about anything, my child. And whatever you say, I will understand it. Whatever you say, it will be the same. Now when I go to swallow your words, nothing will be left over. It is not I who is too old to swallow what is handed to me. Poor me! What are you thinking? Perhaps I am toothless and the meat that you give me is tough. I am finished.

Finally, it has become evident to me that *purung* is a case of that special kind of interpretive system that refers its interpretations to underlying intentional states of knowledge and belief. In the West, this is a feature of modern literature and its interpretations. There is, in *purung*, a great deal of talk about mental states, especially epistemic states, of one's own and of the interlocutor – above, "think then, if you knew what I know my child." It is speech for reconciling differing belief states in a common version by revealing or concealing and interpreting them. In the sense that interpretations formally undertaken are a kind of analysis, oratory is also an analytic procedure that makes use of oratorical language as a tool of analysis. One more example follows:

Well, if we are to be friends, let me say I know the flesh, the humanity of other men; I know what it is to enter my equal human's home. I have a spleen, and though I am a child facing you, I have knowledge enough to give you a share, so I will gossip; I will let you in on my thoughts. . . . I am a child, oddly, by a turn, a child to you, but you know now and you knew before the target of my thoughts, as I have already told you what is in my heart. (M. Rosaldo, 1980, p. 195)

## Chinook myths

Dell Hymes (1981) gives an interesting example of a myth that is a story about the protagonist's effort at interpretation in his book, *In Vain I Tried to Tell You*. The myth, from the Clackamas Chinook, is *about* interpretation – Seal's daughter's interpretation of the behavior of the woman who is her uncle's wife who "goes out like a man." The expression is metaphorical, but it seems to be unambiguous, or is, in any case, disambiguated by the end of the tale. The story might be considered metainterpretive in the sense that it is about the hazards of interpretation itself. Here, then, is an oral genre in which locution, interpretation, and a discussion of interpretation are woven into a story. Please notice that the talk here is mainly about talk itself – talk fixed as locution by being marked as talk itself. The locutions are those both of text and of interpretation taken as text for a second level of interpretation:

They lived there, Seal, her daughter, her younger brother. I do not know when it was, but now a woman got to Seal's younger brother.
They lived there. They would go outside in the evening. The girl would say, she would tell her mother: "Mother! there is something different about my Uncle's wife. It sounds like a man when she 'goes out.'" "Don't say that! She is your Uncle's wife!"
They lived there like that for a long time. They would 'go out' in the evening. And then she would tell her: "Mother! There is something different about my uncle's wife. When she 'goes out' it sounds like a man." "Don't say that!"
Her uncle and his wife would "lie together" in bed. Some time afterwards the two of them "lay" close to the fire, they "lay" close beside each other. I do not know what time of night it was, but something dripped on her face. She shook her mother. She told her: "Mother! Something dripped on my face." "Hm . . . Don't say that. Your uncle and his wife are 'going.'"
Presently then again she heard something dripping down. She told her: "Mother! Something is dripping, I hear something." "Don't say that. Your uncle and his wife are 'going.'"
The girl got up, she fixed the fire, she lit pitch, she looked where the two were lying. Oh! Oh! She raised her light to it. In his bed her uncle's neck was cut. He was dead. She screamed.
She told her mother: "I told you something was dripping. You told me: 'Don't say that. They are "going."' I had told you there was something different about my uncle's wife. When she 'goes out,' it sounds like a man when she urinates. You told me: "Don't say that!" She wept.
Seal said: "Younger brother! My younger brother! They [his house posts] are valuable standing there. My younger brother!" She kept saying that.
But the girl herself wept. She said: "I tried in vain to tell you. My uncle's wife sounds like a man when she urinates, not like a woman. You told me: 'Don't say that!' Oh! Oh! my uncle!" The girl wept.
Now I remember only that far. (Hymes, 1981, pp. 278–9)

## Conclusion

Though we may not have oral systems of text and interpretation in our culture, the appropriate genres having been handed over to writing, many oral cultures seem to have such oral genres in the absence of a system of writing. Moreover, some of those cultures seem to show the same general preoccupation with the nature of interpretation itself that is of concern to literary theorists. In those oral cultures that have them, artful genres are a privileged and valued form of life, one that is an occasion for reflection and for elegance and beauty that go beyond adaptive necessity.

## ACKNOWLEDGMENTS

I want to thank Janet Miller at the Anthropology Archives of the Chicago Field Museum of Natural History for supplying me with the letters and diaries of William Jones. I discussed the ideas in this chapter, before writing it, with Jane Atkinson, William Bright, Renato Rosaldo, and Annette Weiner. My debt to them is far greater than the usual debt of writer to colleague, for I was out of my own field. They were lavishly generous with advice, examples, details, references, and materials, and I am very grateful to them all for their help. I am especially indebted to Renato Rosaldo for inviting me to rummage through his closet of Ilongot materials and letting me borrow an enormous box full of them. I am also grateful to David Olson, who got me interested in this problem in the first place, and who helped me to see the general argument in a way that led me later to formulate the *general claim* discussed herein. Finally, I thank my husband, Jerome Bruner, whose work on narrative informed the discussion here, for many interesting conversations on Ilongot oratory and related matters.

## NOTES

1 For these reasons, though it may make sense for some purposes to think of conversation as an (oral) genre like any other, I have reservations about doing this. Ordinary conversation is not as tightly patterned as the other genres discussed here; it does not focus the listener's attention on the locutions themselves but rather on illocution and perlocution, and it seems to help define the others by contrast as the oral base-level or pre-genre form. Of course, it is not usually seen as an artful (oral) genre as are *purung* and *kiyori*, but this does not explain the whole of the difference. For example, *tuydek* are not artful, but they are highly patterned, and it is, I believe, by virtue of this that they shift the listener's natural focus on illocution to locution. Perhaps careful students of conversation – the ethnomethodologists, for example – would disagree, citing the complexity of conversational patterns, an observation with which I agree. But complexity is not structure, pattern, or rule, and that is what I am after here. In fact, this might be the reason why the ethnomethodologists have had such a stunning lack of success in coming up with any general principles or conversational rules. Perhaps it is the nature of everyday conversation to be a more or less free form in which almost anything can be said in almost any way provided that order and sequence is maintained, topic and comment structure is attended to, and the level of formality and ellipsis is appropriate.

2 Wittgenstein, in the *Investigations*, discusses this view as an illusion held by logicians, "for they see in the essence, not something that already lies open to view and that becomes surveyable by a rearrangement, but something that lies *beneath* the surface. Something that lies within, which we see when we look *into* the thing, and which an analysis digs out. 'The essence is hidden from us': this is the form our problem now assumes" (1953, ¶ 92, p. 43). I suggest that the logicians are not alone in this. The impulse to go

behind the surface of talk and appearance to something "more real" seems to me, like its corollary belief in the existence of a concealed metaphysical reality, virtually universal in human cultures. Our own culture may be one of the more striking exceptions.

The illusionary quality is explained by Wittgenstein this way: "The ideal, as we think of it, is unshakable. You can never get outside it; you must always turn back. There is no outside; outside you cannot breathe – where does this idea come from? *It is like a pair of glasses on our nose through which we see whatever we look at. It never occurs to us to take them off* " (1953, ¶ 103, p. 45, my italics). An illusion having this description seems, to me, a good candidate for a universal of human cognition.

3 I have discussed similar transformations (e.g., of comment to topic) undertaken in order to reflect on the reflection itself as a recursive process of taking the new as the given in Feldman (1987, 1988b).

4 "A related point is that oratory is not, in fact, a genre for communicating information. Typically, participants know 'all the facts' – all the relevant history – before entering a debate. They have rehearsed arguments to counter all of their opponents' strategies for days before the encounter; they have nothing to learn. Among orators, there is no place for adjudication; theirs is a contest of wits" (M. Rosaldo, 1980, p. 86). And, in a footnote to this paragraph, she says further: "In fact, it is impossible to accuse someone – of taking a head, for instance – in oratory."

## REFERENCES

Atkinson, J. (1984). "Wrapped words": Poetry and politics among the Wana of Central Sulawesi, Indonesia. In D. Brenneis & F. Myers (eds.), *Dangerous words: Language and politics in the Pacific*. New York: New York University Press.

Austin, J. L. (1965). *How to do things with words*. New York: Oxford University Press.

Bartlett, F. C. (1950). *Remembering*. Cambridge University Press.

Bloom, H. (1989). *Ruin the sacred truths*. Cambridge, Mass.: Harvard University Press.

Bright, W. (1984). *American Indian linguistics and literature*. Berlin: Mouton.

Chafe, W., & Danielewicz, J. (1987). Properties of written and spoken language (Tech. Rep. No. 5). Berkeley and Los Angeles: University of California, Center for the Study of Writing.

Feldman, C. F. (1987). Thought from language: The linguistic construction of cognitive representations. In J. Bruner and H. Haste (eds.), *Making sense*. New York: Methuen.

(1988a). Untitled. In Selections from the Symposium on "Literacy, Reading and Power." *Yale Journal of Criticism* 2(1): 209–14.

(1988b). Early forms of thoughts about thoughts: Some simple linguistic expressions of mental state. In J. Astington, P. Harris, & D. Olson (eds.), *Developing theories of mind*. Cambridge University Press.

Geertz, C. (1973). *The interpretation of cultures*. New York: Basic.

Goody, J., & Watt, I. (1968). The consequences of literacy. In J. Goody (ed.), *Literacy in traditional societies*. Cambridge University Press.
Havelock, E. (1982). *The literate revolution in Greece and its cultural consequences*. Princeton, N.J.: Princeton University Press.
Hymes, D. (1981). *In vain I tried to tell you*. Philadelphia: University of Pennsylvania Press.
Jakobson, R. (1981). *Selected writings*. The Hague: Mouton.
McLuhan, M. (1962). *The Gutenberg galaxy*. Toronto: University of Toronto Press.
Olson, D. (1986). The cognitive consequences of literacy. *Canadian Journal of Psychology* 27(2): 109–21.
Ong, W. (1982). *Orality and literacy: The technologizing of the word*. London: Methuen.
Rosaldo, M. (1971). Context and metaphor in Ilongot oral tradition. Ph.D. dissertation, Harvard University, Department of Anthropology.
  (1973). I have nothing to hide: The language of Ilongot oratory. *Language in Society* 2:193–223.
  (1980). *Knowledge and passion*. Cambridge University Press.
  (1982). The things we do with words: Ilongot speech acts and speech act theory in philosophy. *Language in Society* 2:203–37.
  (1984). Words that are moving: The social meanings of Ilongot verbal art. In D. Brenneis & F. Myers (eds.), *Dangerous words: Language and politics in the Pacific*. New York: New York University Press.
Rosaldo, R. (1980). *Ilongot headhunting 1883–1974*. Stanford, Calif.: Stanford University Press.
Searle, J. (1969). *Speech acts*. Cambridge University Press.
Wittgenstein, L. (1953). *Philosophical investigations*. Oxford: Blackwell Publisher.

# 4
# Rational thought in oral culture and literate decontextualization

J. PETER DENNY

Although the effects of literacy upon human thought are large, they are often misconstrued and exaggerated. Western thought, to which literacy is a big contributor, is widely believed to be more reflective, more abstract, more complex, and more logical than thought in preliterate agricultural and hunter-gatherer societies. The available research, however, shows that these beliefs are wrong and that Western thought has only one distinctive property separating it from thought in *both* agricultural and hunter-gatherer societies – decontextualization. Decontextualizing is the handling of information in a way that either disconnects other information or backgrounds it. For example, when we teach our kindergarten children the "abstract" shapes, square, circle, triangle, and rectangle, we present diagrams in which the shape is either not connected to any object or other properties of the object are backgrounded.

## A general theory of cross-cultural cognition

To show that Western thought differs only by being decontextualized, it is helpful to have a general theory of cross-cultural differences in thinking that systematizes the available research findings. Most of what we know can be summarized using two variables, differentiation and contextualization. Higher differentiation is making more distinctions *within* a thought unit, whereas higher contextualization, as implied above, is making more connections to *other* thought units. Cross-cultural differences in thought concern habits of thinking, not capacities for thought. All humans are capable of and do practice both differentiated thinking and its opposite, integrated thinking, as well as both contextualized and decontextualized thought. However, different cultures make some of these thought patterns fluent and automatic, whereas the opposite patterns remain unusual and cumbersome.

An oversimplified summary will serve to introduce the known differences. Hunter-gatherer thought is the starting point for later de-

*Rational thought in oral culture* 67

```
high ─────────────△─────────  • differentiation
medium high      ╱ ╲       ╱
               ╱    ╲     ╱
             ╱   ╲ ╲   ╱
           ╱      ╲ ╲ ╱
         ╱         ╲ ╳
low    ╱            ╲╱  ╲   contextualization

      gatherer   hunter  agriculturist  industrialist
```

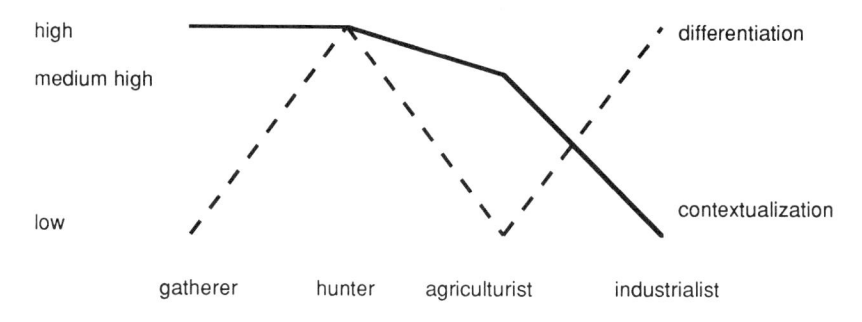

Figure 4.1. Cross-cultural variation in contextualization and differentiation.

velopments, since hunting and gathering tasks were those used to support humans throughout their millions of years of biological evolution. After we became fully evolved 45,000 years ago, these tasks and their associated thought styles continued until agriculture began 8,000 or so years ago. In societies in which gathering predominated, thinking was integrated (low differentiation) and contextualized; where hunting predominated, thinking was differentiated and contextualized. As agriculture developed to middle levels of societal complexity, an integrative thought style was favored as was, according to some research, slightly lowered contextualization. The shift to industrial or "Western" thought, which began in classical Greece, led to a large decrease in contextualization – it is this change that was amplified by literacy. At the same time, differentiation returned to high levels. The changes in these two variables are summarized in Figure 4.1.

### Evidence for the theory and its range of application

The nonlinear function shown for differentiation is based for the most part on the psychological research of Berry (1976): For various samples representing three of the culture types, he has repeatedly found that hunting and Western groups show higher differentiation scores than do African agriculturalists on psychological tests in which the subject's task is to make distinctions within a thought unit, for example, see a simpler visual design as a hidden part of a more complex whole (called "embedded figures tests"). Research by others suggests that very low differentiation is most characteristic of agriculture of middle levels of complexity, in which there are large domesticated animals. Simpler agricultural societies, such as the Amerindian horticulturalists, do not show greatly lowered differentiation: Lonner and Sharp (1983) found embedded figures test scores for Mayan horticulturalists that were only slightly lower than Berry's for hunting and industrial societies. However, other middle-level agricultural groups such as Pacific Islanders do seem to show lowered differentiation: Bishop (1978, p. 187) reports informal results from Papua-New Guinea indicating poor embedded figures test performance. This pattern is confirmed and extended by Lomax's studies of information processing styles in song and dance (Lomax & Berkowitz, 1972): He finds low differentiation (his term is "high integration") for only the middle-level African and Pacific Island agriculturalists, not for simpler Amerindian horticulturalists or for the more complex agricultural societies, the plow agriculturalists of Europe, and the irrigation agriculturalists of Asia.

This research has been tentatively extended to gatherers. For Australian gatherers, McIntyre's (1976) study seems to show that traditional Aboriginal children are lower in differentiation on embedded figures tests than are Westernized Aboriginal children or white Australian children. Similarly, Reuning and Wortley (1973) find that Bushmen gatherers in southern Africa have great difficulty with embedded figures tests, and are therefore most probably integrative in their thought style. These observations are supported by those of Lomax and Berkowitz (1972) who find highly integrative song and dance styles among both Aborigines and Bushmen. To these latter authors, this integrated thought style seems to be the outcome of the predominance of women's gathering over men's hunting in the socioeconomic system of these peoples. For the Aborigines only, another possible explanation comes from the work of Turner (1985), who argues that Aboriginal culture is a fundamentally different alternative to the Amerindian hunting cultures – it remains to work out how this might connect with integrated thinking. For the African gatherers, another possibility is that their integrative thought has come from many centuries of interdependence with neighboring agricultural societies. This appears to be the case for the Biaka hunter-gatherers of central Africa, who were found by Berry et al. (1986) to be almost as integrative in their embedded figures test performance as adjacent agricultural groups. In summary, the nonlinear function in Figure 4.1 shows high integration among gatherers, high differentiation among hunters, high integration among middle-level agriculturalists, and high differentiation in industrial society.

The other function in Figure 4.1 showing the decrease in contextualization from agricultural to industrial society is attested in psychological studies of deductive reasoning. Standard reasoning problems developed in the Western tradition, such as those solvable by modus ponens, i.e., *if p then q, p, therefore q*, are low in contextualization by design; they are supposed to be done without any connections to other information beyond that stated in the problem. To test for this culturally expected decontextualization, psychologists often devise examples that have no connection with the everyday experience of the subjects. Thus, Luria (1974) in the 1930s gave the following example to illiterate peasants in southern Russia: "In the far north, where there is snow, all bears are white. Novaya Zemlya is in the far north and there is always snow there. What color are the bears there?" If processed as a decontextualized package, the answer by deductive reasoning is "white." However, Luria found that his subjects either refused to do such problems because they could think of no appropriate context for the information, or they added contextual information before reasoning. In either case they were scored "wrong." A few young, newly literate subjects had enough Western-style schooling to be able to do the expected decontextualization. Similar effects were found for African agriculturalists by Greenfield (1972) and Scribner (1977). Finally, Hutchins (1980) studied the naturally occurring reasoning in a Trobriand Island (Papua-New Guinea) court case and found massive contextualization – for instance, the judge's decision only alluded to principles of law (which he said all in the court would be familiar with) and did not make explicit their role in his decision; the litigants and spectators were expected to add these principles from context to the information in the judge's statement so as to follow the logic of his decision. In these various studies, agricultural groups showed high contextualization compared to the low contextualization that Westerners apply to such problems.

Equivalent psychological studies of hunter-gatherer groups are not available, but other kinds of research show them to be high contextualizers. Denny (1986) studied the semantics of Eskimo mathematical words and found that number concepts could not be expressed in isolation, that is, there was no equivalent to purely numeric words such as English *one, two, three*. At minimum, the context that has to be expressed is the counting of elements, indicated by the suffix *-t*, or the counting of sets, indicated by *-it*:

pingasut   'three (elements)'     pingasuit   'three (sets)'
sitamat    'four (elements)'      sitamait    'four (sets)'

Frequently, more contextual information is expressed in the number words:

pingasu*iqtaq*tuq        'he did it three *times*'
marru*unaaqtiq*lugik     'two *at a time*'
marru*uqattaq*lugik      'they being *regularly two*'
sitama*ujuut*            'ones that are *usually* four'
sitama*lik*              'the *one with* four'

All these examples show that, in Eskimo counting, numeric information is contextualized by other information. In summary, our evidence shows that hunting and gathering societies are high in contextualization, as are agriculturalists (medium high as research to be reviewed shows), and the Western tradition is low in contextualization.

**Functional basis**

Humans do not change their habits of thought unless there are compelling reasons to do so. Our own decontextualized thought is so natural to us that to discuss why we adopted it, it is necessary to say what is useful about the original contextualized mode of thought found in non-Western groups. Douglas (1966, p. 88) suggests that in small-scale societies, thought has to be employed not just to gain a living but also to support the social structure; without autonomous social institutions such as tax offices, political parties, and armies, everyday thinking must share the burden of maintaining correct social behavior. Consequently, ordinary thought categories are strongly imbued with social information, for instance, a bear is not just an animal but also a spirit who in myths and dreams takes on a human social role.

Another factor encouraging aboriginal contextualization is described by Carpenter (1973): The relatively powerless position of the hunter-gatherer in pursuit of wild animals and plants requires a pervasive watchfulness – all aspects of the evolving and uncontrollable situation must be noted in order to obtain the desired goods from nature. When carrying out this wide-scale monitoring of the environment, each piece of information is only assessed within a much larger context, for example, the significance of a certain wind direction only emerges in the context of season, time of day, spatial location, and so on.

Turning from contextualization to differentiation, we find that the highly differentiated thought style of hunting groups is much like our own and requires less comment. Nonetheless, Carpenter has emphasized the need for fine distinctions concerning environmental conditions if one is to hunt wild animals successfully. As we have reviewed, the integrative style of the gatherers may be grounded in women's predominance or other societal influences that are still poorly understood.

We can now ask what changes took place in human thought as agriculture developed to the middle levels of complexity exemplified in equatorial Africa, characterized by large domesticated animals and crops growing in permanent fields. At this stage there are some, but not many, specialized institutions of social control, such as part-time court officers and part-time soldiers all of whom are still dependent on the family farmstead for their subsistence. The agricultural mode of production requires coordination of a much larger work force at crucial stages than was needed for hunting and gathering, so that requirements for social organization and control are much greater. This is the stage of societal complexity just before the development of full-time *non*agricultural occupations supported by cash payments and taxation, as seen in the plow-agricultural societies of Europe and the irrigation-agricultural societies of the East. Thus, in African agricultural societies, the discrepancy between the need for large-scale social coordination and the availability of specialized personnel for this work is at its maximum. I hypothesize that because of this, the natural connection between practical thought and social behavior found in the contextualizing style of simpler societies is supplemented by a further drastic reshaping of thought in the service of social stability, a change from differentiated to integrated thought. High integration among African agriculturalists is not only shown in Berry's (1976) psychological research, but also shows up in semantic studies: Denny and Creider (1986) describe the enormous diversity of objects grouped together in the Bantu noun classes, and Hawkinson (1979) describes the broad range of situations encoded by Swahili -*a* meaning 'of'.

The fact that African thought is *both* highly contextualizing and highly integrative (i.e., low in differentiation) is particularly well described by Fernandez (1980). Discussing traditional religious sermons among the Fang in West Africa, he points out that "by condensing in one unitary presentation many diverse domains . . . [the sermons] suggest . . . an *integrity*, a relatedness . . . at the same time . . . forcing *contextualization* on the auditor" (p. 53, my emphasis). We can see both tendencies in one of his examples, *life is sugar cane.* To interpret the metaphor one has to formulate an integrative likeness that brings 'life' and 'sugar cane' together as a single unit of thought and downplays the many differentiations that might be made between them. To form this integrated unit one must draw from context prior knowledge about life and about sugar cane: "[life] comes in sections, and if approached section by section it can be consumed with sweet satisfaction" (p. 55). The very high frequency of remote integrations in various genres attests to the highly integrative style of African thought; in my experience, they are, in contrast, quite rare in texts from hunter-gatherer groups, although reliance on context is still very high.

In support of my hypothesis that integrative thought was developed in the service of social integration, it is relevant to note that

Fernandez stresses the social role of integrative thought in Africa. For example, concerning the sermon passage, *the drumming stick is male . . . the drum is female,* he says the "orderliness, the structure, perceived in one domain of experience, that of musical instruments, is used to inform and structure . . . an orderliness in . . . the domain of social . . . relationships" (p. 56). It seems, then, that integrative thought (low differentiation) is added to contextualizing thought to further strengthen social cohesiveness at the middle levels of agricultural complexity. At greater levels of societal complexity, for example, in Europe or China, the paid civil servant takes over the job of social regulation, and the thought style returns to high differentiation. This, as we have seen, is the style of the hunter whose problems of social structure can be coped with by contextualizing alone, as well as the style of complex agricultural states in which special institutions and occupations relieve the thought system of some of the burden of social control. It remains to be seen whether the integrative thought style of gatherers results also from social needs.

Finally, we turn to the functional bases of the change to which literacy contributes, the decontextualization of thought in the Western tradition. Although the widespread popular literacy of Greece produced the most thoroughgoing decontextualization, for example, Plato's advocacy of studying each idea in and of itself, Goody (1977) has shown that partial decontextualization arises from specialized craft literacy in the Near East. However, literacy is not the sole cause of decontextualized thought, but only an amplifier of it. Indeed, at least one case in which literacy is *not* associated with decontextualized thought has been described, that of the Vai in West Africa (Scribner & Cole, 1981).

The general cause of decontextualization, which can apply independently of literacy, is the growth of human societies beyond a size where all members share a common background of information. In small societies most interactions are face to face, between relatives and persons who have known each other all their lives. As societies grow to include thousands and tens of thousands of people, interaction with strangers who may not share background information increases. This means that one must be careful to include all relevant information in the message since the recipient may not be able to add the correct points from context. This is the original impulse to decontextualized thought – providing information that is self-contained for people who lead different lives than one's own, within societies larger than the aboriginal hunting and gathering band.

To test for these beginnings of decontextualized thought, various scholars have looked at a part of language that is necessarily contextual, the spatial deictics, for example, English *here, there, this, that*. To understand these terms, in their basic spatial locative uses, the hearer must know from context where the speaker is located since *here* means 'at the speaker' and *there* 'away from the speaker'. Such terms should be favored in small-scale societies in which context is often shared. Perkins (1980) examined a subtype of spatial deictics, those occurring as affixes (parts) of other words. Using a carefully constructed sample of the world's languages, he found that hunter-gatherers and incipient (slash and burn) agriculturalists have a higher proportion of languages with spatial deictic affixes than do middle-level and complex agriculturalists. Since he also found that morphological affixes of all types decline with societal complexity, his study is mostly sensitive to the earliest phase of decontextualization, that occurring with the development of large agricultural tribes such as many found in tropical Africa or the Pacific Islands. These are all oral cultures, but the social milieu is large enough to discourage reliance on highly context-dependent devices such as spatial deictics. Denny's (1978) study helps make the connection between preliterate and literate decontextualization. Although examining only one hunter-gatherer and one agriculturalist language (Eskimo and Kikuyu respectively), he found that the system of spatial deictic words (independent words, not affixes as in Perkins) was slightly smaller in Kikuyu, pointing again to a moderate amount of decontextualization due to the larger size of preliterate agricultural society. However, the English spatial deictic system (*here, there, this, that*) is very much smaller than either the Kikuyu or the Eskimo one, indeed it is presumably the minimum one that a language can have – only one spatial variable is expressed: 'at the speaker' (*here, this*) and 'away from the speaker' (*there, that*). In contrast, Kikuyu expresses four spatial variables, and Eskimo expresses six spatial variables. The dwindling in the amount of spatial information included in an intrinsically contextualizing system is evidence for the greater decontextualization associated with Western literacy.

The other phenomenon offered as evidence for preliterate decontextualization is relative clause formation. Perkins (1980) reanalyzes the data provided in Keenan and Comrie (1977) and finds that the number of noun phrase positions (subject, direct object, indirect object, oblique [e.g., locatives], etc.) in a language that can be modified by a relative clause increases with increasing complexity of the society speaking the language. The results show some increase in relative clause availability in preliterate but medium-sized societies, with further increases in groups having Western literacy. Perkins bases his explanation of this phenomenon on McNeill's (1976) claim that relative clauses are a device for incorporating contextual information in a message: They express "part of the conceptual structure that otherwise could be available only by relying directly on the context for support" (p. 211). As the community increases in size with the development of agriculture, speakers cannot rely on hearers having such contexts available, so the context is specified in the utterance by relative clauses. Under such pressure the grammar slowly shifts to make more of the noun positions in a sentence modifiable by relative clauses. McNeill also reviews research by others showing that as pidgin languages develop into creoles, relative clause formation rapidly appears, due, he believes, to the pressure of the much larger, Westernizing speech community that the preliterate groups of speakers have joined. Relative clause formation amounts to decontextualization because it allows contextual information to be included in the message instead of being added from context by the recipient. We see from these studies that relative clauses as a decontextualizing device increase as community size increases among preliterates. It is not known if this grammatical device is a function of community size per se or of acquaintance with literate discourse. Scholes and Willis (Chapter 13, this volume) found that the nonliterate Americans they studied could not use relative clauses in their spoken English. This is no doubt an aspect of the "restricted code" (Bernstein, 1962) that they use in their small oral community, since they are blocked from communicating in "elaborated code" within the larger literate community.

An important implication is indicated by our examination of the functional basis for lowered differentiation at middle levels of agricultural complexity, and for decontextualization, beginning at such levels, but greatly accelerating in literate states. Since these are changes made for particular functional reasons, they will never be universal. Within the societies involved, some thought systems, some people, some situations will still show the alternative style of thinking. Thus, although African thought is generally low in differentiation, some highly differentiated systems remain, for example, tense and aspect inflections for verbs (Johnson, 1981). Also, as is well known from Bernstein (1962), within the generally decontextualizing style of Western thought, groups on the margins of industrial society continue to practice the contextualizing style termed "restricted code," that is, restricted to shared contexts. Even among the many nationalities that make up the industrialized West, there are striking differences in the degree of decontextualized thought. Political scientists and historians have long recognized that the United States is the most singularly industrial nation in its social and political culture, that the Western European nations have a less purely industrialized culture, and that the Mediterranean nations are even more weakly industrial. These differences are reflected in degrees of decontextualized thought in a study by Tannen (1980) in which undergraduates from the United States and from Greece were asked to relate what they had seen in a particular (silent) movie. The American students went to great lengths to provide a self-contained account that would not require the hearer to draw from context: Plot and characters were fully delineated, and details of the filming such as camera angles and lighting were reported. However, the Greek undergraduates gave a much more sketchy portrayal of the film, never mentioning the technicalities of filming, leaving a lot for the hearer to fill in from the context of his own knowledge. Instead they concentrated on their personal and aesthetic reactions to the film.

**Why Western thought is solely decontextualizing**

We come now to the main claim of this chapter, that Western thought has only one distinctive feature, decontextualization, and is not the exclusive possessor of many other virtues of human thinking often claimed for it, for instance, being more logical, more abstract, more reflective, more analytical, more objective, and, no doubt some would claim, closer to the mind of God! Our survey of the two variables along which psychological research has shown thinking to vary has set the necessary background: Cultural habits of thought do differ in differentiation, that is, distinctions *within* a thought unit, and in contextualization, that is, connections *among* thought units. To show that they do not differ in other ways will usually involve showing that some supposedly distinctive feature of Western thought is also found in non-Western cultures.

The first of these questions to be studied seems to have been logicality or rationality, and the first investigator to establish non-Western rationality seems to have been the anthropologist Evans-Pritchard (1954). He studied equational statements from Nuer religious thought, such as *a cucumber is an ox*, that were taken by earlier scholars as examples of prelogical or magical thinking; in his opinion, "the reason why it was not readily perceived that the statements that something is something else should not be taken as matter of fact statements is that it was not recognized that they are made in relation to a third term not mentioned in them but understood. . . . A cucumber is equivalent to an ox in respect to God who accepts it in place of an ox" (pp. 147–8), that is, as a sacrifice. We see from this illuminating passage that Western scholars unconsciously assumed that such statements were context free; but this is, of course, their own habit of thought, whereas the Nuer equally unconsciously expected the statements to be contextualized. It is exactly the *unrecognized* difference in contextualization that misled Western scholars to believe that Nuer thought lacked rationality.

More recently, cross-cultural psychologists have come to the same conclusion. Beginning with Luria's (1974) investigations and culminating in Hutchins's (1980) study of highly contextualized logical reasoning, they have gradually seen that standard logical reasoning is used but in a highly contextualized way that obscures it for the Western observer. Along the way, however, the differences in contextualization have sometimes been overinterpreted in ways that I hope to refute. For instance, although Greenfield (1972) was one of the first psychologists to recognize the importance of contextualizing in preliterate thought, she also felt that Western decontextualized thought involved greater abstraction. This is acceptable if abstraction is simply a synonym for decontextualization, that is, a separation of the thought unit from its context; but if any of the many other meanings of abstraction used by social scientists are intended, then it is untrue. Consider two prominent alternative meanings of abstraction: "generality," for example, the difference between animal, dog, and spaniel, and "insubstantiality," for example, the difference between beauty and chair. So far as is known, there are no overall cross-cultural differences in the generality of concepts; all cultures employ highly general concepts, and all languages have some morphemes expressing them. For example, semanticists recognize that occurrences are universally classed into three very general categories: state, process, and event (Lyons, 1977, p. 483). Some languages have separate morphemes expressing these concepts; an example from a hunter-gatherer group, the Cree (Algonquian language family), is *miskw-aa-w*, 'red-state-it' = 'it is red' (Denny, 1985). Similarly for insubstantiality, all cultures and all languages have a rich set of concepts for insubstantial things: In Cree there is a morpheme *-win* used to derive such abstract nouns, for example, *naapewin*, 'maleness,' from *naapew*, 'man'. Consequently, if the term "abstract" is used to describe Western thought one should keep in mind that only decontextualizing abstraction is a distinctive property; generality and insubstantiality are not.

Scribner (1977) made the important discovery that when the contextualized thinking of Kpelle (West Africa) subjects was examined, the conclusion "was found to follow logically from the evidence used" (p. 488). However, she went on to label their contextualized reasoning as "empirical" contrasted with Western decontextualized reasoning, which she called "theoretical." Actually, there is no evidence that an empirical–theoretical difference is involved. Certainly, Westerners apply decontextualization to very empirical matters, as when we supply complete instructions for a new product so that the user need draw a minimum of information from his previous experience. But more importantly, the contextualized thought of non-Western societies can be highly theoretical; traditional myths express theories about the origins and structure of human society, but do so in the context of dramatic stories about individual characters and events (Havelock, 1963).

It is only the most recent cross-cultural psychology of thinking done by Hutchins (1980) that does not suggest other distinctive properties for non-Western thought besides contextualization. Furthermore, he also protests, as I am doing, suggestions about other differences. In particular, he criticizes one of the older anthropological interpretations, that of Dorothy Lee, which also misled me for quite a time (Hutchins, 1979). Lee (1949) claimed that Trobriand Islanders did not customarily think in terms of intentions, causal relations, or temporal relations. Hutchins's research shows that "these claims are absurd" since the native court case that he analyzes is full of these concepts. He suspects that Lee missed their presence in the culture because she only analyzed traditional narratives and magical formulas, two genres in which such concepts play a small role, especially in the explicit surface of the narrative. Even Hutchins was only able to show the full play of logical reasoning in his law case because informants subsequently reported to him the large portion of the thinking that those in the court supplied from context in their minds, but that was not actually uttered.

Another contributor to the line I am pursuing is Feldman (Chapter 3, this volume). She shows that Western literacy is not unique in its property of fixing a text and permitting interpretation of it, which was claimed in Olson (1986). She does so by reviewing oral genres in several societies that involve remembering and commenting upon utterances. Similarly, Narasimhan (Chapter 13, this volume) describes the oral fixing of the *Rigveda* text in classical India and the development of elaborate oral commentaries and analyses of it. As Feldman points out, at most, literacy *facilitates* memory for texts and interpretations, enabling the preservation of more textual material and the development of a longer sequence of commentaries upon commentaries.

We will now review a variety of scholars who have looked at the psychological effects of literacy in order to show that some of them do make erroneous claims about distinctive features of literate thought, but, more importantly, they all agree that the central difference is decontextualization. An instructive example is Ong (1982), who does make several incorrect claims, for instance, that writing facilitates "abstractly segmental, classificatory and explanatory examination" (p. 8) and "frees the mind for more original, more abstract thought" (p. 24). We have discussed abstraction earlier, noting that literacy only enhances the decontextualizing variety of abstraction. We know from the work of Lévi-Strauss (1962) that classificatory thought often takes a different form from the hierarchy of classes favored in the West, namely networks of binary oppositions. Likewise, Lévi-Strauss (1967) has made clear that the oral societies' myths are their explanatory theories. Furthermore, many analyses of oral forms have shown that originality resides in surprising recombinations of familiar materials, whereas the literate notion of originality involves new information. With respect to sequences, Ong later says that the "lengthy sequences that [oral thinkers] produce are not analytic but aggregative." We will see later that analytic means decontextualized, and aggregative means contextualized.

Despite these remarks, Ong is aware of the dangers I am discussing: "The effects of oral states of consciousness are bizarre to the literate mind, and they can invite elaborate explanations which may turn out to be needless" (p. 30). Also, the claims I have criticized are *not* the effects of literacy that he discusses in detail. The main part of his analysis consists of various types of decontextualization each contrasted with contextualization: subordinative–additive, analytic–aggregative, objectively distanced–empathetic and participatory, abstract–situational. The first of these he illustrates very tellingly with the same passage of the Bible in 1610 and 1970 translations. The older one preserves the oral additive style of the Hebrew original in which most sentences are joined by the nonsubordinating conjunction *and*, whereas the recent one substitutes subordinating conjunctions such as *when, while, then,* and *thus* (p. 37). Subordinated sentences are a kind of decontextualization in which the information is partially separated by being backgrounded. In contrast, additive structures allow each piece of information equal weight so that they serve as contexts for each other.

Ong's second contrast, analytic versus aggregative, also involves a special kind of contextualization. Aggregates are fixed clusters of information, such as the Homeric epithets or political terms such as *godless Communists,* in which the main unit is conventionally accompanied by modifiers that provide a context for it. Such fixed contexts aid memory in oral societies (Havelock, 1963) and aid in oral composition (Parry, 1923). However, equipped with writing as an external memory and an aid to composition, literate people find them unnecessary and redundant, preferring instead to analyze out the main unit, for example *communists*. Ong calls his third special type of contextualization empathetic and participatory, contrasting with objectively distanced decontextualization. What he has in mind is the embedding of the story line of an oral epic in the communal values of the audience so that a powerful emotional identification with the hero is felt by everyone. As Havelock (1963) describes, this ensures the effective memorization of the moral values that the epic is supposed to teach. In contrast, objectively distanced written works such as the world's first novel, *The Tale of Genji* (Shikibu, c. 1010) have heroes with a private psychology and convey a critical attitude toward society; the story is partly separated from the communal context of public education.

It is the fourth contrast, abstract versus situational, that Ong describes most fully, presumably because this is decontextualizing abstraction, that is, decontextualization in general. He reviews, as we have done, the work of Luria, Scribner, and Fernandez showing that the oral mode of thought is to embed information in a pertinent situation and the literate mode is to treat information as a self-contained package.

We have seen that although Ong does overestimate the distinctiveness of Western thought, his main account is correctly focused on decontextualization. This is also my evaluation of the other authors I reviewed, notably Havelock, McLuhan, Goody, and Chafe; although they also sometimes claim distinctive properties that are not justified, their main emphasis is upon the decontextualizing nature of literate thought. For example, Goody (1977) concentrates on the effects of Near Eastern craft literacy in producing the new information structures of the list, formula, and table, all of which he describes explicitly as decontextualized because they isolate information from its context in the everyday situation. For example, he describes lists of funeral contributions that give just the donor's name, his contribution, and perhaps his hometown. This information is detached from the complicated context of social interaction during the funeral; in contrast, when such funeral donations are originally experienced and stored in oral memory, "the input is highly contextualized." In a similar way Havelock's (1963) account centers around the decontextualizing nature of literate Greek thought, which he usually calls "abstraction." In most cases, we can see that he means the decontextualizing sense of abstraction because he concentrates on contrasting Homer's oral poetry, in which ideas are contextualized in stories performed with music and dance before audiences, with Plato's philosophy in which each idea is "somehow isolated from its setting and set 'itself by itself' and identified 'per se'" (p. 217).

Likewise, McLuhan (1964) concentrates on the decontextualized thought of literate man, which he conveys by a host of colorful terms, for example, "hot," "fragmented," "aloof and dissociated," "private," "partial and specialized." It is especially clear that he is describing decontextualization in the famous passages defining "hot" as opposed to "cool" media. "A hot medium is one that extends one single sense in 'high definition.' High definition is the state of being well filled with data. A photograph is, usually, 'high definition.' A cartoon is 'low definition' [i.e., cool] simply because very little visual information is provided. . . . And speech is a cool medium of low definition, because so little is given and so much has to be filled in by the listener. On the other hand, hot media do not leave so much to be filled in or completed by the audience" (p. 36).

A last authority on literacy that I will review is Chafe. Like the others, he emphasizes various kinds of decontextualization such as detachment versus involvement. His most recent study (Chafe & Danielewicz, 1987) is uniquely valuable as support for two of the positions taken in this chapter: first, that literacy is only an amplifier of the tendency to decontextualized thought, a tendency that emerges in any society populous enough to involve communication with strangers, and second, that culturally acquired thought habits such as decontextualization never fully replace the contextualizing tendencies of aboriginal thought. Chafe and Danielewicz compare informal and formal speaking, for example, conversations and lectures, to informal and formal writing, for example, letters and academic papers. Some kinds of decontextualization are found in both formal modes, although always enhanced by writing. This is particularly true of their measures of detachment: avoidance of first-person pronouns, avoidance of locative and temporal adverbials, use of abstract subjects, and use of passives. All of these are, for Chafe, ways the reader to detach his message "from the audience, from himself and from concrete reality" (p. 105). From the point of view of this chapter, the fact that this decontextualization is present in *both* formal modes, lectures and papers, although always greater in the written one, indicates that decontextualization is a habit of thought in industrial culture, not an effect directly produced by writing, although it is amplified by writing. Since a formal setting is one in which the sender's compliance with the norms of the society is more seriously assessed, the norm of decontextualizing is more closely adhered to. Also, formal settings usually realize the underlying cause of decontextualization more fully, that is, communicating with strangers who may not share contextual information. The relative lack of detachment in Chafe's results for the two informal modes, conversation and letters, indicates that when circumstances involve shared context, even literate senders revert to the normal human habit of contextualized communication.

The other variety of decontextualization for which Chafe presents data is the avoidance of coordinating conjunctions reviewed earlier from Ong (1982). In oral style, the coordinative joining of sentences means that each one is equally important and each one is contextualized by all the others. In contrast, in literate style a partial decontextualization is achieved by backgrounding some sentences with subordinating conjunctions so that a main sentence is partially isolated. Chafe shows that use of coordinating conjunctions is much lower in both written and formal modes, showing again a decontextualizing habit of thought that is enhanced by writing.

To summarize, all of these authors correctly concentrate on decontextualization as the main style of thought encouraged by literacy, although some of them add other properties that we can see are not distinctive to Western culture. These properties, which I have argued are characteristic of all human thought, are rationality, logic, generalizing abstraction, insubstantial abstraction, theorizing, intentionality, causal thinking, classification, explanation, and originality.

If we accept that Western thought is only distinctive in being decontextualizing, that is, in isolating units of information, we are still left with the task of understanding how this makes our thought appear so different to us. Take the case of logic: If we believe that Hutchins (1980) has shown a universal human logic, we are still confronted by that specialized artifact, the logician's formal logic; surely, there is something distinctive about that. For McLuhan (1964), such specialized knowledge is an outgrowth of decontextualized literate thought, which he termed "specialist isolation." The logician produces at least two novelties that are not found in natural logic, first, a conscious knowledge of what are naturally unconscious processes, and, second, an idealization of processes that are naturally less than ideal. Although all humans can do logic and evaluate and criticize logical reasoning, it is the job of the literate specialist to make a consciously formulated account of the various patterns of reasoning that humans carry out unconsciously. On the second point, Braine (1978) shows how the natural logic of conditional (*if* . . . *then*) statements is converted by logicians into the idealized "horseshoe" connective called "material implication." As he describes it, the natural logic of conditionals consists only of the ability to form thousands of specific conditional propositions, each with considerable contextual content. However, the logicians' idealization is a logical connective that is entirely context free. To conclude, it appears that decontextualized thought is the basis for various derived properties of Western thought.

## Further possibilities in cross-cultural cognition

So far we have reviewed evidence that cross-cultural differences in thought involve two variables, differentiation and contextualization. We have also rejected a number of other differences that have been claimed to be especially characteristic of Western thought. Before closing I want to briefly consider a few other cultural differences in cognition for which there is some evidence, in each case asking whether these are aspects of the two main variables we have discussed or whether they might be additional variables.

The first possible factor concerns different modes of organizing concepts: In complex societies such as the industrial West, people use hierarchical classifications such as animal–dog–spaniel, but many smaller-scale societies use networks of binary opposites instead. An example of one of these remaining in our own thought is "the height of summer and the depths of winter," in which two pairs of opposites are linked. Lévi-Strauss (1962) claims that such binary networks are the main way of linking concepts for many groups and that such networks of opposites can involve hundreds, perhaps thousands, of concepts. As yet there is no method for the psychological study of them. Perhaps the best attempt so far is Lancy's (1983). Recognizing fully that pairing of opposites was a prime mode of organization for his Papua New Guinea subjects, he gave a free-sorting type of picture-sorting task in which subjects could make whatever groups they liked. This did elicit many pairs, but did not allow the description of the way in which pairs are linked into larger networks. There is some evidence that binary organization is an aspect of contextualizing and that hierarchical organization is connected to decontextualizing. In describing binary thought systems as "the science of the concrete," Lévi-Strauss claims that each concept is more strongly connected to other concepts, and more strongly connected to perceptual information, than are concepts organized in hierarchies – this might be a higher degree of contextualizing. On the other side of the contrast, Brown (1979) argues that the most general terms at the top of our hierarchies of botanical concepts, for example, tree, bush, vine, plant, grass, are only developed when societies reach a size and complexity so that a significant portion of the population, normally a ruling class, no longer has much direct contact with plants. This lack of involvement may amount to a loss of contextual information about plants. Thus, a hypothesis for future study would be that binary organization of concepts is a special kind of contextualizing thought.

A second cognitive property that may contribute to cross-cultural differences is the contrast between propositional thinking (expressed in language) and mental modeling (which includes imagery) (Johnson-Laird, 1983). Most typically, this is the contrast between thinking "successively" using words arranged serially in sentences and thinking "simultaneously" using an image. Das, Kirby, and Jerman (1979), who use these terms (successive for propositional thinking and simultaneous for mental modeling), argue that this factor is closely related to the variable of differentiation discussed earlier in the chapter; the arguments are theoretical, because, as he points out, no empirical comparisons have been done yet. Das (1988) summarizes some cross-cultural research for this variable, but these preliminary results do not always fit with the patterns we have been reviewing for differentiation: Although complex agriculturalists from India show high use of successive processing (propositional thought), which may fit with the expectation that such a group would show high differentiation, Cree hunter-gatherers show low use of successive processing, which does not fit with other research showing that they have high differentiation. There is also an important theoretical distinction between the two variables: Propositional thinking (including its linguistic expression) and mental modeling (including imagery) are different cognitive *processes*, whereas differentiation and integration are cognitive *styles*, that is, manners or ways of carrying out any cognitive process. At best then, the relation between the two factors can only be that one of the processes, propositional thinking, favors a differentiating style (each word isolating a thought), whereas the other process, mental modeling, favors an integrative style (an image presenting many pieces of information at once). It is possible for the favored pairings of process and style to be disassociated: Research we reviewed earlier by Denny and Creider (1986), Hawkinson (1979), and Fernandez (1980) reported highly integrative ways of using language to express propositional thinking. All in all, it seems likely that propositional thinking versus mental modeling is a separate factor in cross-cultural variation.

A third property that may be involved in cross-cultural differences in thought is even less studied. One pole of this variable is the emphasis upon hypothetical thinking about imperceptible aspects of nature, such as electromagnetic force, atoms, genetic codes, and so on, which is central to Western scientific thought since the Renaissance. Both Nakamura (1964) and Needham (1969) have stressed that, in contrast, traditional Chinese thought laid great stress on empirical observation of perceptible, concrete aspects of nature, which yielded the many successes of medieval Chinese science and technology. One psychological study, by Bloom (1981), has attempted to demonstrate that one form of hypothetical thinking, the counterfactual conditional, is less fluent among Chinese than American subjects. However, failures to replicate these results (Au, 1983; Liu, 1985) have left the question in abeyance. These two opposite tendencies have, however, been reported for other societies as well. Nakamura describes the hypothetical thinking about abstract imperceptibles that characterized philosophy in classical India. In contrast, Denny and Mailhot (1976) have described the emphasis upon concrete perceptibles that characterizes geographical concepts among the Cree, a hunter-gatherer society of northern Canada. It may be, therefore, that this is another variable along which thinking varies cross-culturally; if so, it is unclear at present whether it is a separate factor or some specialized form of decontextualization – to hypothesize about imperceptibles involves disconnecting one's thinking from the reality that one perceives.

### A case of contextualized thought

Since my overall message is that our contextualizing colleagues in other cultures are just as good thinkers as we are, I will end this chapter with a short example of thought in contextualizing mode. The following passage is the opening of a social commentary given by a Woods Cree woman from northern Manitoba, whose style of discourse is regarded as following traditional patterns of primary orality in Cree. First, I give a very literal English translation and then the text with word-by-word translation.

1. So,
   what I grew up to,
   what I was brought up to,
   I still remember every day.
2. I didn't bother going to school.
3. But it shows my learning,
   that I work with it,
   that I use that learning of mine,
   that I still work at everything my children can use.

1. Kwaani,
   so
   niista kaa-kii-pi-ohpikiiyaan,
   I too [what] I grew up to (*conjunct*)

kaa-kii-pi-isi-ohpikihikawiyaan,
[what] I was thus brought to (*conjunct*)
kiyaapic tahto-kiisikaaw nikiskisin.
still     every day     I remember (*independent*)

2. Mwaa niitha n-ooh-iskooliwin
not   I     I did not bother to have schooling (*independent*)

3. Maaka nookwan             nikiskisinoohamaakoowin,
but     it shows (*independent*) my learning

niista ii-atoskaatamaan,
I too [that] I am working with it (*conjunct*)

ii-aapacihtaayaan            anima nikiskinoohamaakoowin,
[that] I am using it (*conjunct*) that    my learning

kiyaapic ii-atoskiiyaan,
still     [that] I am working (*conjunct*)

tahto     kii-aapacihtaacik       kiikwaan ncawaasimisak.
every    they can use (*conjunct*) thing     my children.

This passage illustrates two types of contextualizing we have discussed earlier, contextualized content similar to that described by Ong and contextualized form of the sort studied by Havelock. The content consists of two clusters of coordinated or conjoined clauses that, by being equally weighted, form mosaics of mutually contextualizing thoughts. The clusters are the two groups of verbs in the "conjunct" mode, which signals more closely linked information than does the other, "independent" mode. Within each cluster of conjunct verbs, coordination is signaled by using identical preverb modifiers: *kaa-kii-pi-* in the first cluster of two verbs in sentence 1 and *ii-* in the second cluster of three verbs in sentence 3. The two conjuncts of sentence 1 describe, in an additive fashion, how she grew up in the way she was brought up, an allusion to the successful teaching by parents in traditional days. After sentence 2 stating that she had no European-style schooling, sentence 3 has a cluster of three conjuncts that combine as equal units to show the value of her traditional learning: She works with it, she uses it, and she works at everything her children can use (the last conjunct is a subordinate part of the third).

The contextualized form involves a patterning of syntactic and lexical devices that Bright (1982) calls poetic; Havelock (1963) regards the addition of poetic structure to an oral communication as providing extra contextual support that ensures the memorability of the oral message. First, the speaker has an elegant patterning of conjunct and independent verbs: She opens with the conjuncts leading to the first independent, then places the second independent (which has no conjuncts) in the middle, and ends with the third independent followed by its conjuncts – a symmetric pattern. She also uses a primary oral device discussed by Havelock (1986, p. 72), repetition with variation. In the sentence 1 cluster, the verb stem *-ohpik-*, 'to grow up', is repeated but varied to *-ohpikih-*, 'to cause to grow up', that is, 'to bring up'. In the sentence 3 cluster, the verb stem *-atoskaat-*, 'to work with, at something', reappears in the variant *-atoskii-*, 'to work', and the inflected verb *ii-aapacihtaayaan*, '(that) I am using it', is repeated but varied to *kii-aapacihtaacik,* '(which) they can use'. Havelock points to the value of repeating for memorability in primary oral culture and the need for variation in the repetitions to ensure that attention does not wander. The subtlest repetition with variation in this passage involves all four conjunct verbs in sentence 3: The verbs 'work' and 'use' are repeated but the relation between them is shifted. First of all, they are parallel actions of her own, *ii-atoskaatamaan*, 'that I use it', *ii-aapacihtaayaan*, 'that I work with it', both involving her learning. Then her working with her learning is related to another kind of using, everything that her children use. Thus, the work-relatedness and usefulness of traditional learning is made interestingly memorable.

**Summary**

This chapter reviews psychological studies of two dimensions along which thinking varies cross-culturally. The first, contextualization, is used frequently in small hunter-gatherer societies. As population size within a cultural group increased through various kinds of agricultural societies to industrial society, decontextualized thought developed because the sender of a message could no longer be sure that the receiver shared much common context. This tendency to send self-contained messages was enhanced by literacy. The second dimension, differentiation, is used frequently among hunters and infrequently among gatherers. In middle-sized agricultural societies, such as those in Africa, problems of social coordination led to the adoption of less-differentiated, integrative thinking. However, in complex agricultural societies, civil servants act as agents of social control, and thought is again highly differentiated.

This chapter also contends that decontextualization is the only distinctive feature of thought in literate Western societies that has been established so far. Other distinctive properties that have been proposed are shown to be also present in nonliterate hunter-gatherer and agricultural groups. These include logic, fixing and interpreting texts, and abstract thinking (other than decontextualizing abstraction), among others. Three other dimensions of cross-cultural variation in thought are reviewed that have some research support; two of them appear to be specialized aspects of contextualization, but the third, propositional thinking versus mental modeling, seems to be a separate variable.

ACKNOWLEDGMENTS

Thanks are due to Jean-Marc Philibert for guiding me to the work of Douglas and of Evans-Pritchard, and to Donna Starks for providing the Woods Cree text.

REFERENCES

Au, T. K.-F. (1983). Chinese and English counterfactuals: The Sapir-Whorf hypothesis revisited. *Cognition* 15:155–87.
Bernstein, D. (1962). Social class, linguistic codes and grammatical elements. *Language and Speech* 5:221.
Berry, J. W. (1976). *Human ecology and cognitive style.* New York: Wiley.
Berry, J. W., van de Koppel, J., Sénéchal, C., Annis, R., Bahuchet, S., Cavalli-Sforza, L. L., & Witkin, H. A. (1986). *On the edge of the forest: Cultural adaptation and cognitive development in Central Africa.* Lisse: Swet & Zeitlinger.
Bishop, A. J. (1978). Spatial abilities and mathematics in Papua New Guinea. *Papua New Guinea Journal of Education* 14(special issue): 172–200.
Bloom, A. (1981). *The linguistic shaping of thought.* New York: Erlbaum.
Braine, M. D. S. (1978). On the relation between the natural logic of reasoning and standard logic. *Psychological Review* 85:1–21.
Bright, W. (1982). Poetic structure in oral narrative. In D. Tannen (ed.), *Spoken and written language,* pp. 171–84. New York: Ablex.
Brown, C. H. (1979). Growth and development of folk botanical life-forms in the Mayan language family. *American Ethnologist,* 6:366–85.
Carpenter, E. (1973). *Eskimo realities.* New York: Holt.
Chafe, W., & Danielewicz, J. (1987). Properties of spoken and written langauge. In R. Horowitz & F. J. Samuels (eds.), *Comprehending oral and written language,* pp. 83–113. New York: Academic Press.
Das, J. P. (1988). Coding, attention and planning. In J. W. Berry, S. H. Irvine, & E. B. Hunt (eds.), *Indigenous cognition,* pp. 39–56. Dordrecht: Nijhoff.
Das, J. P., Kirby, J. R., & Jerman, R. F. (1979). *Simultaneous and successive cognitive processes.* New York: Academic Press.
Denny, J. P. (1978). Locating the universals in lexical systems for spatial deixis. In *Papers from the Parasession on the Lexicon,* pp. 74–84. Chicago Linguistic Society.
    (1985). Semantic verb classes and abstract finals. In W. Cowan (ed.), *Papers of the 15th Algonquian Conference,* pp. 241–71. Ottawa: Carleton University (Linguistics Department).

(1986). Cultural ecology of mathematics: Ojibway and Inuit hunters. In M. Closs (ed.), *Native American mathematics*, pp. 129–80. Austin: University of Texas Press.
Denny, J. P., & Creider, C. A. (1986). The semantics of noun classes in Proto-Bantu. In C. Craig (ed.), *Noun classes and categorization.*, pp. 217–39. Amsterdam: Benjamins.
Denny, J. P., & Mailhot, J. (1976). The semantics of certain abstract elements in the Algonquian verb. *International Journal of American Linguistics* 42:91–8.
Douglas, M. (1966). *Purity and danger.* London: Routledge & Kegan Paul.
Evans-Pritchard, E. E. (1967). A problem of Nuer religious thought. In J. Middleton (ed.), *Myth and cosmos*, pp. 127–48. New York: Natural History Press. (Originally published in 1954.)
Fernandez, J. (1980). Edification by puzzlement. In I. Karp & C. S. Bird (eds.), *Explorations in African systems of thought*, pp. 44–59. Bloomington: Indiana University Press.
Goody, J. (1977). *The domestication of the savage mind.* Cambridge University Press.
Greenfield, P. M. (1972). Oral and written language: The consequences for cognitive development in Africa, the United States and England. *Language and Speech* 15:169–178.
Havelock, E. A. (1963). *Preface to Plato.* Cambridge, Mass.: Harvard University Press.
(1986). *The muse learns to write.* New Haven, Conn.: Yale University Press.
Hawkinson, A. K. (1979). Homonymy versus unity of form: The particle -a in Swahili. *Studies in African Linguistics* 10:81–109.
Hutchins, E. (1979). Reasoning in Trobriand discourse. Reprinted in R. W. Casson (ed.), *Language, culture and cognition*, pp. 481–9. New York: Macmillan.
(1980). *Culture and inference.* Cambridge, Mass.: Harvard University Press.
Johnson, M. R. (1981). A unified temporal theory of tense and aspect. In *Syntax and Semantics*, Vol. 14, *Tense and Aspect*, P. Tedeschi & A. Zaenen (Eds.), pp. 145–75. New York: Academic Press.
Johnson-Laird, P. N. (1983). *Mental models.* Cambridge, Mass.: Harvard University Press.
Keenan, E. L., & Comrie, B. (1977). Noun phrase accessibility and universal grammar. *Linguistic Inquiry*, 8:63–99.
Lancy, D. F. (1983). *Cross-cultural studies in cognition and mathematics.* New York: Academic Press.
Lee, D. D. (1949). Being and value in a primitive culture. *Journal of Philosophy* 8(3).
Lévi-Strauss, C. (1962). *The savage mind.* Chicago: University of Chicago Press.
(1967). The story of Asdiwal. In E. R. Leach (ed.), *The structural study of myth and totemism.* London: Tavistock.
Liu, L. G. (1985). Reasoning counterfactually in Chinese: Are there any obstacles? *Cognition* 21:239–70.

Lomax, A., & Berkowitz, N. (1972). The evolutionary taxonomy of culture. *Science* 177:228–39.
Lonner, W. J., & Sharp, D. W. (1983). Psychological differentiation in a rural Yucatan Mayan Village. In S. H. Irvine & J. W. Berry (eds.), *Human assessment and cultural factors*, pp. 191–209. New York: Plenum.
Luria, A. R. (1974). *Cognitive development: Its cultural and social foundations.* Cambridge, Mass.: Harvard University Press.
Lyons, J. (1977). *Semantics.* Cambridge University Press.
McIntyre, L. A. (1976). An investigation of the effect of culture and urbanization on three cognitive styles and their relationship to school performance. In G. E. Kearney & D. W. McElwain (eds.), *Aboriginal cognition*, pp. 231–56. Canberra: Australian Institute of Aboriginal Studies.
McLuhan, M. (1964). *Understanding media.* New York: McGraw-Hill.
McNeill, D. (1976). Some effects of context on utterances. In S. B. Steever et al. (eds.), *Papers from the parasession on diachronic syntax*, pp. 205–20. Chicago Linguistic Society.
Nakamura, H. (1964). *Ways of thinking of Eastern peoples.* Honolulu: University of Hawaii Press.
Needham, J. (1969). *The grand titration: Science and society in East and West.* London: Allen & Unwin.
Olson, D. R. (1986). The cognitive consequences of literacy. *Canadian Psychology* 27:109–21.
Ong, W. J. (1982). *Orality and literacy.* London: Methuen.
Parry, M. (1923/1971). A comparative study of diction as one of the elements of style in Early Greek epic poetry. Reprinted in A. Parry (ed.), *The making of Homeric verse.* Oxford: Clarendon Press, pp. 421–36.
Perkins, R. V. (1980). The evolution of culture and grammar. Ph.D. dissertation, State University of New York at Buffalo (University Microfilms 8016230).
Reuning, H., & Wortley, W. (1973). Psychological studies of the Bushmen. *Psychologia Africana*, monograph supplement, No. 7.
Scribner, S. (1977). Modes of thinking and ways of speaking: Culture and logic reconsidered. In P. N. Johnson-Laird & P. C. Wason (eds.), *Thinking: readings in cognitive science*, pp. 483–500. Cambridge University Press.
Scribner, S., & Cole, M. (1981). *The psychology of literacy.* Cambridge, Mass.: Harvard University Press.
Shikibu, M. (1010, 1976). *The tale of Genji.* E. G. Seidensticker (Trans.). New York: Knopf.
Tannen, D. (1980). A comparative analysis of oral narrative strategies. In W. L. Chafe (ed.), *The Pear stories*, pp. 51–87. New York: Ablex.
Turner, D. H. (1985). *Life before Genesis.* New York: Lang.

# 5
# Cree literacy in the syllabic script
JO ANNE BENNETT and JOHN W. BERRY

## Introduction

For the past one and a half centuries, the Cree-speaking peoples of northern Canada have been using a syllabic script that is almost unknown outside their homeland. Cree script is unusual for a number of reasons. To begin with, it was not an indigenous creation but rather a prefabricated writing system introduced by a missionary. Nevertheless, it was adopted by the Cree people so enthusiastically that its spread quickly outstripped the proselytizing of the missionaries who introduced it. Knowledge and use of the script were not restricted to a few individuals, but rather, the Cree appear to have achieved something closer to universal literacy in this syllabic script. Remarkably, this was accomplished without the benefit of the institutional supports we usually associate with literacy. The Cree had no paper, pens, or books (at least initially), no teachers, and no schools.

The Cree present us with a situation in which literacy spread almost uncontrollably through a population like an epidemic. The system of Cree syllabic literacy was said to be so easy to acquire that a "clever Indian, on being shown the characters in the morning was able to read the Bible by their use before the sun went down the same day" (McLean, 1890, p. 170). The average Indian, we are told, required no more than one week to accomplish this task, although it was stated (with obvious intellectual ethnocentrism) that the script could be "mastered by any intelligent white man in less than an hour" (p. 164).

The question addressed in this chapter is why knowledge of the script should have spread so rapidly and so easily in previously nonliterate society. We will begin by introducing the script itself, then give a brief account of its invention, early history, present uses, and contemporary position vis-à-vis literacy in English in the roman script. Some of the reasons behind the script's rapid expansion will soon become apparent through this exercise. Others will require additional discussion since they are, and must remain, rather speculative.

Cree literacy in syllabic script

We have engaged in a study of Cree syllabic literacy for the past three years. We have restricted ourselves to an investigation of the script as it is used in four communities in northern Ontario (Figure 5.1): the Cree-speaking communities of Fort Albany and Attawapiskat on the James Bay coast (denoted as West Main Cree in Helm, 1979), and the self-denoted Oji-Cree-speaking communities of Big Trout Lake and Kasabonika in northwestern Ontario. The latter two communities are more properly referred to as "Northern Ojibway" (Helm, 1979), but the appellation is by no means universally accepted (Honigman, 1979; Rogers and Taylor, 1979; Rogers, 1983). When

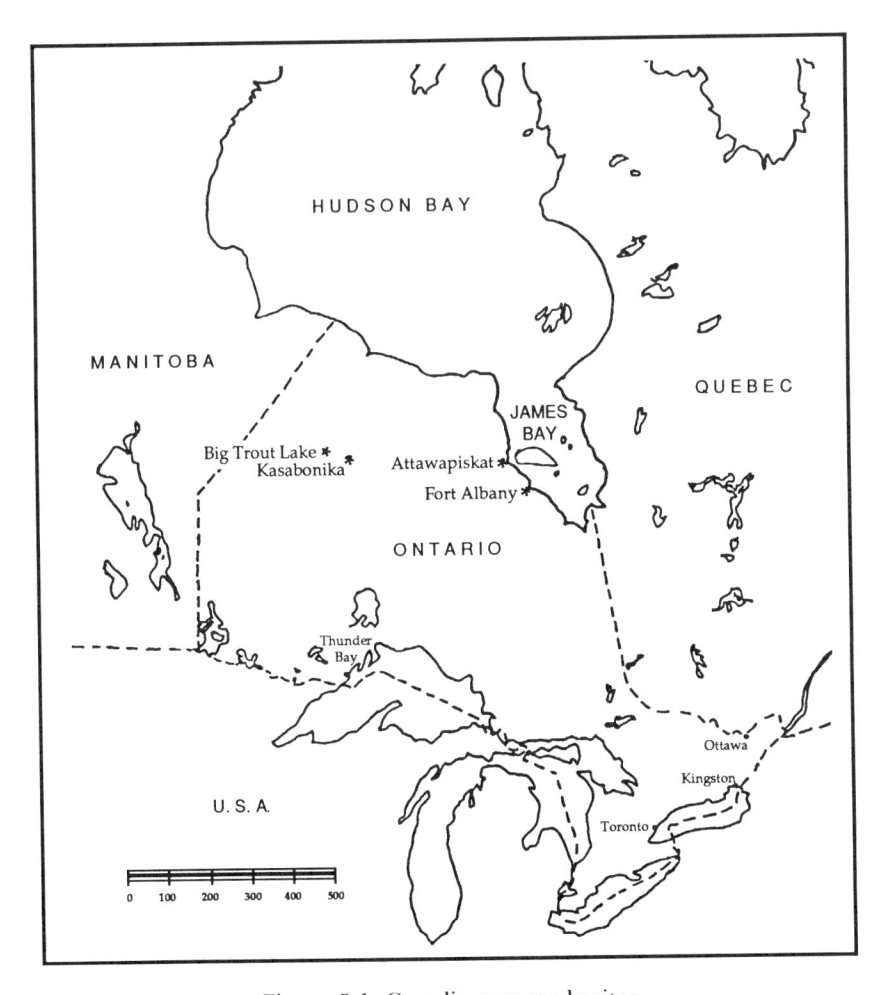

Figure 5.1. Cree literacy study sites.

speaking English, the "Northern Ojibway" usually refer to themselves as "Cree" (Rogers, 1983, p. 86), and for reasons of convenience we will do the same in this chapter.

There are significant social and linguistic differences between the Cree of the James Bay coast and the Inland Northern Ojibway (or Oji-Cree) of northwestern Ontario, but the two groups are sufficiently similar in a broad and general way to be considered together. This is particularly true with respect to the distribution and uses of Cree syllabic literacy.

## The script

The Cree syllabic script was invented in Norway House, Manitoba, in or around 1840 by a Methodist minister, James Evans. (For an excellent account, see Murdoch, 1981, pp. 20–33; also Burwash, 1911.) Evans had long experience with the Ojibway language and considerable experience with Cree, though somewhat less than with Ojibway. Evans was intrigued by the possibility of using a syllabic form of writing for the Cree (and Ojibway) language primarily because most of the naturally occurring syllables in the language consist of a single consonant sound followed by a single vowel.

James Evans, using this phonetic pattern to his advantage, worked out a script that is extremely economical in the number of symbols it employs. Most Cree dialects can be transcribed in the syllabic script using less than a dozen symbols. Many need only nine. This is an extremely small number of characters or symbols, even by alphabetical standards. It is extraordinarily small when compared with other syllabic scripts. For example, the nineteenth-century Cherokee syllabic script contained eighty-five characters (White 1962; Walker, 1969). The Vai script studied by Scribner and Cole in Liberia had over two hundred (Smith 1978; Scribner & Cole, 1981, p. 32).

Although the Cree script relies on a minimal number of characters or symbols, it uses these characters in a unique but systematic number of ways. In the Cree syllabarium (Table 5.1) each major symbol is associated with the sound of what can be thought of as a single consonant in English: /t/, /p/, /m/, and so on. In addition, each of the characters is presented in one of four orientations, corresponding to what would be our own conventional representations of "north," "south," "east," or "west." It is the orientation of the character that gives the vowel quality of the syllable. The number "four" has religious or semireligious significance among many North American Indian groups, and the Cree are no exception. The use of "four,"

Table 5.1. *Cree syllabarium*

|   | E | I | O | A |   | Finals |
|---|---|---|---|---|---|---|
|   | ▽ | △ | ▷ | ◁ |   |   |
| T | ∪ | ∩ | ⊃ | ⊂ | ╱ | ╭ |
| K | ᒥ | ᑭ | ᑯ | ᑲ | ╲ | ╲ |
| N | ⸺ | σ | ⸺ | ⸺ | ⸴ | ⸺ |
| M | ⌐ | Γ | ⌐ | L | ╷ | L |
| Ch | ⌐ | ⌐ | J | ∪ | – | ∪ |
| S | ⌐ | ⌐ | ⌐ | ⌐ | ⌐ | ⌐ |
| Sh | ⌐ | ⌐ | ⌐ | ⌐ | ⌐ | ⌐ |
| P | ∨ | ∧ | > | < | . | ≺ |
| Y | ⊰ | ⊱ | ⊲ | ⊳ |   |   |
| L | ⌐ | ⌐ | ⌐ | ⌐ | ⊤ | ⌐ |
| R | ∪ | ∩ | ⊃ | ⊂ | ⸴ | ⊂ |
| W | ·▽ | ·△ | ·▷ | ·◁ | · | · |

particularly in a way concerned with orientation or direction, was a powerful insight on the part of Evans and may actually have made the script more suitable for the Cree in the sense of being a better psychological "fit." This, of course, remains conjectural. But it is interesting that Evans should choose a basically four-vowel system for Cree, when the language in fact has seven vowels (Darnell & Vanek, 1973). Evans had to rely upon other methods besides orientation to indicate the three additional vowels.

Besides the dozen or fewer main symbols, the Cree syllabarium has a small repertoire of additional signs. A large dot placed over the syllabic character indicates a lengthening of the vowel. Only three of the vowels are lengthened in this way: "I," "O," and "A." (The remaining vowel, "E," is already long.) In this fashion the total complement of vowels is brought up to seven. Likewise, Evans also had to develop signs indicating the insertion of a final consonantal sound at the end of a syllable – for instance, to change /ki/ to /kin/, /pa/ to /pak/, and so on. The latter signs, called "finals," are in fact more "alphabetic" than syllabic. They differ in those areas traditionally under Roman Catholic or Church of England ecclesiastical influence.

*History*

After 1840, knowledge of the Cree syllabic script spread rapidly among the native population of northern Canada. By the 1850s, Catholic missionaries on the James Bay coast, over one thousand miles distant from Norway House as the crow flies – and considerably farther by canoe – were reporting nearly universal literacy among the Cree in a script that they described as a "type of shorthand" (Laverloche, 1851; Garin, 1855). Yet this area, the eastern shore of the James Bay, was said to be so remote that even "the white man had forgotten how to read" (Canton, 1910, p. 173). Reports of the rapid transmission of the syllabic script came from vastly separated regions of Canada at around the same time. It is important to remember that although the Cree syllabic script was invented by a missionary and although the very first "printed" texts (produced by Evans in Norway House on primitive presses about which a plethora of legends have grown up) were religious, it was the case almost everywhere except Norway House that the Native population was able to read and write *before* the arrival of the missionaries and before the missionaries began their extensive translations of religious prose and song into the various dialects of Cree.

*Distribution of syllabic literacy*

Since the end of the Second World War, the introduction of high-tech mass-communication technologies and the rapidly changing economic profile of the north have brought about a vastly increased exposure of the Cree to Euro-Canadian culture. Knowledge of English, a superfluity fifty years ago, is now perceived by most Cree as "necessary for survival in the white man's world." There is an implicit admission here that the once foreign world of southern Canada is now standing on the doorstep. Schools, which were introduced into most communities in the two decades following the Second World War, originally forbade the teaching of syllabics (they also forbade the speaking of the Cree language), so that nearly an entire generation grew up without acquiring literacy in syllabics. However, in the early 1970s this policy was changed. Under the rubric of "Native Culture," instruction in both the Cree language (grammatical fine points and expansion of vocabulary) and the syllabic script was begun in the government-sponsored schools. If Native people are allowed to acquire, as they have been promised, *real* control over their own education, then we may expect to see an increased reliance upon the Cree language in the schools, and possibly an increased use of the syllabic script as well.

In the course of our research, we administered a standardized questionnaire form to 440 people in the four communities in which we worked as well as conducting extensive interviews with people who were literate in the syllabic script. The results of these interviews provided the following picture of the state of syllabic literacy in northern Ontario at present.

Cree remains the primary language of communication in all four communities in which we worked. Adults from the same community speak to each other almost entirely in Cree, with the occasional interjection of an English word or phrase by younger people (from childhood up through the thirties). Children typically arrive in school speaking only a few English words or phrases but with an improved ear for the sounds of the language as a result of exposure to television, radio, video cassettes, and so on.

There is a general inverse weakening of the hold of the Cree language with age. That is, the younger their age, the less likely people are to rely entirely on Cree and the more likely they are to know and use English. The extent to which English is used varies considerably between individuals, but even fluent speakers of English rely primarily upon Cree.

With respect to the distribution of literacy there is a marked difference by age across the population:

1. Cree syllabic literacy is nearly universal among people over forty years of age. Most of these older Cree syllabic literates are completely unfamiliar with written English and many have only a limited comprehension of spoken English.
2. Literacy in English is nearly universal among people under the age of thirty-five or forty. Almost all people of this age have attended school.

In all four communities, the syllabic script is now taught daily in the schools. This has been the case for the past ten to fifteen years, depending upon the community. Nevertheless, the results of the community questionnaire indicate that children learning syllabics in school are not acquiring the ease and proficiency in their own script that their parents acquired outside school. This finding is supported by the observations of native people in those communities.

In each of the four communities there is a "missing generation," that is, a generation of people who are not literate in the syllabic script. They did not learn the script while they were in school because it was not being taught. Neither did they learn it from their parents, because parents had handed over the teaching of their children. The age of this *generation* varies slightly from community to community but always falls somewhere between twenty-five and forty. Many of these people are currently trying to "pick up" syllabics on their own.

*Transmission*

How was the script taught? From extensive interviews with older Cree literates, it has been possible to construct a picture of how knowledge of the Cree syllabic script was passed along in the earlier years of this century. The most striking impression to arise from these interviews was that there was never a "proper way," a "main way," or a "best way" of learning to read and write in the Cree syllabic script. The criterion for successful instruction was pragmatic. If the method of instruction worked, it worked. This, if you like, is a genuine pedagogic tautology.

A small number of older Cree literates learned the syllabic script in an institutional setting – usually from missionaries who set up month-long "schools" in the communities that were summertime gathering places. The rest, however, learned in traditional settings. Most learned at home. They learned the script from those people around them who already knew it. In practical terms this *usually* meant that children learned from their parents. But children also learned from other older relatives or from other children. Adults occasionally learned from adults. We have no recorded instance of an adult learning from a child, but knowing the Cree, there is little reason to doubt that this, too, may have occurred.

The "teacher"–"student" ratio tended to be one-to-one although sometimes there could be more than one student learning at once. This was the case, for example, when people learned in the summer mission schools. Otherwise, however, it was common for each child to be taught separately, even when there were several children being taught in the same family. The frequency and the length of lessons varied enormously. Some people report lessons of five minutes or less. Others say they studied for days on end. Some people worked with the syllabarium every day, others only once or twice a month.

There was as little agreement on "teaching method" as there was on anything else. Thus, some people say they learned the syllabarium first and then moved on to simple names of objects in the environment, only attempting written texts, such as the Bible, when these earlier stages had been mastered. But others say they first learned the names of objects: For example, a mother or father might stop to write in the snow the characters for "rabbit" or "goose" after one of these creatures had been spotted in the bush. Still other people declare that they started learning by "reading" printed material, often biblical texts or particular hymns that they would already have committed to memory.

### "Technologies" for writing

How did the Cree maintain such a strong interest in, and passion for, literacy in a cultural setting without convenient writing surfaces? A script is a visual phenomenon as well as a set of cognitive skills. Until well after World War I, paper was a rare commodity in the north. But the Cree managed by making do with whatever was at hand. Traditional "writing materials" consisted of just about any and every flat surface available in the environment and any and every object capable of inscribing a mark. People wrote with stones, knives, axes, bones, sticks, feathers, charcoal, and fingers on materials as diverse as wood, stone, bark, hide, dirt, snow, and later, of course, paper. They carved their characters into the writing material (with axes and knives), or drew (on the surface of newly split spruce-wood or on birchbark) with pieces of charcoal from the previous night's fire. Using feathers and fingers they wrote with "inks" made from charcoal, crushed stone, stewed plants, fresh animal blood, and even, according to an elderly woman from Attawapiskat, gunpowder. Eventually, of course, pen and paper became available, and today these are used almost exclusively.

### Uses of the script

The Cree employed their syllabic script for many of the same purposes for which we use our own. They wrote letters, sent notes, kept diaries and journals, and they maintained records of both family and business affairs. All of these are fairly private uses and will be considered in more detail later, because it is the private uses that seem to have been crucial in providing the impetus for the spread of the syllabic script.

On a more public scale were such items as the early printing of religious (mainly biblical) texts by outside missionaries. Such books became widely distributed in the north toward the end of the nineteenth century, and today almost all syllabic literates have their own copy of the Bible, often with annotated margins they have filled in themselves. Syllabics were also used for public notices. Occasionally, individuals wrote short "histories" that seem to have been meant to be preserved as documents of interest to the entire community.

What is absent from the above lists, of course, is the extensive accumulation of texts and commentaries that we think of as literature. It probably is not fair to expect a body of literature to develop out of an oral tradition in one and a half centuries nor, for that matter, to expect a nomadic people to develop a large body of texts. Where would they store them? It is only now, in fact, when people are living full-time (or almost full-time) in permanent communities that the legends, stories, and personal recollections of oral tradition are being taped, transcribed, and preserved in written form for future generations.

For most Cree speakers, however, the primary mode of expression remains the spoken and not the written word. Fluency of expression is judged from speech, not from writing. You can frequently hear older people praised for their ability to speak Cree well, just as the lack of such expertise among the young is much bemoaned by the elderly. You seldom hear people praised for their verbal adroitness in syllabics.

*Rapid transmission*

Several things fostered the spread of the syllabic script among the Cree. Some of these have to do with the script itself and with the way in which the script transcribes the Cree language.

The first item, already discussed, is the tremendous economy of the script. A second factor is the inflected, agglutinative nature of the Cree language. Cree constructs words by the addition of numbers of prefixes, suffixes, and infixes onto and into a stem. One word in Cree can be the equivalent of an entire phrase – or even sentence – in English, and a single Cree word may require twenty or more letters when transcribed in the Roman alphabet. Table 5.2 shows a selection of Cree words and phrases transcribed in the Cree syllabic script and in Roman orthography. It also gives the written English equivalent of the Cree words. It is obvious, if only intuitively, that many words in Cree are easier to "see" when written in the syllabic script. This is particularly true when a series of syllables begin with the same consonant as in a word like "*kakikepoko*" (Labrador tea), for which the eye seems to lose track of which "k" it is looking at.

Table 5.2. *Cree words*

| Syllabic script | Roman script | Translation |
|---|---|---|
| ▽σ̇ċ·△ρᐸbσ·ᐊᵇ | E-nihtawikihcikaniwahk | Planting the garden |
| bĊᐊՈLᖊCɑɋ· | Ka-ta-ati-macihtananaw | We might start |
| S·bdᑲ·ᐊᵛ·b | Shikwakolawaskwa | Onions |
| ∧ᵌPCᖊɑ△bσˢ | Piskitasinahikanish | Sentence |

Adapted from Ellis (1983, pp. 643–50).

The economy of the syllabic script and the length of Cree words may explain *how* the rapid spread of syllabic literacy was possible (namely, the relative ease with which it could be acquired and learned), but they do not explain *why* it took place. For this we need to turn to what we referred to as the domain of private or individual use. Here several factors came together to foster the wide acceptance of writing among a previously nonliterate people. The first of these was a previously existing system of trail signs. The second was the scattered settlement pattern of people over the landscape. The third was a cultural predilection for avoiding embarrassing or potentially embarrassing encounters.

*Trail signs.* Although the use of trail signs has nearly ceased today, it was once widespread and is presumed to have predated the spread of literacy (Skinner, 1911, p. 47). Trail signs were three-dimensional symbols made from sticks or other natural objects that were set up at the side of trails to give information to other people following along later. Such information could include the number and (in a gross way) the relative ages of people in a traveling party, the direction in which they intended to travel, whether or not they intended to return, the time of day they had passed by, or the time of day they expected to return. Some of the trail signs shown to the authors resembled in their gross configuration some of the symbols or characters used in the Cree syllabarium. If so, this is unlikely to have been accidental as Evans was well acquainted with Native artifacts when he set out to draw up the script. More importantly, from the viewpoint of literacy, it appears that the Cree were already familiar with the idea that it was possible to communicate with each other, albeit in a limited way, at a remove of space and time. They did not need to get used to the idea that there were other modes besides face-to-face communication.

*Keeping in touch.* Until recently the Cree have been nomadic, following a primarily hunting existence in the boreal forests of northern Canada. Formerly, people lived in small family groups spread thinly over the terrain. This dispersal was necessary because the relative scarcity of game in a severe northern environment simply did not allow large numbers of people to live conjointly for any extended period of time (Rogers, 1969; Steegman, Hurlich, & Winterhalder, 1983). Today most people live in small communities, but even so, settlement patterns are considerably dispersed. Communities of several hundred people are seldom closer than one hundred miles apart.

This is not to say that the Cree prefer things this way. If anything, the opposite is true. Large gatherings are a source of enthusiasm and excitement, and even small-scale family visiting provokes a kind of holiday atmosphere. When such a visit entails a journey (to another community or into the bush), the excitement is almost tangible. The Cree like to be in touch with one another. Their traditional environment impeded this.

Today we can only imagine the kind of isolation experienced by people in tiny groups scattered across the forbidding winter landscape, almost completely out of contact with each other. We can surmise that the desire for communication must have been very great, and we can see in the old system of trail signs evidence of a preliterate attempt to dispel the boreal silence. Magic and divination were also thought to provide a means of getting information at a distance, although they were usually employed to detect and keep track of game and not people.

The Cree syllabic script was a breakthrough in ameliorating the isolation experienced in the bush. With the advent of syllabics it became possible to send letters along with travelers or to leave messages behind in certain likely locations – at the Bay store, or the church, or a trap-line cabin.

Today this function of syllabic literacy is fast losing ground, not so much to a competing form of literacy (English written in Roman orthography) but to a high-tech tradition that bypasses literacy altogether in favor of the spoken word: namely the telephone, radio (particularly two-way trap-line radio and community broadcasts), and, to a lesser degree, television. Linguistic expression is thus firmly back in the oral mode, and the Cree are likely happier with it that way. Cree involvement with telecommunications accounts for some of the (to us) anomalies we see in the northern "town-scapes": a proliferation of satellite dishes scattered among the outhouses, microwave towers surrounded by tipis where fish and meat are being smoked, and so on.

The Cree are devoted users of the telephone. The Northern Ojibway, in particular, can be said to be almost addicted to it, and a monthly bill of two or three hundred dollars is not unusual. For both groups, television has become a necessity, usually running eighteen hours a day, often in conjunction with one or more additional "aural" appliances, that is, a stereo, a tape deck, and a radio, all playing at once. A two-way trap-line radio has become standard equipment for the bush particularly with people who go regularly or stay for extended periods of time.

*Cultural attitudes.* The last question we will explore is how a particular set of cultural attitudes may have worked together to aid the spread of literacy. The Cree have a taste for social harmony that is almost oriental in its dimensions. They combine this with an individualism and fierce egalitarianism that can make social maneuvering a minefield for the unwary foreigner. The issuing of a command, for example, is a formidable breach of etiquette. But even questions are considered impolite particularly if they are put directly (see Black, 1973). The proper mode of interrogation is tangential and vague, so vague that the person being interrogated may choose not to answer without seeming rude.

For example, suppose I know there is to be a Bingo game in the evening. I suspect my friend will be going and I would like to go along with her. Instead of saying to her, "If you're going to Bingo tonight, could I go with you?" it would be far more polite to wait until there are several other people in the room and then say, to no one in particular, "I wonder if there's any Bingo tonight." Everyone will understand that I have asked a question and why. If my friend feels like taking me along with her, she will say something like "I guess there's probably a Bingo game tonight." And *then* I can safely say something as direct as "I wouldn't mind going along sometime."

To turn to another cultural norm, the display of strong negative emotions (anger, sorrow, anxiety) is highly disapproved of. Even milder forms, such as irritation, frustration, or disappointment, are frowned upon. The Cree, for example, almost never swear. (After six years the authors have yet to hear even a "damn.") The most common response to frustration or anxiety is a recourse to laughter, presumably to defuse tension.

The combination of these two attitudes (dislike of direct approach and avoidance of unpleasant emotion) means that making a direct request can be an excruciating experience for the Cree, particularly if the outcome is in doubt. In this kind of situation, what happens, say, when a man wants to marry his neighbor's daughter and is not sure how his request will be met? Probably the easiest thing for him to do is to learn syllabics and write a letter. The use of the written word will allow him to divorce himself from the immediate consequences of his communication and, therefore, from the immediacy of embarrassment should a denial be in order. Another possibility, should his request be unwelcome, would be for everyone to just go along as normal, pretending that the letter was never sent.

In the course of interviews with older syllabic literates, several people mentioned having initiated marriage arrangements by way of a letter. Many people also mentioned sending frequent notes within the community, often to destinations as close as the house next door when it seemed (to me) it would be easier to run over and make the request in person or, simpler yet, to telephone. When pressed for the reasons they wrote these kinds of notes, people often said they sent them "just if you want to ask for something." On her last trip north, after almost four years' acquaintance with the people involved, one of the authors began to receive notes. The first note was a request from a sixteen-year-old chain-smoker (who had been deluged with advice to quit) for money for a pack of cigarettes. She sent the note in with her younger sister from the very next room of the house, a distance not exceeding twenty feet. The second note was a friend's request for a loan of money. It was also carried in from the next room by a child.

These two notes were not, of course, written in the syllabic script, but they were a kind of proof of the vacuum that syllabic literacy (*any* literacy) would have filled and still fills for the Cree. The notes underlined the importance of the emotive, affective underpinnings of literacy as well as the role played by cultural attitudes that, on the face of things, have apparently little to do with learning to read and write.

## Conclusions

The nature of the Cree syllabic script, its economy, and its excellent "fit" with the Cree language ensured that the script would be easy for Cree speakers to learn. Taken alone, however, they do not explain why knowledge of the script spread so rapidly among Cree-speaking people in the middle of the last century.

There is probably no single reason for the rapid transmission of the Cree syllabic script. Knowledge of a preliterate "sign" system may have readied people's minds for the notion of decontextualized communication. Physical isolation and a particular constellation of cultural norms may have provided an intense motivation to learn.

Today, of course, many of these factors no longer apply. Most Cree live for most of the time in communities of several hundred people. In their desire to keep in touch with one another, they tend to rely primarily upon electronic telecommunication technology, so much so that many older people frequently complain of "too much noise" and not enough isolation (they call it "peace"). With respect to the cultural norms concerning suppression of emotion and avoidance of directness, these can be catered for by any form of literacy, whether in Cree syllabics, English, Cree written in roman orthography. The future of the Cree syllabic script is thus at a crucial turning point. Its continued use and viability are not so much a cognitive as a political issue. The future of the script rests with the determination of the Cree people to preserve what they feel is of value in their own traditions.

ACKNOWLEDGMENTS

Research for this project was funded by the Social Sciences and Humanties Research Council. Nearly two dozen native assistants helped us with our work. Deserving of special mention are Evelyn Nanokeesic of Big Trout Lake and Elizabeth Gull of Attawapiskat.

REFERENCES

Black, M. (1973). Ojibwa questioning etiquette and use of ambiguity. *Studies in Linguistics* 23:13–29.
Burwash, Rev. N. (1911). The gift to a nation of written language. *Royal Society of Canada: Proceedings and transactions*, 3rd ser., 5:3–21.
Canton, W. (1910). *A history of the British and Foreign Bible Society, Vol. 4, 1854–1884*. London: Murray.
Darnell, R., & Vanek, A. L. (1973). The psychological reality of Cree syllabics. In R. Darnell (Ed.), *Canadian languages in their social context*, pp. 171–92. Edmonton: University of Alberta Press.
Ellis, C. D. (1983). *Spoken Cree*. Edmonton, Alberta: Pica Pica.
Garin, R. (1855). Lettre du R. P. Garin, O.M.I., à un père de la même société. *Propagation de la Foi* 11:4–17.
Helm, J. (ed.) (1979). *Handbook of North American Indians*. Washington, D.C.: Smithsonian Institute.
Honigman, J. J. (1979). The Westmain Cree. In J. Helm (ed.), *Handbook of North American Indians, Vol. 6, Subarctic*. Washington, D.C.: Smithsonian Institute.
Laverloche, R. P. (1851). Lettre du R. P. Laverloche à un père de sa Congregation Moose Factory, 30 août, 1850. *Propagation de la Foi*, 9:99–104.

McLean, J. (1890). *James Evans: Inventor of the syllabic system of the Cree language.* Toronto: William Briggs.

Murdoch, J. (1981). Syllabics: A successful educational innovation. Unpublished master's thesis, University of Manitoba.

Rogers, E. S. (1969). Natural environment – social organization – witchcraft: Cree versus Ojibwa – a test case. In D. Damas (ed.), *Contributions to anthropology: Ecological essays.* Ottawa: National Museum of Canada, bulletin no. 230:24–39.

(1983). Cultural adaptations of the Northern Ojibwa. In A. T. Steegman, Jr. (ed.), *Boreal forest adaptations: The Northern Algonkians.* New York: Plenum.

Rogers, E. S., & Taylor, G. (1979). Northern Ojibwa. In J. Helm (ed.), *Handbook of North American Indians*, Vol. 6, *Subarctic.* Washington, D.C.: Smithsonian Institute.

Scribner, S., & Cole, M. (1981). *The psychology of literacy.* Cambridge, Mass.: Harvard University Press.

Skinner, A. (1911). Notes on the Eastern Cree and Northern Saulteaux. *Anthropological Papers American Museum of Natural History*, 9, p. 1. Washington, D.C.

Smith, M. (1978). *An ethnography of literacy in a Vai town.* Vai Literacy Project, Working Paper No. 1. New York: Rockefeller University, Laboratory of Comparative Human Cognition.

Steegman, A. T., Jr., Hurlich, M. G., & Winterhalder, B. (1983). Challenges of the boreal forest. In A. T. Steegman, Jr. (ed.), *Boreal forest adaptations: The Northern Algonkians.* New York: Plenum.

Walker, W. (1969). Notes on native writing systems and the design of native literacy programs. *Anthropological Linguistics* 11:148–66.

White, J. K. (1962). On the revival of printing in the Cherokee language. *Current Anthropology* 3:511–14.

# 6
# Literacy: an instrument of oppression

D. P. PATTANAYAK

In this volume, as in many volumes before it, the emphasis is on theorizing about the advantages of literacy. Such theorizing that proclaims the superiority of literacy over orality, rather than the differences between them, has a disabling effect on 800 million illiterates of the world who are thereby branded as second-class citizens. Even Havelock (Chapter 1, this volume), who speaks of the "danger of literacy," and Ong (1982), who speaks of "marginal orality," are playing into the same prejudice. Ananda Coomaraswamy (1947) justifiably calls it "the curse of literacy"; Shirali (1988, p. 91) says that "the power and arrogance of literacy knows no bounds."

Illiteracy is grouped with poverty, malnutrition, lack of education, and health care, while literacy is often equated with growth of productivity, child care, and the advance of civilization. Shankar (1979) has shown that the correlation between literacy and adoption of improved agricultural practices is not significant. Stubbs (1980) has pointed out that we know precious little about the social functions of literacy. There is little evidence that literacy has civilized mankind. Yet not only have the above claims persisted; Western scholars have persisted in their assertion that "literacy played a decisive role in the development of what we may call 'modernity'" (Olson, 1986). Such exaggerated claims have not only resulted in oppressive theorizations, but have provided levers to bureaucrats and managers, policymakers and planners, to perpetuate oppression in the name of literacy and modernization.

In these debates what is missed is the fact that literacy is a strategy for excellence. It is not as though to be nonliterate is to be nonhuman or uncivilized. What has to be seen is the extent and nature of rationality of the illiterate and the nonliterates and then to show how literateness qualitatively widens and enriches it. Both nonliterates and illiterates are placed in the literate milieu, and therefore literate and illiterate modes of discourse complement rather than contrast one another. It is to be understood that literacy is not a solution to all problems, but a problem to be looked into in its own right.

Categories of analysis between oral and written traditions often overlap. Olson (Chapter 9, this volume) has said that literacy involves a series of linguistic, cognitive, and social changes resulting from

1. a system of writing and accumulating texts,
2. institutions for using texts,
3. evolution and acquisition of a metalanguage for talking about texts, and
4. institutions and schools for induction into these literate practices.

Correspondingly, orality can be said to involve

1. a system of reciting, memorizing, and accumulating texts,
2. institutions for using texts,
3. evolution and acquisition of a metalanguage for interpreting and explicating texts, and
4. institutions and schools for induction into these oral practices.

The Vedic tradition in India, the oral historians of Africa, the oral interpreters of epics in Europe and Asia who maintained the oral tradition, developed the metalanguage to talk about texts and propagated the tradition through "schools" that would exemplify the categories postulated for orality. If, as Donne wrote, letters as much as conversations can "mingle souls," then to attribute to letters all the consequences of modernity is an act of oppression. Olson (1986) has claimed that in the preliterate stages of human culture, there was no distinction drawn between text and interpretation; in modern times, he suggested there is only interpretation. This view is possible only if we deny communication of mind with mind through the medium of written word. The present emphasis on interpretation in literary theory is based on the denial of the author. Both at the preliterate stage as well as in modern times, the text meant what it said. As Helen Gardner put it, "Compared with the fruitful enlargement of the capacity to see and think and know and feel, that the experience of reading gives to those who will make the imaginative and intellectual effort to attempt to apprehend the work as its author made it, the sport of 'making texts' and 'importing meanings' is a perverse and barren exercise in ingenuity, a *reductio ad absurdum* of the emphasis which the old New Criticism gave to the importance of readers' response" (Gardner, 1982, p. 7).

In India, there was a tradition of fixing texts orally. This tradition continued for thousands of years. The Buddhists developed greater reliance on written texts than the Hindus. Even then the written and the oral were mutually supportive. In the Hindu tradition, as in Tibetan Buddhism, the word of mouth from the guru was supreme in transmitting knowledge; in the same way, in the present literate society, the lecture of the teacher supplements the book. Narasimhan (Chapter 11, this volume), drawing upon the Tabla Bols, emphasizes the need to look at orality as a distinct system and not mere articulated and written symbols. Between 800 B.C. and A.D. 200, changes took place in the world, beginning with philosophers and religious leaders to thinkers ranging geographically from Greece to China, one of the major effects being the creation of text. There was a creative tension between oral and literate texts to which Narasimhan draws attention by calling it the phenomenon of "literateness," which is based on the dual principles of reflection and technology. If the attention of scholars is drawn to the difference between what Illich (Chapter 6, this volume) distinguishes as scribal literacy and lay literacy instead of focusing attention on establishing the superiority of literacy over orality, then the present undertaking by scholars would have achieved something.

As regards the reorganization of language structure and modification of behavior, it must be recognized that the teaching process is not the mere pushing of propositions and rules into the mind of the child. There are remarkable processes within ourselves leading to internal reorganizations. The complexity of the relations between sound and spelling, as, for example, the difference in the pronunciation of "ea" when it occurs in "read" and "dead," points to individual differences, sometimes leading to effortless reading and sometimes to painful process.

The Cree syllabic writing is an example of a writing system without textual literacy or only textual literacy limited to the Bible. The different rate and frequency of learning and the trail signs among the Cree draws our attention to the fact that the ability to create texts is a socially determined process and that the rationalist system of instruction, starting not with the child but with adults, works well when learned under leisurely conditions. The stress on pedagogy is a feature of the mass society in which the teacher's autonomy to pace instruction is denied. The solution lies somewhere in between.

Adult education *sans* literacy links directly personal experience to objective environment. In adult literacy, writing mediates between personal experience and objective environment. Under conditions of orality, people identify and solve problems by working together. Literacy brings about a break in togetherness, permits and promotes individual and isolated initiative in identifying and solving problems. Literacy brings about a different kind of togetherness, cutting across social groups, establishing new interest groups that manipulate the illiterate for furthering the vested interest of these newly found groups. There is very little structural difference between the language of the literate and the illiterate. The difference appears to be in mental processing of the two groups. In seeking to explain the oppressive role of literacy, we must look for these different modes of processing rather than for two different languages.

REFERENCES

Coomaraswamy, A. (1947). *Bugbear of literacy.* London: Dobson.
Gardner, H. (1982). *In defence of the imagination.* Cambridge, Mass.: Harvard University Press.
Olson, D. (1986). The cognitive consequences of literacy. *Canadian Psychology* 27(2):109–21.
Ong, W. (1982). *Orality and literacy: The technologizing of the word.* London: Methuen.
Shankar, R. (1979). Literacy and adoption of improved agricultural practices. *Indian Journal of Adult Education* 40(3):31–7.
Shirali, K. A. (1988). Ganga Devi: A question of literacy and development. *Canadian Women's Studies* 9:89–91.
Stubbs, M. (1980). *Language and literacy: The sociolinguistics of reading and writing.* London: Routledge & Kegan Paul.

# PART II
Oral and literate forms of discourse

# 7
# Lie it as it plays: Chaucer becomes an author
BARRY SANDERS

## I

Literary inventions and discoveries carry the very same importance as those of science. Informing us about the world, they dazzle with equal brilliance. If I imagine, say, Chaucer transplanted in that other world, he would most resemble Darwin, encountering for the first time those giant turtles – nature's exotics – in the Galapagos Islands. Chaucer is the first Englishman to explore his own beguiling island – that of fiction. Every stance and strategy, virtually every form he adopts is daringly new. He is the first English writer to use the word *author* in its secular meaning; to use the word *tale* in its literary sense; and to use both the words *audience* and *auditor* without their legal implications.[1] He is also the first straight-faced liar in the English language. He has given us our most persistent, powerful, and pervasive oral form: the modern joke. A consummate trickster, he is the first author to have the last laugh. And because he is the first truly literate English author, Chaucer is, above all, the first writer to take on God.

He has to. For the Middle Ages knows only one supreme author and authority, and that is God. From the Logos, the Word or Reason, He created the world, elaborated it, so that by the twelfth century His hand could be read in every aspect of the Book of Nature. Picture the medieval poet dictating to his scribe, who in turn makes visible the spoken word. Surely, the manuscript leaf must have provoked some amusement, the parchment copy a supreme *mendacium* (the word means both "lie" and "forgery") of divine activity. Thus, most medieval writers confined themselves to allegory, or fable, or dream-vision, that is, they rearranged prefabricated parts of the divine *ordo*. They claimed no originality. To do so would demand more than daring and courage: The writer would somehow have to destroy the theological importance invested in the act of creation. Even more fundamentally, he would have to confront the ontological status of the text itself; for with the rise of vernacular literacy, as Franz Bauml points out, "textual as well as pictorial narrative changes its communicative function from commenting on 'reality' to constituting a 'reality'" (1980, p. 245; see also Perry, 1967). But Chaucer does risk originality; the *OED* even credits him with three specific meanings of the word *imagination*, including, in "The Miller's Tale," the familiar connotation of "fancy," what the medievals would call an internal sense, *vis imaginativa*, or *vis phantastica*.[2] At the same time, Chaucer dodges the charge of divine usurpation and iconoclasm by dismantling official, ecclesiastical notions of authority through two devices: lying and joking.

## II

Both moral and literary feigning depend on a person's ability to reshape (in Latin *fingere*, whence "fiction") his own thoughts, which in the late Middle Ages is called narration. Only when a person has become used to thinking as the silent tracing of words on the parchment of his memory can he then detach thought from speech and contradict it. A full-blown lie presupposes a self that thinks, before it says what it has thought. Only when memory is perceived as a text can thought become a material to be shaped, reshaped, and transformed. Only a self that has thought what it does say can say something that it does not think. Neither such a thought as distinct from speech, nor such a thinking self as distinct from the speaker, can exist without speech having been first transmogrified into thought that is stored in the literate memory.

The Old Testament knows of infidelity, broken promises, betrayals, and perjury. It knows of slander, false witness, and, what is worse, false prophecy and the abominable service of false gods. Neither these detestable forms of deceit nor the skillful ruse of a patriarch imply that opposition to an abstract "truth" is essential to what we today call a lie. Neither the Greek *pseudos* (used both for the "liar" and the "lie") nor the Latin *mendacium* (referring also to the emendation of a line on the wax tablet) in classical times comes close to our idea of the untruthful. Both languages lack the words that could oppose the *OED*'s "false statement made with the intent to deceive," to a flight of fancy or feigning. The classical languages barely contain the seed for the full-fledged Western lie and the full-blown Western fiction.

The early Greeks took a sporting attitude toward duplicity. George Steiner comments on an exchange between Athena and Odysseus to make the point: "Mutual deception, the swift saying of 'things that are not,' need be neither evil nor a bare technical constraint. Gods and chosen mortals can be virtuosos of mendacity, contrivers of elaborate untruths for the sake of the verbal craft" (1977, p. 269). And "untruth" is always the telling of *things* that are not, not of *thoughts* that are contradicted! The patron of this cunning craft was Hermes, the trickster, thief, and inventor of the lyre that urges the singer further into the epos. And the hero of that art is the shrewd and wily, generous and noble Odysseus, who according to Plato, in the *Hippias Minor*, is powerful and prudent, knowing and wise in those things about which he is false.

In the realm of orality, one cannot dip twice into the same wave, and therefore the lie is a stranger. My word always travels alongside yours; I stand for my word, and I swear by it. My oath is my truth until well into the twelfth century; the oath puts an end to any case against a freeman. Only in the thirteenth century does continental canon law make the judge a reader of the accused man's conscience, an inquisitor into truth, and makes torture into the means by which the confession of truth is extracted from the accused. Truth ceases to be displayed in surface action and is now perceived as the outward expression of inner meaning accessible only to the self.

In the fifth century Augustine had created a concept that broke with pagan and Christian antiquity by defining every lie as an assault on truth. Intellectual errors of fact are not a moral issue for him in his treatise *On the Lie*. Only the person who says something with the intent of misleading violates the truth. The offense resides in the *voluntas fallendi:* words used with the intent to contradict the truth that the speaker has enshrined in his heart. Even a statement that is factually correct can turn into an assault on the truth if it is proffered with the intent to deceive. Augustine moved the lie into the neighborhood of blasphemy: an act of contempt of God as the only Creator and Author.

For the next eight hundred years, whatever truly exists is there because God has willed it to be. All things man can speak about issue from His creative Word or command. He has brought things into being because He wanted them to be and not because there is something in them that makes it necessary for them to exist. Adam is His "fiction." He molded, shaped, and fashioned him out of the virgin soil of Paradise. The world is henceforth contingent on God's authorship. By every lie a creature usurps authorship reserved to the Creator. Even in the thirteenth century, a cleric who writes down stories has to claim that he is not the story's actual source (its *fons eius*), but only its channel (its *canalis*). Likewise, a person who dictated the story to the scribe must claim that he has not "sucked it from his finger" (*ex suo digito suxit*) – that is, has not invented it – his disclaimer laying bare the intimate connection between fiction, *fingere*, and the manipulation of truth.

Augustine's ban on the arrogation of truth matured, during the

Middle Ages, into the new duty to make truth manifest. In the many-tiered, God-willed order of the twelfth century, to be true in word and in deed came to be perceived as a moral debt. The late patristic prohibition against deceiving the listener was turned by the early Scholastics into the moral obligation of revealing the truth. Augustine feared that the soul could be seduced away from its resemblance to God into the *regio dissimilitudinus* through the "worship of false linguistic idols, signs which hold man in bondage [*sub signo enim servit*] if they do not point to the truth" (Ferguson, 1975, p. 101). Peter Haidu has commented that these "false linguistic idols" subvert what medieval theology "considered its proper function as redeemed language: that of focusing on God's message as inscribed both in Scripture and in the created world. Fiction is man's disruption of language from its divinely ordained intentionality" (1977, p. 885). Removed from serious, religious intent, this kind of language, as Haidu observes, reverberates with parody. It is also ripe for joking. Only against this historical background can we understand what it means to say that the age of European literacy is the world of fiction.

As much as the full-fledged lie, *narratio* presupposes an author and a text that is contingent on his self, his own creation. Neither the epic bard, nor the later storyteller, nor even the highly literate poet is fully an author: He does not pretend to create a world that, by the standards of the early Middle Ages, would be untrue. Chaucer, in the *Canterbury Tales,* is the first English writer who capitalizes on the emerging literate mindset of his courtly audience: Against that background, he fashions his lies into the playful untruth of fiction and himself into an author.

### III

The *Canterbury Tales* may have been written down by a number of scribes, but it was in all likelihood delivered orally, which means that Chaucer's audience was accustomed to listening to their poetry, presumably something they had done, as one of the great ceremonial pleasures of medieval life, many times before. The majority of them, *idiotae,* could not have read the poem, even if they so desired; indeed, very few of them probably had significant access to manuscripts. But Chaucer belonged to a different category: Miniatures show him with a pen hanging from his gown, his "winged words" exemplified by that feathery quill. He was a writer, and he upset his audience's expectations for a more or less improvised poem by flaunting his literate status (see Crosby, 1936; Foley, 1980–1).

He begins the *Canterbury Tales* with a particularly difficult syntactic form for a nonliterate to grasp: a dependent clause.[3] The auditor is required to etch the dependent clause into his mind, postponing its complete meaning as he listens for the independent clause. At the precise moment when he understands the independent clause, he then must connect – literally re-member – it to the subordinate clause, which he has suspended in the back of his mind.

Past, present, and future circulate in a single sentence.[4] These complex sentences are best comprehended through reading. (The word *complex* is derived from the past participle of *complectere*, "to encompass or comprehend.") Only a *reader* knows the luxury of roaming back and forth in a sentence, analyzing it, then moving on. But Chaucer further complicates this temporally confusing construction by beginning the *Canterbury Tales* with not one but two consecutive subordinate clauses: the first from lines one through four, the second from lines five through eleven. He withholds the independent clause, "thanne longen folk to goon on pilgrimages" – and hence leaves dangling the meaning of the earliest part of the poem – until line twelve.

By line twelve, however, Chaucer's audience would undoubtedly not have remembered what came before, or at best retained only a vague sense of it. They would have certainly felt unsettled, for Chaucer has shifted their category, from nonliterate – unable to write and read – to an early kind of illiterate – unable to write and read *and* listen. He has made them feel dumb, in the original sense – stupid because they must remain silent – and blind, for Chaucer is delivering not only the content but also the shape of things. And how can a nonliterate visualize a sentence? Even when nonliterates received information through an interpreter of texts, creating what Brian Stock (1983) calls "textual communities," they were hardly expected to "see" the shape of literacy.

By line twelve, then, Chaucer's audience would have been acutely aware that this oral performance was different, that a text precedes it, and that meaning lies locked in *it*, not in the author – and certainly not in them. If they asked the poet to repeat a line, he would have to back his eye up and give them exactly the same reading, a re-citation, rather than some variant. The author here has in some ways rendered himself superfluous. His written text has shaped this particular poem, a text that casts its shadow before the poem, like a specter, during oral delivery. Presumably, any skillful and literate performer could read it aloud. As Chaucer establishes himself author of the text, then, he naturally functions as a mere reciter in its presence; for the text has now assumed its own, independent authority, one that Chaucer has in effect authorized.[5]

It is appropriate, of course, to compose and deliver poetry using oral devices – formulaic constructions, additions, repetitions – enabling an audience to stay abreast and understand. The oral poet lends his voice to the group; he harmonizes *for* them because he thinks in harmony *with* them. But Chaucer has turned antagonistic, almost nasty. Standing above them, as an authority, he delivers his poem through highly literate techniques – by using two subordinate clauses and so inducing his audience to forget. In effect, he erases the lines of poetry as he reads them aloud. By tricking his audience into forgetting, however, Chaucer sets before them one of the critical concerns of the poem: the imposition of literacy on an inherently oral activity, the composition of poetry. The result produces a brand-new idea: literature.

Inability to remember is thus a crucial Chaucerean strategy. He uses it, first of all, in an aggressive and bossy way to put his audience in their transitional place. Asking them to do the impossible – envision the page as they hear it aloud – he casts them as victims, robbing them of the chance to really "get" the poem. At this point, the poem "gets" them. But his trick is more involved than that. By revealing his *own* inability to remember, he signals an equally important transition – his own – from poet and rhetor, to author and authority.[6]

Chaucer the narrator begins by sketching in details about some thirty-three pilgrims with whom he sat one evening in the Tabard Inn and with whom he set out on the road to Canterbury. He will not, he announces, relate what he has written down or dictated – he will avoid, that is, the tools of literacy, for he intends his poem to be something other than a *memorandum* – in the way twelfth-century documents served merely to record an event. Rather, he will tell us what he has remembered. But for him to use memory as a way of preserving information is archaic: Chaucer only pretends to be part of the oral majority. And we must beware the trickster.

His claim is astonishing: He intends to tell us all four stories the pilgrims recounted on their round trip, "as it remembreth me," in their distinct voices, utilizing their exact metaphors, images, color of language, and idea: *ipsissima verba*. All told, Chaucer promises a hundred and thirty plus stories in over fifteen thousand lines, for the most part meticulously rhymed and metered – certainly a prodigious feat.

So prodigious, in fact, that Chaucer must have known his medieval audience would have believed him, but only up to a point. Indeed, if, as some historians argue, Chaucer was educated at the Inns of Court, he would have learned some mnemonic system – his own Man of Laws learns "ever statute . . . plein by rote" – and so would have been able to retell by memory a large amount of detail. But Chaucer cannot rely on Homer's Mnemosyne, that great treasure bag of phrases and images, into which the rhetor could dip, threading now one and now another on his marvelous loom. Chaucer possesses a literate memory; some of his stories have been miraculously "sucked from his finger." And he boasts of remembering such an abundance of facts and minutiae that an audience – medieval or modern – would be forced to conclude that he is lying to them. No one could possibly remember that much detail with that much precision – mnemonic devices or not. As auditors in the old sense, then, they would have been pulled up short (see Howard, 1976).

Thus Chaucer the narrator becomes deliberately outspoken in his claim to remember all, in order that Chaucer the man can become an imaginative author. No other medieval writer – not Dante, Gower, or Boccaccio – used memory as such a storehouse, a *promptorium*, for fiction. Chaucer's audience would have been alert to a ploy, for he has presented them with such a revolutionary kind of memory. He pushes the limits of orality until they break through their boundary into literacy; he insists on his medieval audience hearing the lines of the *Canterbury Tales* as *grammatica*, as a work of literature. By situating them between orality and literacy, Chaucer forces his audience to confront the process of writing fiction; for if he could not possibly have remembered all that he says he has, he must be making it up, embellishing and shaping some initial bits of source material or sense impression, rather than reworking some other *auctoritas*. He must be telling a story, inventing a tale. That is, he must be fabricating and shaping untruths, or what we call writing fiction.

By assigning to himself the capacity to remember every scrap and nuance, every blink and titter of all thirty-three pilgrims, he sets himself up as a liar,[7] one who does not intend, however, to deceive maliciously, but to delight – with fibs and fables. No other serious literary category exists for him. Chaucer has to create his own.

But he has to walk a fine line. While he needs to be taken as a liar, he cannot be outlandish. He must maintain the fiction that his fiction is factual: Readers enter a fictional dream only when it is seamless. Chaucer achieves his verisimilitude in several ways. By casting himself as one of the pilgrims, Chaucer implies that "I was there, and so I know. I saw all this, I heard them all speak; now let me tell you what they said and did." He gains even more realism by drawing some of the other pilgrims – Harry Bailly the Host, for example – from actual citizenry of fourteenth-century London.

While he needs to inject this kind of realism into his poem, for theological reasons he must also have his audience experience the poem as made up. Thus, he attributes to himself a memory so amazing that it becomes unbelievable, even laughable. He really was not on the road after all. Along the way, he pulls a similar joke: As one of the pilgrims, he tells his own "Tale of Sir Thopas," which turns dull so quickly that the Host orders him to stop – "myn eres aken of thy drasty speche" (1. 113) – demanding a mirthful tale or, as a last resort, even some "doctryne," that is, some knowledge or edification. Alas, Chaucer the pilgrim, unlike Chaucer the narrator, simply cannot muster the rhetorical skill to tell an interesting tale.

The written word constitutes the authorized version, the authenticated truth. But too much truth can get Chaucer into very hot holy water. To cool things off, Chaucer moved his creation into a theologically inert category, into fictive untruth, which he did by allowing his audience to catch him in his straight-faced lie. Chaucer could no longer hide behind the "mumming muse," as Boccaccio calls Mnemosyne, the goddess of recollecting. He had to conjure a new muse – one suited to the literate, joking creator – the goddess of forgetting.

## IV

Storytelling and joking are the Siamese twins of fiction; they are joined by their mutual dependence on untruth.[8] Like metaphor, each suggests that life can be lived between the lines. The vocabulary of narration reveals this delicate balance: Fiction, fable, story, tale – each at times claims to be true, at other times false. Jokes, too, vacillate between lying and the most subtle truth telling. While they start out as lies, innocent and benign, jokes often hit with the stinging accuracy of truth. Even Saint Augustine, not noted for his hilarity, defended their shady character: "Jokes should never be accounted lies, seeing they bear with them in the tone of the voice, and in the very mood of the joker a most evident indication that he means no deceit, although the thing he utters be not true. . . . A person should not be thought to lie, who lieth not" (1984, *De Mendacio*, bk. 1, chap. 2). This shared ambiguity allows both the joker and the author to get away with murder. The joker pleads, "I'm only kidding. It was only a joke," while the author wriggles off the hook by saying, "It's only a story."

In writing fiction, every author weaves an intricately beautiful lie – a metaphoric reality – so that his story will be taken seriously. The author plots in order to perpetrate his story on his audience, to hoodwink them into accepting his fabrication as real. To be successful, the author must take seriously his storytelling and, at the same time, take delight in playing his practical joke on the audience. This is as true for that trickster Mark Twain, as it is for Chaucer, who instructs us, in the prologue to "The Miller's Tale," not to take his brilliant Canterbury *narratio* seriously. He is, he says, only playing a game. Since both author and joker must enjoy being playful, it makes sense that Thoth, the god of writing, is also the inventor of play, the one who, as Jacques Derrida has said, "puts play into play."

This connection was already apparent in England as early as the time of King Aelfric, who uses the word *racu* in some places to gloss the Latin *comoedia* and in other places to gloss *historia*. Anglo-Saxon glossaries thus define *racu* as both "laughter" and "narration." Anglo-Saxon poets are known as "laughter-smiths" and minstrels – singers of stories – as *mimi*, and *scurrae*, but most often as purveyors of laughter, *gleemen* (Wright, 1968).

Medieval England and France developed a rich tradition of jesting and narration, and of course laughter, due in large part to an almost unbelievable range of traveling performers – an *ordo vagorum* of motley players. *Mimi, scurrae, scenici,* Goliards, *poetae,* parasites, *tragoedi, comoedi, comici, joculares, jocistae, corauli, cantatores, joculatores, histriones, cytharistae, thymalici* – all of whom played, juggled, and recited, with great fanfare and elaboration, bawdy *iocare* (jests) and *facetiae* (witty stories) (Reich, 1903; Nicoll, 1931; Tatlock, 1946; Adolf, 1947).

By the thirteenth century these various entertainers, ultimately all derived from the *mimi* of ancient Greece, were being described by one French word, *jongleur,* modern English *juggler,* derived in turn from the same Latin root as *joke, iocare.* Traveling from place to place, these juggler-raconteurs left a trail of laughter across the *terra ridentum.* It is clear from the account books of colleges and monasteries, from councils, Synods, and the Capitularies of someone like Charlemagne, that bishops, abbots, and abbesses, forbidden to own hunting dogs, falcons, and hawks, were also denied the company of *joculatores.* These Capitularies, denouncing the ribald stories being recited by these troops of itinerant players, make clear that their *gesta* are only thinly disguised *iocistae.* Besides, many are preserved under the name that Cicero gave them, *facetiae* – short, mostly funny, and bawdy vignettes. They resemble the modern joke in subject but not yet in form (see Faral, 1910; Ogilvy, 1963; Bowen, 1986a, b).

Petrarch was the first to collect them, which he published as an addendum to his *Rerum Memorandum Libri* (1343–5), an obscure little book appropriately enough on memory and eloquence. The most influential and probably the most original collection, however, was assembled by that grand Renaissance humanist, Poggio Bracciolini, in 1470, who claims that he heard his 273 short jokes and stories while serving as Apostolic Secretary in the Roman Curia. Poggio further tells us that these jokes were told by the secretaries in the *Bugiale* (from the Italian *bugia,* "a lie"), a "workshop of lies" established by the papal secretaries themselves to pass the time and to attack "those things which we disapproved of; very often we took the Pope himself as the starting point of our criticism" (Salemi, 1983, p. 3).

The style of these jest books betray their upbringing in orality, marked as they are by a great use of homonyms, repetitions, and other rhetorical devices. For the most part, however, when they were published and circulated, the jest book put an end to the *facetiae* as an oral form. Something more powerful had supplanted it, the joke, still our most unpredictable and frolicsome form of oral entertainment. Nearly everyone, even those who cannot tell stories, delights in recounting an occasional joke. We owe this extraordinary invention, at least in English, to Chaucer, who brings together the history of jesting, narration, and laughter in one grand climax by creating the first modern joke, "The Miller's Tale."[9]

Chaucer not only assumed a jesting, ironic stance toward writing itself. In a stroke of literary brilliance, he transformed the physicality of the practical joke into the verbal punch line. Added to the *facetiae*, the punch line turned the listener into a target, a butt, no longer knocked over bodily with a physical blow but now bowled over emotionally or psychically with an image or a line. Chaucer had already played his own practical joke on his courtly audience, victimizing them with highly literate techniques. In "The Miller's Tale," he has drawn the curtain and offered them a glimpse into the literate future, the practical joke transformed. While the Miller tells a story that revolves around several practical jokes – a fake flood, a misdirected kiss, a perfectly aimed fart, a burned arse – his tale itself constitutes a colossal, nasty joke, about gullibility and cuckoldry, fired at the Reeve.

Derisive jesting in the classical world was characterized as *aculi*, "barbed," "arrow-like" (a shift forward from the feathery end of the shaft, as Homer's "winged words" imply); the word *butt* quite appropriately means "target." These words reveal something crucial: The punch line cannot work effectively as a literary device unless the target appears as a developed character, his vulnerability made fleshly palpable. The Miller must be close enough to the Reeve to know, as we say, where he "lives." A joke misfires unless it finds a personality rife with consciousness and sensibility. Idiots, dolts – *stupidus* of all kinds – will simply miss the point; or the point will miss them – go by without so much as a glancing blow or pass over their heads. Corralling the joke into a literate context forced Chaucer into becoming a modern writer, into dropping traditional, familiar stereotypes in favor of dramatic characters. In short, by writing jokes, Chaucer had to become a serious author.

Chaucer understood that the tremendous power and sophistication of this oral form could be harnessed to effect the most profound social change, to realign status and relationships. The ultimate effect of Chaucer's accomplishment is staggering. Because of him people still tell aggressive jokes and for precisely the same reasons, for the history of joking records the outbreak of an uncivil war. Unwitting victims keel over, break up, fall apart, double up – all with laughter. If no one ever stumbled or fell, never slipped or got butted, we would, if jokes provide any evidence, still try to knock them over – either physically (with practical jokes) or verbally (with well-aimed "punch" lines).

Without formally analyzing "The Miller's Tale," I would now like to extract the pattern of joking from that tale; in so doing, I have to at least mention the tale that immediately follows it, "The Reeve's Tale," for after all, the Miller directs his jokes at a victim, the Reeve. The Miller has no tale, in effect, without him.

## V

While we play practical jokes to establish our power and exercise control, we crack aggressive jokes against our neighbors out of envy, a connection first pointed out by the earliest analysis of laughter in Western thought, in Plato's *Philebus*. Usually, we envy the other person's higher social status or better situation. The Miller and the Reeve have clearly been rivals for some time: One rides at the head of pilgrimage, the other at the hind end. The Miller slowly reveals that he envies the circumstances of the Reeve's marriage – quite predictably, the Reeve's young and pretty wife. He can rectify this inequity in one of two ways: by raising himself or lowering the Reeve. Jokes accomplish both simultaneously. The joke teller elevates himself by displaying, to everyone's delight, a keen and clever wit, and lowers the other person by showing him to be a dunce. Try as he may, the jokee rarely ever second-guesses – and thus is unable to defuse – the punch line. Placing himself so diligently on guard, of course, the jokee renders himself even more unstable and precarious, a wobbly target easily knocked over.

In the way Chaucer uses it, joking acts as a socially acceptable form of justice, a self-styled people's court. The Miller can in an instant "get even" by humiliating the Reeve. While the joker necessarily satisfies his needs at the victim's expense, the victim too can win approval but *only* by pulling himself out of his humiliation (literally, "to become like the earth," *humus*). If he becomes angry or leaves in a rage, he lowers himself even further – buries himself – by prompting the audience to laugh *at* him. He can of course retaliate, return the fire, by telling a joke back on his aggressor. But it had better be a clever one, more clever than the one the joker told, not like the Reeve's feeble escalation.

The victim can survive socially in one way only, by standing his ground and laughing the joke off, thus demonstrating that he knows how to play the game like a good sport. The audience reinforces his magnanimity by laughing along *with* him, supporting him in his effort at being a "big" man. Through the power of literacy, jokes contextualize social relationships. But that is only half their power.

A collection of fifteenth-century sermons titled *Jacob's Well* explains that mercy is the virtue that opposes and converts envy, and the sermons counsel us to remove the "ooze of envy" from our souls. For a moment, by balancing the pans of justice, the joker has rid himself of envy and thus gained satisfaction. And while it may not *yet* be heartfelt, both teller and victim must at least act as if they have dropped their grudges and inch their way toward forgiveness.

The audience, too, benefits from this spirit; as Chaucer says about his pilgrim audience, after they hear the Miller's *jape:* "For the moore part they laughe and pleyde." Laughter promotes feelings of community. The experience resembles a religious one, perhaps a more efficacious one in fact than religion can offer. In this embrace of *communitas,* each person relates to the other as an equal. The temporary effect of joking, then, is to create a feeling that things are even-Stephen; or, more accurately, to use the Clown's phrase, the master of laughter in *Hamlet,* that all is "even-Cristen," a state in which every soul is equal under God's vision. Mary Douglas is apt here: "Whatever the joke, however remote its subject, the telling of it is potentially subversive. Since its form consists of a victorious tilting of uncontrol against control, it is an image of the levelling of hierarchy, the triumph of intimacy over formality, of unofficial values over official ones" (1975, p. 98).

Jokes may even spread the Good News faster than religion. They communicate such delight that as soon as we "get" a joke – and the more clever the joke, the more deeply we are apt to "get" it – we immediately have the urge to pass this gift of pleasure on, to collar the nearest person, embellish and retell the joke, increasing its value by adding our own "interest" to it. Gift giving is particularly refreshing at a time when wage labor is on the rise: It startles by breaking the cash nexus.[10] We are rarely ever presented with the opportunity, especially today, of keeping a gift in circulation.

## VI

Hermes, the patron trickster for the early Greeks, gets nudged aside in the early Middle Ages by Merlin, the patron saint of letters. This shape shifter leaves his epigrams "on tombstones, swords, boats, and hermes scattered throughout the realm" and sends his letters "which circulate between lovers, between enemies, between Arthur and his barons" (Bloch, 1983, p. 2). More than prolific, he is capable of performing the wildest feats of magic, as well as seeing into the future. Legend knows him best of all as a trickster, a riddler – revealing the truth in apparent lies – and a profound practical joker. In the second *Life of St. Kentigern,* Merlin serves as a clairvoyant fool in King Rederich's court and with his "foolish words and gestures . . . excites to jokes and loud laughter the lords themselves and their servants" (Welsford, 1935, p. 105). For Merlin, writing results, above all else, in laughing matter.

If Merlin acts as the patron saint of playful writing, Chaucer is its incarnation. He is attracted to joking not because of his keen sense of humor, but because he is in the very marrow of his bones a writer. He delights in what Ezra Pound calls *Logopoeia,* "the dance of the intellect among words." To acknowledge Chaucer's connection between joking and storytelling is to recognize a most remarkable, buried fact about the history of literature: joking is first cousin to medieval *narratio,* fiction, a genre that culminates so eloquently in the modern novel. Indeed, the first great European novelist, Rabelais, confesses that he was inspired by a cosmic punch line, and immediately after hearing God's laughter began writing his own lengthy, brilliantly conceived joke, *Gargantua and Pantagruel.*

Chaucer's development of the joke points to an elaborate interdependence between orality and literacy; it demonstrates the way forms can be taken out of orality, analyzed and reshaped in literacy, then sent back on their way into orality – with renewed, restrengthened life.[11] Literacy, as Walter Ong (1982) suggests, can enhance orality, and Chaucer presents us with a prime example. Jokes persist as our most lively form of oral, unscripted performance. And because he is the first major English author whose stories emanate from the shape of *narratio* in a text, rather than from a text that has trapped elements from orality, like a sieve, Chaucer forces his audience to do the impossible: to listen with their mind's eye. From this point on, the word *audience* sometimes means *reading* audience, creating a category as strange as "oral literature." Chaucer encourages the strangeness. He recites using literate constructs; he tells the truth with lies; he speaks in the present through the past and future tenses. Amid this confusion, anything – especially a new *narratio fabulosa* – is possible.[12]

But great authors always deliver more than they promise, and Chaucer is no exception. If we listen carefully, we can hear him, like that wickedly delightful heroine of "The Miller's Tale," Dame Alice, laughing "tee hee" long after the tale is over. Chaucer laughs last, because he has us both ways. If we want to really understand the intricate skill of "The Miller's Tale," we have to read it. But if we want to participate in its spirit, we have to remain strongly connected to orality – best of all through our own joke telling.

## VII

Peasants and folk peoples may have lived and died without leaving much of a written record, but they did not disappear without making a sound. We will never understand their place out of history until we understand their laughing place in it;[13] for laughter announces more than the mere presence of people – their voice print. It unmasks their attitudes and tastes, their anxieties and outright fears. In short, it lays bare their sensibilities. Dismantling barriers of language, sex, nationality, even age, laughter is surefire. It is the Esperanto of the people, their *Ursprache*. By celebrating raw humanity, laughter levels every stratum of society into boisterous hoi polloi. More than any other oral form, it most economically sets relations in order, fuels rivalries, resolves conflicts, and defuses and sets off a chain reaction of power. In influence, speed, and effect, jokes surpass every printed and electronic medium.

In virtually every subject, we have to guard against imposing modern definitions on historical activities. This holds even for something that seems as unmistakable as "reading"; but we know, for example, that when Charlemagne uses the phrase "I have read," he sometimes means Bishop Alcuin has read aloud to him. But who can mistake the sound of a laugh? Surely, it is the most heartfelt sign that Chaucer has been "heard."

## NOTES

1 For *author*, see "The Legend of Good Women": "Of manye a geste as autorys seyn" (l. 88). The word *tale* is used as early as the thirteenth century as a "story or narrative, true or fictitious, *drawn up so as to interest or amuse* [my emphasis], or to preserve the history of a fact or incident; a literary composition cast in narrative form" (*OED*). But not until Chaucer "is the meaning unequivocally that implied in the italicized words of the definition" (Duncan, 1972, p. 2). For *audience*, see *Troilus and Criseyde:* "Now I am gone, whom yeve ye audience?" (l. 235). For *auditor*, see "The Summoner's Tale": "Who folweth Cristes gospel and his foore, / But we that humble been, and chaast, and poore, / Werkeris of Goddes word, nat auditors?" (ll. 1935–7). I am currently compiling a list of first meanings the *OED* attributes to Chaucer.
2 The *OED* cites "The Legend of Good Women" for the following definition of *imagination:* "The mental consideration of actions or events not yet in

existence," and cites *The House of Fame*, 2: 220, for the "operation of the mind generally." Even when the *OED* refers to *imagination* as "poetic genius," the citation points to Chaucer: "Upon hys ymaginacyon He made also the tales of Caunterbury" (Hawes, *Past Pleasures*). Chaucer's use is all the more remarkable if we consider that the imagination was distrusted in the Middle Ages because it falsified reality (see Bundy, 1927; Bloomfield, 1962).

Thomas Ross, the editor of the variorum "The Miller's Tale," surveys Chaucer's possible sources and analogues for that tale only to announce, "In the absence of a direct source, we must conclude that to Chaucer belongs the laurels for this masterpiece of narrative" (1983, p. 6). But Chaucer's fiction is also original in the sense that his stories can stand as pure entertainment. One does not have to rehabilitate them by reading allegorically in an attempt to uncover their scriptural message. Utilizing this kind of reading, the Middle Ages – particularly in the twelfth century – defended most *fabulae* (Dronke, 1974).

3 See Scholes and Willis, Chapter 13, this volume. See also Ong (1982). Harris (1986) cautions against "significant over-simplification" in the binary opposition of clause types – subordinate and independent – but does point out the complexity of subordination.

So clearly bound by the rules of time, and so far removed from eternality, complex sentences exemplify Augustine's "fallen syntax" into the *regio dissimilitudinus*. Consider Augustine on time: "Every part of the past is forced out by the future, and every part of the future moment is created and flows from that which is the Everlasting Present. Who will hold the heart of man, that it may stand and see how eternity, as it stands still and is neither past nor future, determines the future and past times?" (1984, "Soliloquies," bk.12, chap. 11).

4 In a commentary on the Sphere of Sacrobosco, Robertus Anglicus forecasts the invention of the mechanical clock with verge escapement and foliot; the manuscript is dated 1271 (Thorndike, 1941).

Perhaps because they require the same kind of abstraction, complex sentences appear at the same time as the mechanical clock, which also indicates time in a fuguelike manner: While we know that the clock always indicates the present, its hands continually erase the past, while pointing toward the future. Nonliterates do not *tell* time. The sun, the seasons, some important festival or cosmic event tells *them* the time.

5 Writers like Nicholas of Trevisa made important distinctions in the late Middle Ages between *assertio* and *recitatio*. "An auctor was supposed to 'assert' or 'affirm' while a compilator 'repeated' what others had said or done" (Minnis, 1984, p. 193).

6 Lydgate conferred the title of rhetor on Chaucer (with a pun) a decade after his death: "And eke my maister Chaucer is now in grave / The noble rethor poete of brytayne" (*Life Our Lady*, 34).

Robert Burlin sees Chaucer's fiction in the *Canterbury Tales* as an oscillation between "experience and auctoritee": "The first group of poems promotes the illusion of authorial experience, the second works from the premise of authoritativeness" (1977, p. 14). I want to argue that *all* the tales – indeed their premise – derives from literacy: the authority of the written word. Experience in Chaucer's fiction must by definition always be trumped up – in its fullest sense, both heralded and fabricated.

7 Judith Ferster describes the reception of medieval fiction: "Either fiction leads audiences into falsehood and evil, and writers are liars, or fiction urges its audience toward salvation, and writers are aligned with philosophers and saints" (1985, p. 16). I argue that with the rise of literacy, a third category emerged – authors are liars – *and* still lead their audience to the truth.

8 Augustine: "Almost everyone who tells a joke, tells a fable" (1984, "Soliloquies," bk. 1, chap. 1, p. 14).

9 Medievalists constantly argue away Chaucer's playfulness. Glending Olson (1982) insists that Chaucer's play serves a practical end by providing a refreshing respite, necessary to carry out serious work. Richard Lanham (1976) argues that Chaucer must have seen the world as a game and people as players. Stephen Manning (1979) holds a similar view.

10 The classic work on gift exchange is still Marcel Mausse (1923–4). For a more recent, provocative study on the nature of gift economies, see Lewis Hyde (1979). The ultimate gift we can pass on, of course, is life itself – through offspring – just as we ourselves "pass on." Perhaps the phrase "passing on" once indicated this precious gift.

11 The opposite movement also occurs: "It is remarkable how many episodes from the annals of early British history owe their preservation in popular tradition to the wit and playfulness of the words in which they were recorded" (Frank, 1972, p. 207).

12 Macrobius defines *narratio fabulosa* as tales in which "truth is expressed through fictional devices" (see Dronke, 1974). Middle English *fable*, ultimately derived from Latin *fabula*, refers to any invented plot. On the question of medieval genre in general, see Kahrl (1965) and Strohm (1971, 1980). These critics all try to deal with Chaucer's "fiction" by assigning each tale to a specific genre, a strategy that may work for the early Middle Ages. I want to show *how* Chaucer fights to leave these traditional classifications.

13 Keith Thomas (1977) argues a similar point in his provocative article on laughter.

REFERENCES

Adolf, H. (1947). On medieval laughter. *Speculum* 23(2):251–3.
Augustine, Saint. (1984). *Selected writings*. New York: Paulist Press.
Bauml, F. (1980). Varieties and consequences of medieval literacy and illiteracy. *Speculum* 55(2):237–65.
Bloch, H. (1983). *Genealogies: A literary anthropology of the French Middle Ages*. Chicago: University of Chicago Press.
Bloomfield, M. (1962). Piers Plowman *as a fourteenth-century apocalypse*. New Brunswick, N.J.: Rutgers University Press.

Bowen, B. C. (1986a). Renaissance collections of *facetiae*, 1344–1490: A new listing. *Renaissance Quarterly*, 1:1–15.
(1986b). Part two: 1499–1520. *Renaissance Quarterly*, 2:263–75.
Bundy, M. W. (1927). *The theory of the imagination in classical and medieval thought*. University of Illinois Studies in Language and Literature, Vol. 12. Urbana: University of Illinois.
Burlin, R. (1977). *Chaucerian fiction*. Princeton, N.J.: Princeton University Press.
Crosby, R. (1936). Oral delivery in the middle ages. *Speculum* 11(4):99–110.
(1938). Chaucer and the custom of oral delivery. *Speculum* 13(4):413–32.
Douglas, M. (1975). *Implicit meanings: Essays in anthropology*. London: Routledge & Kegan Paul.
Dronke, P. (1974). *Fabula: Explorations into the uses of myth in medieval platonism*. Leiden: Brill.
Duncan, E. H. (1972). Short fiction in medieval English: A survey. *Studies in Short Fiction* 9:1–28.
Faral, E. (1964). *Les jongleurs en France au moyen age*, 2nd ed. Paris: Champion.
Ferguson, M. (1975). Saint Augustine's region of unlikeness: The crossing of exile and language. *The Georgia Review*, 29(4):842–64.
Ferster, J. (1985). *Chaucer on interpretation*. Cambridge University Press.
Foley, J. M. (1980–81). Oral literature: Premises and problems. *Choice* 18: 487–96.
Frank, R. (1972). Some uses of paranomasia in old English scriptural verse. *Speculum* 47:207–26.
Haidu, P. (1977). Repetition: Modern reflections on medieval aesthetics. *Modern Language Notes* 92:875–87.
Harris, M. B. (1986). Aspects of subordination in English and other languages. *Bulletin of the John Rylands University* (Library of Manchester), 69(1):195–209.
Howard, D. (1976). *The idea of the* Canterbury Tales. Berkeley and Los Angeles: University of California Press.
Hyde, L. (1979). *The gift: Imagination and the erotic life of property*. New York: Random House.
Kahrl, S. (1965). Allegory in practice: A study of narrative styles in medieval exempla. *Modern Philology* 63:105–10.
Lanham, R. (1976). *The motives of eloquence: Literary rhetoric in the Renaissance*. New Haven, Conn.: Yale University Press.
Manning, S. (1979). Rhetoric, game, morality, and Geoffrey Chaucer. *Studies in the Age of Chaucer* 1:105–18.
Mausse, M. (1923–4). Essai sur le don: Forme et raison de l'échange dans les sociétés archaiques. *L'Anne Sociologique* 1:30–186.
Minnis, A. J. (1984). *Medieval theory of authorship: Scholastic literary attitudes in the later Middle Ages*. London: Scolar.
Nicoll, A. (1931). *Masks, mimes and miracles*. New York: Harcourt, Brace & World.
Ogilvy, J. D. A. (1963). Mimi, scurrae, histriones: Entertainers of the early Middle Ages. *Speculum* 38(4):603–19.

Olson, G. (1982). *Literature as recreation in the later Middle Ages.* Ithaca, N.Y.: Cornell University Press.
Ong, W. (1982). *Orality and literacy: The technologizing of the word.* London: Methuen & Co.
Perry, B. E. (1967). *The ancient romances.* Berkeley and Los Angeles: University of California Press.
Reich, H. (1903). *Der mimus.* Berlin: Weidmann.
Ross, T. (1983). *Variorum The Miller's Tale.* Norman: University of Oklahoma Press.
Salemi, J. S. (trans.) (1983). Poggio's *Facetiae. Allegorica* 8:1,2.
Steiner, G. (1977). *After Babel: Aspects of language and translation.* Oxford University Press.
Stock, B. (1983). *The implications of literacy: Written language and models of interpretation in the eleventh and twelfth centuries.* Princeton, N.J.: Princeton University Press.
Strohm, P. (1971). Some generic distinctions in the *Canterbury Tales. Modern Philology* 68:321–8.
    (1980). Middle English narrative genres. *Genre* 8:379–88.
Tatlock, J. S. P. (1946). Medieval laughter. *Speculum* 31:289–94.
Thomas, K. (1977, Jan. 21). The place of laughter in Tudor and Stuart England. *Times Literary Supplement,* pp. 77–81.
Thorndike, L. (1941). Invention of the mechanical clock about 1271 AD. *Speculum* 16(2):242–3.
Welsford, E. (1935). *The fool: His social and literary history.* London: Faber & Faber.
Wright, T. (1968). *Anglo-Saxon and Old English vocabularies.* 2nd ed. Darmstadt: Wissenschaftliche Buchgeselschaft.

# 8

## The invention of self: autobiography and its forms

JEROME BRUNER and SUSAN WEISSER

Nothing would seem more "natural" than talking about oneself. After all, we all do it and, it would seem, do it with scarcely a psychic strain. The exceptions to this seeming ease come only when self-report encroaches on taboo or when it threatens the mutual deterrence treaty by which the ego, superego, and id manage to live with the same tenement of clay. Or, at least, so it would seem.

But having now spent several years listening to people of many different ages talking about themselves and their lives, I want to offer several very different theses. Put at its starkest, the first is this: Almost from the start of language, self-report is framed by stylistic conventions and by rules of genre. From very early in life (as we shall see) to the far reaches of literary autobiography, we are bound by strong conventions regarding not only *what* we say when we tell about ourselves, but *how* we say it, to whom, and so on. Indeed, the conventions of style and genre are so strong that they even carry over into such lone activities as bedtime soliloquies and writing in our diary.

My second thesis is that the shape of a life is as much a function of the conventions of genre and style in which it is couched as it is, so to speak, of what "happened" in the course of that life. And turning points in a life are provoked not by actualities, but by revisions in the story one has been using to tell about life and self, the most drastic of these being genre changes prompted from within. This leads me to propose, then, that in some important sense, "lives" are texts: texts that are subject to revision, exegesis, reinterpretation, and so on. That is to say, *accounted* lives are taken by those who account them as texts amenable to alternative interpretation. When people reinterpret their life accounts, they do not deny the prior "text" (as I shall define that word in a moment), but deny the interpretation they have placed upon it. And as I shall try to show presently, it is a lifelong habit.

What sort of a "text" is the report of a life? Obviously, when it is written down as literary autobiography (a rare enough act), this is

This chapter was prepared jointly by the two authors, but it was decided that it should be composed in the first person by the senior author.

presumed to pose no problem. But it would be careless to say that *unless* one writes it down, one has no textual account of one's life – just as careless as it would be to say that a literary autobiography is the one and only text of a life. Rather, I wish to equate "text" in this sense with a conceptually formulated narrative account of what a life has been about. That it is an account carried in memory, or carried in memory in such a way as to be capable of generating shorter or longer versions of itself, does not exclude it from status as a text open to alternative interpretations.

I think Hayden White's (1981) discussion of historical accounts may be of some use to us here. He distinguishes, after the French school, between *annales, chroniques,* and *histoires.* The first consist of selected events roughly fixed in date, as say, in the *Annals of St. Gall:*

709. Hard winter. Duke Gottfried died.
710. Hard year, deficient in crops.
712. Floods everywhere.
714. Pippin, Mayor of the Palace, dies.
718. Charles devastated the Saxons.
721. Theudo drove the Saracens out of Aquitaine.
725. Saracens came for the first time.
731. Blessed Bede, the presbyter, died.
732. Charles fought the Saracens at Poitier.

The list is constructed of "happenings," and the blank dates are years in which "nothing" happened. Yet as White remarks, there must obviously be some covert impulse or criterion that leads to Pippin's death making the list rather than, say, the conviction of some peasant for stealing. The events, nonetheless, fall short of being "narremes," constituents of a superordinate story form, even though they vaguely suggest that the annalist in question was a trouble collector, but that is not enough (in Hayden White's words) "to impose a meaning on the events."

As for the *chronique,* its function is to create what we might call "clots" of meaning for sets of events, what all that trouble was *about.* It may still not "end the story," or console in Frank Kermode's (1967) sense, but chroniques do have plots, if only little ones. They would make it clearer why Pippin mattered. But they, in turn, only achieve their full meaning or interpretation when embodied in a *histoire* that in its fullness, includes a systemic account of the nature of the moral order of things in which the dramatic *chroniques* are unfolding. Never mind that today's *histoire* is tomorrow's hypocrisy.

Self-reports are like that: suspiciously motivated recall of *annale*-like events ("the strict teacher in the third grade"), given meaning by *chroniques* ("my battle against authority in school"), imbedded in a more or less vague *histoire* ("my lifelong search for autonomy in a conformity-demanding culture"). Later, I want to take up again this "text-making" process of motivated memory, and I hope the account up to here gives you some inkling of the point to which I am heading.

I must say a word about what I intend by the idea of genre to which I have referred, commenting that self-tellings are structured in genre. As Jonathan Culler (1986) and many others before him have pointed out, genre is a way of characterizing a text in terms of certain formal and content properties, but it is also a way of characterizing how a reader or listener *takes* a text, whatever its actual content and its formal characteristics may be. Mary McCarthy's (1957) *Memories of a Catholic Girlhood* first appeared in the form of short stories and were later brought together as "autobiography" (with italicized interstitial metachapters). It is perfectly possible to read the autobiographical volume *not* as autobiography, but as a postmodernist novel, treating the story narrator and the interstitial essayist as a canny novelist simulating an epistemic crisis. It is equally possible to read Ms. McCarthy's allegedly *non*-autobiographical stories and novels as autobiography. The point I want to make, simply, is that genres exist not only as modes of writing or speaking but as modes of reading and listening. We can read a comic text as satire or social commentary, a Gothic tale as a psychoanalytic record, and so on. I had the occasion, some years ago, of accompanying some native fishermen on a sailing *pirogue* off the coast of Senegal. To make conversation as we were changing location, I pointed west and announced that there was where my home was. My companions looked puzzled for a moment, and then the headman broke into laughter, nodding in mock agreement. He had taken it as a great joke. For the remainder of the day, until we finally beached the *pirogue* and said farewell, nearly everything I said was found to have something amusing in it. I had become an instant success as a comic – for the listeners!

What is especially interesting about autobiography is that we can tell or write our own autobiography in one mode or genre and later read or recall it in terms of another or several others. Indeed, it is the rare life in which this does not happen, as when we recall a prior "soul baring" as not the "real" truth but an exercise in self-pity, self-aggrandizement, or whatever. Paul John Eakin (1985), in his stunning recent book, *Fictions in Autobiography: Studies in the Art of Self-Invention*, quotes William Maxwell (1980) as saying, "In talking about the past, we lie with every breath we draw" (p. 27).

But I am not trying to belittle autobiography as tendentious self-report. Rather, I want to make the point that autobiography constitutes a form of "rhetorical strategy," and whoever gives a report of himself, in whatever medium, knows it necessarily to be so, more or less explicitly. It is the *first* experience most of us ever have with the crucial distinction between a text and its interpretation. It is what leads a perceptive poet like Joseph Brodsky (1986), commenting on a deliberately false self-report in childhood, to conclude that lying is the origin of consciousness. Well, "lying" is probably the wrong word, for the consciousness that emerges when one recognizes the distinction between what has "happened," how one has reported it, and how else it might have been interpreted is not entirely a matter of being aware of "mistruth" but, rather, of being aware of alternate interpretations that are possible. And once one commits oneself to a particular "version," the past *becomes* that version or becomes inflected toward that version.

There is a unique epistemological and psychological circumstance that makes inevitable this kind of disjunction between the self-reporter and his report about himself, a disjunction that virtually forces us to adopt a strategy of discourse; for the act of self-reporting, as every thoughtful autobiographer since Saint Augustine has remarked, separates the self who is *telling* from the past self or "selves" who are being *told about*. In Emile Benveniste's (1971) austere terms, the "I" that speaks or writes lives in the "instance of discourse" in which he attempts to impersonate a self created out of memory from the past. The narrator and his subject "share the same name, but not the same time and space" (Howarth, 1980). The strategic task in the telling – whether the story is told for the consumption of others, or for oneself, and it is always both – is to make the narrative believable. And providing one is not deliberately lying or, as fiction writers must, using a fragment of memory for elaboration into a story, we strive for a verisimilitude that will satisfy ourselves and our auditors. The ultimate objective of any narrative is verisimilitude. But *how* we achieve it is also determined by the rules of the genres of autobiography in terms of which we operate and is not given by some "nothing-but-the-fact" dictum. A claim to self-transparency, for example, might have bestowed verisimilitude upon a self-report *before* but not after the coming of Freud! We know very little, besides, about the techniques whereby we make our accounts of ourselves believable to ourselves. And even such excellent analyses of self-deception as Polonoff's (1987) do not quite manage to capture what it is about alternative self-accountings that gives some accounts more verisimilitude than others.

But even beyond verisimilitude, the discourse strategy of self-report must serve other needs in order to meet the requirements of genre – ones even as detailed as syntax. Genre imposes crucial choices: tense, the option between stative and action verbs, reliance on prolepsis or analepsis. We shall see later how crucial these decisions may be in shaping what we take our "realities" to be. As Jean Starobinski (1971) so brilliantly demonstrated a generation ago, in autobiography, style "satisfies the conditions of the genre" and is not merely an ornament or the expression of social class. And obviously, discourse strategy requires a massive decision about theme: Is the self-report to be organized around love, duty, self-reliance, shame, a thwarted search for moral truth, what?

Genre, style, theme, convention – it is impossible to launch into self-report without making decisions about them. There is no way in which one can, so to speak, lapse into an "aboriginal" noninterpretive self-reportorial form. Autobiography *forces* interpretation. The interpretation requires management. How it is managed is what forms "mind" in the culture – whether it is "modern" mind or the mind of the member of a classic Greek *polis*.

But what is this interpretation? What is it an interpretation *of*? And what is it *for*? Let me consider the last of these first. The ultimate function of autobiography is self-location, the outcome of a navigational act that fixes position in a virtual rather than real sense. Through autobiography, we locate ourselves in the symbolic world of culture. Through it, we identify with a family, a community, and indirectly with the broader culture. It is the only way we have of relating to our conspecifics after we come out from under the shield of infantile mechanisms that allow us our prolonged human immaturity (Bruner, 1972). But at the same time that our autobiographical acts locate us culturally, they also serve to individuate us, to define what later I shall call *agency*. If the "inside" complexity of autobiography is given by the disjunction between self as narrator and self as subject, the "outside" complexity is assured by this Janus-like requirement of declaring both cultural allegiance and independence in the act of autobiography.

And what is an autobiography a representation *of*? A representation of memory, one will say (e.g., Neisser, 1986; Rubin, 1986). But what is the "memory" from which our autobiographical constructions are constituted? Memory, to look at it as abstractly as possible, is one of three ways in which the human past can be transmitted. The other two ways are through the genes and the instructions they transmit, and through culture with its corpus of symbolized knowledge and procedure into which people enter when they master its semiotic system. We need not pause over genetic transmission; we already know enough to be able to make up and send forward arbitrary messages without quite knowing what quite constitutes a natural message. With respect to cultural "transmission," anthropology has finally shaken itself from the slumbers of the past and has begun to consider transmission models that are considerably more interesting than the old "learning-imitation" mechanisms (e.g., Dollard, 1935; Whiting, 1941) or the more fanciful ones derived from psychoanalytic theory (e.g., Kardiner, 1939). Today, the emphasis is upon "mind-shaping" devices by which a culture continues itself. They include such cognitive-shaping devices as stories and "heroes" and how these give form to our conception not only of the world, of possible lives, but also conceptions of self – as in Michelle Rosaldo's (1980) account of the Ilongot (and many others: Geertz, 1973; Renato Rosaldo, 1980; Shweder, 1990). What we already know is that one of the chief means for cultural transmission is through schematizing systems that affect and shape individual perception, memory, and thought. So the issue of human memory becomes the more important.

Human memory seems, itself, to be served by three different transmission systems. The first, roughly, is managed through habit mechanisms: through the acquisition of skills, habituation, discrimination, and so on. It was what most of "learning theory" in the past generation was about. Habits, so-called, preserve adaptations accomplished in past encounters with the world. The second system is usually referred to as "episodic memory": It is the system through which specific past events, impressions, and so on are acquired, stored, and retrieved. It is highly unstable, notoriously selective and governed by interest and attitudes, only moderately accurate, even when it is one of those vivid "flash-bulb" memories (e.g., Neisser, 1982), and enormously useful for coping with the details of life – like the recognition of friends and family, memory for telephone numbers, vivid images of the face of your counselor at camp, and so on. It assures us access, albeit biased, to the events that make up the *annales* of our autobiographies.

The third of the human memory systems – usually called "semantic memory" (e.g., Tulving 1972) – is the most interesting in the present context. Put crudely, it traffics in memory for meaning and generality, and as one might well imagine, its sphere is on the borderline between what in common sense is called "thought" and what is ordinarily referred to as memory. In semantic memory, for example, we recall the results of categorizing and inferential activity, rather than the raw inputs (e.g., Bruner, Goodnow, & Austin, 1956). We remember, for example, that there were "a lot of people helping," though we are hard put to remember who they were or what they were doing exactly, though we can sometimes fill in if pressed. A bright Oxford undergraduate, answering a rather leaden finals question about the difference between episodic and semantic memory, remarked that semantic memory was there so that the culture could take over mind. The rest of his answer was indifferent, but I gave him an alpha on it anyway; for what we have learned about memory since Sir Frederic Bartlett's classic *Remembering* in 1932 is that it contains an enormously powerful schematizing function that is not only capable of selecting and organizing vast quantities of stored material into meaningful patterns, but capable, as well, of reverting to Sir Frederic's term, of "turning around" on already formed schemata and reorganizing them according to intentions and "attitudes" presently in play. Our memory system, then, provides *annales* but has a built-in system for converting them into *chroniques* and *histoires,* and there is enough flexibility in the system to alter the *annales* to make them fit into the *chroniques.*

On the basis of the foregoing, scandalously brief sketch of memory, I would want to conclude that the process of "making an autobiography" is a canny act of putting a sampling of episodic memories into a dense matrix of organized and culturally schematized semantic memory. The mix is reminiscent not only of Hayden White's description of history, but of W. V. Quine's (1978) famous quip about physics: one percent observation, ninety-nine percent speculation.

I must put in an aside here, if I am to avoid later misunderstanding. I do not wish to make the claim that, in view of what I have said, all there is to life is one's autobiography of it. For one thing, anyone can reel off multiple autobiographies of his own life – that is, can include different materials, organize it around different themes (within limits), make it match different moods, slant it for different audiences, and so on. And, indeed, one's told (or implicitly "held") autobiography can omit crucial matters that may yet have a powerful effect on one's contemporary behavior – omit them willfully or because they are made inaccessible by repression or some kindred mechanism. Or the organization of one's account may be such as to "misrepresent" powerful sources of motivation that drive one to act in certain ways that seem inexplicable to one. That is to say, the interpretation that is inherent in any autobiography may be more or less "right" in accounting for one's past, present, or future behavior. Such "rightness," is, of course, calculable by various criteria – truth or accuracy, predictability, agreement with the account of others viewing one from the outside, the degree to which the account gives its teller comfort, narrative plausibility, and so on. Talking cures, like psychoanalysis, are designed to help people make a better match between what they think and tell about themselves and how they feel or behave. But note that even among contemporary psychoanalysts, there is a raging battle in progress about whether that "match" between self-report on the one hand and feeling and acting on the other is a matter of "getting the record straight" (mnemonic archeology, so to speak) or of telling a usefully predictive and satisfying narrative (see Spence, 1982, 1987). I raise the point here not because it is a deep one – for it is little more than folk wisdom – but rather to make clear how typically interpretive is the nature of self-reporting. Indeed, this is the proper place to announce that for the rest of this chapter, I shall eschew the expression "self-report" altogether and use instead the more accurate one of "self-accounting."

What this amounts to, then, is that many things besides one's "implicitly held" or overtly told autobiography may affect how one actually behaves or feels. The point, rather, is that self-accounting is one of the powerful forces that orchestrates and gives direction and style to the myriad of factors that are capable of influencing human behavior. One of the principal ways in which it has this effect is through its reconstruction of memory. Once memory undergoes such reconstruction (or reinterpretation), it becomes possible to draw inferences, make predictions, take risks and so on in a manner that would often not be possible under priorly operative conditions. Self-accounting, then, becomes a major form not only of taking the past (selectively) into account, but of freeing oneself from earlier established modes of responding and of organizing one's response to the future.

Let me quickly sum up where I have come before moving on. The act of autobiography, rather than "life" as stored in the darkness of memory, is what constructs the account of a life. Autobiography, in a word, turns life into text, however implicit or explicit the text may be. It is only by textualization that one can "know" one's life. The process of life textualization is a complex one, a never-ending interpretation and reinterpretation. Its textual status is not in the strict sense determined exclusively by acts of speaking and writing, but depends instead upon acts of conceptualization: creating schemata of interpretation by which semantic memory gives coherence to elements of episodic memory. Schematization is guided by rules of genre and cultural convention, which in turn impose rules of linguistic usage and narrative construction. Finally, by virtue of its function as a"locational device," autobiography creates needs for identification and individuation and, at the same time, satisfies these needs if the autobiography can achieve "rightness" of representation.

I would now like to examine the interpretive activity and the genre making involved in spontaneous, unwritten narratives about self. I think I will be able to show that such interpretive activity is of a very high order, even in the unwritten form. I would have liked to have turned now to autobiography and its *literary* genres to show the sorts of specialization imposed by "publication." That story, I think, is more sociological than psychological. But limitations on space do not permit. As you can surmise, I think that in self-accounting, "textualization" is a primary process. Or, to let the cat out of the bag a little, it is the form or genre of the reflexive act involved in self-consciousness that matters, not the nature of the printout that ensues from it. In order for self-consciousness to be expressed at all, it must be couched interpretively and subordinated to the generic, stylistic, and cultural constraints of interpretation. Self-consciousness, I shall argue at the end, is perhaps the most primitive form of interpretation and may be a component of all other forms of interpretation. That is to say, insofar as *any* interpretation involves a reflective turning inward to one's own thoughts, it would be the case that such reflection necessarily entails an element of self-consciousness.

The first case I would like to discuss will seem an unlikely one for a book that contains "literacy" as one of its terms; for it relates to the self-accountings of a small child, Emmy, between her second and her third birthdays. We were in luck. Her parents reported to a colleague of ours, midway into the child's second year, that their daughter carried out extended soliloquies after lights were out at bedtime. Our colleague, Professor Katherine Nelson, to the good fortune of posterity, immediately supplied the parents with a first-class tape recorder and (as it turned out) a very considerable supply of cassettes, for Emmy was indeed a chattering night owl. These were duly and painstakingly transcribed, one of the most enthralling corpora of speech imaginable, whether you come to them as a psychologist, psychoanalyst, or linguist – and all three have worked together in interpreting them (Nelson, 1989).

In the analysis that I want to describe, Dr. Joan Lucariello and I (Bruner & Lucariello, 1989) selected only those of Emmy's utterances that dealt with accounts of activities in which she had actually engaged or was imminently planning to engage. These were all autobiographical comments. They constituted about a quarter of her soliloquizing, for she also spent time puzzling out odd matters she had encountered, told stories to her stuffed animals and to herself, sang songs, and even indulged in *l'esprit d'escalier* with respect to what she had said or might have said to her parents and friends. The irrepressible Emmy, you might say, was the born memoirist.

And she had plenty to brood about in her soliloquies, for early in her third year, her brother Stephen was born, displacing her from her room, her bed, and from the exclusivity of parental attention that she had enjoyed before his carefully heralded arrival. And then, shortly thereafter, she launched forth into nursery school, where she had to cope with punch-ready little boys, complicated parental ferryings, puzzling relationships, and the rest. If, in Sidney Hook's (1943) phrase, hers was not an event-making life, it certainly was an eventful one.

Her task, every child's task, was to locate herself in the stream of events. But to do so, she also needed (as we shall see) to get some sense of fit between what was happening to her and what she was doing, how she was feeling, and what she was thinking. It is a formidable interpretive task and, I believe, cannot be accomplished without the aid of language. But here is the crucial point – it is not just language per se. *It is a specialized genre that is required* and that she seems to be seeking.

It is a specialized genre that is shot through with stylistic features, one that she begins to master in the course of her third year. It is with this development that we shall be concerned. Let me characterize it rather abstractly first in terms of certain key stylistic features in her soliloquies, features that are undergoing systematic generic change. The first is a form of SEQUENCE, and it is crucial. At first, sequencing is like the *annale* making to which I earlier alluded. Initially, her sequencing is linear and marked predominantly by the use of temporally ordering conjunctives: A occurred and B occurred and then C occurred, and so on. *And* and *and then* are its terms. At a more evolved level, more temporally focused terms enter: *before, after, yesterday, pretty soon.* To these are finally added causal terms that go beyond mere temporal ordering: *because* and *so*.

A second feature is CANONICALITY: the steadiness, predictability, or appropriateness of a sequence of events that has been recounted. The most primitive canonicality term is a frequency-recurrence marker like *once, sometimes, again*. At the next level there are variability markers, disjunctives such as *or* and *but*. Necessity markers are next: *have to, gotta*, and the like. And finally come deontic appropriateness markers: *supposed to* and kindred terms. These are ways in which Emmy deals not only with temporal and causal ordering, but with the steadiness and appropriateness of events she is encountering.

The final feature is PERSPECTIVALISM – one's stance, affective and epistemic with respect to the matters under discussion. These include terms indicating doubt and certainty, preference, emphasis, time perspective, and the like: *maybe, don't know, like, for a little while, all day,* as well as emphatic stresses and emphasis-marking repetitions. Through perspective, she puts herself into the world of events, or simply takes stances.

We compared Emmy's self-accounts from the first and the second halves of her third year. They are set out in Table 8.1. There is little question that by the second half of the year, her self-accountings are much more tightly sequenced, much more marked for canonicality, and much more perspectival. A first response to this finding is that it merely reflects her increasing mastery of the language, and this is undoubtedly true. But it is not the whole truth, for there is one other stylistic feature that goes with this generic self-accounting.

In a sense, it is derivative of what we have called canonicality and consists of rendering an event not in the past or future (when it happened), but in a timeless present. Timelessness marks universality. We were interested to note, to begin with, that matters of routine daily concern tended more often to be tense marked, whereas matters of some pitch were more likely to be timeless. Compare

Daddy did make some cornbread for Emmy have

with the following charged item relating to her diaper-changing prerogatives after the birth of brother Stephen:

Sometimes Mommy, Daddy put Emmy down with home. Sometimes Mommy, sometimes Tanta puts Emmy down with the home. Sometimes Jeannie and Annie and Tanta and Emmy and Mormor and my Daddy and Carl, Daddy and Carl. Mommy. Then comes Tanta and Jeannie come over. And sometime Jeannie take off my old changing table at home and my get that diaper and put it on. . . . Sometimes Jeannie change my diaper.

If we now compare Emmy's tense-marked self-accountings in the first and second halves of the year (Table 8.2), we see no difference in the three narrative genre features mentioned earlier (SEQUENCE, CANONICALITY, PERSPECTIVALISM). If, however, we compare her self-accountings that are given in the timeless mode (Table 8.2), we see a marked increase in the second half of that year in narrative markings. That is to say, her tense-marked utterances show little change in narrative marking; her timeless utterances show great change.

Table 8.1. *Percentage of Emmy's narrative soliloquies containing one or more narrative elaborative markers*

|  | 22–23 months | 28–33 months |
| --- | --- | --- |
| Causality markers | 6 | 35 |
| Canonical markers | 33 | 52 |
| Perspective markers | 33 | 71 |
| Number of narrative episodes | (18) | (17) |

Table 8.2. *Strong narrative marking in "timeless" and tense-marked soliloquies (expressed as percentage of episodes containing markers)*

|  | Timeless | | Tense-marked | |
| --- | --- | --- | --- | --- |
|  | 22–23 mos. | 28–33 mos. | 22–23 mos. | 28–33 mos. |
| Causal sequence | — | 76 | 17 | 29 |
| Affect perspect | — | 47 | — | 29 |
| Epistem perspect | — | 56 | 17 | 29 |
| Emphatic perspect | 17 | 67 | 8 | 14 |
| Number of episodes | (6) | (9) | (12) | (7) |

I take this to mean that Emmy has indeed begun to swing into an autobiographical genre style of timelessness, causality, canonicality, and perspective. She has, as it were, begun to master the interpretive style and, in the process, seemingly located herself, her feelings, her actions in the stream of events through which she is moving. She has located herself more steadily in the sense of assigning causality, has placed events in terms of their recurrence and legitimacy, and has taken a stance with respect to them. And once Emmy hammers a soliloquy theme into its right genre form, more likely than not it will simply drop out and not appear again. I would hazard the guess that now it is in a form that can constitute an internalizable conceptual representation of herself in her world. Or to invoke a Vygotskian theme, we can say that rendering events in one's life into an appropriate genre form is a requisite to making such event representations fully amenable to thought. But that need not concern us here.

Now let me turn to adult autobiography. I commented earlier that autobiography is a locational, almost navigational activity. Recognizing the danger of doing so, I nonetheless want to pursue that metaphor a little. Navigation is not usually conducted just for your own benefit, although like all forms of mental activity, it can become a solo amusement. Rather, you ordinarily locate your course or position with a view to delivering a cargo somewhere in particular. Or you locate yourself in order to be able to tell your position to rescuers should your mast break, your gas run out, or your wing fall off. Besides, it is comforting to you as a member of the human species, I suppose, to know where you are with respect to where your conspecifics are, however much pleasure there may be in being on your own.

To locate yourself with all these navigational requirements in mind, you need to become a member of a consensus: to be party, for example, to an agreement about a map projection, know what time it is at Greenwich, know about Channel 16 or about 2182 kilohertz, know how to take a fix and interpret it in the almanac of celestial ephemera, and so on. You usually need a mentor as well as books to lead you from the dry world of precepts to the wet world of practice. It is not as important that everything you know be absolutely right than that it be agreed upon, like agreeing whether to drive on the right or on the left.

Early in life, as we have seen, we learn how to talk about our lives. It is eminently a consensual exercise. We learn in the circle of the family, which, after all, is where we must first locate ourselves. We learn the family genre: the thematics, the stylistic requirements, the lexicon, the Austinian procedures for offering justifications and making excuses, and the rest of it – and we learn surprisingly early (Dunn, 1988). The self-accounting discourse mode of the family provides not only a model, but a set of constraints. A great deal of family talk is concerned not so much with giving full accounts of life, but with accounting on the *annales* level (with implicit criteria for how to make events more comprehensible on demand in terms of larger chronicles). We early on learn how to invent our lives for the sheer necessity of getting on in the family.

With such matters as these in mind, we have been collecting autobiographies – not written ones, but spoken ones (Bruner & Weisser, in press). We have simply asked our subjects to tell us the story of their lives in an hour, and when they are done, Dr. Weisser (for she conducts the interviews) asks them some informally worded, but carefully formulated questions. People have no difficulty with the task, indeed rather enjoy it. Nobody has been thunderstruck at the request, and that is, come to think of it, a nontrivial finding for starters. Many people find it hard, or so profess, and even children seem to show some awareness of the multiple routes one can travel in going about the task. Most recently, Dr. Weisser and I have taken to interviewing independently the members of the same families, parents and offspring alike. I want to tell now about one such family of six: a father, a mother, and their two daughters and two sons who range in age from twenty-four to forty-two. I shall not be able to do justice to the six complicated individuals involved or to the family culture in which they operate. But I can at least illustrate some points.

The father is in his sixties, a heating contractor of modestly comfortable means. He is a reflective man, a hard worker, and dedicated to helping others. The mother, a few years younger, went back to work four years ago (after a life as a housewife and mother) working at her husband's office, but drawing a salary. The family has lived in the same section of Brooklyn for thirty years where Mrs. Goodhertz (for we shall call the family Goodhertz) has been active in the local Catholic Church and the local Democratic Party. The eldest daughter, Nonny, married young to a man who became an alcoholic whom she divorced after eight years. She has a ten-year-old daughter, is remarried, has bounced back, and now sells advertising space for a trade journal. The next eldest child, Rod, a few years younger than Nonny, was also married rather young and, after a disastrous and brief marriage, his wife divorced him, taking their young son, shortly after which he lost his job with the city for losing his temper once too often. He has a job now in an import wharehouse, is suing the city to recover his old job, and suing his wife for partial custody of their child. Describing himself as angry and unhappy, he gives one the sense of being rather in limbo. The next son, Carl, again a couple of years younger than Rod, went swiftly through a Catholic school and college, into the Catholic peace movement, on to graduate school out of New York where he recently earned his Ph.D. in neurophysiology. He now has a job at a university laboratory in the city, is often at loggerheads with his boss over who should get credit, but is effective at his work. Donna, at twenty-four the youngest member of the family by a stretch of six years, is by consensus the "baby of the family." The family is given to a chunky heaviness, Nonny and Rod both being heavily overweight – all save for Donna, who is slim, pretty, and vivacious. She, after an indifferent and somewhat unhappy time in college, has been studying to become an actress, has had minor parts, and is newly enrolled in a first-class drama school.

Mrs. Goodhertz is a second-generation Italian-American, daughter of a father she describes very briefly as of the old school: a poor provider, a drinker, unfaithful to her mother. Mr. Goodhertz's father was also a poor provider, left his mother so that the son had to be looked after part-time by nuns and then begin work part-time and leave school at an early age. Both parents, by any standard, had tough childhoods, and each was determined to spare their own children a repetition. They are a close-knit family. Donna still lives at home, the home she came back to from the hospital where she was born. So now does Rod. Nonny does sometimes, and is presently living close by, Carl is a frequent visitor and Sunday diner. The family is given to sitting round the kitchen or dining room table where, each of them tells us independently, you can talk out any problem that is bothering you, "no topics barred."

I want to touch on two major self-accounting themes in the family's culture – all too briefly, and in apology for the brevity, I refer you to a recent article about some of the Goodhertzes (Bruner, 1987). Let me say first what I mean by a theme. In effect, it is composed by juxtaposing idealized but contrastive possible worlds in terms of which one can orient an account of oneself. To achieve the contrast, one uses not only thematic sources, but linguistic means for highlighting contrast and analogy – tropes, lexicon, syntactic devices. The first theme, for example, is constructed around the distinction between "real world" and "home": when and how and why one should be one place or the other. Its lexico-syntactic realization depends heavily on locatives, on nouns of place, and on verbs of motion. The second theme relates to the contrast between conformity and autonomy, allegiance and independence. Its core concern is the nature, achievement, and uses of the two contrasting elements: independence to the limit of "wild" impulsiveness, on the one hand, and steady, willing accepted responsibility, on the other. How can they be balanced in one's account of one's life? One sees its linguistic expression in the antiphony between the optative and the obligatory modes; *want, wish, just did it,* in contrast to *had to, must, should.* It not only has its chosen modals but some chosen adverbs that almost have the force of disjunct adverbials that "express an evaluation of what is being said" (Quirk & Greenbaum, 1973). The prime example is the adverb *just* used to indicate the inevitability of impulse, as in "I just wanted to tell him off that once." It is never used in the obligatory mode.

Consider "home" and "real world" first. Obviously, it is an ancient theme, a contrast whose meaning changes with historical circumstances (see Rybczynski, 1986). Imagine only its altered meaning as one moves from the cottage-centered European farm village of the late eighteenth century to the urbanized setting of the Industrial Revolution that followed. But whatever its abstract meaning as a cultural contrast, the distinction has its effect on people's minds not through its abstract meaning, but through some idiosyncratic version of it that grows out of one's "local life." The abstract cultural distinction is "contained" in the local instantiation. So while home and real world have an abstract representation in our conception of the culture at large, the representation in the minds of those under the sway of it is of a much more personal (indeed, psychological) order.

What is amazing about a distinction of this kind is that those who use it or encounter it, even in its idiosyncratic and local forms, recognize each other as sharing a kindred dilemma or plight. What binds people in a community is this shared recognition, this sense that "I know that you know that I know what you mean." The more closely knit, the more presuppositionally sharing the community, the smaller is it likely to be – and the more powerful will be its effects on those it holds in its circle. The family, of course, is the quintessential example, virtually the limiting case.

Consider now the psychic geography of our Goodhertz family. For them, home is inside, private, forgiving, genuine, intimate, safe. The real world is anonymous, hypocritical, unpredictable, chancy. But explicitly for the children and implicitly for the parents, home is also to be "cooped up" and bored, restricted by duties and obligations; the real world is excitement, opportunity, challenge. Early on in her autobiographical account, the mother says of the children, "We spoiled them for the real world," and the father speaks of "getting them ready for the real world."

It is not just the theme but the language that locks them to the distinction. Their autobiographical accounts are drenched with metaphors of space and location, with locatives and spatial deictics. Carl, for example, is full of in–out, here–there, coming from–going to. His *Bildungsroman* is framed almost as "travel" in the great tradition of Doughty and Freya Stark (though crossed with Lucky Jim): moving outward concentrically to find the right "place to grow," or "feeling out of place," or "gaining a special place in the Department" until you find a "privileged place" that "provides opportunities." For Carl, "special places" are homelike enclaves in the real world, but even at that they are uncertain, Icarus-like: "I'm a kid from Brooklyn who should not be where he is. I got lots of breaks, though I don't know why. I don't know how I got where I am or whether I'll stay." Each in their own way sounds the same spatial theme: Donna with thirty-seven of her first one hundred sentences containing spatial metaphors or locatives as she tells how she has been "going into the City on my own since I was fourteen," or Nonny for whom "moving up" is the root metaphor of her escape from an alcoholic husband into a new life of enterprise – even selling "space" as a way of moving that way. Rod describes himself as "stuck, like an animal in a cage": He has lost control of his movement.

The "sharp divide" that marks this family travel theme has deep and idiosyncratic psychological roots: Home is what the parents constructed as their buffer against the guarded secret of their own abused childhoods; the real world is compounded of those unspoken secrets and, so to speak, the blandishments of life on the town. But for all its idiosyncrasy, the distinction "matches" a cultural "fact," one that still holds together a neighborhood in the boondocks of Brooklyn, just as surely as it welds the Goodhertz family into a mode of discourse that gives them ways of speaking their part in a theme. It does not matter so much where they come out in managing the contrast;

## The invention of self

what matters is that they attend to it, justify in terms of it, and so on. Agreement is not the issue; common focus is.

About the antiphony of autonomy and allegiance, I want to make only one brief comment. There is surely no society whose socialization procedures are powerful enough to suppress entirely the conflict between social duty and personal impulse. Whenever knowledgeable anthropologists muse about their "people" outside the austere pages of their monographs, they strike a common refrain. Fitting in yet staying free is everywhere a dilemma. Are there ever societies so closed down and circumscribed that they leave no options, no alternative possible worlds, no detours around responsibility and ritual?

Again, how the dilemma expresses itself will, even within a simple society, be idiosyncratic and focal, yet nonetheless recognizable as a general cultural plight, a bell that tolls for all who have an ear to listen. So Mr. Goodhertz broods that though he has dedicated himself to helping others, both in and out of his family, he sometimes wonders whether he has not missed out on intimacy in life. And his wife, nearing sixty, goes back to work for pay to reclaim an entitlement to do what she wants. Rod curses the darkness into which he feels cast for failing the responsibilities he did not (or maybe he did?) fulfill. Carl wants tenure one day, but his boss must recognize and credit his "specialness." Or he tells how he left the California golden girl with whom he lived one summer, leaping from her bed one morning to fly back East, eschewing "the life of a lotus eater" so that he could mix his pleasures with his duties more equably. Nonny, asked what she expects of life, says "more," but is unclear whether it is more self-expression or more pay and recognition. Donna forever "wants": parts to play, "not to be cooped up with four kids inside four walls," to experience the world, to give people a piece of her mind as she sees fit. And as the Goodhertzes sit around that kitchen or dining table, each frames their self-account in a way and with a lexicon that they have learned the others will understand, even to the point of agreeing that Donna has not yet tested what it is like to be autonomously out of the nest. And in the process, each enters a communal genre of autobiography, though all describe their process of exchange as "completely free," "no topics barred." But, one senses, the topics are given, and it is principally about these that they may feel free.

Let me restate my principal thesis again and then offer some tentative conclusions. Mind is formed to an astonishing degree by the act of inventing self, for in the prolonged and repetitive acts of self-invention, we define the world, the scope of our agency with respect of it, and the nature of the epistemology that governs how the self shall know the world and, indeed, know itself reflexively. Self-invention, by its very nature, creates disjunctions between a recounting self in the instant of discourse and the selves schematized in memory.

The task of self-accounting begins with the very onset of language. Our self-accounts quickly become generic, losing their occasion relatedness. In the case of Emmy, her self-telling soliloquies move speedily in her third year toward expression in a language and a mode of thought featuring timelessness, causality, canonicality, and perspectivalism. They change not only in content, but in style. She is engaged in that self-making task of getting straight through narrative the relation between what she thinks, how she feels, and what she does – lining up her intentions with their outcomes where possible and marking them by doubt where the effort fails. In the process, Emmy begins to textualize her life in a way that leaves it open always to interpretation and reinterpretation. I have no doubt that an Ilongot child would have done it differently and that some of what we witnessed reflects the high literacy of Emmy's culture. Her parents, after all, were university dons. An Ilongot child, bred in a different family, would probably, even by three, have begun to show some different features in her soliloquies.

That is why I turned next to the relationship of family and autobiography: to indicate in what measure the family continues, as vicar of the culture, to perfect and refine the genres of life accounting. It is not that the family *shapes* in any direct sense the form of a life. Rather, by posing the thematic structures in terms of which life can be accounted for, by setting the linguistic contrasts and defining the dilemmas, it constrains the management of self-consciousness and agency. To the antinomy of self as Narrator and self as subject, it adds those of home and world, and responsibility and individuality. And these it constrains as well.

My general argument is that the historical transformation of this kind of self-consciousness in the West is the primary determinant of the modern mind – the forms of self-accounting genres that it has brought into being. On this reckoning, the decline of serfdom and feudalism, the abstractions inherent in the use of money, and the idea of surplus resources and savings could have as much impact on these oral, highly interpretable forms, as did literacy (Bruner, 1990).

Having said that, however, I must now say that I readily agree that where literacy becomes an instrument of more self-conscious, more agentively oriented self-accounting, the change toward modernity is doubtless hastened, but that is not, in my view, the prime mover.

Recall that the digging stick in the archeological horizons of the East Africa of *Australopithecus* was in use for tens of thousands of years before it was put to its full use and before it had much if any effect on forms of agriculture (Lewin, 1988). Writing systems, as among the Vai, do not seem to have had much effect on thought in that culture (Scribner & Cole, 1981). The Mayans of Yucatan had perfected the wheel and axle but used them in the construction of prayer wheels whilst their laborers hauled shaped stones by ropes without pullies. It may very well be as Lev Vygotsky (1987) urged in the spirit of Francis Bacon, that neither hand nor mind alone amounts to much and that they require instruments and auxiliaries to perfect them. I would only argue, in extension of that important truth, that to get ahead you need a good theory and that theories most often begin inside. The most important one is a theory about yourself.

REFERENCES

Bartlett, F. C. (1932). *Remembering*. Cambridge University Press.
Benveniste, E. (1971). *Problems in general linguistics*. Coral Gables, Fla.: University of Miami Press.
Brodsky, J. (1986). *Less than one: Selected essays*. New York: Farrar, Straus & Giroux.
Bruner, J. S. (1972). The nature and uses of immaturity. *American Psychology* 27(8):1–22.
  (1987). Life as narrative. *Social Research* 54(1):1–32.
  (1990). *Acts of Meaning*. Cambridge, Mass.: Harvard University Press.
Bruner, J. S., Goodnow, J. G., & Austin, G. (1956). *A study of thinking*. New York: Wiley.
Bruner, J. S., & Lucariello, J. (1989). Monologue as narrative recreation of the world. In K. Nelson (ed.), *Narratives from the crib*. Cambridge, Mass.: Harvard University Press.
Bruner, J. S., & Weisser, S. (in press). *Autobiography and the construction of self*. Cambridge, Mass.: Harvard University Press.
Culler, J. (1986). Some meanings of genre. Paper presented at a seminar on "Genre" at New York University.
Dollard, J. (1935). *Criteria for the life history*. New Haven, Conn.: Yale University Press.
Dunn, J. (1988). *The beginnings of social understanding*. Cambridge, Mass.: Harvard University Press.
Eakin, P. J. (1985). *Fictions in autobiography: Studies in the art of self-invention*. Princeton, N.J.: Princeton University Press.
Geertz, C. (1973). *The interpretation of cultures*. New York: Basic.
Hook, S. (1943). *The hero in history*. New York: John Day.
Howarth, W. L. (1980). Some principles of autobiography. In J. Olney (ed.), *Autobiography: Essays theoretical and critical*. Princeton, N.J.: Princeton University Press.

Kardiner, A. (1939). *The individual and his society.* New York: Columbia University Press.
Kermode, F. (1967). *The sense of an ending: Studies in the theory of fiction.* Oxford University Press.
Lewin, R. (1988). *In the age of mankind.* Washington, D.C.: Smithsonian Institute.
Maxwell, W. (1980). *So long, see you tomorrow.* New York: Knopf.
McCarthy, M. (1957). *Memories of a Catholic girlhood.* New York: Harcourt Brace.
Neisser, U. (1982). Snapshots or benchmarks? In U. Neisser (Ed.), *Memory observed: Remembering in natural contexts.* San Francisco: Freeman.
(1986). Nested structure in autobiographical memory. In D. C. Rubin (ed.), *Autobiographical memory.* Cambridge University Press.
Nelson, K. (ed.) (1989). *Narratives from the crib.* Cambridge, Mass.: Harvard University Press.
Polonoff, D. (1987). Self-deception. *Social Research* 54(1):45–54.
Quine, W. V. (1978). Other worldly [review of Nelson Goodman, *Ways of worldmaking*]. *New York Review of Books*, Nov. 23.
Quirk, R., & Greenbaum, S. (1973). *A concise grammar of contemporary English.* New York: Harcourt Brace Jovanovich.
Rosaldo, M. (1980). *Knowledge and passion: Ilongot notions of self and social life.* Cambridge University Press.
Rosaldo, R. (1980). *Ilongot headhunting, 1883–1974: A study in history and society.* Stanford, Calif.: Stanford University Press.
Rubin, D. C. (ed.) (1986). *Autobiographical memory.* Cambridge University Press.
Rybczynski, W. (1986). *Home: A short history of an idea.* New York: Viking-Penguin.
Scribner, S., & Cole, M. (1981). *The psychology of literacy.* Cambridge, Mass.: Harvard University Press.
Shweder, R. A. (1990). Cultural psychology: What is it? In J. Stigler, R. A. Shweder, & G. Herdt (eds.), *Cultural psychology: The Chicago symposium on culture and human development.* Cambridge University Press.
Spence, D. P. (1982). *Narrative truth and historical truth: Meaning and interpretation in psychoanalysis.* New York: Norton.
(1987). *The Freudian metaphor: Toward a paradigm change in psychoanalysis.* New York: Norton.
Starobinski, J. (1971). The style of autobiography. In S. Chatman (ed.), *Literary style: A symposium.* Oxford University Press.
Tulving, E. (1972). Episodic and semantic memory. In E. Tulving & W. Donaldson (eds.), *Organization of memory.* New York: Academic Press.
Vygotsky, L. (1987). *Thought and language.* Cambridge, Mass.: MIT Press.
White, H. (1981). The value of narrativity in the representation of reality. In W. J. T. Mitchell (ed.), *On narrative.* Chicago: University of Chicago Press.
Whiting, J. (1941). *Becoming a Kwoma.* New Haven, Conn.: Yale University Press.

# 9
# Literacy and objectivity: the rise of modern science

DAVID R. OLSON

While the belief that the Protestant Reformation is related in some way to the rise of modern science (Merton, 1970; Rousseau, 1966; Weber, 1930), the hypothesis linking these social movements and the development of widespread literacy is relatively new and may be traced to the writings of Innis (1951), McLuhan (1962), Havelock (1963), Goody and Watt (1968), Eisenstein (1979), and Stock (1983). These writers and others have all acknowledged that changes in the forms of communication have altered human activities and cultural forms. The explanations of these changes have tended to run in one of two directions.

One group interprets cultural changes associated with changes in the forms of communication in terms of changed social and institutional practices while assuming that the cognitive processes of individuals remain much the same. In this camp I would put such writers as Scribner (1977), Scribner and Cole (1981), Leach (1966), Douglas (1980), Eisenstein (1979), and Street (1984). The other group interprets these same cultural changes in terms of psychological changes, altered forms of representation and forms of consciousness. In this camp I would put McLuhan (1962, 1964), Havelock (1963), Goody (1977), Greenfield (1972), Ong (1982), Stock (1983), and myself (Olson, 1977).

One should not make too much of this difference, but it may be illustrated by contrasting the work of Eisenstein (1979), who examined the importance of printing to the rise of Protestantism and to the rise of modern science, with that of Stock (1983), who examined the role that literacy played in setting the stage for the changes described by Eisenstein. In the first case, the emphasis falls upon changing technologies and their uses; in the second, on newly evolving forms of literate competence.

Eisenstein (1979) was primarily concerned with the role of the printing press as an agent of change. As her account is extremely rich, it is difficult to state her resulting theory briefly. Yet central to her account is her demonstration of the role of the printing press in both the Reformation and the rise of modern science. She summarizes as follows: "Intellectual and spiritual life were profoundly transformed by the multiplication of new tools for duplicating books in fifteenth-century Europe. The communications shift altered the way Western Christians viewed their sacred book and the natural world" (p. 704). First, for Reformation theology, the printing press placed a copy of Scripture in the hands of every reader and thereby circumvented the role of the Church. One could encounter God through the simple practice of reading for oneself without the mediation of the priest. An analogy is the way that U.S. presidents may appeal to the public directly via radio and television rather than through the elected representatives in Congress. Second, the printing press provided an important means for spreading the gospel to a rapidly growing reading public.

For modern science, Eisenstein suggests that printing was primarily responsible for placing an "original" copy of a text, free from copyist errors, into the hands of hundreds of scholars who could study, compare, criticize, and update them. New discoveries could be incorporated into newer editions. In this way printing contributed to the development of an accumulative research tradition. Hence, the developments in both science and religion were produced more by exploiting the new opportunities afforded by printed materials, whether books, diagrams, charts, or maps, than by any particular alteration in modes or forms of thought.

However, because Eisenstein focuses her attention on printing and the different roles it played in science and religion, she overlooks an important aspect of the relation between the Reformation and the rise of modern science. The relation she overlooks, I suggest, may be crucial to detecting a way in which change in the medium of communication could produce a genuine change in the structure of cognition. She argues that until the Reformation, science and religion were closely related, whereas after the rise of modern science, they went their own separate ways. They did so because "the effect of printing on Bible study was in marked contrast with its effect on nature study" (p. 701). Science, she suggests, used printing for the consensual validation of observations, the rise of objectivity, whereas religion used it primarily for the spread of glad tidings. Because of their different uses, "the changes wrought by printing provide the most plausible point of departure for explaining how confidence shifted from divine revelation to mathematical reasoning and man-made maps" (p. 701).

Indeed, the apparently different ways that religious and scientific traditions were affected by the communications revolution, suggested to Eisenstein (1979, p. 701) "the futility of trying to encapsulate its consequences in any one formula." Printing neither led from words to images – McLuhan's eye for ear formula – nor from images to words.

*Literacy and objectivity*

The effects call for "a multivariable explanation even while stressing the significance of the single innovation" (p. 702).

Admittedly, Eisenstein provides abundant evidence that printing (and writing) did serve different purposes in religion and science, yet a second look reveals a deeper relation between them than she allows. To see this we must distinguish skill in the medium of writing, that is literacy, from the technology of printing (Postman, 1985). Printing may indeed have been used in quite different ways by science and religion as Eisenstein suggests. Yet writing as a medium of communication and the required competence with that medium – literacy – played much the same fundamental role in the Protestant Reformation as it did in the rise of modern science. In both cases I would like to suggest, it permitted the clear differentiation of the "given" from the "interpreted." Literacy generally, and printing in particular, fixed the written record as the given against which interpretations could be compared. Writing created a fixed, original, objective "text"; printing put that text into millions of hands.

Eisenstein quotes Sprat as making precisely this point in his joint defense of the Church of England, of which he was a bishop, and the Royal Society, of which he was the historian. Both, he claimed, had achieved a Reformation:

Both have taken a like course to bring this [Reformation] about; each of them passing by the corrupt copies and referring themselves to the perfect originals for instruction; the one to Scripture, the other to the huge Volume of Creatures. They are both accused unjustly by their enemies of the same crimes, of having forsaken the Ancient Traditions and ventured on Novelties. They both suppose alike that their Ancestors might err; and yet retain a sufficient reverence for them. (Sprat, 1966)

Why this search for the perfect originals? Because the original would be the "given" against which any interpretation would be compared. The given in religion was the *word* of God, the given in Nature was the *work* of God, as Bacon (1857–64) would say. This was the distinction that underlay both Reformation hermeneutics and the rise of scientific epistemology. Both were centered on the conceptual distinction between that given by God, whether in Scripture or in nature, and those interpretations made by humans, only some of which strictly accorded with the given. Changing means of communication, writing and printing, accompanied by developing skills of literacy, could therefore be used as a single explanation for developments in two apparently different traditions – religion and science. It is this common role for written texts which Eisenstein, so far as I can tell, overlooks.

The changing beliefs and concepts that accompanied the rise of literacy is the precise concern of the second group of scholars mentioned at the outset, the most relevant one for our present purposes being Stock (1983). In his work, Stock shows how the legal system changed when courts began to use written records rather than oral testimony as evidence, how theology changed when it came to be text rather than church centered, and how these changes set the stage for the great modern reformations, the Protestant Reformation and the rise of modern science.

The changing role of written texts in the administration of justice is representative. Until the twelfth century complaints were delivered orally; the breach of law was stated and compensation was demanded. The defendant replied to the charge and the local "doomsman" indicated the type of validation to be used to decide the case. This decision was not a matter of weighing the evidence in the attempt to arrive at an abstract "truth." Rather it was a matter of fairness, of allowing some clue to indicate the defendant's innocence or guilt. This, of course, is trial by ordeal. The innocent, it was assumed, could survive some horrible ordeal; the guilty would perish by ordeal, lose the duel, or whatever. A physical sign, losing the duel, was a sign of guilt.

In the twelfth and thirteenth centuries, written documents began to replace oral memory and oral testimony. Stock (1983) and Clanchy (1979) have both detailed how the scrutiny of written documents and records came to provide the evidential base permitting legally competent judges to pronounce on the innocence or guilt of the accused. Stock shows that changes in understanding of Scripture, of the sacraments, and of nature underwent a corresponding transformation under the impact of literacy. The fundamental tenet of the later Middle Ages, Stock (1984–5, p. 24) points out, was "the identification of objectivity with a text. As a consequence . . . questions also began to be asked about the validity of hearsay testimony, oral family record, and collective memory."

Here, I believe, we have our link between literacy and modernity – the systematic distinction between something that is taken as given, fixed, autonomous, and objective and something that may be construed as interpretive, inferential, and subjective. My hypothesis is that the contrast between texts and their interpretations provided the model, more than that, the precise cognitive categories or concepts needed for the description and the interpretation of nature, that is, for the building of modern science. To state this somewhat grandly, hermeneutics, the interpretation of texts, provided the conceptual categories needed for scientific epistemology, what I referred to as the interpretation of nature. Let me spell out the relation and provide some evidence for the hypothesis.

## The objectivity of texts

The Reformation, the rise of modern science, and mentalistic psychology are, of course, social movements, but they all rested, I argue, on a new conceptual distinction. What is that distinction and how was it derived from writing and literacy? A written text preserves only part of language, the form, and the meaning has to be regenerated from that form by the reader. The preserved part we will talk loosely of as being "given," "fixed," "permanent"; the reconstructed part we can call, roughly, the meaning, the intention, the interpretation.

That distinction is implicit in speech, but the relation between a text and an interpretation becomes especially problematic in literacy. In oral language the form and meaning form an indissoluble pairing. When we do not understand an utterance, we normally ask, "What do *you* mean?" rather than "What does *it* mean?" focusing on the person doing the communicating, not on the sentence. Furthermore, we use much beside the linguistic form to gather a person's intentions with the result that it is virtually impossible to distinguish what was said, the form, and what was meant by it, the meaning. In speech, then, form and meaning are perceived as indissolubly linked by speakers. Literacy is instrumental in pulling them apart by freezing the form into a text.

Writing involves the preservation of a part of language – what was actually said, the given, which could be contrasted with the interpretations assigned and the intentions that lie behind it. In an oral society, there are, of course, "texts," fixed bodies of ritual and poetry, along with intentions and interpretations as Feldman (Chapter 3, this volume) has pointed out. All language necessarily involves all of those. But literacy provides the means for splitting those things apart, fixing part of its meaning as the text and permitting interpretations to be seen for the first time as interpretations. Goody (1986) has shown how religious reform movements rely upon just this distinction, calling for the abandonment of interpretations and a "return to the book."

The shift in the understanding of interpretation that has been studied most carefully is the change in interpretation associated with the Reformation and the Counter-Reformation. As Stock has shown, the problem of heresy in the Middle Ages was almost exclusively associated with literacy: "Heretics had a highly-developed, if somewhat personal, style of 'rationality' which depended on individual interpretation of theological texts" (pp. 110–20). Heretics considered the teachings of the Church to be mere interpretation, if not fabrication. Yet while heretics recognized the interpretations of the Church as interpretations – as man-made – they did not recognize their own interpretations as merely interpretations. They, like the medieval church, took their interpretations to be the ones intended by God, and hence, they died, apparently happily, at the stake for them. The Church's view of interpretation before the Reformation, as expressed for example in Aquinas's *Summa Theologia* (written 1267–73/1968–70), was that Scripture had several levels of meaning including literal meaning, spiritual meaning, and moral meaning. All levels of meaning were "given" in the text. Reformation theology, as exemplified in Luther, denied that all these meanings were in the text: The literal, historical meaning was in the text, all the rest was "tradition" and "dogma." Reformation theology, in a word, involved a sharp distinction between what was given by the text and the interpretations that one could make of a text. The latter were suddenly seen as subjective, fanciful, and a product of the imagination. Thus, part of the meaning was moved from being seen as given by the text to being seen as invented by the reader. The interpretive principle of the Reformation, as expressed for example in Luther's attitude to Scripture, was that Scripture is "autonomous," it does not need interpretation, it needs reading; it means what it says. All the rest is made up, a product of fancy or tradition. It was this distinction between the given and the interpreted that launched the Reformation and, a century later, opened "the book of nature" to modern scientists, to make it readable to anyone "with a faithful eye" as Robert Hooke (1665/1961), one of the first of the seventeenth-century British empiricists, said.

### The objectivity of nature

The hypothesis connecting hermeneutics with scientific epistemology is that hermeneutics provided the conceptual distinction between something taken as fixed or given and something else taken as interpretation. The scriptural text and its interpretation were seen as exactly parallel to the natural world and its interpretation.

It was commonplace in the Middle Ages to speak of nature as God's book. But the metaphor came to have a new meaning in the seventeenth century. Francis Bacon (1620/1965) spoke of "the book of God's word and the book of God's work." Thomas Browne, a seventeenth-century British cleric, talked of God's two great books, Scripture and nature (Aarsleff, 1982). Galileo (1638/1974) complicated the story by claiming that the book of nature was written in the language of mathematics. At first we may be tempted to believe that this is a mere metaphor. However, it may be argued that modern science was the product of applying the distinctions evolved for understanding the book of Scripture, namely that between the given and the interpreted, to the book of nature. For modern science, the *given* was the world of observed facts; all the rest, hypotheses, final causes, interpretation, and inferences were invented, made up by man. These distinctions are fundamental to scientific epistemology. Modern science rests on the distinction between observation and inference, observations being objective and reliable while inferences are theoretical interpretations of those observations. In modern times the distinction has come in for considerable revision, but it has not been abandoned. I shall return to that problem later.

The modern scientists – Galileo, William Harvey, Robert Hooke, Robert Boyle, Isaac Newton, and Francis Bacon – consistently and systematically distinguished facts from "hypotheses." Science, Bacon said, consisted of the "statement of observed facts." It involved no interpretations. William Harvey added: "For in every Science . . . a diligent observation is required" (1653, p. 1). Bacon (1620/1965) said it most strongly: "God forbid that we give out a dream of our imagination for a pattern in the world" (p. 323). The split was complete. Observation provided direct access to the "given"; theory and interpretation was the work of the imagination. Bacon again: "All depends on keeping the eye steadily fixed upon the facts of nature and so receiving their images simply as they are" (p. 323). Hooke (1665/1961): "The Science of Nature has already too long made only a work of Brain and the Fancy: It is now high time that it should return to the plainness and soundness of Observation on material and obvious things" (Preface b). They not only said it, they acted on it. Galileo and Newton are replete with denials of the relevance of purposes, goals, and causes in the explanation of motion and machines; they sought factual description, not theoretical interpretation.

So "reading" the book of nature – that is, science – was simply applied hermeneutics. The distinctions worked up for reading and interpreting Scripture could be applied, essentially without revision, to reading and interpreting the book of nature. Recall Bacon's plea: "God forbid that we give out a dream of our imagination for a pattern in the world." In science the distinction takes the form of observation versus inference, fact versus theory, evidence versus claim and a whole set of related concepts such as hypothesis, conclusion, conjecture, assertion, assumption, and inference, concepts that are critical to modern scientific thought.

Moreover, as interpretive procedures used in reading text change, the forms of written discourse change. That is, as readers begin to make a sharp given–interpretation distinction, they begin to write texts in a different way. The historian of the Royal Society of London, Thomas Sprat (1667/1966), describes how the forms of discourse came to reflect the society's attitudes to Scripture and nature. The society was concerned "with the advancement of science and with the improvement of the English language as a medium of prose." The Society demanded a mathematical plainness of style free from all "amplifications, digressions, and swellings of style" (p. 56). Godzich and Kittay (1987) have traced the beginnings of prose in France to the twelfth century when written prose came to be a "signifying practice" that could substitute for oral verse. They quote Franz Boas as saying, "The form of modern prose is largely determined by the fact that it is read, not spoken, while primitive prose is based on the art of oral delivery and is, therefore, more closely related to modern oratory than to the printed literary style" (p. 194). That written literary style, I suggest, is characterized by its attempt to clearly distinguish the given from the interpretation and to make texts that, while not composed primarily of "statements of observed fact," marked observations in such a way as to distinguish them from inference and interpretations (see also Hutchins, 1980).

There is another prong to the argument that I shall discuss here only in passing. It is that if interpretations are not in the text, where do they come from? Interpretations came to be seen increasingly as subjective, that is, made up by the reader of texts or the observer of nature. It was this new subjectivity, I suggest, that provided the bases for Descartes's mind–body dualism and the priority of the mental: "Cogito, ergo sum" ("I think, therefore I am"). Bishop Berkeley's new theory of vision identified the reality with the workings of the mind – to be is to be perceived – the priority of the mental. Descartes, Locke, and Berkeley, I suspect, were as much a product of Lutheran hermeneutics as Bacon and Galileo were. Saenger (1982; Chapter 12, this volume) connects the rise of notions of private consciousness and reflection with the development in the tenth to the thirteenth centuries of silent reading, a suggestion that fits in well with this account.

In the past few years my colleagues and I (Olson & Astington, 1987; Olson & Torrance, 1987) have been engaged in a program of research that is directed toward examining the given–interpretation distinction and its development in a variety of contexts. If the distinction is a literate one, one invented for interpreting written texts, we should expect to find that members of traditional, that is, nonliterate, societies will tend to conflate what is said with what is meant by it; that is, that they fail to distinguish the given from the interpretation. We read the anthropological literature, and we ourselves conducted experiments with preliterate children. Of course, it is dangerous to compare those two sources, for two reasons. First, young children are not only nonliterate, they are immature. Second, by comparing nonliterate adults with young children, we are perhaps inadvertently encouraging the myth that nonliterates are childlike. But if the critical factor is the set of assumptions held about language and texts, we may treat data on adult nonliterates and child preliterates as similar.

What we find varies from one traditional society to another somewhat, but several researchers have reported findings that bear on the hypothesis. Evans-Pritchard (1937) was surprised to find that what a suspected witch actually intended by his speech made no difference to his accusers who interpreted it to their own ends. There was no sharp distinction between the text, what was said, and the interpretation. Similarly, Duranti (1985) in a recent study of the interpretive strategies of the Samoans, reported that there is no obvious, perhaps even detectable, distinction between what is said, the given, and the interpretation that is assigned: "A certain meaning is possible because others accept it within a particular context" (p. 47). Hence, a Samoan speaker will not "reclaim the meaning of his words by saying 'I didn't mean it'" (p. 49). Generalizing, there is little indication of a given–interpretation distinction. Surprisingly, not only is there no distinction pertaining to meaning, there are no ways for referring to intentions or for treating intentions and meanings as internal mental events. Consequently, "Samoans, as perhaps members of Polynesian cultures in general, don't seem to have the western notion of 'self'" (p. 48; see also Levy, 1973). Rosaldo's (1982, 1984) study of speech acts in Ilongot, a traditional Philippine society, found a corresponding absence of concepts of intentionality and of self. McKellin (1986), too, discusses how Papuan speakers in making offers and complaints allow that what is uttered means only what the speaker takes it to mean; the spoken "text" does not have a meaning separated from the way it is taken up by the listener. McCormick (1989), in examining the influence of Spanish on Quechua, a Peruvian language, reports that Quechua

is rather vague in the area of speech acts and mental states. Bilinguals borrow freely from Spanish for anything other than "say," "know," and "tell." Believe, think, etc. are commonly [expressed in] Spanish in our area. Other more complex inferences seem to be rarely used. When translating from Spanish to Quechua, for example, our Quechua friends seem to have no ready phrases to express mental states – "deny" comes out "say it is not true," or [else the term used is] Spanish.

Yet she is quick to point out that we must not interpret such findings as *lacks*, but rather as indications of cultural differences (Luria, 1976). As Feldman (Chapter 3, this volume) shows, many oral cultures do "fix" texts by oral means and subject such texts to talk and to interpretation. Whether such interpretations are seen as being "in the text," that is, as given, or in the mind of the interpreter, an issue central to the hypothesis under consideration, remains unclear.

All linguistic groups talk, tease, lie, tell secrets, and appear to have some devices for referring to talk (Heath, 1983; Schieffelin & Cochran-Smith, 1982), and they all have some ways of referring to the status of pieces of knowledge through the use of "evidentials" (Chafe, 1985). These devices are somewhat equivalent to English speech-act terms – that is, verbs of saying – and mental-state terms – that is, verbs of thinking. Hence, it appears that concepts for referring to what was said and what was meant by it are not absent in nonliterate societies; rather, it is the range and explicitness of these concepts that varies. Literacy, I suggest, gives these implicit distinctions conceptual status and turns them into basic categories of thought (Havelock, 1982, p. 290).

In our empirical studies of young children, we can detect the beginnings of their recognition of these intentional states and their acquisition of the metalinguistic and metacognitive verbs that mark these states. Hence, we can observe more directly the consequences of the presence or absence of these concepts. In a typical study, my colleague Nancy Torrance read stories or acted out events in which an ambiguous utterance is misinterpreted by a listener. She noted how children responded to the misinterpretation. Here is a sample:

One Saturday night, Lucy and Charlie Brown were going to a party. Lucy was all dressed in her brand new red party dress, but she didn't have her shoes on. She wanted to wear her *new* red shoes to go with her party dress. Linus was upstairs so she called up to him, "Linus, bring me my red shoes." Linus went to Lucy's closet where she kept her shoes. Now Linus picked up the *old* red shoes and rushed down the stairs with them. He said, "Here are your red shoes" and gave the shoes to Lucy. "Good grief," said Lucy, "how can you be so stupid?" and she gave him a whack on the head.

We followed such stories with a series of questions. Here is how a typical five-year-old responds:

Experimenter: Did Linus bring the shoes that Lucy wanted?
Child: No.
E: Did he do what Lucy said to do?
C: No.
E: What did Lucy tell him to bring?
C: The red party shoes.
E: What were the exact words that Lucy said? She said "Linus, bring me . . ."
C: My new red shoes.

Of course, the new red shoes are what Lucy meant, we would say, not what she said. All she said was "red shoes." The child conflated the given with the interpretation and consequently, when asked what was said, reported, instead, the interpretation. By the time they are eight, most children make this distinction spontaneously, and all of them can make it when it is pointed out to them. Subsequent studies indicate that children as young as four or five years can make these distinctions under optimal circumstances (Ruffman, Torrance, & Olson, 1989; see also Beal & Flavell, 1984; Robinson & Robinson, 1977, 1980).

At about the same time that they are sorting out the difference between a text and its interpretation, they are also sorting out the difference between what is in their own minds, their prior knowledge and beliefs, and what is present and visible in the world. Janet Astington and I (Olson & Astington, 1987) posed a series of questions to children as to what they see when they look at ambiguous displays and what other people, holding different beliefs, see when they look at the same display. To illustrate, young children assume that if they know that a cat picture is red and if they see a red patch through a window as the cat, they assume that someone else, not knowing that the cat is red, would also see the red patch as a cat. The striking feature is that until they are about five years old, children tend not to acknowledge the role of beliefs, of a private mental life that differs from person to person, in their perception. This is related to what Piaget called "ego-centrism." Only when they are six or seven do they begin to acknowledge that another person, holding different beliefs, would see things differently than they themselves do. About this time they begin to mark the difference with mental verbs in such sentences as "He doesn't *know* that the cat is red" or that "She *thinks* that it is something else." A rich literature of children's developing understanding of these concepts has recently developed (see Wimmer & Perner, 1983; Chandler & Helm, 1984; Astington, Harris, & Olson, 1988; Taylor, 1988).

Both of these forms of the given–interpretation distinctions may exist in embryonic form in preliterate children and in nonliterate adults. We need to check out these possibilities more exhaustively. But what is clearly the case is that these interpretive categories become the focus of a great deal of elaboration and development in a literate society during the middle school years. To illustrate, Astington and I took a sample of some thirty of the principal verbs, technically speech-act and mental-state verbs, that mark and elaborate the distinctions in question. There are three points to note about these verbs. First, they are verbs that make up the "literate standard" language; they are not a part of the lexicon of many fluent speakers of English. Second, they were largely borrowed from learned Latin in the fifteenth and sixteenth centuries as English became the literate language of religion and government (see Traugott, 1987; Olson & Astington, 1990). And third, and I think this is the most promising aspect of this work, these verbs are not completely discontinuous from the simple verbs of saying and thinking that children acquire when they are two or three years old; thus, the verb *interpret* can be analyzed into something like "to think that it means"; *understand* can be analyzed into "to know what something means."

The evolution of a literate tradition, then, involves more than the accumulation of knowledge or the development of an accumulative research tradition. It involves a new way of classifying and organizing knowledge. First, it involves the systematic distinction between what a text says and what it means, that is, between a text and its interpretation, and hence, between facts and theories, observations and inferences. But second, it sets up the possibility of collecting and organizing the former into complex knowledge systems. That is what authoritative texts aspire to be: compilations of the given. "Knowledge is learned as an 'ideal text', something which so far as the learners are concerned is given not created" (Hoskin, 1982). Seen as repositories of a society's valid and objective knowledge, textbooks are taken as above criticism (De Castell, Luke, & Luke, 1989).

## Conclusion

We began with the well-documented inference relating literacy to the social and psychological changes that occurred with the invention of alphabetic literacy in Greece and, more particularly, with the growth of literacy in the late Middle Ages and the early Renaissance. I argued that while the relation is well known, there was no theory connecting the Reformation with the rise of modern science or with Cartesian mentalism. I advanced the notion that the three were by-products of literacy and offered, as a mechanism for the change, the new conceptual distinction between what was given in a text and the interpretations a reader brought to or assigned to a text. I called it the given–interpretation distinction. I could as well have called it the reading–interpretation distinction (see Havelock, 1976) or the form–meaning distinction (McLuhan, 1988). It was the hypothesis that something was given, invariant, and autonomous about a text and that that givenness could be contrasted with the interpretations of that text which were subjective, fallible, and the product of the imagination. That distinction I say was invited by literacy because writing, in fact, split the comprehension process into two parts, that preserved by text, the given, and that provided by the reader, the interpretation. Printing sharpened just this distinction. With the exact duplication of the original text, free from copyist errors, what was given in the text was more readily distinguished from the interpretation brought to the text by the reader. In a single move the layers of meaning of Scripture that Aquinas had claimed to be in the text were suddenly taken by Luther to be mere additions, accretions, and interpolations. Galileo followed the lead, taking Aristotle's notion of "final causes" as mere interpretation of motion, quite independent of the laws of motion themselves. The distinction between the given and the interpreted, then, invented for reading and interpreting texts, was simply borrowed for "reading" the book of nature. The result was modern science, science built on the notion of a discontinuity between observation and inference, facts and theory, claims and evidence. Modern scientific epistemology was, therefore, a by-product of Reformation hermeneutics and objectivity, a by-product of literacy.

## ACKNOWLEDGMENTS

I am grateful for the support of the SSHRC, the Spencer Foundation, and the Ontario Ministry of Education through its Block Transfer Grant to OISE.

## REFERENCES

Aarsleff, H. (1982). *From Locke to Saussure*. Minneapolis: University of Minnesota Press.
Aquinas, Saint Thomas (1968–70). *Summa theologia* (Latin/English ed.). London: Blackfriars/McGraw-Hill. (Originally published in 1267–73.)
Astington, J. W., Harris, P., & Olson, D. R. (1988). *Developing theories of mind*. Cambridge University Press.
Bacon, F. (1857–64). The advancement of learning. In J. Spedding, R. Ellis, & D. Heath (eds.), *The works of Francis Bacon* (Vols. 1–14). London.
  (1965). The great instauration. In S. Warhaft, *Francis Bacon: A selection of his works*. London: Macmillan. (Originally published in 1620.)
Beal, C., & Flavell, J. (1984). Development of the ability to distinguish communicative intention and literal message meaning. *Child Development* 55:920–8.
Chafe, W. (1985). Linguistic differences produced by differences between speaking and writing. In D. Olson, N. Torrance, & A. Hildyard (eds.), *Literacy, language, and learning: The nature and consequences of reading and writing* (pp. 105–23). Cambridge University Press.
Chandler, M. J., & Helm, D. (1984). Developmental changes in the contribution of shared experience to social role-taking competence. *International Journal of Behavioral Development* 7:145–56.
Clanchy, M. T. (1979). *From memory to written record*. London: Arnold.
De Castell, S., Luke, A., & Luke, C. (1989). *Language, authority and criticism: Readings on the school textbook*. London: Falmer.

Douglas, M. (1980). *Edward Evans-Pritchard.* Harmondsworth: Penguin Books.
Duranti, A. (1985). Famous theories and local theories: The Samoans and Wittgenstein. *Quarterly Newsletter of the Laboratory of Comparative Human Cognition* 7:46–51.
Eisenstein, E. (1979). *The printing press as an agent of change.* Cambridge University Press.
Evans-Pritchard, E. (1937). *Witchcraft, oracles and magic among the Azande.* Oxford University Press.
Galilei, Galileo (1974). *Two new sciences.* (S. Drake, trans.). Madison: University of Wisconsin Press. (Originally published in 1638.)
Godzich, W., & Kittay, J. (1987). *The emergence of prose: An essay in prosaics.* Minneapolis: University of Minnesota Press.
Goody, J. (1977). *The domestication of the savage mind.* Cambridge University Press.
 (1986). Writing, religion, and revolt in Bahia. *Visible Language* 20(3):318–43.
 (1987). *The interface between the oral and the written.* Cambridge University Press.
Goody, J., & Watt, I. (1968). The consequences of literacy. In J. Goody (ed.), *Literacy in traditional societies* (2nd ed.). Cambridge University Press. (Originally published in 1963.)
Greenfield, P. M. (1972). Oral and written language: The consequences for cognitive development in Africa, the United States and England. *Language and Speech* 15:169–78.
Harvey, W. (1653). *Anatomical exercitations concerning the generation of living creatures.* London.
Havelock, E. (1963). *Preface to Plato.* Cambridge, Mass.: Harvard University Press.
 (1976). *Origins of western literacy.* Toronto: Ontario Institute for Studies in Education.
 (1982). *The literate revolution in Greece and its cultural consequences.* Princeton, N.J.: Princeton University Press.
Heath, S. (1983). *Ways with words.* Cambridge University Press.
Hooke, R. (1961). *Micrographia.* New York: Dover. (Originally published in 1665.)
Hoskin, K. (1982). Examinations and the schooling of science. In R. MacLeod (ed.), *Days of judgement: Science, examinations and the organization of knowledge in late Victorian England.* Naefferton, England: Duffield.
Hutchins, E. (1980). *Culture and inference.* Cambridge, Mass.: Harvard University Press.
Innis, H. (1951). *The bias of communication.* Toronto: University of Toronto Press.
Leach, E. R. (1966). Ritualization in man in relation to conceptual and social development. *Philosophical Transactions of the Royal Society of London* 251:403–8.

Levy, R. I. (1973). *Tahitians: Mind and experience in the Society Islands*. Chicago: University of Chicago Press.
Luria, A. R. (1976). *Cognitive development: Its cultural and social foundations.* Cambridge, Mass.: Harvard University Press.
McCormick, P. (1989). Intentionality and language: Is belief possible without the language of belief? *Periodically* (the newsletter of the McLuhan Program in Culture and Technology and the Consortium on Literacy), 12:4–5. Toronto.
McKellin, W. (1986). Intentional ambiguity in Mangalese negotiations. Unpublished manuscript, University of Toronto.
McLuhan, M. (1962). *The Gutenberg galaxy.* Toronto: University of Toronto Press.
  (1964). *Understanding media: The extensions of man.* New York: New American Library.
  (1988). The role of new media in social change. *Antigonish Review* 43–9, 74–5.
Merton, R. (1970). *Science, technology and society in seventeenth century England.* New York: Fertig.
Olson, D. R. (1977). From utterance to text. *Harvard Educational Review.* 47(3):257–81.
Olson, D. R., & Astington, J. W. (1987). Seeing and knowing: On the ascription of mental states to young children. *Canadian Journal of Psychology* 41(4):399–411.
  (1990). Talking about text: How literacy contributes to thought. *Journal of Pragmatics* (in press).
Olson, D. R., & Torrance, N. G. (1987). Language, literacy, and mental states. *Discourse Processes* 10(2):157–167.
Ong, W. (1982). *Orality and literacy: The technologizing of the word.* London: Methuen.
Postman, N. (1985). *Amusing ourselves to death.* New York: Viking-Penguin.
Robinson, E., & Robinson, W. (1980). Understanding about ambiguous messages: A symptom of learning to distinguish message from meaning. Report written for Bishop Road Infant School. University of Bristol School of Education.
  (1977). Children's explanations of failure and the inadequacy of the misunderstood message. *Developmental Psychology* 13:151–61.
Rosaldo, M. Z. (1982). The things we do with words: Ilongot speech acts and speech act theory in philosophy. *Language in Society* 11:203–37.
  (1984). Toward an anthropology of self and feeling. In R. A. Shweder & R. A. LeVine, *Culture theory: Essays on mind, self and emotion.* Cambridge University Press.
Rousseau, J. (1966). *Essay on the origin of language.* (J. Moran, trans.). New York: Ungar. (Originally published in 1749.)
Ruffman, T., Torrance, N., & Olson, D. R. (1989). Children's understanding and interpretation of a speaker's ambiguous message. Unpublished manuscript. Ontario Institute for Studies in Education, Toronto.

Saenger, P. (1982). Silent reading: Its impact on late medieval script and society. *Viator*, 13:367–414.
Schieffelin, B., & Cochran-Smith, M. (1982). Learning to read culturally: Literacy before schooling. In H. Goelman, A. Oberg, & F. Smith (eds.), *Awakening to literacy*. Exeter, N.H.: Heinemann.
Scribner, S. (1977). Modes of thinking and ways of speaking: Culture and logic reconsidered. In P. N. Johnson-Laird & P. C. Wason (eds.), *Thinking: Readings in cognitive science*. Cambridge University Press.
Scribner, S., & Cole, N. (1981). *The psychology of literacy*. Cambridge, Mass.: Harvard University Press.
Sprat, T. (1966). *History of the Royal Society of London for the improving of natural knowledge*. (J. I. Cope & H. W. Jones, eds.). St. Louis: Washington University Press. (Originally published in London, 1667.)
Stock, B. (1983). *The implications of literacy*. Princeton, N.J.: Princeton University Press.
(1984–5). Medieval history, linguistic theory, and social organization. *New Literary History* 16:13–29.
Street, B. (1984). *Literacy in theory and practice*. Cambridge University Press.
Taylor, M. (1988). The development of children's understanding of the seeing–knowing distinction. In J. W. Astington, P. L. Harris, & D. R. Olson (eds.), *Developing theories of mind*. Cambridge University Press.
Traugott, E. C. (1987). Literacy and language change: The special case of speech act verbs. *Interchange* 18(1 & 2):32–47.
Weber, M. (1930). *The Protestant ethic and the spirit of capitalism*. (T. Parsons, trans.). (Originally published in 1905.)
Wimmer, H., & Perner, J. (1983). Beliefs about beliefs: Representation and constraining function of wrong beliefs in young children's understanding of deception. *Cognition* 13:103–28.

# 10
## Thinking through literacies
JEFFREY KITTAY

One of the major problems in the understanding of literacy is our failure to specify what its properties are independent of writing.[1] Recent research in the vernacular literature of medieval France as it became increasingly literate has been helpful in thinking through what literacy or literacies are. As the capacities literacy calls upon are taken to be inspired by writing, we tend to see them as unique to writing itself and are discouraged from investigating those aspects of the understanding of writing that call upon capacities which may exist irrespective of writing, but which writing may be the first to engage, and with far-reaching consequences. Put differently, it seems clear that if we are going to distinguish between mere decoding and some fuller kind of literacy − in French, the distinction between an illiterate as an *analphabet* and one who is an *illettré* − we shall have to delve into realms of cognition, often murky or hypothetical realms, that writing may seem to encourage but that are nonetheless potential mental capacities.

It is clear that any kind of literacy is initially dependent upon a given graphic code or set of codes. If that were all there was to it, however, then encoding and decoding techniques between the grapheme and the phoneme would exhaust literacy. The introduction of graphemes does not lay innocently upon the complex of preexisting codes. It assumes some of the representational burdens of preexisting codes but is powerless with respect to others, and a reshuffling goes on. Each channel of communication depends for its complete decipherment on what it excludes as well as what it includes of the total communicative act. When channels change, when one goes from one kind of medium to another, for example from sonorousness to silent writing, there is a redistribution between what is explicitly represented or notated and what is not. The necessary dyad of cognition between utterance and situation, or text and context, involves the boundary between channels (e.g., text as verbal, context as nonverbal), but that boundary is specific to the culture at the time. When a culture changes historically, the channel it uses for specific kinds of messages, the relations between utterance and situation, are brought to the fore and possibly radically reconstrued. When the codes or channels functioning as background or as foreground are redistributed because of a material change in the means of communication, perceptual and cognitive patterns change as well.[2]

So it is not just a question of encoding techniques between the grapheme and the phoneme, but more appropriately the following question: Literacy is the knowledge of encoding from *what* into writing? decoding from writing into *what*? The simple answer is "orality," but "orality" may be a more troublesome term than we think, because while it has one meaning as everything that is spoken, it has, in the distinction with the literate tradition, another meaning that is purely residual only: everything a literate culture looks back upon, everything that is communicated, whether sounded by mouth or not, as long as it is uninscribed. Albert Lord used it to characterize societies without writing, and it continues to be so used.[3] Having an opposition between something called literacy and something called orality tends to divide the world of communication into these two separate spheres. We have been saved from this mistake by recent work showing that what we know as literacy and orality interpenetrate and interdepend, less opposites than, say, something like differing modes of experience available to us. Literacy and whatever it is not both enclose and operate within all kinds of signifying behavior and discourses (not to mention situational types, patterns of unconscious inference, and cultural norms). The skill of reading and writing is neither an innocent supplement to oral communication nor necessarily confrontational with respect to it. To understand how its role is created, limited, and extended demands a broader understanding of communication in general, one that we are only beginning to acquire.

Literacy is much more than encoding and decoding the oral, which in turn is much more than the spoken. And we meet the question of the difference between that which remains necessary but outside the decoding of oral utterance (what pragmatics wonders about) and that which remains necessary but outside of the decoding of written utterance. To be more precise, what is the difference between that which remains outside the decoding of the oral utterance (but which we must nonetheless understand and which the oral utterance operates within, implies, depends upon, and makes possible) and that which remains outside the decoding of the written utterance (but which we must nonetheless understand and which the written utterance operates within, implies, depends upon, and makes possible)? In some instances there is no difference, and in others the difference is crucial. It depends on the distribution of literate practices within a culture.

One stance sees writing as fundamentally lacking certain elements necessary in nonwritten communication. Those are commonly called "context"; writing is seen as "decontextualized," and thus an understanding of writing calls upon compensatory mechanisms. The writer must write *in* those aspects of the oral communication that are not themselves uttered but are prerequisites for the successful conveyance of the message, so that, for example, what is an oral deictic must in writing be specified, because the reader will not be in the situation of the writer, will be bereft of the system of possible denotations, and thus will not know what a simple "now" or "here" or "that" means. This is more difficult than it sounds because much of that which needs further specification or glossing is not signaled by such devices as deictics. But let us leave that aside.

The problem is whether terms and discourses actually exist for that which is unspoken and whether, even if they did exist, it would be appropriate for such terms and discourses to have a place in a written utterance. There are forces in conflict here: There is, on the one hand, a drive to explicitness,[4] to bring to the surface and articulate in writing that which is unwritten and unsaid, and there is, on the other hand, not only the necessity to effect a communication with economy and dispatch, but also something that we might call appropriate covertness, or maybe verisimilitude, which recognizes the enormous investment communication in general has in implicitness as such, so that even if we did have the terms for that which remains unspoken in a given situation, we could not use them all because some of them are to remain unwritten.

Ethnomethodologists and sociolinguists run into this practical problem. They seek to fill in what is implied, to gloss and make explicit, but become quickly aware both that to do so is an open-ended, impossible task and that it is distorting in and of itself, for if all these things were actually communicated "in so many words," much incongruity or even evidence of such things as devious motivation would result (Garfinkel & Sacks, 1970). Rendering explicitly and in so many words what an *analysis* shows to be implicit in an interaction (from a family dinner discussion to a session of psychotherapy) can in fact destroy a certain ambiguity that is essential to the interaction (see Labov & Fanshel, 1977).

A writer cannot utter those things unless he or she has devised a place for them "to come from," *a discourse or set of discourses in which such things could be uttered while remaining in an important sense unspoken,* one not based on the practices of speech performance. That is, they will remain unwritten and thus unuttered (and thus the communication will depend on a preceding, e.g., oral, situation as an underlying given) until the writer succeeds in finding a special and appropriate place for them in the text. A writing narrator, as opposed to a speaking one, can innovate in creating classes of utterances that remain unspoken, or that are at least alienated in some sense from prevailing speech models. A simple but unassailable example is the rubric, the adding of chapter and section titles in medieval manuscripts that are transcriptions of performance. Although rubrics can be spoken and are in recitations of some sorts, they mark an exclusively *scribal* position (see Huot, 1987). What kind of position that is, its appropriateness, and the relation between what a rubric does and what a teller would do, are all issues that cannot be raised in a preliterate culture. The same goes for free indirect discourse, which is neither direct nor indirect quotation.[5] It is a particular kind of filtered immediacy that was virtually impossible in medieval oral genres of telling.

The more we understand the peculiarities and constraints upon communication in a speech situation, the more we can see how a writer's emulation of the speech situation can actually function as a limit upon the kinds of communication to which writing can aspire. So a second stance is of writing, aiming not to compensate for the lack of explicitness, but to elaborate a different kind of mode or representation of experience and reality, by containing in a different fashion the communications it finds and by discovering within itself, like at an interlinear space where they could be a rubric, new kinds of communication. But while one culture may embrace rubrication and another may embrace the gloss, a third may find either practice at best superfluous and at worst perverse. What opportunities does the latter culture leave available?

If we try to find out how writing comprises a class of utterances that is *distinct* from other coexisting communicative practices, we encounter two different kinds of theoretical difficulties. The first is an *intrinsic descriptive* difficulty to the oral–literate distinction, irrespective of how it is embodied, because different media do use each other, act as inversions of each other, supplement and cede to each other. And there is always, to a certain extent, a translatability from one to the other, that is, speech can be transcribed and read, and writing can be put in quotes and recited. Media have a certain mutual permeability and can diffuse through one another, if it is desirable and no steps have been taken to prevent it. (Jewish sacred tradition specifically prohibits, for example, that oral commentary be written, and also that the Scriptures, the written, be recited by heart: Even if portions have been memorized, they should be spoken only as an out-loud reading, eyes scanning the Torah; they must be given as a deciphering from the written.)

The second is the *empirical* difficulty of not finding things in a pure or universal form, but relative to factors specific to a given culture.

What is cognitively innovative about literacy is not universally exploited by all cultures with writing. If we look around, we find a polyglot quality to literacy. It depends on relative factors, such as (1) how open a culture is to new kinds of communication, for which it could look to writing and (2) what the specific material factors of the medium are that can be exploited. This goes from the differences in the *physical* material of writing (clay tablets, papyrus, print, and the cathode ray tube) to the *graphic* arrangements and rearrangements that writing offers, such as juxtapositions of words in space (e.g., lists, tables, indexes), juxtapositions that are inimical to speech. One striking difference is the way cultures deal with the absence of the utterer: Is it to be compensated for or cognitively exploited?

The process of writers removing themselves from the context of song and performance is a gradual one, and particularly appears so because of the permeability and translatability spoken of earlier. The reworking and transforming of writing does not happen all at once. If one looks at cultures in early stages of literacy, one can see writing only gradually extending the net of its dominion beyond that of already existing communicational techniques.

The French Middle Ages are a model of what happens when a culture reaches a higher level of understanding of the properties of writing, so that new kinds of utterances and new ways of understanding them become desirable and necessary. A recent book (Godzich & Kittay, 1987) focuses on the moment in French history when verse, which had comprised virtually all of French writing, is relatively abruptly considered to be no longer the medium for historical truth; in fact it is abruptly considered to distort and lie. The culture decides to resort to something new, prose, which had not existed in French up to this time and which emerges at this point as a newly authoritative communicative practice.

It happens that tied to the shift from written verse to written prose in the Middle Ages is a realization of some of the consequences of the fact that reading can beneficially do without the presence of an utterer, and that an utterer, and all the implications of speech performance, should not be *read into* all texts. The book shows that what is most profound about prose as it is rediscovered in the Middle Ages is not its lack of formal markings (rhyme, meter). Rather it is acceptance of the condition that writing permits communication in the absence of the utterer, which need not be compensated for because that absence, at that time, brought with it an effect of a more stable truth and authority. To be literate in this new prose was to learn how to read it without conceding a speaker-performer equivalence.[6] It is to read for no final and embracing physical speaker behind the text but to see speech performance as enclosable, within quotes and local, surrounded by a more marginal, unlocatable, or somehow more "objective" source, like that behind such things as a rubric or a piece of free indirect discourse (see Kittay, 1988).

So writing, even a specific material form of writing (like the alphabet on paper, say) is not only one discovery. As it comes to serve more and more diverse kinds of communication, and begins to do so in a uniquely writerly fashion, a new competence is called for, the competence to read and to bring this all to some kind of meaning. A new literacy is in the offing. The interesting puzzle for me is the way in which writing draws upon different kinds of discourses and puts them together in a way that only writing, not speech, would do it.[7] In so doing, writing has created a new vantage point which has also become, and crucially for us, a unique epistemological situation. Thus, we have a literacy beyond decoding. This is why teachers of reading and writing begin to consider themselves teachers of such things as "critical thinking."[8]

Goody, Ong, and others have shown the way lists, tables, and codices enable the written to disconnect and abstract parts of utterances, parts that speech and performance tend to lock together. Writers can manipulate and rearrange pieces of utterance in what are potentially cognitively innovative and valuable organizations and conceptual schemes. (This is an effect of working with notational codes, not unlike working with mathematical, computer, or musical notation. We have to understand what notation is, what operations it offers, and which of writing's possibilities are strictly due to its notational dimension.) The kind of manipulability of utterance that writing allows is due both to the quality writing has of being repeatable and rereadable – its ability to generate multiple and simultaneously discrepant messages – and to the effect that it *can* have of being relatively neutral with respect to, and thus potentially neutralizing of, preexisting enabling conditions of utterance (again, to a possible effect of objectivity). It has also been shown that writing does not inevitably do this, that certain cultures restrict it from these kinds of uses. I am interested in a different, but related kind of exploitation of writing having to do with the cognitive value of a written text since, as its reception is in the absence of its writer, it can come from an impossible place. This cannot be developed in a chapter of this scope, but it can be illustrated, and it is with such an illustration that I will conclude.

An archeologist is surveying the ruins of an ancient town on a hillside. Let us say that the archeologist knows from historical evidence that there was first a high wall, built to defend a larger piece of territory, then there were a few small passages in the wall, and around those passages, on both sides of the wall, a town gradually built itself up, perhaps as a way station around the passageway. The town was destroyed, and later the wall tumbled down and is now marked by a line of remaining rocks and footings. The archeologist stands astride the line of rocks and looks at the layout of the roads and remnants of dwellings that make up the ancient town.

As an archeologist in such a position, what does one see, what can one think about what one sees? One sees the town and thus can, by means of one's training, begin to mentally reconstruct it as it was lived in. In fact, let us say that the position where the wall was and where one now is, is an ideal vantage point from which the whole town can be visually surveyed. And yet, standing as one is in a place where nobody could have stood when the town was occupied, one sees the town as nobody could then have seen it. The vista is impossible, unreal for the townspeople. Standing there, however, helps the archeologist see some aspects of the town that lead her, she believes, to a more profound understanding of the town's layout as it was. All the townspeople were somewhere in that town as it was, but she is standing strictly nowhere in that town, and yet she senses that she may have access to at least some kind of understanding of their situation by virtue of her impossible position.

The knowledge of this archeologist is of a privileged but difficult kind. It is a cognitive advance, but only if she acknowledges and gauges her distance from the view of the townspeople. We, to whom the conclusions will be conveyed, must also gauge the distance if we are to read what she has written from that vantage point. We also have to understand what is said or written, what is cognized; we have to appreciate the unique perspective or the way it organizes other perspectives, in spite of its impossibility. Not that the perspective comes from a zero point or an average point or a neutral point (all of which are just as distortion-prone as this one), but that it comes from no point of perception as given or preconceived, which makes it questionable perhaps but also possibly of special value.

This is the kind of cognitive possibility that cultures can find in new media exploited to certain lengths, like writing. Such writing must have its corresponding literacy: It has to be understood in terms of where it "comes from," even if that is a kind of nowhere in comparison to the usual sites from which events and situations are usually described. (All archeology mobilizes this kind of understanding: We must give such writing at least one reading through the temporal break, which sees the author as a visitor from the future; otherwise, we will not be literate with respect to that writing, no matter how well we decode.) But a culture – one that, say, already has writing for some purposes – will have access to that kind of cognitive possibility in writing only if there is some sort of need for or attraction to an abstraction of position, or to a particular kind of positionlessness, analogous to that of the archeologist astride the wall. It is obvious that archeologists of any era could physically stand in the position so described with respect to a habitation of an earlier era, but it is far from clear that such a vantage point would have some unique interest: In other words, that kind of position is not of universal interest, not even of universal hypothetical interest (which is the way, of course, in which I am using it).[9] One cannot assume that every archeologist would find it desirable to represent the town from there, or would even know how to go about simply *speaking from* there, rather than, say, finding the place grotesque, uninformative, or impossible (as we might judge perspectives such as hanging upside down from a tree or being down a well).

Writing allows utterances to be situated in an analogously impossible way.[10] This because, with the potential to be free of utterance situations *in presencia*, it can combine perceptually based utterances (analogous to where the townspeople could stand) with perspectivally based ones (analogous to the position "within" the wall, or in retrospection). However, a culture, because of its tolerance or even hunger for certain kinds of displacements (and why it should have such tolerance or hunger is *the* most fascinating question), may recognize in that peculiar perceptual position (standing where no one could have stood) a particular perspectival value with respect to life in the town. Writing, as cleft between the spatiotemporal coordinates of its inscription and those of its reading, as a production that is both nonspoken and nonpresent at its reception, removes the writer from the constraints of the manifold conditions of actual presence and speech performances, leaving possible perspectival opportunities ready to be discovered.

Free indirect discourse is one significant example. Certain cultures for certain purposes will let this come to be, will see such discourse, for example, as even truer under certain circumstances than direct discourse.[11] There is a strong argument that the prerequisite for such kinds of discourse, and whatever they bring anew, is not just the ability to write or the ability to read, but a certain kind of literacy.

NOTES

1 An early draft of this chapter was presented at the *Third International Conference on Thinking*, Honolulu, Hawaii, January 1987.
2 Such changes are often indicated by the surfacing of some pragmatic indicators (like deictic expressions) and the disappearance of others.
3 As only one example: "By 'oral' I shall mean to indicate a tradition which arose without written record, which could prosper only in the absence of

fixed texts, and which was in part committed to writing near the end of the oral culture's tenure" (Foley 1977, p. 145).
4 Degree of explicitness is often put forward as a distinction between written and spoken language.
5 E.g., "She knocked. John opened the door. *How beautiful she was.*"
6 Involved in the book's thesis is a narrowing of the meaning of the term "prose" such that it does not apply across the board to all unversed utterances.
7 Though, again, speech could always quote it, as we do to authors all the time. But what may not have begun as dialogue might well come out as such when cited – or as aphorism.
8 It would be an error, however, to consider all critical thinking to be literate critical thinking.
9 Involved here is also the question of what kind of freedom we grant to those institutions and sign systems in authority. Who is allowed to elucidate, and how much latitude do we allow elucidators? There is a kind of professional "license" (like "poetic license") that makes us accept elucidation from certain sources and in certain situations, in spite of apparent distortions, and not in others, and might make us grant only to an archeologist the ability to speak from that special place. I am thinking of how, in the Middle Ages, Latin could elucidate Scripture (thereby allowing Latin almost necessarily some leeway, some interstitial place to stand), whereas John of Salisbury denied an elucidative function to the vernacular.
10 I am not speaking here of a universal or absolute impossibility, just of certain traditional Western attitudes toward secular utterances. Cross-cultural studies will show that some of the things writing can do here, other *media* (including the plural of the human "medium") can do at other times and places.
11 One might say that free indirect discourse is better than giving the *words* of John opening the door to Mary (see Note 5), since he is not "speaking" his thoughts anyway, and in that sense the words are not his to begin with.

REFERENCES

Foley, J. M. (1977), The traditional oral audience. *Balkan Studies* 18:145–53.
Garfinkel, H., & Sacks, H. (1970). On formal structures of practical actions. In J. C. McKinney & E. A. Tiryakian (eds.), *Theoretical sociology: Perspectives and developments* (pp. 337–66). East Norwalk, Conn.: Appleton-Century-Crofts.
Godzich, W., & Kittay, J. (1987). *The emergence of prose.* Minneapolis: University of Minnesota Press.
Huot, S. (1987). *From song to book: The poetics of writing in old French lyric and lyrical narrative poetry.* Ithaca, N.Y.: Cornell University Press.
Kittay, J. (1988). Utterance unmoored: The changing interpretation of the act of reading in the Middle Ages. *Language & Society* 17:209–30.
Labov, W., & Fanshel, D. (1977). *Therapeutic discourse.* New York: Academic Press.

# PART III
Oral and literate aspects of cognition

# 11
# Literacy: its characterization and implications
R. NARASIMHAN

**The literacy hypothesis and the Indian tradition**

In the past twenty-five years or so, in a series of highly influential articles and books, Havelock (1963, 1982), Goody and Watt (1962), Goody (1977), Ong (1982), Olson (1977, 1986), and others have argued persuasively that Western European culture changed in an essential way after the invention of alphabetic script by the Greeks a few centuries before Plato's time. These studies contrast the alphabetic literacy of post-Homeric Greece with the oral traditions of Homeric and pre-Homeric Greece and draw some far-reaching conclusions. Among others, for instance, it is claimed that alphabetic literacy was an essential enabling factor in the Greek democratic tradition in ordering society and politics; in the Greek analytic tradition in the development of logic; and in the Greek skeptical and critical tradition in the study of nature and history. Writing is also claimed to have been an essential force in the emergence of an autonomous psyche making up the inner world of individual human beings: The hallucinations of Homeric heroes gave place to the reflective introspections of the post-Homeric Greek tradition.

Writing and subsequently, to an even greater extent, printing made it possible to draw a clear distinction between "utterance" and "text." A "text" as an invariant fixed entity carried its meaning within itself. And, as Luther argued later, anyone could learn to interpret the *true* meaning that a text carried within itself. Hermeneutics thus came to replace rhetoric as the principal methodological tool to recover truth. Olson (1986; Chapter 9, this volume) traces the early beginnings of the scientific tradition to an application of hermeneutics to nature, looking upon it as the book of God's work. He argues "that the contrast between texts and their interpretations provided the model, or more than that, the precise cognitive categories or concepts needed for the description and interpretation of nature, that is, for the building of modern science" (p. 152).

This *literacy hypothesis*, its wide-ranging scope notwithstanding, has have argued in detail that literacy per se does not engender cognitive changes. Gough (1968) has made a preliminary analysis of Indian and Chinese experiences and argues that the consequences of literacy have been very variable in these two cases and do not support the conclusions drawn by Havelock and others based on Greece and Western Europe. A more systematic and contrastive study of the Indian tradition should be of great interest and value in this context because of the many singular features this tradition exhibits.

The sacred and the ritual literature of India – the Vedas and the early commentaries on them including the earliest grammars – were all products of an oral milieu. They were all meant to be memorized and recited. There has been much inconclusive argument on whether this entire corpus was actually composed without any recourse to writing. Whatever doubts one may have about the strictly oral compositional nature of the later works (c.g., Panini's grammar, c 500 B.C.), there is fairly convincing internal evidence to establish that the earliest of the Vedas, the *Rigveda* (c. 1500 B.C.), is made up of orally composed hymns.[1] Before its redaction into a text, different versions of the *Rigveda* seem to have existed and were used in practice by different "schools." But after the redaction (before 600 B.C.), only a single, standardized version of the *Rigveda* has been preserved and transmitted faultlessly from generation to generation through purely oral means. The efficacy of the mnemotechnics evolved to preserve the authenticity of the text of this veda is attested to by the fact that a systematic comparison of the orally preserved renderings of the text from different parts of India has shown that there is no variation in the text of these renderings. One is able to assert the authenticity and the fixity of the Rigvedic text because what has been preserved and is available through recitation is not only the main text in its continuous (free-running) form, but also a variety of transformations of this text: for example, the text as a sequence of separated words, the words as sequences of consonants and vowels, various rule-governed transformations of the text built out of prescribed permutations of words within segmented word sequences, and so on.[2] The recitations from various parts of the country could be checked against one another on the basis of these analyzed and/or transformed texts.

There can be no argument the *Rigveda* as preserved constitutes a "text" in every sense of this term. It is an autonomous and fixed corpus. A whole textual tradition grew up around this text. Grammatical rules to analyze and segment it into words and to reconstruct the text from the word sequence were formulated. Compilations of lists of various kinds relating to the text were prepared: for example, groups of synonyms, difficult vocables, a classification of the divine

*Literacy: characterization and implications* 179

names occurring in text. Etymological interpretations of such words in these lists were provided. Indexes of the hymns constituting the text of the *Rigveda* – in terms of their composers, their meters, the number of stanzas in them, the number of hymns in the various sections of the *Veda* – were compiled.[3] It is of interest to note that most of these works were themselves composed in the form of memorizable texts, committed to memory for preservation, and handed down from generation to generation in the oral mode. A commentarial and interpretative tradition developed and flourished around the Vedic text right from very early times.[4] Six auxiliary subjects of study, which later on developed into autonomous disciplines, acquired special status within the Vedic tradition, namely, phonetics, metrics, grammar, etymology, ritual practice, and astronomy.

As already mentioned, the mnemotechnics evolved for the preservation of the *Rigveda* in its authentic form were again put to use for the oral preservation of much of these auxiliary products of the textual tradition. But, more significantly, analogous mnemotechnics were evolved to support the development, teaching, and preservation of structurally complex performing art forms, vocal and instrumental music, dance, and so on.[5] In other words, although the Indian tradition, in the large, was oral, it functioned within a highly literate framework. Despite undervaluing *writing* as a technology, articulations usually unavailable to oral societies were made accessible within the Indian tradition through a variety of intellectually sophisticated techniques. These "literate" underpinnings of the oral tradition in India remain to be systematically studied.

However, for our present argument, the point to note is that in spite of the availability of a textual tradition involved in active textual literacy practices, the kinds of scientific and technological developments at the social level, and cognitive developments at the individual level, that a textual tradition is supposed to result in did not materialize in India at the global level. Indian tradition, in the large, continued to remain an oral one in its psychosocial aspects. There was no effort to discriminate systematically between myth and history; between beliefs in the supernatural and a rational analysis of natural phenomena; between disputatious, polemical arguments, and comparative, critical, analytical studies; between a didactic approach to inquiry and a reflective approach to it. The important question to ask is "Despite its literate underpinnings why did the Indian tradition continue to exhibit these 'nonliterate' characteristics?"

It would appear that what is of relevance is not the existence of a textual tradition per se but the kinds of conceptualizations and critical analytical techniques such a tradition develops and makes use of in its textual studies. Olson's claims (quoted earlier) that the interpretative textual tradition of medieval Europe gave rise to the empirical scientific tradition there presupposes that the cognitive and conceptual categories in terms of which that textual tradition functioned were immediately transferable to the analysis and study of natural phenomena, and more significantly, there was an intellectual urge to do so. This does not seem to have happened in the case of the textual tradition in India. The reasons for this need to be systematically studied. We shall take up this point again later in the chapter.

For our present purpose, these criticisms of the literacy hypothesis would seem to suggest that literacy must be looked at in a much broader perspective. We need a more ramified characterization of literacy and its practices without limiting ourselves narrowly to the presence or absence of script literacy, textual literacy, and so on. Such a broader, more ramified characterization of literacy will be our concern in the rest of the chapter.

*Characterizing "literacy": some general considerations*

Our concern in this section will be to analyze the issues that underpin the literacy hypothesis from a more general perspective and see whether we can formulate a more ramified characterization of literate behavior instead of limiting it exclusively to the capability to read and write. We shall approach this task in two stages. First we shall consider briefly how the availability of language enables human beings to engage in reflective behavior that is outside the reach of other animals. Literacy can then be studied as an extension and augmentation of the potentialities of the oral mode of behavior. This would then enable us to determine what new ways of dealing with the world and the self are made available in moving from the oral to the literate mode of behavior. These are the "consequences of literacy in the small." We shall see that through institutionalizing and technologizing some of these ways of dealing with the world and the self, the consequences of literacy are made available to wider groups of people. These are the "consequences of literacy in the large."

Language behavior is able to bring about a qualitative change in the communication capability of human beings because of its intrinsic potential to *articulate* the aspects of the world that are being dealt with. This ability to articulate situational aspects – aspects of objects, agents, and events constituting a situation and their interrelationships – is an essential prerequisite to *specifying* and *instructing*. Through specifications and instructions, one is able to plan and program activities of the world. Articulated self-expression plays a crucial role in complex programming of one's own behavior. Through language behavior, human beings are able to deal not only with the world that is immediately available for interaction, but with worlds distanced from them in space and time. Moreover, they are able to deal not only with the actual world out there that is given, but with (imagined) possible worlds and counterfactual situations. With language behavior, one is not restricted to performing actual experiments but can take recourse to *gedanken* experiments.[6]

The specific claims that have been made about the consequences of alphabetic literacy in post-Homeric Greece may be reformulated as claims that alphabetic literacy brought about qualitative changes among the post-Homeric Greeks in their perception and understanding of, and consequently in their capacity to grapple with, the notions of *time, space, nature,* and *self* (including *society*). The nature of this change may be seen to be the acquisition of the capacity to *externalize* (or *depersonalize*) these notions and deal with them as objectifiable concepts.

Two questions arise at this stage for consideration: First, was or is alphabetic literacy (or even literacy in the sense of writing) an indispensable prerequisite to trigger the externalization of these concepts? Second, is the particular manner of externalization attributed to the Greeks a unique Greek contribution, or is that an inevitable consequence of the very externalization process?

We saw earlier that a characterizing feature of language behavior is that it enables one to articulate aspects of the world and the self. Insofar as language behavior underpins orality, the medium by itself, whether it is speech or writing, cannot completely account for the externalizing capability. We need to look more closely at the compulsions for externalization that the medium imposes, and also the nature and extent of articulation that is the result of the externalization process.

Havelock, Ong, and others have emphasized in their writings that in the oral mode, the interpersonal interactions are very situation bound (i.e., context bound), and since the interaction takes place face to face, there is very little motivation to articulate explicitly all the details of the situational context one is dealing with. Consequently there is very little inclination to reflect on these and, thus, develop a capability for articulation.

Writing, however, is intrinsically a distanced activity. One writes for an audience that is separated from oneself in space and time. Hence, writing enforces articulation of the situational aspects one is concerned with as a prerequisite to achieving successful communication. Since writing makes explicit the need for articulation, it opens the way to reflect on *methodologies* for articulation and levels and structurings of articulations.

Coming now to the second of our questions, were the specific forms of articulations of post-Homeric Greece a unique Greek contribution? This question really concerns the *representational* aspects of the results of the articulation or externalization process. Were the particular modes of representation of the Greeks a unique contribution? This would seem to be so.[7] This, in fact, is the thrust of Gough's evaluation of the Chinese tradition that we referred to in the previous section: "Further progress was arrested due to the failure to incorporate knowledge in formal theories and test them through systematic experiments." The Greek representational techniques seem to have favored the development of an empirical scientific tradition more effectively than either the Chinese or the Indian. This criticism relates to the inadequacy not only of the representation of their articulations by the Chinese and the Indians, but also of the verificational criteria adopted to validate the nature of the articulations and their interrelationships. Such inadequacies are likely to arise if articulations and their representations are motivated by ideologies (or philosophies, or metaphysical predilections) that are not concerned with material control of the real, physical world.

Historically, in Western European culture, representations of articulations and the *uses made* of these representations have played a determining role in the development of methodologies for world articulation and self-articulation. Use has been the prime mover here. The principal thrust has been to understand the world in terms of representations and their structurings so that these representations could be acted on (i.e., manipulated, transformed) to create new, engineered worlds. In the language of representations and their uses, the orality–literacy contrast reveals itself as the contrast between craft techniques based on apprenticeship and tradition and engineering techniques based on theorized science.

Historically, the use of natural language in the oral mode and the use of writing (in the sense of using a script) have both turned out to be inadequate to cope with the complex representational needs of engineering and engineered worlds. New notations, new formalisms, and new languages have had to be devised, and new visual–graphic techniques innovated, to come to grips with these abstractions and to manipulate and transform them. Many of these ideas and techniques are in the leading edge of current theorizing and research. Much of this work makes essential use of computational formalisms and computer technology.

Once articulation has been cultivated as a methodology for looking

*Literacy: characterization and implications* 183

at and dealing with the world and the self, insofar as it can be talked about in natural language, this methodology can be made available to some extent for use in the oral mode. Such feedback can make the consequences of literacy available to those functioning in the oral mode.[8] A question that arises is, What are the limits to such feedback?

The limits are determined by the representational issues relating to the relevant articulations. Without script literacy, by limiting feedback communication to natural language exclusively, what can be accomplished is bound to be highly circumscribed. Script literacy makes more ramified feedback possible. Arguments, reasoning, deductions, explanations, and so forth, when they are long and complex, cannot be communicated perspicuously without the help of writing. As Goody observes (1977, p. 44), "It is . . . the *form* in which the alternatives are presented that makes one aware of the differences, forces one to consider contradiction, makes one conscious of the 'rules' of the argument" (my italics).

However, even in the absence of script literacy, by resorting to visual–graphic aids, much more than in the purely oral mode may be feasible. It is known that graphic symbols and representational techniques based on these have been deployed, in lieu of script writing, with considerable success in some traditional societies.[9] The Indian tradition seems to have resorted to other kinds of literate devices to underpin articulated behavior: We shall refer to some of these in the next section. Currently, computer technology is opening up entirely new possibilities. By structuring feedback through computer-supported visual–graphic representations, qualitatively new levels of articulations should become available to serve as aids to narrow the gap between orality and literacy.

A second form of feedback occurs when literate ideas and practices diffuse into the cultural milieu through institutionalizing and technologizing such ideas and practices. Pacey (1974) gives an extremely interesting and significant illustration of this in his account of the development of architectural technology in Western Europe during the period A.D. 1100–1300. He discusses how architecture – primarily in the context of cathedral building – started as a craft (i.e., execution based on acquired skill) and gradually transformed itself into a technology when it became design centered, the designs being based on increasingly articulated principles. These principles themselves, which, to begin with, were based on mystical considerations, came increasingly to be based on technical and, later, engineering considerations. He traces the evolution of this transformation from models based on empirically determined parameters – supported by rules of thumb charts, tables, approximate formulas – to models generated criticisms from several quarters. Scribner and Cole (1981) based on more theoretical considerations. For our present argument, a more significant aspect of this transformation was the use of drawings in the building construction as it changed from a craft into a technology. Starting from rough sketches without any indication of dimensions, successive use was made of drawings not to scale but with dimensions indicated, drawings to scale, and, finally, three-dimensional visualizations based on multiple projections. Pacey also points out how the introduction of measurement techniques (linear measures, angles, weights), when applied to drawings, led to perspective representations; when applied to astronomy, led to the discovery of errors in the geocentric model; when applied to map making, led to the exploration of new sea routes to familiar places.

Clanchy (1979) has described in detail how the institutionalization of written-record keeping for administration and jurisprudence subsequent to the Norman conquest in England laid the foundation for lay literacy and the use of literacy in practical everyday living. Technologizing of book production was, of course, the outcome of the introduction of printing through the use of movable type in mid-fifteenth-century Europe. The wide-ranging consequences of this have been extensively discussed by various specialists.[10]

We can summarize our general discussion so far of literacy and its consequences in the historical context by noting that it was not writing or script literacy per se that was the cause of social, cultural, and technological changes in Western Europe. The causes were much more complex but depended centrally upon efforts at articulating aspects of the world and the self, as well as the specific forms and manner of representation of these articulations and the uses made of these representations to create engineered new worlds. So far as the majority of the people were concerned, profiting from literacy came about indirectly, that is, not in terms of the initiatives they took as individuals, but because of literacy practices that were institutionalized and technologized.

The framework just outlined provides a ramified account of literacy. By comparing and contrasting the specific forms of articulations, their representational aspects, and the uses made of these representations we should be able to compare the transformations that have come about historically in various cultures. In order to characterize levels of literacy among individuals and societies more explicitly, it is necessary to discuss at a cognitive level the nature of the articulation process and the issues that arise in the representation of the products that are the outcome of this process. We shall now consider both these questions, although only in a tentative way.

## Characterizing literacy: cognitive-level considerations

Goody (1977, p. 44) points out that "less 'traditional' societies are marked not so much by the absence of reflective thinking as by the absence of proper tools for constructive rumination." Both these observations underpin the following thesis, which we shall formulate to characterize literacy at a cognitive level:

*Reflection* is the basis of literate behavior. "Literateness" is characterized by the kinds (forms) of reflective processes deployed in one's interaction with the world, the inner world as well as the outer one. Literacy is the underpinning of literateness with appropriate (effective) technologies. Literacy not only strengthens literateness but qualitatively widens its scope depending on the nature of the technologies deployed.

Levels of literateness and levels of literacy are determined by the varieties and kinds (forms) of reflective processes in use as well as the kinds of technologies that underpin them.

The thesis, it will be noticed, tries to avoid setting up a polarization between orality and literacy. Literateness constitutes a continuum from primary orality at one end to literate behavior underpinned by the most sophisticated technologies conceivable at the other end. In the standard definition of literacy, the technology that underpins literateness is writing using a script: this is script literacy. But one would like to see a general cognitive model of literacy capable of coping with other forms of literacy (i.e., literacy underpinned by other kinds of technologies) such as visual literacy, computer literacy, and so on. The thesis takes into account such needs for broadening the scope of literacy.

Technology enters the picture in two ways, first, by assisting and/or augmenting the reflective processes and, second, by enabling the *representation* of the outcomes of the application of the reflective processes. Let us for the present concentrate on the latter role of technology. Notice, to begin with, that a representation constitutes a *model* of the aspect of the world that has been reflected on. Let us use the generic term "text" to refer to such representations (i.e., to a modeled world). In this sense, a map is a text, and so is a poem or a song. It is clear that a model is an abstraction. The process of going from an actual to a modeled world is an *abstracting* process. Going the reverse way – from the model, or text, to reality – is *interpretation*.

There are, then, three behavioral modes available to human beings. The first is functioning exclusively in the real world. This is the oral or commonsense mode of behavior. Ordinary language is the medium of communication as well as of cognition. Abstraction and representation are restricted to what is possible in ordinary language.

In its extreme unarticulated form, this mode of behavior remains tacit, habit driven, and perceptual.

The second mode involves moving back and forth between the real world and more or less formalized modeled versions of it. This calls for continuous efforts at abstraction and representation. Specialized tools for abstracting, and also formalized schemes for representing the abstractions, are innovated to aid these efforts. This is preeminently the mode of behavior in the empirical sciences. Through education this becomes also the mode available to many literate individuals. Formal schooling is essentially concerned with developing this mode of behavior.

The third mode is functioning exclusively within the modeled world. Texts, then, become the analogs of the phenomenology of the real world, and abstracting and interpretation go from texts to "models" of texts and back again. This may be called the textual or hermeneutic mode of behavior. It is a fully articulated, puzzle-solving, and cognitive mode of behavior. The professional behavior of academics (especially, of humanists) is prototypical of this mode.

To take the cognitive level characterization of literate behavior further, we would have to consider in detail the particularities of the reflective process, on the one hand, and the techniques relating to representations and the implications of these techniques, on the other hand. Isolating and identifying the reflective processes and characterizing them in computational (i.e., information processing) terms are, clearly, very much open problems. These are precisely the issues that much of artificial intelligence research is preoccupied with.

As regards representation (i.e., the modeled world or the world of texts), three possibilities arise depending on the modality of the representations. These modalities could be (1) temporal, (2) spatiotemporal, or (3) spatial. In Table 11.1, representational possibilities in these three modes are illustrated. Note that the spatiotemporal scale approximately corresponds to the literacy–orality scale. But the correspondence is, at best, a notional one, for highly abstract articulations can be represented in the temporal mode also. So the spatiotemporal scale does not mirror in any straightforward manner the "literateness" levels giving rise to these abstractions.

This is precisely the anomaly that shows up in the Indian tradition when the methodologies that support the practices in the tradition are analyzed carefully. We discussed earlier the elaborate mnemotechniques that were devised to preserve the authenticity of the *Rigveda* as a text as it was handed down through the generations purely through oral means. The details of these mnemotechnics reveal an

Table 11.1. *Representational models for articulated abstractions*

| Modality of existence | Medium of representation | Form of representation |
|---|---|---|
| Temporal | Word sequences (chanted, sung, recited, or spoken) | Prayer, poem, proverb, epigram, ballad, sutra, etc. |
| | Rhythmic syllable sequences (chanted, sung, recited) | Indian oral notational schemes, e.g., Bol, Sollu-Kattu, etc. |
| | Music (for voice, instrument) | Musical compositions in various forms |
| Spatiotemporal | Staged live | Rituals, dance, drama, opera, etc. |
| | Filmed, taped, computer generated | Live action sequences, computer animation, etc. |
| Spatial | Script writing | Text in various forms (letter, essay, etc.) |
| | Two-dimensional images | Diagram, schema, chart, map, picture, etc. |
| | Three-dimensional images | Sculpture, architecture, etc. |

exceptionally thorough metalevel grasp of the generative grammatical bases of the reciting process, on the one hand, and of the text that was being memorized and recited, on the other hand.[11] This feature is characteristic of the entire Indian intellectual tradition. While at one level it was highly speculative, at another level the tradition has been very conscious of the specificational needs to preserve the authenticity of performances – in rituals, recitations, and the performing arts. Explicit grammars defining correct performances have been elaborated and techniques perfected to pass on practices in an uncorrupted form from generation to generation through oral instructional means.

In the case of music teaching and practice, for example, in the absence of written notational schemes, oral notational schemes were invented and successfully used in teaching and for setting lessons to the student to facilitate rehearsal and practice. In the playing of the *tabla* – a percussion instrument that provides rhythmic accompaniment to vocal and instrumental music performance – this oral notational scheme is known as Bol (literally, "the spoken"). In the Appendix to this chapter, a brief description of this oral notational scheme is given. Similar oral notational and other mnemonic aids were devised to assist teaching, rehearsal, and practice in the case of vocal and instrumental performances also. Ranade (1984) gives an informative account of the oral dimensions of teaching classical music in the North Indian tradition. Analogous considerations apply to the teaching and learning of classical Indian dances like Bharatanatyam.

Notwithstanding the sophistication of these representational techniques in the temporal domain devised by the Indian tradition, the fact remains that from a cognitive point of view, representations in the spatial domain are ultimately vastly more powerful. The primary reason for this would seem to be the way human beings, considered as information processing systems, are put together. Our ability to *integrate*, that is, perceive gestalts, see and match patterns, schematize, and so on, are vastly superior in the spatial domain than in the temporal domain. An important and significant consideration here is the potentiality for *scaling* in the spatial domain. One can make a scaled-down version of a wall-sized world map that can be held in the palm of one's hand; the scaled version would nevertheless preserve a good deal of the spatial relationships in the original. The smaller version helps in perceiving patterns much more readily than the larger version. It is significant that there is no analog of scaling in the temporal domain. One cannot make a two-minute summary of a Beethoven symphony. But notice that a summary of the principal themes *can be* displayed on one page if a notational scheme is devised for *writing out* the symphony. Such a spatial summary would readily assist in perceiving patterns and interrelationships between those themes. Such considerations would seem to suggest that at least one reason for the failure to make much headway by the theoreticians of the Indian tradition was their exclusive dependence on the temporal domain to represent their abstractions, both descriptions and specifications.[12]

It is also of some interest that spatial representations tend, in general, to be decontextualized and affect delinked (see Table 11.1). However, temporal and spatiotemporal representations tend to be contextualized and affect linked. This feature, of course, has been noted and emphasized by Havelock (1982), Ong (1982), and others as an essential difference between orality and literacy. The abstractions arrived at and encoded in the temporal domain in the Indian tradition, for example, were very context bound; and *within* the tradition, no attempt seems to have been made to look at these representations contrastively, delinked from their contexts, in order to articulate the methodological issues underpinning these efforts and accomplishments.

The cognitive superiority of the spatial representations explains why writing (scripts, diagrams, charts, maps, written notational schemes, etc.) is so much more effective in supporting reflective thinking than oral discourse, miming, dramatic play, music, and so on. But it still remains to be explained why, out of all media of representation in the spatial domain, script writing is so much more cognitively effective and consequential. Perhaps this is because it combines the best of two worlds. While being spatial, decontextualized, and affect delinked, it is also able to reproduce the discursive nature of speech. In other words, it can help ratiocination and generate a reasoned discourse. Images by themselves cannot accomplish this. However, it is to be emphasized that script writing combined with diagrams (images) is vastly superior to script writing alone.

These considerations emphasize again the importance of analyzing the contributions of technologies that support the reflective processes. The orality–literacy contrast, and also the consequences of literacy both in the small and in the large, cannot be meaningfully discussed without analyzing simultaneously the contributions of the technologies and institutions that are the outgrowth of the reflective and representational activities. In the absence of systematic and detailed studies along these lines of ancient traditions like the Chinese and Indian, it would be difficult to understand the differences between these traditions and the Western European one and to account for the absence of the various innovations that characterize the Western European past in these other ancient cultures.

## Conclusion

Criticisms of the literacy hypothesis led us to look at the characterization of literacy from a much wider perspective. Starting from the reflective use of (natural) language behavior in world articulation and self-articulation, we postulated the thesis that the basis of literateness is reflection; and literacy is a consequence of underpinning literateness by appropriate and effective technologies. The most effective such technology, in the historical context, has turned out to be writing using a script. This results in script literacy.

A cognitive-level discussion of the modalities available for representing our articulations of the world and the self showed that representation in the spatial mode offers cognitively many advantages. Correspondingly, the possibilities for representations in the temporal mode suffer from many disadvantages. We discussed how the Western

European tradition (following Greece) and the Indian tradition opted to depend on the spatial and temporal modalities, respectively, for representing their articulations.[13] We argued that this difference in their choices was one major factor accounting for the differences in the cultural developments of these two traditions in the historical context. We also argued that the consequences of literacy in the small and in the large are linked by feedback mechanisms resulting from institutionalizing and technologizing world articulations and self-articulations.

In the past decade or two, a variety of scholars have been studying the Western European cultural milieu from around 1000 A.D. onward in an attempt to delineate the role of literacy in the conceptual and social changes that have been taking place there. Three classes of literacy practices seem to have made major contributions to the transformation that Western European culture has gone through during this period. These are the following:

1. Concern with the interpretation assignment process that is involved in assigning meaning to a text; articulating one's conceptualizations of this process as a system of rules, verificational procedures, and so on; building aids to assist this process, for example, dictionaries, indexes, concordances; devising appropriate vehicles to communicate the meanings arrived at, for example, dialogues, commentaries, essays, and so on; in short, a general concern with method.
2. Concern with printing technology; publishing and distribution of books involving literate activities such as authoring, editing, translating, and so on; consequent creation of an increasingly large, informed, and literate reading community.
3. Concern with schooling and the instructional process, especially as this process applies to teaching engineering practices; conceptualizations relating to this process; devising aids to this process; and so on.

In the light of our discussions, it is important to look at these three classes of literacy practices in terms of their articulations, the institutionalized structures these practices gave rise to, and the technological supports that were built up for them.[14] Detailed analyses in these terms should enable cross-cultural comparisons in revealing ways.

A corresponding study and analysis of the Indian tradition should throw much light on the developmental differences between this tradition and the Western European one. We saw earlier how a textual tradition has flourished in India for at least 2,500 years, and yet texts have remained strictly products in the oral domain. Highly sys-

## Literacy: characterization and implications

tematized interpretation assignment techniques were developed to deal with such orally transmitted texts. These interpretations, as well as the aids to arrive at these interpretations, were themselves composed as further texts for memorization, transmission, and preservation. This mode of functioning continued to be the tradition for a long time, well after the introduction of writing to support these literate activities. Writing, for the most part, was looked upon as a support to memory and recall.

Quite naturally, only a small part of the population was involved in these activities. In the absence of widespread script literacy, literate aids to conceptualization and to behavior in the large could have arisen indirectly and through feedback from this textual tradition. The interesting issues to analyze in this context are these.

1. Was there any such feedback? If so, what were its characteristics?
2. How does this feedback, if any, contrast with the corresponding one in the Western European culture, for example, in administration, jurisprudence, science, engineering, craft, art, and so on?
3. In contrast to the situation in Europe, were there intrinsic differences and limitations in the functioning of the textual tradition itself that could be attributed to its exclusively oral nature? If so, how did these manifest themselves in the feedback process?

Analogous studies of the Chinese tradition should be of much comparative value since that tradition, unlike the Indian one, used both script and images (diagrams) as representational media. In this sense China was closer to Europe. Nevertheless, the early achievements of China do not seem to have led to later developments comparable to those in Western Europe. One would like to understand the reasons for this.

### Appendix: an oral notational scheme for *tabla* playing

*Tabla* is a percussion instrument that provides rhythmic accompaniment to vocal and instrumental music performance in the North Indian classical (or semiclassical) style. The instrument consists of two independent units: *dhaga* for the left hand and *tabla* for the right hand. Each unit is made up of three distinct surface regions (Figure 11.1). The rhythmic notes are produced by striking on the regions marked 1, 2, 3 with identified fingers and, sometimes, the palm.

*Tabla* playing can be analyzed into primitive strokes for striking the *dhaga* and the *tabla* and sequences made up of combinations of these

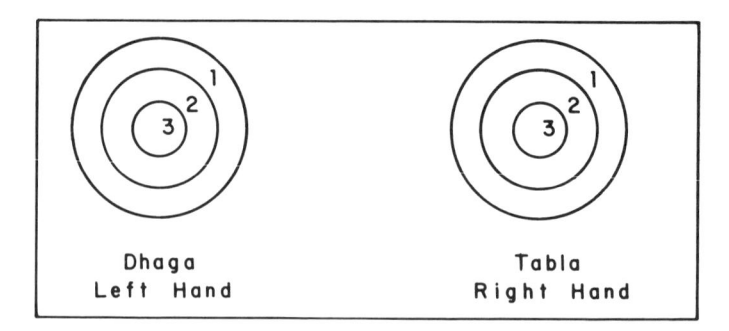

Figure 11.1. Percussion instrument used in North Indian classical style. Numbers indicate regions struck by different fingers.

primitive strokes. The sequences make up phrases at the first level and the phrases, sentences at the next level. Each sentence constitutes a cycle, and the structure of beats in a sentence characterizes the different *tal*s. For instance, the most frequently used Teen tal has sixteen beats made up of four phrases of four beats each. A large variety of stroke sequences can be innovated to make up each phrase of four beats. Hence, a very large repertoire of sentences can be built up – each sentence conforming to the sixteen-beat timing constraint – for Teen tal. Learning to play the *tabla* consists, then, in the following:

1. learning the primitives for the left and the right hands,
2. learning combinations of these primitives,
3. learning the characteristic sentences for each *tal*, and
4. building up a repertoire of sentences for a given *tal*.

In order to devise a notation, the straightforward written approach would be to assign a distinct symbol for each left- and right-hand primitive and then write out the *tal* pattern as a sequence of these symbols structured into phrase units making up a sentence. This is illustrated in the following:

*Right-hand primitives*
$f_1^1$: index finger on region 1
$f_1^2$: index finger on region 2
$f_1^3$: index finger on region 3
$f_2^3$: middle finger on region 3

*Left-hand primitives*
$f$: tips of index and middle fingers on region 2 with the palm curved
$p$: flat palm on regions 1 and 2

*Literacy: characterization and implications* 193

One pattern for Teen tal (sixteen beats) is divided into four phrases of four beats each (the dots signifying half-beats):

*tabla:*  $(f_1^1 \cdot f_1^1 \cdot f_2^3 f_1^3 \cdot f_1^3)\ (f_1^1 \cdot f_1^1 \cdot f_1^2 \cdot f_1^1 \cdot)$
*dhaga:* $(f \ \cdot (f \cdot \cdot \ \ \cdot \ \ p \ \cdot )\ (f \ \cdot f \ \cdot \cdot \ \ \cdot \cdot \ \ \cdot)$
*tabla:*  $(f_1^1 \cdot f_1^1 \cdot f_2^3 f_1^3 \cdot f_1^3)\ (f_1^1 \cdot f_1^1 \cdot f_1^2 \cdot f_1^1 \cdot)$
*dhaga:* $(\cdot \ \cdot \cdot \ \ \cdot \cdot \ \ \cdot \ \ p \ \cdot)\ (f \ \cdot f \ \cdot f \ \cdot \cdot \ \ \cdot)$

The Indian oral notation is constructed by assigning a distinct utterable syllable or syllable sequence to each primitive and to combinations of primitives. The phrases and the sentences, then, are built up out of these basic syllables and syllable sequences. A specific mapping is illustrated in the following (some configurations are mapped onto more than one syllable sequence):

$f_1^1 \to t\bar{a}, n\bar{a}$ $\quad\quad$ $f_2^3 \to ti$
$f_1^2 \to nil$ $\quad\quad\quad$ $f \ \to go$
$f_1^3 \to ta$ $\quad\quad\quad\ $ $p \to ki$
$\begin{matrix}(f_1^1 \ \cdot)\\(f \ \ \cdot)\end{matrix} \to dha$ $\quad\ \ \begin{matrix}(f_1^2 \ \cdot)\\(p \ \ \cdot)\end{matrix} \to tina$

$\begin{matrix}(f_2^2 f_1^3)\\(\cdot \ \ \cdot)\end{matrix} \to tita$ $\quad\quad \begin{matrix}(f_1^1 \ \cdot)\\(\cdot \ \ f)\end{matrix} \to n\bar{a}go$

$\begin{matrix}(f_1^2 \ \ \cdot)\\(f \ \ \ \cdot)\end{matrix} \to dhina, dh\bar{\imath}$
$\begin{matrix}(f_2^3 f_1^3)\\(f \ \ \cdot)\end{matrix} \to dhita$
$\begin{matrix}(f_2^3 f_1^3 \ \cdot \ \ f_1^3)\\(\cdot \ \ \cdot \ \ p \ \ \cdot)\end{matrix} \to tirakita, titakita$
$\begin{matrix}(f_2^3 f_1^3 f_2^3 \ \cdot)\\(\cdot \ \ \cdot \ \ \cdot \ \ \cdot)\end{matrix} \to trka$

With the use of this mapping, the Teen tal pattern illustrated earlier is transformed into the following text, which is memorized and recited while actualizing the stroke sequence:

(*dhā  dhā  titakita*)  (*dhā  dhā  tina  nā*)
(*tā   tā   titakita*)  (*dhā  dhā  dhna  nā*)

Here is a variant pattern for Teen tal in both types of notations. Each phrase of four beats is divided into sixteen parts, the dots signifying quarter-beats:

tabla:  $(f_1^2 \cdot f_1^1 \cdot \ f_1^1 \cdot \ f_2^3 f_1^3 \cdot \ f_1^3 f_1^1 \cdot f_1^2 \cdot f_1^1 \cdot)$
dhaga: $(f \ \cdot \cdot \ \cdot f \ \cdot \cdot \ \cdot p \cdot \ f \ \cdot f \ \cdot \cdot \ \cdot)$
tabla:  $(f_1^1 \cdot f_2^3 f_1^3 \cdot \ f_1^3 f_1^1 \cdot \ f_1^2 \cdot \ f_1^1 \cdot f_1^2 \cdot f_1^1 \cdot)$
dhaga: $(f \ \cdot \cdot \ \cdot p \cdot \ f \cdot \ f \ \cdot \cdot \ \cdot p \ \cdot \cdot \ \cdot)$
tabla:  $(f_1^2 \cdot f_1^1 \cdot \ f_1^1 \cdot \ f_2^3 f_1^3 \cdot \ f_1^3 f_1^1 \cdot f_1^2 \cdot f_1^1 \cdot)$
dhaga: $(p \ \cdot \cdot \ \cdot \cdot \ \cdot \cdot \ \cdot p \cdot \ f \cdot f \ \cdot \cdot \ \cdot)$
tabla:  $(f_1^1 \cdot f_2^3 f_1^3 \cdot \ f_1^3 f_1^1 \cdot \ f_1^2 \cdot \ f_1^1 \cdot f_1^2 \cdot f_1^1 \cdot)$
dhaga: $(f \ \cdot \cdot \ \cdot p \cdot \ f \cdot \ f \ \cdot \cdot \ \cdot f \ \cdot \cdot \ \cdot)$

(dhīna  dhā  tirakiṭa  dhā  dhīnā)
(dhā  tirakiṭa  dhā  dhīnā  tīnā)
(tīnā  tā  tirakiṭa  dhā  dhīnā)
(dhā  tirakiṭa  dhā  dhīnā  tīnā)

The sixteen quarter-beats in each phrase are grouped as follows in the words:

(4  2  4  2  4)
(2  4  2  4  4)
(4  2  4  2  4)
(2  4  2  4  4)

The mappings given here are not exhaustive but only indicative of the principles on which the oral notational system is constructed. It is readily seen that in a performing-art context, the oral notational scheme offers many advantages – especially for percussion playing. The patterns are internalized as recallable texts, and the actualizing of the rhythms with the hands is quite analogous to paralinguistic gesturings that accompany speech. Also, other performance indicators such as speed, intensity, manner of finger contact, and so on, can be mapped onto and expressed through the prosodic aspects of the recitation of the text. In this sense, this oral notational scheme, while retaining a simple form, is capable of specifying a desired performance more comprehensively and precisely than the written version.

A somewhat analogous (although possibly not a complete) oral notational system, called Sollu-Kattu, has been evolved for specifying the foot work in the classical Bharatnatyam dance performance. This and other such notational aids to performance evolved within the Indian tradition are yet to be systematically analyzed and studied.

### ACKNOWLEDGMENT

I am greatly indebted to Mr. Ashoka Divakaran for assistance in analyzing the grammar underlying *tabla* playing and for examples of Teen tal patterns (referred to as Bol or Kayda).

*Literacy: characterization and implications* 195

## NOTES

1 See Gonda (1975, pp. 193-7), specifically his analyses of the structure of the Rigvedic hymns under the heading "Similarities and Repetitions." Gonda's discussion of the Vedic corpus – especially the *Rigveda* text – and related exegetic literature in this book is exceptionally encyclopedic. All the details given here are taken from this book.
2 The word-separated text is called *padapatha*. If we denote by "a, b, c, d, e, f, . . ." The sequence of words in the *padapatha*, then three of the more important transformed texts are the following: *kramapatha:* ab, bc, cd, de, ef, . . . ; *jatapatha:* abbaab, bccbbc, . . . ; *ghanapatha:* abbaabccbaabc, bccbbcddcbbcd,. . . .
3 See Gonda (1975, pp. 26-38), where these "appendices and auxiliary literature" are discussed in detail.
4 See Gonda (1975, pp. 39-42). The earliest of the exegeses from a ritualistic viewpoint are contained in the *brahmanas*, associated with the *Rigveda*. Gonda (chap. 8, pp. 339-442) discusses in great detail the interpretative and argumentative style of the *brahmanas*.
5 These are discussed further below. An explicit illustration of a notational scheme for oral-aural use may be found in the Appendix to this chapter.
6 For a more detailed discussion of this mediating role of language behavior, see Narasimhan (1981).
7 Barnes (1982, p. 86) sums up the Greek influence as follows: "An account of Aristotle's intellectual afterlife would be little less than a history of European thought. . . . even those radical thinkers who were determined to reject Aristotelian views found themselves doing so in Aristotelian language." See also the relevant essays in Finley (1984) for more detailed discussions.
8 See Cressy (1983) for a discussion of such feedback in the historical context in England and New England.
9 It is well known that picture writing preceded the invention of script-based writing systems. For a detailed discussion see Gelb (1952).
10 A comprehensive account may be found in Eisenstein (1979). See also Clanchy (1983) for somewhat differing views on the role of printing technology in Europe.
11 For a review of the achievements of the Indian grammatical tradition see Scharfe (1977). Scharfe notes the influence of the Indian conceptualizations and formalizations in the study of phonetics on modern European phonetics. In earlier times the Indian ideas seem to have influenced the Chinese in the East and the Arabs in the West.
12 This is most readily seen in the case of mathematical notations. It is extremely unlikely that mathematics in the West would have made much progress if a two-dimensional symbolic notation had not been devised for routine use. Consider, for example, the power of matrix and tensor notations, and the cumbersomeness and difficulties caused by the need to write these out in a strictly linear mode for purposes of computer programming.

13 See the fascinating account by Yates (1966) of the "art of memory" in the Western European tradition based on visual–spatial mapping techniques. She discusses the continuous elaboration of these techniques starting from 500 B.C. in Greece and relates such efforts to seventeenth-century attempts at constructing universal languages. These visual–spatial mnemotechnics contrast sharply with the oral–aural mnemotechnics developed within the Indian tradition.

14 The works by Clanchy, Cressy, and Eisenstein already referred to are of immediate relevance here. Pacey (1974) gives an informative account of the sociocultural background to the development of technology in Western Europe and discusses the concerns with education and training in this context. Yates (1966) relates the "art of memory" to later concerns with "method." Stock (1983) traces the connection between the growth of textual communities and efforts at a scientific understanding of "nature" in the late Middle Ages in Europe.

REFERENCES

Barnes, J. (1982). *Aristotle*. Past Masters Series. Oxford University Press.
Clanchy, M. T. (1979). *From memory to written record: England 1066–1307*. London: Arnold.
  (1983). Looking back from the invention of printing. In D. P. Resnick (ed.), *Literacy in historical perspective* (pp. 7–22). Washington, D.C.: Library of Congress.
Cressy, D. (1983). The environment for literacy: Accomplishments and context in 17th century England and New England. In D. P. Resnick (ed.), *Literacy in historical perspective* (pp. 23–42). Washington, D.C.: Library of Congress.
Eisenstein, E. L. (1979). *The printing press as an agent of change*, 2 vols. Cambridge University Press.
Finley, M. (1984). *The legacy of Greece: A new appraisal*. Oxford University Press.
Gelb, I. J. (1952). *A study of writing*. Chicago: University of Chicago Press.
Gonda, J. (1975). *Vedic literature: Saṃhitās and brāhmaṇas*. In J. Gonda (ed.), *A history of Indian literature* (Vol. 1, Fas. 1). Wiesbaden: Harrassowitz.
Goody, J. (1977). *The domestication of the savage mind*. Cambridge University Press.
Goody, J., & Watt, I. (1962). The consequences of literacy. *Comparative Studies in Society and History* 5:304–45.
Gough, K. (1968). Implications of literacy in traditional China and India. In J. Goody (ed.), *Literacy in traditional societies*. Cambridge University Press.
Havelock, E. A. (1963). *Preface to Plato*. Cambridge, Mass.: Harvard University Press.
  (1982). *The literate revolution in Greece and its cultural consequences*. Princeton, N.J.: Princeton University Press.
Narasimhan, R. (1981). *Modelling language behaviour*. Series on Language and Communication, Vol. 10. Berlin: Springer.

Olson, D. R. (1977). From utterance to text: The bias of language in speech and writing. *Harvard Educational Review* 47:257–81.
(1986). The cognitive consequences of literacy. *Canadian Psychology* 27:109–21.
Ong, W. J. (1982). *Orality and literacy*. London: Methuen.
Pacey, A. (1974). *The maze of ingenuity*. London: Lane.
Ranade, A. (1984). *On music and musicians of Hindoostan*. New Delhi: Promilla.
Scharfe, H. (1977). *Grammatical literature*. In J. Gonda (ed.), *A history of Indian literature* (Vol. 5, Fas. 2). Wiesbaden: Harrassowitz.
Scribner, S., & Cole, M. (1981). *The psychology of literacy*. Cambridge, Mass.: Harvard University Press.
Stock, B. (1983). *The implications of literacy*. Princeton, N.J.: Princeton University Press.
Yates, F. A. (1966). *The art of memory*. London: Routledge & Kegan Paul.

# 12
## The separation of words and the physiology of reading
PAUL SAENGER

The activity of reading, like any human activity, has had a historical development (Saenger, 1982; Chartier, 1986; Boureau et al., 1987, pp. 7–18, 191–227). Because particular cognitive processes enable today's reader to decipher the written page, it should not be assumed that these same cognitive activities have been used throughout human history. It is also clear that the format in which written thought has been presented to the reader to be deciphered has undergone many changes to reach the form that the modern reader now views as immutable and nearly universal. Contemporary evidence for the first of these assertions can be drawn from the observation of diverse cultures throughout the world in which literate men and women use different cognitive skills to read written and printed text. These skills vary as the format of text itself varies from culture to culture.

The different cognitive skills required for the decoding of text reflect, on a more profound level, a variety of physiological processes that readers in different civilizations have employed to extract meaning from the written or printed page. Two factors intrinsic to all read documents determine the nature of these physiological processes and, in turn, the type of pedagogy by which individuals are taught to read in each culture. The first is the structure of the language in which the text has been composed and set down (Meillet, 1938). For example, the frequency of polysyllabic words, the absence or presence of inflection, and the absence or presence of conventions for word order all have ramifications on the requisite mental capacities required for the decoding of both oral and written languages (Meillet, 1921/1938, pp. 601ff.; 1923/1938, pp. 246ff.; Vendryes, 1921). The second factor is the way the language is transcribed, by which I mean the full range of graphic conventions used for its representation. It is the latter that forms the central focus of this chapter.

The conventions for the transcription of language are quasi-independent from linguistic structure. Languages that are linguistically closely related frequently have, over the course of history, been transcribed by radically disparate forms of notation. Examples of this phenomenon are numerous among the languages of the world today. Chinese and Vietnamese, languages closely related in origin and structure, have historically been transcribed by radically different systems of writing (Reischauer & Fairbank, 1973, pp. 39–44; Alleton, 1970). Chinese has since earliest times been transcribed logographically while Vietnamese, since the seventeenth century, has been transcribed phonetically, using a version of the Roman alphabet employed according to conventions first introduced by Italian and Portuguese Jesuit missionaries (Cohen et al., 1963, pp. 47, 319). Thus, to engage in a study of the history of reading, the scholar must take into account the discrete historical developments of both the structure and transcription of language. The primary sources for writing the history of reading are not simply the texts of the past, the literary abstractions that are the record of language itself, but also the artifacts that have conveyed texts and that form the primary documents for the conventions of transcription. Specifically, the historian of reading in the West must examine not only the modern editions of texts but also the rolls, codices, lapidary inscriptions, and paintings or the photographs and microfilms of the objects that preserve texts in their original state. For this purpose, institutions, like the great national libraries of Western Europe and the Institut de recherche et d'histoire des textes in Paris, which collect not only the printed editions but also photographs of the artifacts that have transmitted texts, offer unique, invaluable, and indeed essential resources in the quest of reconstructing the history of reading.

If ancient and medieval books and documents as artifacts are the primary source material for the history of transcription, the research conducted by modern psychologists in transcultural comparative reading provides important analytical techniques for the interpretation of this corpus of source material. For example, laboratory experiments and clinical studies have strongly suggested that the reading of Chinese requires for the identification of Chinese character-morphemes a somewhat different allocation of cerebral functions between the left and right hemispheres of the brain than that used for word recognition by readers of Western European and Oriental phonetic scripts (Ehri, 1980; Tzeng & Hung, 1980; Taylor & Taylor, 1983, pp. 71–4, 245). It has been observed that because of the structure of the Chinese language and the direct morpheme–image correspondence characteristic of Chinese logographs, readers of Chinese, at least for the reading of single syllabic words, which constitute over fifty percent of those in normal use, have a direct visual access to the meaning of the word without the mediation of either physical or mental phonic articulation (Tzeng & Hung, 1981; Taylor & Taylor,

1983, pp. 34–5, 45, 52–3, 226). This capacity for direct visual access to meaning, while it plays a role in the reading of modern European languages, is less systematically exploited than in Chinese and is itself a phenomenon resulting from an historical evolution that began with a format of the Latin written antithetical to such a mode of reading (Vachek, 1973, pp. 12–13, 55; Taylor & Taylor, 1983, p. 107).[1] Parallel research in the discipline of educational psychology indicates that the Chinese graphic tradition of logograms provides optimal conditions for rapid lexical access and allows for the development of silent reading in China at an earlier age than in the West. As an apparent consequence, skilled adult Chinese readers are able to achieve a proficiency in silent reading unequaled in modern Occidental languages (Gray, 1956; Taylor & Taylor, 1983, p. 138).

The relationship between the cognitive skills characterizing reading in a given national or ethnic tradition and the conventions of graphic representation has been further elucidated by experiments conducted in Japan. In contrast to Chinese, Japanese has a dual structure of transcription, one logographic (*kanji*) and one phonetic (*kana*) (Sakamoto & Makita, 1973; Taylor, 1980; Taylor & Taylor, 1983, pp. 77–91). A Japanese text may be transcribed pictographically using Chinese logograms or phonetically using *kana* or syllabary characters. Clinical studies of Japanese patients with cerebral lesions have identified individuals apparently unable to read either ideographic or syllabic transcriptions depending on which areas of the brain had been affected (Sakamoto & Makita, 1973, 1981; Meodell, 1981; Paivio & Begg, 1981; Renzi, 1982, pp. 18–19; Taylor & Taylor, 1983, pp. 73–4; Hasuike, Tzeng, & Hung, 1986, pp. 275–88).[2] This correlation, if it is correct, implies that the cerebral processes necessary for decoding ideograms, as opposed to phonetic transcriptions, have physiologically distinct loci within the brain. Furthermore, it suggests the existence of discrete mechanisms of decoding with different allocations of cognitive resources for the reading of different kinds of script. Evidence also suggests that the right hemisphere plays a more active role in reading scripts in which each word has a discrete word image. The recent introduction of proton emission tomography scanners, which allow technicians to observe the inner workings of the brain during cognitive activities, may one day explain much more precisely the differences in hemispheric functions that result from different conventions of graphic transcription (Phelps, 1983; Phelps & Maziotta, 1985).

Abundant examples exist of modification in reading pedagogy based on the differing reading skills required for the deciphering of particular languages. In general, graphic systems that eliminate or reduce the need for a cognitive process prior to lexical access facilitate the early adaptation of young readers to silent reading, while written languages that are more ambiguous necessitate the manipulation of phonetic components to construct words. These latter graphic systems require a longer training period in which oral reading and rote memorization play a prominent role, enduring even into adulthood. First, in the dual system of transcription used for Japanese, syllabic characters, limited in number, are used to instruct young children (Sakamoto & Makita 1973; cf. Wang, 1981). The exclusive use of a syllabary method of presenting text to novice readers, necessitating the oral reconstruction of words from their phonetic components by means of a limited set of cues corresponding to sounds, makes this mode of transcription preferable, in the initial phase of elementary education, to the use of a logographic system in which the much larger number of Chinese word characters is required.

However, the Japanese syllabary transcriptions contain no word separation and impose on the young reader the formidable burden of word recognition through the synthetic reconstruction of words from initially ambiguous phonic signs offering no distinction between word and syllabic boundaries. To aid the young Japanese reader, group oral recitation is an essential aspect of elementary reading instruction (Sakamoto & Makita, 1973). As the young reader progresses, he soon begins to read more difficult texts that are increasingly transcribed in Chinese characters, and syllabary transcription is relegated to a secondary role. The prevalence of Chinese characters in these more difficult texts is predicated on the greater mnemonic capacity of a physically more mature reader to retain lexical images. The infusion of logographs also, in effect, divides many, if not all, Japanese words for the reader and largely eliminates the task of word reconstruction based on a synthetic combination of phonetic elements (Sakamoto & Makita, 1973; Taylor & Taylor, 1983, pp. 70, 114). The increased presence of Chinese characters accompanies the transition to rapid silent reading and is particularly efficacious for reference reading by which I mean the rapid perusal of text in the quest for specific information (Sakamoto & Makita, 1973, pp. 440–65). The skills associated with reference reading are characteristic of advanced civilizations in both Occident and Orient. Thus, a blend of syllabary and logographic transcription in the Japanese language allows pedagogues to lead pupils in a smooth transition from an oral mode of reading, suitable to young readers but irksome to adults, to one that, while still making use of the initially learned syllabary decoding skills, is better suited to the rapid silent reading required of experienced readers in a modern industrial society. This more efficient mode of reading is, however, too difficult for young readers to master in the initial phase of instruction.

Another graphic tradition in which oralization as a cognitive activity preliminary to word recognition is more important for young readers than it is in modern English is that of modern Hebrew (Feitelson, 1973). In Hebrew, the similarity in the form of many characters, even in the presence of both vowels and regular spacing, makes word recognition by word shape, especially for young readers, more difficult than in languages transcribed with Roman characters. As a result, Israeli educators in the 1960s came to reject the emphasis on the global recognition of words as images. This technique had been borrowed from the Anglo-Saxon and Danish "whole-word method" of reading instruction where it had been effective because of the large number of silent letters and letter combinations in these languages, which on the one hand help to distinguish the entire word and on the other hinder consistent decoding of a word through the synthesis of phonetic cues (Feitelson, 1973, p. 434).[3]

The vernacular languages of India provide yet another example of a modern graphic tradition in which oral processes are more important for achieving lexical access than in the modern languages of Western Europe (Commen, 1972). In Hindi, syllabic characters accompanied by vowels are admirably suited for accurate transcription of the component sounds of words, but because of the similarity of numerous signs, the Indian characters fail to bestow upon each word a unique and unequivocal global image even when they are set off by interword space as they are in modern script and printed books. This ambiguity in transcription has resulted in a pedagogical tradition for young readers that stresses synthetic reading, oral recitation, and rote memorization of texts. In India, recitation from memory while holding an open book is an activity commonly regarded as a form of reading. Still another and historically more pertinent example is Liberia, where the Vai ethnic and linguistic group use a form of phonetic syllabary transcription, which originated as an attempt to emulate the written documents of Portuguese explorers of the sixteenth century, but which subsequently developed as an autonomous written language in total isolation from European or Arabic influence (Scribner & Cole, 1981). In Vai, we find the rare instance of a modern language, polysyllabic in its structure, transcribed syllabically without word separation, punctuation, or the presence of initial capital forms. The general appearance of a page of Vai script, therefore, strikingly resembles the opening of an ancient Greek or Roman roll or codex written in *scriptura continua* (Steffens, 1929; Ullman, 1969). In both the ancient Greek and Roman books and in Vai, the reader encounters, at the first glance, rows of discrete phonetic symbols that first have to be manipulated within the mind to form properly articulated and accented entities equivalent to words. In all three languages, the phonetic components of words have at best only limited consistent meanings. In a written language such as Vai, requiring extensive activity of a phonetic character prior to understanding a word's meaning, it is not surprising to find that oral recitation not only forms an important part of elementary reading instruction but also, in the form of mumbling and sounding out a text, is a normal part of the habits of experienced adult readers. In this respect, the reading habits of the Vai people and of the ancient Greeks and Romans reflect similar modes of decoding polysyllabic languages written in unseparated script. In historically unrelated circumstances, similar reading processes exploit common cerebral structures and mental capacities, which have remained biologically unchanged during the brief period of recorded civilization, to resolve analogous forms of graphic ambiguity (Saenger, 1982).

The correlation between the propensity to read aloud and the threshold in the duration of cognitive activity needed to achieve lexical access is a recurrent phenomenon in reading in various cultures that is in need of further elucidation, historically on the basis of literary evidence and experimentally in the laboratory and in anthropological on-site investigation. It is evident that modern readers would consider a script written without word separation to be exceedingly difficult to decipher. Indeed, to most modern readers, the idea of reading lines of script without word separation is unimaginable. The experiments performed on English-speaking readers confirm that the suppression or obfuscation of spatial boundaries between words is one factor that both slows down reading and encourages vocal and subvocal activity (Sokolov, 1972). Specifically, laboratory tests show that the suppression of space between words causes a reduced field of vision or tunnel vision in adults characterized by eye movements similar to children who have not yet mastered the techniques for the silent rapid perusal of text (Fisher, 1976, pp. 417–55). Readers under these conditions also experience a radically reduced span of peripheral vision, the field in which preliminary details of words or letters can be recognized (Levin & Addis, 1979, p. 42). The phenomenon of a generally reduced visual field can be precisely observed by measuring the eye–voice span, the variable quantity of text that a reader has decoded but not yet pronounced at any given moment during oral reading. Laboratory tests also show that without spaces to use for guideposts, the reader needs more than twice the normal quantity of fixations per line of printed text. The reader of unseparated printed text also requires a quantity of ocular regressions for which there is no parallel under normal reading conditions in order to verify that the words have been correctly separated (Fisher, 1976, pp. 422–3, 426). The reader's success in finding a reasonably appropriate meaning acts as a final test that the separation has been accurately performed.

To understand the processing significance of interword space, it is useful to think in terms of an analogy to a computer program written to verify correct spelling. For such programs, the use of a typed space to signify word termination is an essential component. A program to correct orthography, were it to be written so as to be applicable to text written without word separation, would be infinitely more complex, for it would have to incorporate a thesaurus of licet syllables and syllable divisions as well as syntactical, grammatical, and contextual constraints for controlling all the phonetically plausible, but inappropriate points for dividing continuous text. All artificial reading devices make use of space as a fundamental cue, and it is improbable that current technology could produce a machine capable of the oral pronunciation of unseparated text. However, the brain of the ancient reader confronting unseparated script had to perform precisely these tasks, which modern readers are no longer called upon to perform and which are even deemed too difficult and laborious for the computer.

Psychologists specializing in experimentation involving unseparated text concede that a reader who habitually read unseparated writing might adapt to some extent and improve his reading rates over time. However, they maintain that the increased ocular fixations and the regressions would always be required to compensate for an inherently more difficult cognitive activity (Senders, Fisher, & Monty, 1978; Downing & Leong, 1982, p. 33). Of necessity, the radically reduced field of vision and increased number of fixations implies that the quantity of written text perceived at each of the reader's fixations is proportionately reduced. This reduction in the length of each unit of textual intake means that at the end of each fixation, the reader's memory retains in place of the coded images of the contours of one, two, or three words, as is customary when reading modern separated text, the phonic trace of series of syllables, the boundaries of which themselves need identification and verification. These syllables sometimes correspond to monosyllabic or bisyllabic words or sense-conveying syllabic prefixes or suffixes, but especially in intellectually difficult texts (like those of ancient Greece and Rome that were typically written with longer words), they frequently correspond to syllabic fragments of words of which both the termination and the sense are apt to remain uncertain during the moment between ocular saccades. This ambiguity was increased by ancient grammatical structures that, relying on inflection, lacked conventional word order and frequently failed to group words that were syntactically related. In these circumstances, the ancient reader in daily life reacted by reading orally because both overt physical pronunciation and, to a lesser extent, covert slow mental pronunciation aid the reader to retain a series of phonemes of ambiguous meaning (Taylor & Taylor, 1983, pp. 227–32). Oral activity thus helped the reader to hold in short-term memory that fraction of a word or phrase that had already been decoded phonetically while the cognitive task of syllable and word recognition necessary for understanding the sense of the initial fragment proceeds through the decoding of the subsequent section of text (Chartier, 1986, p. 126).[4] In this manner ancient readers of unseparated writing were able to retain and understand a section of written text in a fashion somewhat comparable to that which modern silent readers of separated text can retain visually. But given the processing constraints of his medium, there existed no incentive for the ancient reader to suppress the exterior voice in reading, for such a conscious effort, even if it did not interfere with the mnemonic function of some mature readers, could not greatly increase the speed of the reading process. Thus, Ambrose when he read silently could not, given the constraints of ancient writing, have read in the manner of the modern silent reader. When the ancients read silently, they did so to enhance their privacy by concealing the content of what they were reading and not to enhance reading speed (Balogh, 1926–7, pp. 92–3, 100–101; Pugh, 1973; Levin & Addis, 1979, p. 25).

Thus, the unimaginable idea of reading without the benefit of word separation an ancient classical language text, with all its inherent grammatical and syntactical complexities, was in fact a reality. Specialists of antique and early medieval culture have long known that for over a millennium, Latin and Greek texts were written without word separation, and as has been suggested, the ancient techniques for deciphering the unseparated texts were consonant with the physiological constraints that laboratory experimentation tells us such unseparated text imposed. It was the very absence of word boundaries that made the technique of the identification and memorization of those sequences of letters that represented licit syllables a fundamental aspect of both ancient and medieval pedagogy. The only way in which ancient scribes aided the reader in the task of grasping letters for syllable recognition was by regularly placing relatively more space between letters than is customary for medieval or modern handwritten or printed separated text.[5]

A modern equivalent of the ancient technique of oral reading by syllables is found among children who are just learning to read. The widely observed phenomenon of lip movement by young readers is the continuation of a habit that originated because the child initially pronounced words orally syllable by syllable in order to gain access to their meaning. Laboratory measurements of the eye–voice span of beginning readers indicates that the number of characters perceived during each of their more numerous ocular fixations often falls within the limits of longer words. This observation confirms that oralization aids readers with narrow fields of vision in the process of reconstituting words from their phonetic components. When these young readers are obliged to read silently, many encounter difficulties in comprehension. The suppression of interword space, however, does not affect such readers. The pattern of their ocular movements, unlike those of proficient adult readers, remains unchanged by the absence of cues whose use has not been mastered (Levin & Kaplan, 1970, p. 119). The fact that publishers of textbooks for beginning readers place more interletter and interline space in texts intended to be read orally by beginning readers, in a fashion somewhat analogous to ancient scribes, is a graphic indication of a profound similitude between the reading habits of young readers and those of adult readers in ancient times (Tinker, 1965). However, unlike in ancient books, the spaces between words, which are always present in modern texts, enable young Occidental readers, in a manner analogous to young Japanese readers progressing from syllabary characters to ideographs, to readily evolve from reading skills based on a synthetic recognition of words through their syllabic components to the global recognition of the word as an entire unit with a single meaning and pronunciation. Such a possibility for cognitive evolution was not offered to ancient readers, whose reading habits by virtue of the medium in which they read remained arrested at a subword level.

The uninterrupted writing of ancient *scriptura continua* was only possible in the context of a writing system that had a complete set of signs for the unambiguous transcription of pronounced speech. This occurred for the first time in Indo-European languages when the Greeks adapted the Phoenician alphabet and added symbols for vowels. The Graeco-Latin alphabetical scripts, employing vowels with varying degrees of modification, were used for the transcription of the old forms of Romance, Germanic, Slavic, and Hindu tongues, all members of the Indo-European language group in which words were polysyllabic and inflected. For these Indo-European languages, the reader's immediate identification of words was not essential for the type of reading they engaged in, but the reasonably swift identification of syllables was fundamental for the comprehension of text (Adams, 1981, p. 197–221). These graphic systems were based on consistent and sufficient codes for sounds that different readers would construe in the same way because vowels permitted the reader to identify syllables swiftly. Before the introduction of vowels to the Phoenician alphabet, all the ancient languages of the Mediterranean world, whether syllabic or alphabetical, Semitic or Indo-European, were written with word separation by either space, points, or both in conjunction (Cohen, 1958; Wingo, 1972). After the introduction of vowels, space between words was no longer necessary to eliminate an unacceptable level of ambiguity.

In the antique Mediterranean world, there existed a direct historical correlation between the achievement of unambiguous reproduction of the sounds of speech through the use of vowels and the adoption of *scriptura continua*. The ancient writings of Mesopotamia, Phoenicia, and Israel invariably contained separation, for, lacking vowels, had the spaces between words been deleted and the signs written in the format of *scriptura continua*, the resulting visual presentation of the text would have been analogous to today's lexogrammatical puzzles. Such written languages might have been decipherable, given conventions for syntax, closely defined rules of grammar, conventions for word order, and contextual clues, but only after such extensive cognitive activity prior to lexical access as to make reading as we know it impractical. While the very earliest Greek inscriptions were written with separation by interpuncts, Greece soon thereafter became the first ancient civilization to employ *scriptura continua* (Lejeune, 1954, p. 429; Harder, 1960, p. 101). The Romans, who borrowed their letter forms and vowels from the Greeks, maintained the earlier Mediterranean tradition of separating words by points far longer than the Greeks, but they too, after a scantily documented period of six centuries, substituted *scriptura continua* for separated script in the decades preceding A.D. 200. In Hebrew, the introduction of vowels in the manuscripts of the High Middle Ages resulted in the evolution of unseparated medieval Masoretic script, modeled on the unseparated writing of the contemporary Latin West (Gottwald, 1959, pp. 40–8). In India, the Brahmi syllabary alphabet, whose ultimate relationship to ancient Greek is uncertain, but whose Mideast origin appears likely, incorporated vowels that consequently permitted Sanskrit to be transcribed in its own form of *scriptura continua* (Basham, 1959, 394–9; Filliozat, 1963, 147–66). The various vernacular dialects transcribed in writing derived from the Greek, including Coptic, Glagolitic, and Cyrillic, and from Sanskrit also have long medieval traditions originating in antiquity of transcription without intratextual space. In contrast, the Semitic languages when written without vowels, notably Hebrew, Aramaic, Arabic, and Syriac, were always written with word separation in antiquity and continued to be so transcribed into modern times with, however, the quantity and even the mode of separation varying according to the epoch.

The parallel development of vocalic writing without separation and consonantal transcription with separation seems at first glance to be paradoxical, and this dual phenomenon has long puzzled students of the history of writing who have condemned the dominance of *scriptura continua* in late antiquity as a retrograde development in human history. From the modern point of view, it does seem inexplicable that two modes for facilitating lexical access, the use of vowels and word separation, were not combined at an early date to form a hybrid method of transcription that would have had many of the redundant cues for word recognition that characterize the modern separated written page. However, in contradiction to our expectation, the Roman Empire, which for a time enjoyed the widespread if not universal use of separated script with vowels, chose to discard that form of writing for *scriptura continua*.

The failure to achieve a lasting hybridization of separated consonantal script with unseparated vocalic script in any of the ancient Indo-European languages cannot be explained away by the ignorance of the scribes in one language of the conventions of the other, for the survival of numerous bilingual papyri fragments clearly suggests that the Romans, the Greeks, and the Hebrews were in late antiquity aware of each other's differing graphic traditions including word separation (Wingo, 1972, p. 15). The answer to our query lies rather in an analysis of the unique features of ancient reading habits and the social context in which ancient reading and writing took place. Stated summarily, the ancient world did not possess the desire, characteristic of modern civilizations, to make reading easier and swifter because the advantages, which the modern world perceives as accruing from easier reading – the swift effective retrieval of information in reference consultation, the ability to read swiftly a great many difficult technical, logical, and scientific texts, and the greater diffusion of literacy throughout all social strata of the population – were never or seldom viewed as advantages by the ancients.[6]

As we have seen, the reading habits of the ancient world were profoundly oral and rhetorical by taste as well as by necessity and were focused on a limited and intensely scrutinized canon of literature. Precisely because those who read aloud relished the mellifluous sounds of pronounced text and were not interested in the swift intrusive consultation of books, the absence of interword space in Greek and Latin was not perceived to be an impediment to effective reading as it would be to the modern reader who strives to read swiftly (Balogh, 1926–7, pp. 84–109, 202–40). Moreover, the oralization, which the ancients savored esthetically, provided mnemonic compensation through enhanced short-term recall for the difficulty in gaining access to the meaning of unseparated text. Long-term memory of frequently read-aloud texts also compensated for the inherent graphic and grammatical ambiguities of the languages of late antiquity. The notion that the greater portion of the population should be autonomous and self-motivated readers was entirely foreign to the elitist literate mentality of the ancient world. For the literate, the reaction of the difficulties of lexical access arising from *scriptura continua* did not spark the desire to make script easier to decipher, but resulted instead in the delegation of the labor of reading and writing to skilled slaves who acted as professional readers. It is in the context of a society with an abundant supply of highly skilled intellectual slave labor that the profoundly different ancient attitudes toward reading must be comprehended and the ready and pervasive acceptance of the suppression of word separation throughout the Roman Empire understood; for, even during the period when the Romans separated words by interpuncts sometimes accompanied by space and the Greeks did not, the philosopher Seneca viewed this difference in graphic presentation to be a result of differing styles of oratorical delivery. He attributed the Roman use of the interpunct to the Latin emphasis on rhythmically measured prose and expressive oral delivery of written text in contrast to what he deemed the gushing quality of Greek rhetoric. In this way, he curiously suggested that interpuncts slowed the reader's cadence rather than augmenting the speed of decoding (Seneca, *Epistulae* 40.11).

However, a century after Seneca's death in A.D. 65, the global image of the Roman page was to become increasingly similar to that of Greek, when the Romans gave up separation by interpuncts and adapted the Greek convention of *scriptura continua*. The similarity of the Greek and Roman page was further enhanced by the adoption of uncial script, which was an emulation, if not in its specific *ducti*, at least of the general visual impression of unseparated Greek script that subsequent paleographers have also labeled uncial. The Romans, however, were reluctant to emulate other Greek practices that helped the Greek reader to control unseparated text. Foliation and pagination, not uncommon in Greek papyri, seem never to have been employed by the Romans, and paragraphing was received into Latin only with hesitancy and then confined to certain genres of texts (Lehmann, 1936, pp. 333–61, 411–42; Turner, 1977, p. 75). At the end of antiquity, in both Greek and Latin texts, intratextual space had ceased entirely to serve as a code to separate words and had become instead an occasionally used code for the punctuation of texts. Most late Roman and Greek texts were written totally without intratextual space or other sign of punctuation (Müller, 1964).

The absence of interword space and interpunctuation at the end of antiquity was a reflection of the particular relationship of the antique reader to the book. The reintroduction of word separation in the early Middle Ages by Irish and Anglo-Saxon scribes marks a dramatic change in that relationship. It is, therefore, the introduction of word separation that constitutes the great divide in the history of reading between antique cultures and those of the modern Occident. It is clear from the evidence of any Gothic page, chosen at random in a northern European university book of the thirteenth century, that for Latin, the practice of placing an easily perceptible unit of space between every word, including monosyllabic prepositions, pronouns, conjunctions, and enclitic particles was the norm of scholastic culture. The examination of Greek texts copied in the medieval West, in Italy in the fifteenth century, and in Greece in the second half of the sixteenth century reveals how the separation of words originated in Greek manuscripts copied by Irish and Anglo-Saxon scribes and became standard practice in Renaissance Italy and France before becoming normal in Byzantium for both the written and printed page (Cohen et al., 1963, pp. 180–1).[7] In the Slavic languages, written in the Cyrillic alphabet, word separation became standard only at the beginning of the seventeenth century (Vallant, 1963, pp. 301–12). For the Indian languages devolving from Sanskrit, word separation seems to have become standard only in the modern period (Burnell, 1878, p. XXXIIb).

While the general chronological configuration of the geographic dissemination of word separation throughout the world of the Indo-European languages is apparent, it is still not known when and by what route word separation, rejected by the literate culture of late antiquity, came to be the unfailing hallmark of the written Latin of the central Middle Ages where it also provided the model for the quantity of space used to separate Hebrew and Arabic and for the ultimate reintroduction of separation into Greek. Clearly during the course of the eight centuries following Rome's fall, the task of separating written text, which had been for half a millennium a cognitive function of the reader, became instead the task of the scribe. But how and when did this change fundamental to the history of reading transpire? Its importance was great, for the introduction of word separation freed the intellectual faculties of the reader, permitting him to read all texts silently and, therefore, more swiftly and in particular to understand greater numbers of intellectually more difficult texts with greater ease. Word separation, by altering the physiology of reading and thereby simplifying the reading process, enabled the reader to simultaneously perceive the meaning of the text and the coded information pertaining to its grammatical, musical, and intellectual interpretation.[8] For these reasons, separated written text became the standard medium of written communication of a civilization characterized by superior intellectual rigor. Because of both its intrinsic intellectual advantages and its allure as a sign of a civilization marked by a high order of intellectual attainment, word separation was emulated first by non-Latin languages within Eastern Europe, then in the Near East, and finally in South Asia. The acceptance of word separation within the Latin culture of the Middle Ages, which originated in northern Europe in the regions most remote from the center of Roman Imperial civilization, gradually became the standard medium for all the written Indo-European languages in the modern epoch.

NOTES

1 An example of French would be à and a, and où and ou, in which distinctions of word meaning are conveyed by unpronounced grave accent marks. In English, certain variations in spelling and silent spellings denote ideas directly (Vachek, 1973). The number of words more explicit in their graphic form than in their pronunciation is far inferior to written Chinese (Taylor & Taylor, 1983).
2 The transcription of English into braille also results in an apparent redistribution of cerebral functions (De Renzi, 1982). Recent research suggests that a crude model of right hemisphere reading for idiographic script and left hemisphere reading for syllable and alphabetical scripts is inadequate (Hasuike, Tzeng, & Hung, 1986).
3 For the similarity of Danish and English pedagogy, see the contribution of Mogen Jansen in Feitelson (1973).
4 The ancients complained about such unexpressive reading in which the reader's voice betrayed he had not grasped the meaning of words before pronouncing them. In early modern Europe, peasants and other members of the lower classes have frequently been described in literature and represented in paintings as reading aloud in order to understand. See the lines of Labiche's *La cagnotte* cited by Chartier (1986).
5 The space contained within the letter O provides a useful unit of measurement for comparing interletter space in ancient and modern script.
6 The most fundamental of reference tools, the dictionary, was absent in Roman and Greek antiquity, although glossaries existed in China from ancient times.

7 This generalization is based on an examination of the photograph of the Greek manuscript collections in the Bibliothèque Nationale.
8 The ancient Romans had no musical notation. The birth and spread of medieval music notation is closely related to the introduction of word separation.

## REFERENCES

Adams, M. J. (1981). What good is orthographic redundancy? In O. Tzeng & H. Singer, *Perception of print: Reading research in experimental psychology.* Hillsdale, N.J.: Erlbaum.
Alleton, V. (1970). *L'écriture chinoise,* 3rd ed. Paris: Presses Universitaires de France.
Balogh, J. (1926–7). Voces paginarum. *Philologus 82.*
Basham, A. L. (1959). *The wonder that was India.* New York: Grove.
Boureau, A., Chartier, R., Docreux, M.-E., Jouhavd, C., Saenger, P., & Velay-Vallantin, C. (1987). *Les usages de l'imprimé: XV$^e$-XIX$^e$ siècle.* Paris: Fayard.
Burnell, A. C. (1878). *Elements of south-Indian palaeography.* London: Trābner.
Chartier, R. (1986). Les pratiques de l'écrit. *Histoire de la vie privée: tome 3, De la Renaissance aux Lumières.* Paris: Seuil.
Cohen, M. (1958). *La grande invention de l'écriture et son évolution.* Paris: Klincksieck.
Cohen, M., et al. (1963). *L'écriture et la psychologie des peuples.* Centre International de synthèse, XXII$^e$ semaine de synthèse. Paris: Colin.
Commen, C. (1972). India. In J. Downing, (ed.), *Comparative reading: Cross national studies of behavior in reading and writing.* New York: Macmillan.
De Renzi, E. (1982). *Disorders of space exploration and cognition.* New York: Wiley.
Downing, J., & Leong, C. K. (1982). *Psychology of reading.* New York: Macmillan.
Ehri, L. (1980). The role of orthographic images in learning printed words. In J. F. Kavanagh & R. L. Venezky, *Orthography, reading and dyslexia.* Baltimore: University Park Press.
Feitelson, D. (1973). Israel. In J. Downing, *Comparative reading: Cross national studies of behavior in reading and writing.* New York: Macmillan.
Filliozat, J. (1963). Les écritures indiennes: Le monde indien et son système graphique. In M. Cohen (ed.), *L'écriture et la psychologie des peuples,* Centre International de synthèse, XXII$^e$ semaine de synthèse. Paris: Colin.
Fisher, D. F. (1976). Spatial factors in reading and search: The case for space. In R. A. Monty & J. W. Senders (eds.), *Eye movement and psychological processes.* Hillsdale, N.J.: Erlbaum.
Gottwald, N. K. (1959). *A light to the nations: An introduction to the Old Testament.* New York: Harper & Row.
Gray, W. S. (1956). *The teaching of reading and writing: An international survey* (monograph). Paris: UNESCO.
Harder, R. (1960). *Kleine schriften.* Munich: Beck.

Hasuike, R., Tzeng, O., & Hung, D. (1986). Script effects and cerebral lateralization: The case of Chinese characters. In J. Vaid (ed.), *Language processing in bilinguals: Psycholinguistic and neuropsychological perspectives.* Hillsdale, N.J.: Erlbaum.
Lehmann, P. (1936). Blätter, seiten, spalten, zeilen. *Zentrablatt für Bibliothekswesen* 53:333–61, 411–42.
Lejeune, M. (1954). Review of Marcel Cohen et al. *L'écriture in Revue des études anciennes,* 56:429.
Levin, H., & Addis, A. B. (1979). *The eye-voice span.* Cambridge, Mass.: MIT Press.
Levin, H., & Kaplan, E. L. (1970). Grammatical structure and reading. In H. Levin & J. P. Williams (eds.), *Book studies on reading.* New York: Basic.
Meillet, A (1921/1936–38). Remarques sur la théorie de la phrase. *Journal de Psychologie,* Reprinted in A. Meillet, *Linguistique historique et linguistique générale,* 2. Paris: Champion.
 (1923/1938). Le caractère concret du mot. *Journal de Psychologie,* p. 246. Reprinted in A. Meillet, *Linguistique historique et linguistique générale,* 2. Paris: Champion.
 (1938). *Esquisse d'une histoire de la langue latine* (4th ed.). Paris: Hachette.
Meodell, P. (1981). Dyslexia and normal reading. In G. T. Pavlidis & T. R. Miles (eds.), *Dyslexia research and its applications to education.* New York: Wiley.
Müller, R. W. (1964). *Rhetorische und syntaktische interponkion: Untersuchungen zur pausenbezeichung im antiken Latein.* Inaugural dissertation. Tübingen.
Paivio, A., & Begg, I. (1981). *Psychology of language.* Englewood Cliffs, N.J: Prentice-Hall.
Phelps, M. E. (1983). Position computed tomography for studies of myocardial and cerebral function. *Annals of Internal Medicine* 98:339–59.
Phelps, M. E., & Maziotta, J. C. (1985). Proton emission tomography: Human brain function and biochemistry. *Science* 228:799–809.
Pugh, T. (1973). The development of silent reading. In William Latham, (ed.). *The road to effective reading: Proceedings of the Tenth Annual Study Conference of the United Kingdom Reading Association.* Totley, Thornbridge: Lock.
Reischauer, E. O., & Fairbank, J. K. (1973). *East Asia: Tradition and transformation.* Boston: Houghton Mifflin.
Saenger, P. (1982). Silent reading: Its impact on late medieval script and society. *Viator* 13:367–414.
Sakamoto, T., & Makita, K. (1973). Japan. In J. Downing (ed.), *Comparative reading: Cross national studies of behavior in reading and writing.* New York: Macmillan.
 (1981). Language structure and optimal orthography. In O. Tzeng & H. Singer, *Perception of print: Reading research in experimental psychology.* Hillsdale, N.J.: Erlbaum.
Scribner, S., & Cole, M. (1981). *The psychology of literacy.* Cambridge, Mass.: Harvard University Press.
Senders, J. W., Fisher, D. F., & Monty, R. A. (1978). *Eye movement and higher psychological functions.* Hillsdale, N.J.: Erlbaum.

Seneca, *Epistulae.* 40.11.
Sokolov, A. N. (1972). *Inner speech and thought.* New York: Plenum.
Steffens, F. (1929). *Lateinische paläographie.* Berlin: de Gruyter.
Taylor, I. (1980). The Korean language: An alphabet: A syllabary, a logography? In P. A. Kolers, M. F. Wrolstad, & H. Bauma (eds.), *Processing of visible language* 2. New York: Plenum.
Taylor, I., & Taylor, M. M. (1983). *The psychology of reading.* New York: Academic Press.
Tinker, M. A. (1965). *Bases for effective reading.* Minneapolis: University of Minnesota Press.
Turner, E. G. (1977). *The typology of the early codex.* Philadelphia: University of Pennsylvania Press.
Tzeng, O., & Hung, D. (1980). Reading in a nonalphabetic writing. In J. P. Kavanagh & R. L. Venezky, *Orthography, reading and dyslexia.* Baltimore: University Park Press.
(1981). Linguistic determination: A written language perspective. In O. Tzeng & H. Singer, *Perception of print: Reading research in experimental psychology.* Hillsdale, N.J.: Erlbaum.
Ullman, B. L. (1969). *Ancient writing and its influence.* J. Brown (ed). Cambridge, Mass.: Harvard University Press.
Vachek, J. (1973). *Written language: General problems and problems of English.* The Hague: Mouton.
Vallant, A. (1963). L'écriture cyrillique et son extension. In M. Cohen, *L'écriture et la psychologie des peuples.* Centre International de synthèse, XXII[e] semaine de synthèse. Paris: Colin.
Vendryes, J. (1921). *Le langage: Introduction linguistique à l'histoire.* Paris: Renaissance du Livre.
Wang, W. S.-Y. (1981). Language structure and optimal orthography. In O. J. L. Tzeng & H. Singer, *Perception of print: Reading research in experimental psychology.* Hillsdale, N.J.: Erlbaum.
Wingo, E. O. (1972). *Latin punctuation in the classical age.* The Hague: Mouton.

# 13

# Linguists, literacy, and the intensionality of Marshall McLuhan's Western man

ROBERT J. SCHOLES and BRENDA J. WILLIS

## Linguists

The science of language has, at least in this century, treated language and language users as though orthography had never been invented, limiting and even equating language to speech. The two most influential linguists of the first half of this century, Edward Sapir and Leonard Bloomfield, were clear in their views. Sapir defined language as "a purely human and non-instinctive method of communicating ideas, emotions, and desires by means of a system of voluntarily produced symbols . . . [which] are, in the first instance, auditory" (1921, p. 8). Written language, for Sapir, was clearly secondary and of interest only in that each element of the written system corresponds to an element in the oral system (ibid., pp. 19, 20). Bloomfield was equally disinterested in orthography and literacy, asserting, "Writing is not language, but merely a way of recording language [by which he means, of course, speech] by means of visible marks" (1933, p. 21).

The most influential of contemporary linguists is unarguably Noam Chomsky. While his interests are not affected by limitations on linguistic knowledge of the type discussed below, it is nonetheless true that his repeated characterization of the domain of his grammatical studies as an "ideal speaker-hearer" (e.g., Chomsky, 1965) has done nothing to encourage linguists to consider the contributions of literacy to linguistic competence.

The identification of language with speech continues unchecked and largely unchallenged. At present, the most widely used introductory textbook in linguistics, Fromkin and Rodman's *An Introduction to Language*, equates linguistic knowledge (i.e., one's "grammar") with speech in the following way: "The grammar includes everything speakers know about their language – the sound system, called *phonology*; . . . the rules of word formation, called *morphology*; and the rules of sentence formation, called *syntax*" (1988, p. 17). One of our purposes in this chapter is to show that such claims, as understood by most linguists, are seriously flawed.

Before pursuing this goal, one caveat must be noted. The term "grammar" as used in contemporary linguistics is ambiguous. It refers both to a person's knowledge of language and to a (linguist's) description of that knowledge (see Chomsky & Halle, 1968, p. 3, for an explicit statement of this ambiguity). In the presentation to follow, we will in no way criticize or challenge the ability of a trained linguist to describe a person's knowledge in terms of phonemic, morphemic, and syntactic constructs of whatever type seem most interesting, efficient, or well motivated by considerations of internal consistency. What we do challenge is the accuracy (i.e., the external consistency) of such descriptions for particular knowers of language. In an attempt to avoid confusion, we will try to stick with the term "linguistic competence" when speaking of the knowledge of language possessed by a user and "linguistic description" when speaking of the linguist's characterization of that knowledge.

Given the prevailing attitude among linguists equating linguistic description with the knowledge of language possessed by its speakers, it is not surprising that extensions of their discipline – studies of language acquisition, language impairments due to neurological damage, and the search for behavioral concomitants of linguistic constructs – should maintain this view.

Studies of the acquisition of language, particularly those mapping this development after the age of five (e.g., Palermo & Molfese, 1972), have ignored the role played by the attainment of reading skills and literacy in this process. Where they have been considered in relation to developing linguistic competence, it has generally been assumed that poor reading results from delayed or aberrant oral language acquisition (e.g., Bond, Tinker, Wasson, & Vogel, 1974; Hall & Ramig, 1978; Fletcher, 1981; Wasson, 1984). Few reading specialists appear to have considered the possibility that failure in learning to read may have a limiting effect on the acquisition of oral language (notable and admirable exceptions may be found in Patel, 1981; Ehri, 1985).

Aphasiologists and neurolinguists assign aphasic patients to various linguistically based syndromes (Broca's, Wernicke's, conduction, etc.) on the basis of posttrauma language behavior generally without consideration of the possible effects of pretrauma literacy on such abilities (e.g., Goodglass & Kaplan, 1972; Heilman & Scholes, 1976). Of particular interest in this context is the syndrome known as "agrammatism" (Scholes & Willis, 1984; Kean, 1985). Agrammatism is characterized by an inability to deal (in production or comprehension) with "function words" and inflectional affixes. As will be shown later, the adult illiterate is also agrammatic. (Although such morphemes occur in speech, their syntactic import is not a component of the illiterate's linguistic capability.) As a consequence, we would expect that illiterate aphasics would present with agrammatism no matter what the nature of the neurological damage might be. (For a review of studies that at least recognize literacy as a possible factor in aphasiological analysis, see Lecours & Parente, Chapter 14, this volume.)

The bulk of research in psycholinguistics has been exclusively concerned with the linguistic performance of literate subjects. The justly famous work demonstrating that phonetic continua are perceived in terms of discrete (phonemic) categories (Liberman, Harris, Hofmann, & Griffin, 1957; Fry, 1964) has not (at this date) been attempted with prereading children or nonreading adults despite the fact that we have had reason to doubt that such behavior would obtain in nonreaders since 1964 (Bruce, 1964). The large body of work demonstrating reaction time and/or mnemonic indicators of various aspects of morphology and syntax (see, among many volumes on the subject, Hayes, 1970; Slobin, 1971; Taylor, 1976; McNeill, 1987) is likewise largely limited to studies of literate adults. Given the data on the syntax and morphology of illiterate adults reviewed later it would be suspected that the bulk of psycholinguistic investigation concerns the linguistic performance not of speakers, but of readers.

We will have more to say about each of these areas of language study in the closing sections of this chapter, including some mention of scholars who have acknowledged the role of literacy in language acquisition and knowledge, some comments on the revisions that would appear to be appropriate once the role of literacy is incorporated, and a brief discussion of the role that literacy plays not only on the body of knowledge that the linguist's description purports to describe, but on the constructs that the literate linguist brings to bear on the description of both literate and nonliterate language users. First, however, we intend to show that the description appropriate to the linguistic knowledge of nonliterate native speakers of English is unlike that of the adult literate native speaker in phonology, morphology, and syntax.

### Literacy

In this section, we show how the results of a set of experiments on the linguistic performance of nonreading native speakers of English fail to verify the claims of isomorphic phonemic, morphemic, and syntactic knowledge of all speakers of a language.[1] In this present context, we will be concerned with nonliterate adults; more detailed descriptions of the specific tests as well as results of their employment with primary school children are found in Scholes and Willis (1987b).

The results reported here are based on a population of twenty-one nonliterate adults. The subjects were found and tested in adult literacy programs in several locations within the state of Florida. The group ranged in age from eighteen to sixty-two (mean age 42.6 years); there were thirteen males and eight females, six whites and fifteen blacks. In education, two had had no formal schooling at all, while one had completed the twelfth grade, and the mean number of years of school completed was 6.04. None of these factors (age, sex, ethnicity, or schooling) affected the results reported below. The reading ability of the members of this group was minimal. Many did not know the alphabet, while some could laboriously "sound out" single simple words.

*Phonology*

Fromkin and Rodman are clear in their teaching concerning the phonemic knowledge shared by all speakers of English. They assert, "A speaker of English 'knows' that there are three sounds in the word *cat*, the initial sound represented by the letter *c*, the second by *a*, and the final sound by *t;* yet physically the word is just one continuous sound. You can *segment* the one sound into parts because you know English " (1988, p. 32). Obtaining evidence for such knowledge would appear to be quite straightforward – ask the speaker what you get if you remove the /k/ from "cat." If she knows the segmental structure described by Fromkin and Rodman, there should be no difficulty in responding with "at." Such a task, called *phoneme deletion*, has now been done in a variety of languages with a variety of subjects and has consistently failed to verify Fromkin and Rodman's claim.

For quite some time before we personally became involved in research of this type, others had made the basic discoveries. These fundamental facts were that phoneme deletion tasks could be done easily by subjects who could read alphabetic orthographies. They could not be done, however, by prereading English-speaking children (Bruce, 1964; Lieberman, Shankweiler, Fischer, & Carter, 1974; Karpova, 1977), nor by older children who read languages whose orthography is not alphabetic (Read, Zhang, Mie, & Ding, 1986), nor by precocious readers of English (Patel & Patterson, 1982). This work (reviewed in Bertelson, 1986; Bertelson & DeGelder, 1988) strongly suggested that phonemes are a component of a speaker's awareness of language only if that person can read an alphabetic representation of his language. Our own work is just a set of confirmations and extensions of that fact.

As a preliminary to our own phoneme deletion tasks, all subjects were given a minimal pairs test. This is a test of the listener's ability to detect minimal differences in words where the difference is assignable to a single pair of phonemes, as, for example, in "flagrant" and "fragrant." The nonliterate adults averaged two errors in the twenty-four trials of this test. As the items included nonsense forms (e.g., "flun" "frun") as well as relatively uncommon forms such as the pair just above, this result shows that the group had adequate auditory acuity and could easily hear whole words as being the same or different on the basis of wholistic configurations.

In the phoneme deletion task, test items were arranged in terms of three levels of difficulty, and the subjects were scored in terms of the highest level attained. Success was defined as three correct answers on the five trials at each level. The test and the subject's responses were, of course, entirely oral. The easiest set of five trials in the phoneme deletion test was as follows:

1. "fly" take away /f/
2. "flat" take away /l/
3. "bite" take away /t/
4. "past" take away /s/
5. "beaver" take away /v/

Of the twenty-one subjects, seventeen could not do this task at all. Of the four who got at least three of these simplest items, none were able to do at least three of the five trials on the next more difficult level (items such as "driver" take away /v/). With some exceptions, then, it may be said that adult nonliterate native speakers of English are unable to do phoneme deletion.

Phoneme deletion tasks are easy for literate speakers of English. Even third-graders – provided they are readers – can do them without difficulty (Scholes & Willis, 1987b). It would appear, then, that when literate adults are asked to make phonemic judgments about words, these judgments are based on the written (not acoustic) forms of these words. When an alphabetically literate subject is asked to delete /r/ from "grow," for example, the written form of the word "grow" is internally visualized, the letter "r" is deleted, and the result pronounced.

If this is how alphabetically literate people do phoneme deletion tasks, then they should have some difficulty when the phoneme to be deleted is not directly represented in the written form of the word; for example, in deleting the /k/ sound from "fixed." This prediction was verified in an experiment using thirty highly literate native speakers of English (college students). For these subjects, stimuli were presented orally, and the responses were written. The items used, and the percent of correct responses were:

"taxed" take away /s/ (tacked/tact)   43%
"fixed" take away /k/ (fist)   40%
"coughed" take away /f/ (caught)   37%

The prediction that these would be difficult was confirmed. Well over half of the subjects could not delete phonemes that were not biuniquely represented in the spelling of the word.

Further, if literates are asked to do phoneme deletions in cases where the resulting word is one thing if phonemic processing is used and another thing if orthographic processing is employed, responses should show that the written form of the word has been accessed in a large number of cases. An example of such a test case is in deleting the /š/ onset from "share." If purely phonemic processing is involved, the response should be "air"; if the written form of the word is used, then the subject might respond with "are."

The same thirty college undergraduates were asked to do phoneme deletion for five stimuli for which either a phonemic or a literal response was possible. These are listed below with the words that would be given as answers for phonemic or literal processing:

| Stimuli | Phonemic | Literal |
|---|---|---|
| "flower" take away /fl/ | our | ower |
| "share" take away /š/ | air | are |
| "hungry" take away /gri/ | hung | hun |
| "defined" take away /fain/ | did | deed |
| "liked" take away /k/ | light | lied |

The subjects' responses were almost evenly divided between phonemic and literal processing: 48 percent phonemic, 43 percent literal, and 9 percent responses that did not fit these categories.

The results of the phoneme deletion research are convincing. Speakers of English are able to manipulate phonemes only if they can read. The acquisition of the alphabetic representation of language enables the language knower to transfer this way of representation (i.e., sequences of discrete sublexical elements) to speech. In short, we know about phonemes because we know about letters.

## Morphology

In Fromkin and Rodman's teaching, the "grammar that is internalized by the language learner includes the morphemes and the derived words of the language" (1988, p. 152). The morphemes that are held to be elements of the competence of any native speaker include both those morphemes that map onto real-world phenomena and those inflectional and derivational affixes and so-called function words that serve to signal syntactic function, status, and relationships of and among content forms. The fact that there are a number of language users whose grammars contain no entities we would wish to label "words," as well as the orthographic basis for such a construct, has been dealt with before (e.g., Gelb, 1952); our own research concerns the ability of speakers to demonstrate knowledge of the morphemic constituents of derived words.

This knowledge is here taken (parallel to the operational criterion for phonemic knowledge) to imply an ability to manipulate such elements – to delete them or add them or otherwise show that complex words can be segmented in terms of the concatenated morphemes. In our research with nonliterate adults, we asked the subjects to do two fairly simple tasks of morphological analysis. First, they were given five compound words ("stopwatch," "touchdown," "redcap," "daytime," and "lighthouse") one at a time and asked what two smaller words made up each compound. All but three of the twenty-one subjects were able to do this task without error. One subject made a single error, and two were unable to do this task at all. The second task asked subjects to report the "smaller word" inside each of these complex words: "misspelling," "rewriting," "reaction," "discovery," and "uncertainty." When this task is run with literate college student subjects, they respond with the stem morpheme (i.e., "spell," "write," "act," "cover," and "certain," respectively). The twenty-one nonliterate adults, in dramatic contrast, produced stem morpheme responses for only 23 percent of the trials. Just four of these subjects managed at least three of the five stimuli. While some of the responses from nonliterate adults were syllabic (e.g., "miss," "scove," "sir," etc.), the most common response was a look of confusion.

Since, with the possible exception of the two subjects who were not successful in separating constituent words in compounds – the notion of "word" and the process of isolating and identifying words was demonstrated in the previous task – it would appear safe to say that the problem faced by the nonliterate adults in isolating stem words in complex forms is a morphological one, that is, they cannot do morphemic analysis. (We are aware that expected responses for the compound stimuli could be obtained by syllable segmentation, but no clear cases of such a strategy – for example, "date" and "I'm" for "daytime" – occurred.)

By way of contrast, these same tasks were run with third-grade and fifth-grade children with various degrees of reading skill. The reading children were able to do these tasks quite well, with all fifth-graders (average readers) tested able to perform perfectly on the stem word isolation task (Scholes & Willis, 1987b).

These results provide evidence that nonliterate adults are not aware of the morphemic elements in complex English words. As with segmental phonemes, access to these constructs appears to be gained through literacy.

*Syntax*

The syntax of a language is the component of a grammar that deals with sentence structures and the relationships between overt properties of sentences and the underlying, semantically and functionally interpretable propositions. In understanding sentences, the comprehender must be able to perform the grammatical analyses that convert utterances into their underlying propositions in order to understand what the sentences mean. This process of converting overt sequences of elements into underlying propositions is, it turns out, a very different kind of system in nonliterate adult users of English than it is in the literate adult.

In our test of sentence comprehension, subjects were asked questions whose syntactic structure was designed to show how particular sentence structures are interpreted by the listener. There were fifteen questions in the full test, but we will report on just a few of the more characteristic and illuminating of them here (the full set of questions is given in Scholes & Willis, 1987b).

Among the most interesting cases are a pair of sentences that contrast the syntactic structures inherent in the verbs "tell" and "promise." Our questions were "If John tells Bill to go away, who goes away?" and "If John promises Bill to go away, who goes away?" The twenty-one adult nonreaders responded (correctly) with "Bill" in 100 percent of the "tell" cases, but in just 50 percent of the trials with "promise" was the response the correct "John." Another quite dramatic result occurred in the responses to the question "What does a man-eating lion eat?" Seventeen of the twenty-one nonliterate adults responded with "lions." Our final illustration is the question "If a girl watching a man drawing pictures of a young boy runs away, who runs away?" Fifteen of the twenty-one subjects responded, "the boy."

As these examples show, there are syntactic rules that are properly in the competence of literate users of English that are not part of the syntactic component of the competence of nonliterates. When nonliterate adults are faced with comprehending such complex structures as the nominalized proposition in "man-eating lion," sentences in which clauses intervene between a subject and its predicate, or sentences containing verbs such as "promise" that take sentential objects rather than noun-phrase objects, they tend to misinterpret the subject–verb relationships. The nonliterates tend to employ strategies for interpreting sentences. For the structures just illustrated, the comprehensional strategy used by the nonliterate is to take the noun phrase immediately preceding a verb as the subject of that verb. Structures for which this strategy yields the correct analysis (as with "tell") are correctly understood, while those that do not follow this pattern (where the subject follows the verb or where the subject precedes it but is separated from it by intervening noun phrases) are interpreted differently by nonreaders than by readers.

Syntactic strategies of this type (i.e., sentence interpretation based solely on the sequence and adjacency of words) are not only characteristic of adult speakers who do not read, but are also found in prereading children (Scholes, 1970, 1978; Scholes & Klepper, 1982), congenitally hearing-impaired people (Russell, Quigley, & Power, 1976; Scholes, Cohen, & Brumfield, 1978), certain types of aphasics (Heilman & Scholes, 1976; Scholes, 1978), and to a significant extent, people who read English but do not normally use it for oral communication (Willis, 1988).

These data suggest that the syntactic rules of the grammars of speakers of English that permute subject and object noun phrases or embed clauses within other clauses do not obtain for speakers who are not literate. Rather, the syntax of adult nonreaders retains the sequential strategies associated with prereading children (Palermo & Molfese, 1972; Russell, Quigley, & Power, 1976). In short, it would appear that the attainment of many of the transformational syntactic rules commonly employed by linguists in the description of the language of all adult native speakers of English is not found in those who do not acquire literacy.

*The grammar of nonliterate speakers*

We take these results as evidence that some of the claims of linguists concerning the components of descriptions of the elements and processes by means of which all speakers of a language generate and comprehend utterances are more accurately viewed as claims about literate users of a language. Based on the linguistic abilities assessed in the research described above, the differences appear to be that the constructs that describe the knowledge of language possessed by nonliterates do not include phonemic or morphemic representations of lexical items and that the syntactic rules that describe the generation of sentences do not contain metathesizing and embedding transformations. In short, the descriptions of the linguistic competence of nonliterates contain gestalt lexical entities and syntactic rules based on sequencing and adjacency. Such characteristics of the description of linguistic knowledge, previously associated with preschool children, agrammatic aphasics, and the hearing impaired, are now seen to be retained throughout life in the absence of the acquisition of literacy.

**Intensionality**

The distinctions between the linguistic skills of literate and nonliterate speakers of English can, we believe, be best characterized and unified within the context of a contrast between extensional and intensional elements. We define "extensional elements" of a language as those elements having reference to extralinguistic real-world phenomena. They are the terms that allow linguistic propositions to be about something. "Intensional elements," however, we define as elements having no reference to anything outside of the linguistic system itself. Their meanings are found within the grammar itself. (For additional discussion of this concept, see Scholes & Willis, 1987a; 1987c; 1989.)

Applying this distinction to morphemes of English, such forms as the "to" infinitive marker, the "by" that marks subjects of passivized sentences, and articles ("a" and "the") are intensional. They have no reference to anything other than the facts of the structure of English that they denote. Morphemes such as "man," "see," "beside," and so on are extensional in that they name objects, actions, spatial relationships, and other observable phenomena. In contrast to usage of the term "intensional " in philosophy and logic (Wilkes, 1988; Zalta, 1988) and its previous usage in linguistic theory (Partee, 1982), we consider elements to be extensional even when the phenomena they denote are fictional (e.g., for us, "unicorn" is an extensional term). The distinction we intend here is strictly between elements that refer to linguistic constructs (intensional) and those whose reference is outside of and independent of the particular grammar by means of which they are expressed.

To see how the distinction captures the observed differences in literate and nonliterate language, consider first the inability of nonliterates to analyze morphologically complex words. For the stimuli in our test of morphological analysis, the affixes appended to stems in "misspelling," "rewriting," "reaction," "discovery," and "uncertainty" are intensional. The suffixes "-ing," "-ion," "-y," and "-ty" are purely intensional in that their meaning is "this word is a noun" (i.e., there is no object, event, state, or property of the universe outside of English that is an "ing" or a "ty"). More technically, the reference of "-ion" is a nonterminal node of a structural description of the full word. Similarly, the prefixes "mis-," "re-," "dis-," and "un-" are largely intensional in that their meanings are functions such as "it is not the case that" and "iteration." If, then, we posit that the nonliterate cannot deal with intensionality, these speakers would have no way of identifying and processing the intensional affixes in these words and, consequently, no way of separating such elements from the extensional stems to which they are affixed.

The same analysis can be applied to the nonliterate's syntax. In the pairs of sentences below, we have indicated the extensional morphemes by capitals and intensional morphemes by lower case:

1a. If MARY PUSHes JOHN, WHO does the PUSHing?
1b. If JOHN IS PUSHed by MARY, WHO does the PUSHing?
2b. If a GIRL WATCHes a MAN DRAW PICTURES of a YOUNG BOY RUNning AWAY, WHO RUNS AWAY?
2b. If a GIRL WATChing a MAN DRAWing PICTURES of a YOUNG BOY RUNS AWAY, WHO RUNS AWAY?
3a. WHAT does a MAN EATing a LION EAT?
3b. WHAT does a MAN-EATing LION EAT?
4a. If JOHN PROMISES that BILL GOES AWAY, WHO GOES AWAY?
4b. If JOHN PROMISES BILL to GO AWAY, WHO GOES AWAY?

If, again, we posit a speaker lacking the ability to process intensional morphology, each of these pairs of sentences becomes structurally synonymous. Without the intensional elements to tell the listener what terms of each sentence are intensionally marked as subject and/or object of particular verbs, the comprehender must rely on some comprehensional strategy. Generally, the strategy employed involves adjacency and sequence (e.g., the noun phrase most immediately preceding a verb is the subject of that verb).

While such strategies have been noted and described for quite some time in studies of children, aphasics, and the hearing impaired (see earlier references), what has not been previously noted, to our knowledge, is that strategies are viable only given the absence of the ability to process intensional terms. If a language user has the ability to understand and incorporate intensional elements in his derivation of the structure of sentences (and words, for that matter), strategies are not needed. Since strategies are used as a matter of course by young children, agrammatic aphasics, hearing-impaired signers, and (now) nonliterate adults, it would appear that an absence of intensional processing ability is common to all of these language users.

Positing that the nonliterate adult is unable to employ intensionality in sentential and lexical analysis, then, provides a reasonable and unifying explanation of both morphological and syntactic behavior. However, the unifying power of the view that intensionality is absent in these speakers goes even further. Phonemes are intensional. Dividing the continuum of speech into discrete sublexical, subsyllabic units involves using mental constructs that have no reality in the physical world. The reference of any phoneme is its function in the phonemic system in which it obtains; a phoneme is, by definition, not a sound but a set of contrasts, it has an intensional interpretation. Any system of graphic symbols by means of which phonemes are represented is, then, likewise intensional. Alphabetic letters, in their function as representations of phonemes, are intensional.[2]

If, then, a language user lacks the ability to process intensional elements in performing various linguistic tasks, this inability would include the isolation and manipulation of phonemic elements. Such an inability is observed in the performance of nonliterate adults (and, as previously noted, preliterate children as well as readers of nonalphabetic orthographies).

The unifying capacity of the concept of extensional and intensional linguistic processing allows us to formulate two levels of linguistic knowledge and two types of descriptions of that knowledge. The distinction – which would otherwise require a list of components and processes describing phonological, morphological, and syntactic differences between readers and nonreaders – can now be expressed much more succinctly: The linguistic knowledge of literates employs both extensional and intensional elements and processing while the linguistic knowledge of nonliterates is limited to extensional elements and processing. The descriptions and the competencies associated with this difference may, then, be labeled as "intensional grammar" and "extensional grammar."

### Marshall McLuhan's Western man

By the meaningless sign linked to the meaningless sound we have built the shape and meaning of Western man. (Marshall McLuhan, *The Gutenberg Galaxy*)

McLuhan's dictum surely ranks with the great one-liners in all of literature, fiction or nonfiction. It has that elegant terseness of truth about it that is suggestive not so much of finality as of genesis. It provokes more than decides, generates more than terminates.

In particular, it has provided us with a context in which to view not only phylogeny, but ontogenetic development as well; and it has been an exciting and illuminating investigation. Interpreted within the context of language acquisition, it provides a characterization of the distinction between the literate mature language user and the preliterate child or nonliterate adult – provided that an important amendation is made.

The fault in the McLuhan statement is the characterization of letters and sounds as meaningless. They are not meaningless; they are intensional. A more accurate (if clumsier) rendering of the intent, then, would be: By the intensional graphic sign (i.e., the written letter) linked to the intensional unit of sound (i.e., the phoneme) we have built the shape and meaning of Western man.

McLuhan was apparently well aware of intensionality and its place in considerations of literacy and cognitive function since he also says, "The role of phonetic literacy in the creating of the techniques of . . . formal logic . . . is well known" (1962, p. 36). (It is, of course, in the context of formal logic that the distinction between intensional operational terms and extensional variables is best known.) Where we may be parting intellectual company from McLuhan is that his statement (or, at least, our rewording of it) implies that the ability to read an alphabetic orthography necessarily entails intensional competence. Such a view would be somewhat misleading since the ability to comprehend alphabetically represented words does not, in and of itself, indicate that the reader is processing the intensional values of the letters.

Other writers have noted the distinction between the ability to read words written with letters and the ability to interpret letters as intensional symbols (see Besner, Davelaar, Alcott, & Parry, 1984, for a review). Alphabetically written words can be recognized and interpreted as gestalt shapes for which it is the overall configuration that matters, not the specific sequence of letters that make up that shape. This, of course, is the reason we can read English passages written in a variety of scripts and hands – the styles alter the shapes of individual letters (often to the point where they can no longer be identified), but they do not distort the relative shapes of the whole words. As lexical gestalts, alphabetically represented words are not different from ideographic and lexicographic writing systems such as Chinese. There are, then, sizable numbers of people who have intensional competence but who do not employ alphabetic orthographies, and conversely, there are people who employ alphabetic orthographies but who do not have intensional competence. The former group includes the majority of the literate peoples of the world; the latter group includes most children in the early stages of reading (first- and second-graders) (Perfetti, 1984) and, apparently, readers of English (e.g., Kenyan school children) who are not native speakers of the language and do not employ it as an oral language (Willis, 1988).

Similarly, as is shown by the research reported above, it is quite normal for individuals to be able to perceive differences in the overall sound patterns between words (minimal pairs) without being able to isolate the phonemic segments in which these differences reside. It is not, then, the fact that either graphic or acoustic shapes of linguistic units may be analyzable in terms of intensional elements that grants intensional capability to their users; either form may be dealt with as gestalts.

It is not, then, the ability or inability to read that best captures the differences in language and cognition between literates and nonliterates. It is, rather, the ability or inability to process intensional constructs, to think like Western man. In addition to the extensional grammar that represents their linguistic abilities, the absence of intensional logic and reasoning shows up in various other limitations in nonliterates (Akinnaso, 1981). They do not recognize sentences as being well or ill formed by virtue of usage of intensional morphemes, but, instead, will accept or reject sentences on the basis of purely pragmatic properties. They will say, for example, that "John hit Mary" is a bad sentence because John shouldn't do that and that "John be give flowers of Mary" is a good sentence because that is a nice thing for John to do. They do poorly on tasks that require the use of analogy. For example, in a test paradigm like "If you speak today and you did the same thing yesterday, then yesterday you spoke. If you drive today and you did the same thing yesterday, then what did you do yesterday?" nonliterate adults are liable to respond with things like "Well, I watched TV and then I went to the store." In a more general cognitive context, they appear unable to classify things on the basis of geometrical categories or other abstract properties (Luria, 1976; Nickerson, 1986). Nonliterate adults employ, we would suggest, the same concrete operational (Piaget, 1955; Flavell, 1963) processing as preliterate children.

The type of person, then, that McLuhan characterizes as "Western," that Chomsky calls "ideal," and that Olson (1988, 1989) describes as someone having the ability to treat "knowledge as an object" is perhaps most informatively labeled "intensional man."

**Caveats and heuristics**

Intensionality is not all or none. Our studies of adult illiterates suggest that not all nonreaders lack the ability to process speech intensionally, and it is clear that there are many reader-writers of English who do lack this competence to varying degrees.

It is not at all difficult to find samples of written English that are highly communicative but lacking consistently correct usage of intensional morphology and syntax; words are spelled on the basis of wholistic form, and punctuation is used in an elocutionary fashion. Failure to comprehend the intensional functions of internal punctuation is in fact rather widespread among literate native speakers of English. In some recent studies of ours, we found, to take one illustrative case, that more than 30 percent of college students (and about 50 percent of the general population) did not see the intensional (syntactic) significance of the presence or absence of the comma in "John helped the young girl and the old man read the instructions" versus "John helped the young girl, and the old man read the instructions."

Nor does the all-or-none characterization apply to linguists and literacy. There have been a number of scholars identified with the field who have recognized the usefulness of English orthography as linguistic data (e.g., Chomsky & Halle, 1968), and there are linguists who reject the identification of language and speech (e.g., Baron, 1981) as well as those who have seriously considered relationships between literacy and linguistic competence (e.g., Ferguson, 1978; Chafe, 1985; Givon, 1985; Kalmar, 1985). To our knowledge, however, there has been only one published claim that knowledge of orthography ought to be overtly represented in the linguist's description of the competence (i.e., in the grammar) of literate language users – that by Fred W. Householder, Jr. (1966).

Further, only Ranko Bugarski (1970), apparently, has seriously considered the implications of Benjamin Lee Whorf's (1940) "linguistic relativity hypothesis" for linguistics itself. Whorf's claim was that one's grammar (competence) serves as a filter through which one views the world. Applied to linguistics, it suggests that the description of a language user having extensional, concrete, pragmatic competence constructed by a linguist having intensional, formal sophistication is more likely to reflect the competence of the linguist than that of the informant. In the context of literate linguists characterizing illiterate speaker-hearers (present or past), Whorf's hypothesis is surely true.

More important, by far, than concerns with how well or poorly the science of language has performed its function is the issue of the impact of illiteracy on individuals and society. If the data we have presented and our interpretation of them are valid, it is then clear that the handicap of illiteracy is far more profound than is suggested by the inability to read. Illiteracy is more accurately seen as a complex of linguistic and cognitive competencies qualitatively unlike those of literates. How this complex of competencies may be linked to reading skill may have to do with the linguistic function of orthography.

As Bugarski (1970) points out, orthographies are representations of the linguistic intuitions of the users of a language. Orthographic conventions may, then, be seen as ways of representing linguistic constructs – words, phrases, clauses, subjects and predicates, sentences, morphemes, phonemes, and so on. A writing system, in this sense, is a grammar – a description of a language.

The distinction between literates and illiterates can now, given this insight into orthography and the theory of intensionality, be formulated in a manner having some heuristic value. What distinguishes the person of formal, intensional competence from the person of extensional, concrete competence may well be that the former has been able to acquire the grammatical significance of the written form of language while the latter has not (either by being quite ignorant of writing or of having acquired a knowledge of it as merely a way of representing speech). We are confident that a review of the history of writing (e.g., Gelb, 1952) as well as studies of the relationships between the acquisition of reading skill and the development of intensional competence in contemporary children and adults from the perspective of orthography as grammar will prove both intellectually rewarding and pedagogically significant.

NOTES

1 Despite our considerable respect for his judgment, we have rejected the editor's (D.R.O.) suggestion that we use the term "metalinguistic" to describe our tasks and the subjects' skills in performing these tasks. Our rejection is based largely on the fact that the term is already used in the field in two well-understood senses. In one sense (the most widely used one), metalinguistic refers to using a language to describe itself, that is, using terms such as the English word "noun" to talk about the linguistic construct "noun." With the possible exception of our test of morphological analysis, where one might claim that knowledge of the reference of the term "word" is crucial to the performance of the task, we do not see how

knowledge of metalinguistic terminology is involved. It is certainly not involved in the questions testing syntactic comprehension (e.g., If John promises Bill to leave, who leaves?) nor the phonemic analysis task (e.g., What do you get if you take [r] away from [gro]?). For further elucidation of the metalinguistic view see Olson, Chapter 15, this volume.

The other established usage of the term is in the sense of metatheory, where a "metalinguistic theory" is a theory of "big L," that is, a theory governing all human natural language, in which context a linguistic theory, or "grammar," is a theory of some specific language, English, for example. In this sense of the term, we do deal with metalinguistics – our concepts of intensionality and extensionality are metalinguistic in that they are intended as concepts governing all human linguistic competence.

The sense in which the editor wanted us to use the term is that found in such sources as Read (1978) and Cazden (1976). Cazden defines it as "the ability to make forms opaque and attend to them in and for themselves," and Read characterizes a metalinguistic skill relevant to some linguistic construct as "knowing that one knows it." Defined in this way, metalinguistic skill would appear to be the kind of skill demonstrated by a linguist writing a grammar of some language – a sense comparable to the first established usage discussed above – and not, as these same authors actually use the term, descriptive of the behavior of subjects in tests of language analysis and comprehension. Again, we do not believe that the skills we are tapping in our subjects are at all comparable to the skills we employ in designing the tests or interpreting the results.

If one has to distinguish between things one knows about a language and overt demonstrations of that knowledge, the field has two perfectly good terms for just that purpose, i.e., linguistic competence (knowledge) and linguistic performance (overt demonstration). We reject even this characterization of our work. We feel, quite seriously, that if a speaker's linguistic competence included knowledge of the structural significance of, say, the intensional morphemes "-ing" and "-s" in "the girl watching the boy runs away," the speaker would not – could not – understand that the boy runs away. Since that is, in fact, what many speakers of English do take the sentence to mean, we can only conclude that intensional competence (not performance) is lacking.

We therefore refer to our tasks and our subjects' behavior as "linguistic," and we assert that what we are studying and characterizing are variations in linguistic competence.

2 The distinction between an overt phonetic property of the speech continuum and the phoneme is parallel in a very interesting way to the distinction between note and interval in music. In music, notes are obviously extensional, referring to things one can hear, while intervals are intensional, constructs whose values are confined to the particular musical system in which they function. It has always intrigued us that music is apparently processed in the right, nondominant hemisphere of the untrained but in the left, dominant hemisphere among trained musicians (Bever & Chiarello, 1974). This finding is, given the intensionality theory, entirely

consistent with the finding that children lacking the left hemisphere are constrained to extensional language acquisition and competence (Dennis & Whitaker, 1976). The suggestion that extensionality is compatible with either hemisphere of the brain, while intensionality is confined to the dominant hemisphere is also consistent with studies of split-brain patients and with Jaynes's (1982) characterization of the origin of consciousness.

On another level, we should note that studies of the segmentation of speech among preliterate and nonliterate speakers consistently find that the syllable is the minimal unit of analysis, not the "speech sound" (Peters, 1985). This makes the creation of alphabetic (i.e., phonemic) orthography and the abandonment of syllabic scripts an event of greater significance and mystery than even McLuhan may have imagined. It clearly suggests, in a way that parallels the origin of word and morpheme boundaries and the creation of geometry, the development of an intellectual insight that can only have a rationalist etiology, that is, it had to spring not from some heightened talent for observation of the physical world but from a totally new way of conceptualizing that world.

## REFERENCES

Akinnaso, F. N. (1981). The consequences of literacy in pragmatic and theoretical perspectives. *Anthropology & Education Quarterly* 12(3):163–200.

Baron, N. S. (1981). *Speech, writing, and sign.* Bloomington: Indiana University Press.

Bertelson, P. (1986). The onset of literacy: Liminal remarks. *Cognition* 24:1–30.

Bertelson, P., & DeGelder, B. (1988). Learning about reading from illiterates. In A. Galaburda (ed.), *From neurons to reading.* Cambridge, Mass.: MIT Press.

Besner, D., Davelaar, E., Alcott, D., & Parry, P. (1984). Wholistic reading of alphabetic print: Evidence from the FDM and the FBI. In L. Henderson (ed.), *Orthographies and reading.* Hillsdale, N.J.: Erlbaum.

Bever, T., & Chiarello, R. J. (1974). Cerebral dominance in musicians and nonmusicians. *Science* 185:137–9.

Bloomfield, L. (1933). *Language.* New York: Holt, Rinehart & Winston.

Bond, G. B., Tinker, M. A., Wasson, B. B., & Wasson, J. B. (1984). *Reading difficulties: Their diagnosis and correction.* New York: Prentice-Hall.

Bruce, D. J. (1964). The analysis of word sounds by young children. *British Journal of Educational Psychology* 34:158–9.

Bugarski, R. (1970). Writing systems and phonological insights. Papers from the Sixth Regional Meeting of the Chicago Linguistic Society.

Cazden, C. (1976). Play with language and meta-linguistic awareness: One dimension of language experience. In J. S. Bruner, A. Jolly, & K. Sylva (eds.), *Play: Its role in development and evolution.* New York: Basic.

Chafe, W. L. (1985). Linguistic differences produced by differences between speaking and writing. In D. R. Olson, N. Torrance, & A. Hildyard (eds.),

*Literacy, language, and learning: The nature and consequences of reading and writing.* Cambridge University Press.

Chomsky, N. (1965). *Aspects of the theory of syntax.* Cambridge, Mass.: MIT Press.

Chomsky, N., & Halle, M. (1968). *The sound pattern of English.* New York: Harper & Row.

Dennis, M., & Whitaker, H. A. (1976). Language acquisition following hemidecortication: Linguistic superiority of the left over the right hemisphere. *Brain and Language* 3(3):404–33.

Ehri, L. C. (1985). Effects of printed language acquisition on speech. In D. R. Olson, N. Torrance, & A. Hildyard (eds.), *Literacy, language and learning: The nature and consequences of reading and writing.* Cambridge University Press.

Ferguson, C. A. (1978). Patterns of literacy in multilingual situations. In J. E. Alatis (ed.), *Georgetown University round table on languages and linguistics.* Washington: D. C.: Georgetown University Press.

Flavell, J. H. (1963). *The developmental psychology of Jean Piaget.* New York: Van Nostrand Reinhold.

Fletcher, J. M. (1981). Linguistic factors in reading acquisition: Evidence for developmental changes. In F. J. Prozzolo & M. C. Wittrock (eds.), *Neuropsychological and cognitive processes in reading.* New York: Academic Press.

Fromkin, V., & Rodman, R. (1988). *An introduction to language*, 4th ed. New York: Holt, Rinehart & Winston.

Fry, D. B. (1964). Experimental evidence for the phoneme. In D. Abercrombie, D. B. Fry, P. A. D. MacCarthy, N. C. Scott & J. L. M. Trim (eds.), *In honor of Daniel Jones.* London: Longmans.

Gelb, I. J (1952). *A study of writing*, rev. ed. Chicago: University of Chicago Press.

Givon, T. (1985). Function, structure, and language acquisition. In D. I. Slobin (ed.), *The crosslinguistic study of language acquisition*, Vol. 2. Hillsdale, N.J.: Erlbaum.

Goodglass, H., & Kaplan, E. (1972). *The assessment of aphasia and related disorders.* Philadelphia: Lea & Febiger.

Hall, M. A., & Ramig, C. J. (1978). *Linguistic foundations for reading.* Westerville, Ohio: Merrill.

Hayes, J. R. (ed.) (1970). *Cognition and the development of language.* New York: Wiley.

Heilman, K. M., & Scholes. R. J., (1976). The nature of comprehension errors in Broca's, conduction, and Wernicke's aphasia. *Cortex* 12:258–65.

Householder, F. W., Jr. (1966). Phonological theory: A brief comment. *Journal of Linguistics* 2:99–100. Reprinted in V. B. Makkai (ed.) (1972). *Phonological theory: Evolution and current practice.* Lake Bluff, Ill.: Jupiter Press.

Jaynes, J. (1982). *The origin of consciousness in the breakdown of the bicameral mind.* Boston: Houghton Mifflin.

Kalmar, I. (1985). Are there really no primitive languages? In D. R. Olson, N. Torrance, & A. Hildyard (eds.), *Literacy, language, and learning: The nature and consequences of reading and writing.* Cambridge University Press.

Karpova, S. N. (1977). *The realization of the verbal composition of speech by preschool children.* The Hague: Mouton.
Kean, M.-L. (ed.) (1985). *Agrammatism.* New York: Academic Press.
Liberman, A. M., Harris, K. S., Hofmann, H. S., & Griffith, B. C. (1957). The discrimination of speech sounds within and across phoneme boundaries. *Journal of Experimental Psychology* 54:358–68.
Lieberman, I. Y., Shankweiler, D. F., Fischer, W., & Carter, B. (1974). Explicit syllable and phoneme segmentation in the young child. *Journal of Experimental Child Psychology* 18:201–12.
Luria, A. R. (1976). *Cognitive development: Its cultural and social foundations.* Cambridge, Mass.: Harvard University Press.
McLuhan, M. (1962). *The Gutenberg galaxy* (1969 ed.). New York: New American Library.
McNeill, D. (1987). *Psycholinguistics: A new approach.* New York: Harper & Row.
Nickerson, R. S. (1986). Literacy and cognitive development. In M. E. Wrolstad & D. F. Fisher (eds.), *Toward a new understanding of literacy* New York: Praeger.
Olson, D. R. (1988). Discussion in *Periodically* (the newsletter of the McLuhan Program in Culture and Technology and the Consortium on Orality and Literacy), 2:1–2. Toronto.
Olson, D. R. (1989). Literate thought. In D. M. Topping, C. Crowell, & V. N. Kobayash (eds.) *Thinking across cultures: The Third International Conference.* Hillsdale, N.J.: Erlbaum.
Palermo, D. S., & Molfese, D. L. (1972). Language acquisition from age five onwards. *Psychological Bulletin* 78:409–48.
Partee, B. H. (1982). Intensional logic and natural language. In T. W. Simon & R. J. Scholes (eds.), *Language, mind, and brain.* Hillsdale, N.J.: Erlbaum.
Patel, P. G. (1981). Impaired language mechanisms in specific reading disability: An exploratory synthesis of research findings. *Indian Educational Review* 16(2):46–64.
Patel, P. G., & Patterson, P. (1982). Precocious reading acquisition: Psycholinguistic development, IQ and home background. *First Language* 3(2):8, 139–53.
Perfetti, C. A. (1984). Reading acquisition and beyond: Decoding includes cognition. *American Journal of Education* 93(1):40–60.
Peters, A. M. (1985). Language segmentation: Operating principles for the perception and analysis of language. In D. I. Slobin (ed.), *The crosslinguistic study of language acquisition*, Vol. 2. Hillsdale, N.J.: Erlbaum.
Piaget, J. (1955). *The language and thought of the child.* New York: New American Library.
Read, C. A. (1978). Children's awareness of language, with emphasis on sound systems. In A. Sinclair, R. Jarvella, & W. Levelts (eds.), *The child's conception of language.* New York: Springer-Verlag.
Read, C. A., Zhang, Y., Mie, H., & Ding, B. (1986). The ability to manipulate speech sounds depends on knowing alphabetic writing. *Cognition* 24:31–44.

Russell, W. K., Quigley, S. P., & Power, D. J. (1976). *Linguistics and deaf children.* Washington, D.C.: Alexander Graham Bell Assoociation for the Deaf.

Sapir, E. (1921). *Language* (Harvest Books ed.). New York: Harcourt Brace & World.

Scholes, R. J. (1970). On functors and contentives in children's imitation of word strings. *Journal of Verbal Learning and Verbal Behavior* 9:167–70.

(1978). Syntactic and lexical components of sentence comprehension. In A. Caramazza & E. B. Zurif (eds.), *The acquisition and breakdown of language: Parallels and divergences.* Baltimore, Md.: Johns Hopkins University Press.

(1989). Language, literacy and LAD: An exposition of the intensionality hypothesis, In D. R. Olson & P. McCormick (eds.), *Periodically* (the newsletter of the McLuhan Program in Culture and Technology and the Consortium on Literacy), 12:4–5. Toronto.

Scholes, R. J., Cohen, M., and Brumfield, S. (1978). On the possible causes of syntactic deficits in cogenitally deaf English users. *American Annals of the Deaf* 123(5):528–35.

Scholes, R. J., & Klepper, B. R. (1982). The comprehension of double object constructions in psycholinguistics and neurolinguistics. *Language and Speech* 25(1):55–73.

Scholes, R. J., & Willis, B. J. (1984). Grammars and agrammatism. *Language and Communication* 4(1):1–25.

(1987a). Language and literacy. *Journal of Literary Semantics* 16(1):3–11.

(1987b). Age and education in oral language skills. *Developmental Neuropsychology* 3(3 & 4):239–48.

(1987c). The illiterate native speaker of English: Oral language and intensionality. In J. Klesius & M. Radenich (eds.), *Links to literacy* (Proceedings of the 1987 Florida Reading Association Conference).

(in press). Invisible speech: Oral language abilities in blind braille readers. *Interchange.*

Slobin, D. I. (1971). *Psycholinguistics.* Glenview, Ill.: Scott Foresman.

Taylor, I. (1976). *Introduction to psycholinguistics.* New York: Holt, Rinehart & Winston.

Vogel, S. A. (1974). Syntactic abilities in normal and dyslexic children. *Journal of Learning Disabilities* 7(2):47–53.

Whorf, B. L. (1940). Science and linguistics. *Technological Review* 42(6):229–31, 247–8. Reprinted in *Language, thought and reality: Selected writings of Benjamin Lee Whorf.* Cambridge, Mass.: MIT Press.

Wilkes, K. V. (1988). Mind and body: Some forms of reductionism. In G. H. R. Parkinson (ed.), *The handbook of Western philosophy.* New York: Macmillan.

Willis, B. J. (1988). *Aspects of orality and literacy in the language acquisition of Kenyan primary school children.* Unpublished doctoral dissertation. Gainesville: University of Florida.

Zalta, E. N. (1988). *Intensional logic and the metaphysics of intentionality.* Cambridge, Mass.: MIT Press.

# 14
# A neurological point of view on social alexia

ANDRÉ ROCH LECOURS and MARIA ALICE PARENTE

## Introduction

In the field of psychobiology, one of the most important discoveries of the nineteenth century was that, in a very large majority of human beings, articulated language behavior is governed predominantly by the left cerebral hemisphere. As far as we know, this discovery should be credited to Marc Dax (1865) and Paul Broca (1865). The latter should also be credited for having been the first to suggest that left *cerebral dominance* for language is genetically constrained.[1] It is now widely accepted that Broca's innateness intuition was correct, and there are, from the functional standpoint, reasons to suggest that human neonates show evidence of incipient left-brain specialization for language hardly a few days after birth at term (Entus, 1977). Nonetheless, it remains that full actualization of this particular genetic program cannot occur without environmental exposure to language (wolf-children do not talk). The minimal intensity and duration of such exposure is not precisely known and neither is the extent of eventual variations from one individual to another. However, it is now known that left cerebral dominance for language is seldom if ever an absolute phenomenon (Bradshaw & Nettleton, 1983; Joanette, Lecours, Lepage, & Lamoureux, 1983; Hannequin, Goulet, & Joanette, 1987). In other words, although aphasia is nearly always the result of left-brain damage, it is generally accepted that a certain degree of ambicerebrality of language representation exists in most human beings: Cerebral dominance for language is therefore to be conceived as a stronger or weaker gradient in favor of the left hemisphere. In this regard, however, many of the factors determining the relative participation of each hemisphere remain to be further defined. This is particularly true of environmental factors (as opposed to biological ones).[2]

For example, it is not known whether exposure to oral language alone is sufficient to determine, with regard to linguistic abilities, full actualization of the functional lateralization potential. It is a question bearing on this problem that we raise in the present chapter: Does the acquisition of reading and writing skills play a role in this process? In our opinion, the issue is of undeniable interest: just as studies of the developmental dyslexias and alexias (Critchley, 1964; Galaburda, 1988), studies of the acquired dyslexias and alexias (Coltheart, Patterson, & Marshall, 1980; Patterson, Marshall, & Coltheart, 1985), and studies of social dyslexia and alexia might help to blaze a trail in assessing the impact of essentially historical and social influences on human brain cybernetics.

### Illiteracy and aphasia

Soon after the turn of this century, a German physician by the name of Ernst Weber (1904) claimed that the acquisition of reading and writing skills is more crucial than exposure to spoken language as a social determinant of functional lateralization for language. He founded his assertion on the clinical observation of a few illiterates and semiliterates in whom left-brain damage had not disturbed language behavior, or else had resulted in minor and short-term language disturbances. Unless our reading of Weber's argument is incorrect, he did not intend to challenge Broca's postulate as to the human left brain being genetically predisposed to act as the biological substratum of language behaviors. Formulated in general terms, his implicit assumption was rather that interaction is needed between the human organism and its environment in order for complete functional actualization of this particular genetic program to occur, which is reasonable. More specifically, Weber's idea was apparently that alphabetization is the main environmental influence at stake in this interaction, which would no doubt have been more appropriately presented as a cautious suggestion rather than a germane claim. Three years later, in his famous inaugural dissertation, François Moutier (1908) mentioned illiteracy as a characteristic of several of the subjects whom he presented as exceptions to Broca's doctrine (posterior left third frontal lesions without aphasia): Moutier was aware of Weber's idea (he quotes him in his dissertation) but did not discuss his "exceptions" in relation to it. To our knowledge, it was only half a century later, in 1956, that Weber's question was revived when Macdonald Critchley wrote that the German physician's postulate was no doubt of interest although the problem he had raised was indeed "complex" (which did not particularly enlighten the debate but had the merit of preventing Weber's idea from falling into oblivion). The following year, Viktor Gorlitzer von Mundy (1957) reported on the case of his Indian right-handed butler who displayed persistent right hemiplegia as the result of left-brain damage but showed no evidence of aphasia. In his report,

Gorlitzer von Mundy insisted that, as a military physician in India, he had been struck by the fact that right-handed illiterates with left-brain damage either presented with mild and transitory forms of aphasia or else showed no evidence of aphasia whatsoever. Gorlitzer von Mundy's conclusions were (1) that the acquisition of reading and writing skills does play a role in the process of left-brain specialization for language and (2) that the cerebral representation of language remains ambilateral in illiterates, "as in young children." The latter, according to him, explained the differences between illiterates and readers as to the effects of left brain damage. At the occasion of a "table-ronde" on aphasia, which took place a few years later in London (De Reuck & O'Connor, 1964), Jon Eisenson asserted that aphasia was "relatively unknown amongst [the U.S.] low-level military population" and that American soldiers of this category made "very remarkable recoveries" if they became aphasic at all as the result of gunshot wounds to the left cerebral hemisphere (p. 259); Roman Jakobson objected that his own experience was different, for he had observed World War I veterans of Russian origin from "rural areas" who were and remained "typical aphasiacs with the usual speech impairments caused by [left] brain lesions" (p. 259). In another context, Ron Tikofsky (1970) suggested that the distinction between normalcy and aphasia might be finer in illiterate than in school-educated subjects, the former "having normally a much smaller vocabulary" than the latter. More recently, Adam Wechsler and Jean Métellus each reported on one case of aphasia in a right-handed illiterate subject. In the former case (Wechsler, 1976), the patient presented with crossed aphasia, and the author suggested that right-hemisphere representation of language might in this case have been related to illiteracy. In the latter (Métellus, Cathala, Issartier, & Bodak, 1981), a massive left Sylvian lesion resulted in mild transitory aphasia, and the authors, although unaware of Gorlitzer von Mundy's contribution,[3] followed essentially the same trend of thought as had the latter in 1957. Finally, at the occasion of a discussion with Jacques Mehler and one of us (A.R.L.), Ovid Tzeng (personal communication, 1985) mentioned a report from mainland China telling about a high incidence of crossed aphasia among Chinese dextrals. (It seems that no mention of the literacy parameter nor, for that matter, of the tone-language parameter [Lecours, Basso, Moraschini, & Nespoulous, 1984], was made in this report.)

Beyond "clinical tales" and discussions among aficionados, systematic research on the literacy–lateralization issue has been pursued and reported by Cameron, Currier, and Haerer (1971) in Mississippi and by Damasio, Castro-Caldas, Grosso, and Ferro (1976) in Portugal. The

Mississippi study bore on the hospital records of sixty-five adults with a left Sylvian stroke and right hemiplegia. These records were considered to be those of "literate" ($N = 37$), "semiliterate" ($N = 14$), or "illiterate" ($N = 14$) individuals. The average duration of school education, within the three groups, was respectively 10.6, 5.6, and 2.5 years. The comparative incidence of aphasia[4] within these groups was the object of this research. It turned out that the neurologists at the University of Mississippi Medical Center in Jackson, when examining left-stroke adults with right hemiplegia, reported the existence of an associated aphasia less frequently when patients were "illiterates" than when they were fluent readers.[5] Now, it is more than likely that asserting the existence of aphasia in the context of this study depended on nonstandardized bedside examination, pursued without pencil-and-paper calculation of any sort; and there is little doubt that any seasoned clinician testing patients for aphasia in this manner will, knowingly or otherwise, require less – by reference to an implicit ideal norm – from an illiterate than from a school-educated patient (which makes intuitive good sense if one does not have the opportunity or the habit of referring to explicit and presumably reliable norms). In conclusion to their work, Cameron et al. (1971) suggested that "language is not as well 'planted' in the dominant hemisphere in illiterates as it is in literate persons" (p. 163).

The Lisbon study, however, bore on the expertly noted aphasiological records of 247 subjects with unilateral brain lesions. These records were either those of fluent school-educated readers ($N = 209$) or those of totally unschooled illiterates ($N = 38$). As in the Mississippi study, the comparative incidence of aphasia within the subgroups was the explicit object of the research. However, a primordial difference existed between the two studies since, in the case of the Portuguese one, attributing the label "aphasia" was no longer a matter of clinical flair only but mostly one of carefully pondering various exact measures – such as verbal production rate, number and types of errors in repetition and naming, ciphered results of word– and sentence–picture-matching tasks, and so forth – by reference to BDAE-like predefined standards (Goodglass & Kaplan, 1972). Following this explicit methodology, Damasio, Castro-Caldas et al. (1976) found that 114 readers (55.2%) and 21 illiterates (54.2%) presented with "aphasia." Twenty of the latter were right-handed and had suffered left-brain damage.[6] All of the illiterates with language disorders could be classified either as "global" ($N = 4$), "Broca's" ($N = 10$), or "fluent" ($N = 7$) aphasics. The Token Test (De Renzi & Vignolo, 1962) was used for further evaluation of the 20 right-handed illiterate aphasics as compared to a group of 20 school-educated aphasics "matched for age, sex, type of aphasia, and localization of the lesion" (p. 300): No significant differences in performance were found. The Portuguese researchers therefore concluded that aphasia is the result of left-brain damage in the illiterate as well as in the fluent reader, that it is equally frequent in both, and that "brain specialization for language does not depend on literacy" (p. 300).

### Guggenheim research

We will, at this point, summarize the results of a research project funded by the Harry Frank Guggenheim Foundation (New York). This project aimed at studying the effects of unilateral cerebral lesions among illiterates, and it was led by the authors of this chapter in collaboration with Professor Jacques Mehler[7] and several speech pathologists and neurologists from Brazil and Portugal. The results of this research have been reported elsewhere in detail (Lecours, Mehler, Parente, & collaborators, 1987a, 1987b, 1988).

*Experimental population*

Two hundred and ninety-six persons (153 men and 143 women), all of them absolute or preferential right-handers, all unilingual Lusophones, and all forty years of age or older, served as the subjects of our research. One hundred and fifty-seven of them were totally unschooled illiterates, and 139 had received at least four years of school education and thereafter retained writing skills and reading habits; 108 were neurologically healthy, and 188 were seen less than two months and, as a rule, more than two weeks after a unilateral stroke (109 left and 79 right), involving in nearly all cases the territory of the middle cerebral artery.[8] Brain-damaged individuals reported no past history of neurological illness (stroke included).

The experimental population therefore comprised six groups: on the one hand, sixty-two healthy, forty-eight left-stroke, and forty-seven right-stroke unschooled illiterates; on the other hand, forty-six healthy, sixty-one left-stroke, and thirty-two right-stroke school-educated fluent readers. These six groups were statistically homogeneous with regard to age[9] (averages between 58.2 and 64.3 years) although not with regard to sex distribution;[10] nonetheless, the sex distribution was comparable in the illiterate and the school-educated left-stroke groups[11] as well as in the illiterate and school-educated right-stroke groups.[12] Finally, the three groups of the literate subpopulation were statistically homogeneous with regard to number of years of school education[13] (averages of 8.3, 8.6, and 8.3 years).

## Neurological data

When tested, 184 of the 188 brain-damaged subjects presented with hemiparesis or hemiplegia. An obvious bias in favor of prerolandic and global Sylvian lesions therefore existed within the stroke subpopulations, no doubt indicating greater probability of admission to the wards of overcrowded public hospitals for a stroke patient with, as opposed to one without, hemiplegia. With regard to somesthesia and visual fields, the attending neurologists were requested to note their observations in terms of "deficit absent," "deficit present," or "deficit impossible to assess with a reasonable degree of confidence." Considering that assessing sensory disorders depends to a large extent on the clinician succeeding to establish communication with his or her patient, it might be of interest to note that the "unassessable" notation was used slightly less often in left-stroke illiterates than in left-stroke readers, and it is striking that it was used more than twice as often in right-stroke illiterates than in right-stroke readers (15% versus 6% of cases).

## Aphasia testing

Each subject of the Guggenheim population was administered (at least the spoken language components of) a Portuguese adaptation of the Protocole MT-86 d'Examen Linguistique de l'Aphasie (Version Alpha) (Lecours, Nespoulous, Joanette, Lemay, Puel, Lafond, Cot, & Rascol, 1986). MT-86 Alpha is designed as an elementary bedside aphasia screening test. It is comprised of a directed interview and seven scored subtests: (1) spoken word– and sentence–picture matching, (2) written word– and sentence–picture matching, (3) word and sentence repetition, (4) word and sentence reading, (5) word and sentence dictation, (6) word and sentence copy, and (7) naming. Only the results of subtests (1), (3), and (7) (Lecours et al., 1987a, 1988) will be systematically considered in the present chapter.

*Matching.* The matching tasks include a total of eleven stimuli. In word–picture matching, the subject is requested to point at the one of six and, in sentence–picture matching, at the one of four line drawings that corresponds to a stimulus uttered by the examiner. For each item, the iconographic material is presented in a single display (15 × 21 cm). Scoring bears on first (or absent) response only. The verbal stimuli in word–picture matching are five nouns such as *pente* (comb) and *faca* (knife). Each iconographic display is made up, beside the target, of a drawing related to a semantic foil, of one related to a phonological foil, of one constituting a formal foil (a drawing of an object visually similar to the target), and of two without linguistic or visual kinship to the target (neutral foils) (e.g., with the comb drawing, five foils representing a wig, a bridge [*ponte*], a rake, a carrot, and a key). In sentence–picture matching, verbal stimuli are three intransitive propositions or "simple" stimuli such as *A menina anda* (The girl is walking), and three reversible transitive propositions or "complex" stimuli, such as *O cavalo puxa o menino* (The horse is pulling the boy). Symmetrically distributed in quadrants, the four drawings in each display share iconographic and semiotic features – same or related actors, same or related actions, eventually same or related accessories – in a way such that each of the three nontarget drawings constitutes a semantic, syntactic, phonological, formal foil to the target one (e.g., with the walking-girl drawing, three foils representing a girl running, a boy walking and a boy running).

*Repetition.* The repetition subtest is comprised of eleven stimuli, that is, eight words such as *cavalo* (horse), *cruzeiros* (money), and *embarcaçao* (boat), and three sentences, one of which is *Nos lhe daremos desde que ela reclame* (literally, We it-to-her will-give when that she requires). Scoring bears exclusively on the subject's first (or absence of) response. Not taking phonetic distortions into account, two scores are defined in relation to word repetition: (1) total number of inadequate behaviors (absence of response, phonemic deviations, verbal deviations, and so forth) and (2) total number of phonemic deviations. Not taking phonetic distortions into account, two scores are also defined in relation to sentence repetition: (1) total number of inadequate behaviors (absence of response, verbal deviations, phonemic deviations, and so forth) and (2) total number of verbal deviations (word substitutions, deletions, additions and/or displacements).

*Naming.* The naming subtest aims at the production of twelve nouns and proceeds from a set of simple line drawings (each 15 × 21 cm). These are presented one after the other, and the subject is requested to utter the corresponding nouns, for instance, *sino* (bell), *violao* (guitar), and *cachimbo* (pipe). Scoring bears exclusively on the subject's first complete response (if any within five seconds) and does not take phonetic distortions and phonemic paraphasias into account. Three scores are defined in relation with naming: (1) total number of inadequate behaviors (absence of response, neologistic responses, verbal deviations, and so forth), (2) total number of absences of response within five seconds ("anomia score"), and (3) total number of verbal deviations such as semantic paraphasias and referential circumlocutions ("paraphasias score").

*Results*

Whether one considered the scores of neurologically healthy controls, or else those of either of the two stroke subpopulations, cultural differences were obvious between the illiterate as opposed to the school-educated subgroup, that is, global error scores were always greater in the former than in the latter. These differences were statistically significant in all – matching, repetition, and naming – tasks[14] (see Scholes & Willis, Chapter 13, this volume).

*Matching.* Absence of response in a matching task was exceptional in all six subgroups (13 absences of response, altogether, versus 1,601 actual matches, "correct" or otherwise). Mismatches were frequent in illiterate controls (Lecours et al., 1987a) and in all pathological subgroups, more so among left-stroke than among right-stroke subjects. Two particularly frequent mismatches among illiterate controls, although not among school-educated ones, were "walking-girl → running-girl" and "horse-pulling-boy → boy-pulling-horse." When statistical analyses were restricted to dimidiated displays (sentence–picture matching) and took target lateralization into account, that is, when errors that could be attributed to unilateral visual neglect were excluded (Lecours et al., 1987b), significant differences were found, by reference to appropriate controls, for both left-stroke subgroups but for neither of the two right-stroke ones.[15] On the whole, these auditory comprehension results are consistent with the tenets of classical aphasiology (Lecours et al., 1988).

*Repetition.* Two very frequent repetition errors among illiterate controls and subjects of the two right-stroke subgroups bore on grammatical morphemes as in *'pratos'* → *"prato"* and *'cruzeiros'* → *"cruzeiro"* (Lecours et al., 1987a). These two and other deviations were observed in left-stroke illiterates and literates (e.g., *'trem'* → *"tem," 'pratos'* → *"ratos," 'cruzeiros'* → *"cruzeivinho," 'embarçaco'* → *"embraçao,"* etc.). On the whole, the most frequent errors in sentence repetition, more so among left-stroke illiterates and school-educated subjects, were deletions of attributes and/or functionals. By comparison to appropriate controls, statistically significant differences were found in word repetition for both left-stroke subgroups but for neither of the two right-stroke ones.[16] Sentence repetition generated large numbers of inadequate responses in all three groups of the illiterate subpopulation and in left-stroke readers. In this respect, the only statistically significant difference that was documented is that left-stroke readers produced more inadequate responses than their controls.[17] On the whole, these repetition results are consistent with the tenets of classical aphasiology (Lecours et al., 1988).

*Naming.* Among illiterate controls, most inadequate behaviors in the naming task were of the anomic type and seemed related to a difficulty in visual decoding of the iconographic substrata of the test (Lecours et al., 1987a). Similar behaviors were observed within the four pathological subgroups, more so among the illiterates, together with varying numbers of circumlocutory responses and semantic paraphasias (e.g., 'cat' → "dog," 'pipe' → "cigar," 'pipe' → "man," 'whiskers' → "hair," 'banana' → "fruit," 'banana' → "sugarcane," and so forth). By reference to appropriate controls, statistically significant differences were found in overall scores for left-stroke illiterates and readers.[18] A significant difference was also found between illiterate controls and right-stroke illiterates, although not between school-educated controls and right-stroke readers.[19] Using the same statistical procedure, it was found that right-stroke illiterates – whose behavior in naming was not expected in view of the tenets of classical aphasiology (Lecours et al., 1988) – differed from their controls with regard to paraphasia score although not with regard to anomia score.[20]

*Discussion*

Our Guggenheim results can be summarized by asserting that they confirm the tenets of classical aphasiology insofar as matching and repetition data are concerned; the same is true of naming data among left-stroke illiterates and readers but not, as underlined above, of naming data among right-stroke illiterates. The possibility that the latter data are linked to visual neglect having been ruled out (Lecours et al., 1987b, 1988), two tentative hypotheses can be put forward. On the one hand, given that a difficulty in decoding iconographic materials was documented to exist among neurologically healthy illiterates (Lecours et al., 1987a), one might suggest that the naming results of right-stroke illiterates are witness to more of the same difficulty rather than to anomalies in lexical access. Of course, since the difference with appropriate controls is observed in right-stroke illiterates but not in fluent readers with similar lesions, this hypothesis would entail the existence of an illiteracy-specific picture-decoding pathology. But our data could also be taken as indicative of word-finding difficulties in right-stroke illiterates, that is, as related to more diffuse – more ambilateral – representation of lexicon among illiterates than among fluent readers. Since even the scholastic form of left cerebral "dominance" for lexico-semantic abilities is relative (Hannequin, Goulet, & Joanette, 1987) and since the paraphasia scores seem to be critical with regard to the naming behavior difference between right-stroke illiterates and their controls (cf. above), we tend, for the time being, to favor the second hypothesis above.

Although Weber's 1904 claim has never been integrally revived to our knowledge, the notion of some influence being exerted by written language acquisition on functional lateralization for language has occasionally been defended on the basis of aphasiological data or speculations (Critchley, 1956; Gorlitzer von Mundy, 1957; Eisenson, in De Reuck & O'Connor, 1964; Cameron et al., 1971; Currier, Haerer, & Farmer, 1976; Wechsler, 1976; Métellus, 1981). It is also on the basis of aphasiological data or speculations that this notion has been rejected (Jakobson, in de Reuck & O'Connor, 1964; Tikofsky, 1970; Damasio, Castro-Caldas et al., 1976; Damasio, Hamsher et al., 1976).[21] This being said and not taking our work into account, only two published studies (Cameron et al., 1971; Damasio, Castro-Caldas et al., 1976) have gone beyond the anecdote or the expression of personal beliefs.

For some reason, these two studies have been considered to have yielded irreconcilable results, which has led to controversy (Currier, Haerer, & Farmer, 1976; Damasio, Hamsher et al., 1976). In our opinion, this controversy was unfounded given the methodological differences between the two studies. As a matter of fact, our own results are compatible with the conclusions given to both studies. On the one hand, we found no difference between illiterates and readers as to the incidence of "aphasia" following left-brain damage (between 55% and 60% of cases in both subgroups using the MT-Alpha screening procedure; cf. above).[22] We therefore agree with Damasio, Castro-Caldas et al. (1976) that left cerebral dominance for language does not primarily depend on literacy. On the other hand, given that our pathological data were in each case compared to appropriate controls, we were able to document the existence, among right-stroke illiterates, of a naming anomaly that was not apparent in neurologically healthy illiterates. We therefore agree with Cameron et al. (1971) that, as a rule, left cerebral dominance for language could be less exclusive among illiterates than among school-educated individuals.

Out of the three published dichotic studies aiming at the study of functional lateralization in illiterates as opposed to school-educated readers (Damasio, Damasio, Castro-Caldas, & Hamsher, 1979; Tzavaras, Kaprinis, & Gatzoyas, 1981; Castro & Morais, 1987), the one led by Damasio et al. (1979) has yielded a result that is also compatible with less absolute cerebral dominance for language among the illiterates: When the dichotic stimuli were pairs of phonologically similar meaningful words differing only in their initial consonants (such as *ponte-fonte* and *caneta-maneta*), a right-ear advantage was found in fluent readers and a left-ear advantage in "dysliterates." It was therefore suggested that the latter might present "less mature dominance, calling for particular perceptual strategies in specific circumstances" (p. 337). We agree again.

It is now largely accepted that the right hemisphere of school-educated dextral adults is involved in a number of (highly efficient) linguistic behaviors (Bradshaw & Nettleton, 1983; Joanette et al., 1983; Hannequin et al., 1987); our current view is that illiterates have a lower threshold in this respect, that is, must resort to right-hemisphere-based strategies in order to attend efficiently to tasks – such as those involved in accessing frequent concrete nouns from simple line drawings (cf. above) or else discriminating phonologically similar words (Damasio et al., 1979) – which literate subjects can attend entirely on the basis of left-hemisphere activities.

Given that the notions of analphabetism and that of total absence of school education were in complete overlap within our Guggenheim population,[23] our data provide no indication as to whether more "mature" functional lateralization to the left should be linked to the literacy parameter per se or to school education as a whole (or else to some other aspect of it). Although it has been shown that alphabetization can indeed modify certain aspects of language processing, such as syllabic versus phonemic segmentation (Morais, Cary, Alegria, & Bertelson, 1979), the studies led by Scribner and Cole (1981, p. 238, on "literacy without education" among Liberians of the Vai community) and by one of us (indicating that the copy of a two-dimensional cube by healthy young adult illiterates regularly shows evidence of "constructional apraxia" [Parente, 1984]) can be taken to mean that school education as a whole rather than alphabetization per se is at stake in this respect. In either case, it would seem justified to assert, with regard to the biology of language, that interaction does occur between a species-specific genetic tendency toward left–right asymmetry in brain function and sociohistorical factors such as generalized availability of school education (which, up to a point, is an archetypical *lapalissade*).

ACKNOWLEDGMENTS

The authors' research on the effects of unilateral brain lesions in illiterates was supported by the Harry Frank Guggenheim Foundation, by the Conseil de la recherche médicale du Canada, and by the Brazilian Conselho Nacional da Pesquisa.

## NOTES

1 Broca's (1865) assertion in this respect was found on Louis-Pierre Gratiolet's (1854) description of asymmetries in the ontogenesis of the human brain (earlier cortical sulcation in certain regions of the left as opposed to the right cerebral hemisphere).
2 For instance, right-hemisphere participation is said to be relatively greater in children as opposed to adults (Lenneberg, 1967), in women as opposed to men (McGlone, 1980), and in left-handers and ambidextrals as opposed to right-handers (Hécaen & de Ajuriaguerra, 1963).
3 They implicitly claimed to be the first to discuss the issue.
4 As noted in each patient's record.
5 $\chi^2$ test, $p = .02$.
6 The remaining one was left-handed and had suffered a right stroke.
7 Directeur de recherche, Centre d'étude des processus cognitifs et du langage, Laboratoire de psychologie (Ecole des hautes en sciences et Centre national de la recherche scientifique), Paris.
8 It is this artery that irrigates the components of the "speech area" and their homologues of the other cerebral hemisphere.
9 Kruskall–Wallis Test, $H = 7.7$, df = 5, $p = .17$ (Siegel, 1956).
10 $\chi/u2 = 14.5$, df = 5, $p = .013$.
11 $\chi^2 = 1.10$, df = 1, $p = .29$.
12 $\chi^2 = 0$, df = 1, $p = 1$.
13 Kruskall–Wallis Test, $H = 0.18$, df = 2, $p = .92$ (Siegel, 1956).
14 Mann–Whitney Test: $p < .02$ in all cases (Siegel, 1956).
15 Sentence–picture matching: mismatches of left-stroke illiterates in left halves of displays ($\chi^2 = 7.6$, df = 1, $p = .0057$); of left-stroke readers in left halves ($\chi^2 = 3.8$, df = 1, $p = .05$); of right-stroke illiterates in right halves ($\chi^2 = 3.1$, df = 1, $p = .8$); of right-stroke readers in right halves ($\chi^2 = 0$, df = 1, $p = 1$).
16 Word repetition: dysechophemia of left-stroke illiterates ($\chi^2 = 20.6$, df = 1, $p < .0001$); of left-stroke readers ($\chi^2 = 6.24$, df = 1, $p = .013$); of right-stroke illiterates ($\chi^2 = 0.22$, df = 1, $p = .64$); of right-stroke readers ($\chi^2 = 0$, df = 1, $p = 1$).
17 $\chi^2 = 7.85$, df = 1, $p = .005$.
18 Naming: left-stroke illiterates ($\chi^2 = 10.35$, df = 1, $p = .001$); left-stroke readers ($\chi^2 = 10.7$, df 1, $p = .001$).
19 Naming: right-stroke illiterates ($\chi^2 = 8.09$, df = 1, $p = .004$); right-stroke readers ($\chi^2 = 1.88$, df 1, $p = .17$).
20 Paraphasia score ($\chi^2 = 5.12$, df = 1, $p = .02$); anomia score ($\chi^2 = 2.03$, df = 1, $p = .15$).
21 For a review, see Lecours et al. (1988).
22 In this respect, one might mention that blind a posteriori assessment of a subject of tape-recorded interviews led an experienced speech pathologist to suspect the presence of "mild aphasia" in nine of twenty right-stroke illiterates and in four of twenty-three neurologically healthy illiterate controls.

23 As a matter of fact, the notion of illiteracy and that of personal and maternal malnutrition were also in large overlap within our experimental population. In this respect, one may note that malnutrition does not seem to interfere substantially with the genetic program leading to "dominance" of the left cerebral hemisphere for language.

REFERENCES

Bradshaw, J. L., & Nettleton N. C., (1983). *Human cerebral asymmetry.* Englewood Cliffs, N.J.: Prentice Hall.
Broca, P. (1865). Sur le siège de la faculté du langage articulé. *Bulletin de la Société d'anthropologie* 6:337–93.
Cameron, R. F., Currier, R. D., & Haerer, A. F. (1971). Aphasia and literacy. *British Journal of Disorders of Communication* 6:161–3.
Castro, S. L., & Morais, J. (1987). Ear differences in illiterates. *Neuropsychologia* 25:409–18.
Coltheart, M., Patterson, K., & Marshall., J. C. (eds.) (1980). *Deep dyslexia.* London: Routledge & Kegan Paul.
Critchley, M. (1956). Premorbid literacy and the pattern of subsequent aphasia. *Proceedings of the Society of Medicine* 49:335–6.
(1964). *Development dyslexia.* London: Heinemann.
Currier, R. D., Haerer, A. F., & Farmer, L. J. (1976). Letter to the Editor. *Archives of Neurology* 33:662.
Damasio, A. R., Castro-Caldas, A., Grosso, J. T., & Ferro, J. M. (1976). Brain specialization for language does not depend on literacy. *Archives of Neurology* 33:300–301.
Damasio, A. R., Hamsher, K. de S., Castro-Caldas, A., Grosso, J. T., & Ferro, J. M. (1976). Letter to the editor. *Archives of Neurology* 33:662.
Damasio, H., Damasio, A. R., Castro-Caldas, A., & Hamsher, K. de S. (1979). Reversal of ear advantage for phonetically similar words in illiterates. *Journal of Clinical Neuropsychology* 1:331–8.
Dax, M. (1865). Lésions de la moitié gauche de l'encéphale coincident avec l'oubli des signes de la pensée. *Gazette hebdomadaire de médecine et de chirurgie* 33:259–62 (manuscript submitted for presentation at the Congrès méridional de médecine, Montpellier, 1836).
De Renzi, E., & Vignolo, L. A. (1962). The Token Test: A sensitive test to detect receptive disturbances in aphasics. *Brain* 85:665–78.
De Reuck, A. V. S., & O'Connor, M. (eds.) (1964). *Disorders of language.* London: Churchill.
Entus, A. K. (1977). Hemisphere asymmetry in processing of dichotically presented speech and nonspeech stimuli by infants. In S. J. Segalowitz & F. A. Gruber (eds.), *Language development and neurological theory,* pp. 63–73. New York: Academic Press.
Galaburda, A. (ed.) (1988). *From neurons to reading.* Cambridge, Mass.: MIT Press.

Goodglass, H., & Kaplan, E. (1972). *The assessment of aphasia and related disorders*. Philadelphia: Lea & Febiger.
Gorlitzer von Mundy, V. (1957). Zur Frage der paarig veranlagten Sprachzentren. *Der Nervenartz* 28:212–16.
Gratiolet, L. P. (1854). *Mémoire sur les plis cérébraux de l'homme et des primates*. Paris: Bertrand.
Hannequin, D., Goulet, P., & Joanette, Y. (1987). *La contribution de l'hémisphère droit à la communication verbale*. Paris: Masson.
Hécaen, H., & de Ajuriaguerra, J. (1963). *Les gauchers*. Paris: Presses Universitaires de France.
Joanette, Y., Lecours, A. R., Lepage, Y., & Lamoureux, M. (1983). Language in right-handers with right-hemisphere lesions: A preliminary study including anatomical, genetic and social factors. *Brain and Language* 20:217–48.
Lecours, A. R., Basso, A., Moraschini, S., & Nespoulous, J. L. (1984). Where is the speech area and who has seen it? In D. Caplan, A. R. Lecours, & A. Smith (eds.), *Biological perspectives on language*, pp. 220–46. Cambridge, Mass.: MIT Press.
Lecours, A. R., Mehler, J., Parente, M. A., & collaborators. (1987a). Illiteracy and brain damage: 1. Aphasia testing in culturally contrasted populations (control subjects). *Neuropsychologia* 25:231–45.
  (1987b). Illiteracy and brain damage: 2. Manifestations of unilateral neglect in testing 'auditory comprehension' with iconographic materials. *Brain and Cognition* 6:243–65.
  (1988). Illiteracy and brain damage: 3. A contribution to the study of speech and language disorders in illiterates with unilateral brain damage (initial testing). *Neuropsychologia*, 27(4):575–89.
Lecours, A. R., Nespoulous, J. L., Joanette, Y., Lemay, A., Puel, M., Lafond, D., Cot, F., & Rascol, A. (1986). *Protocole MT-86 d'Examen Linguistique de l'Aphasie (Version Alpha)*. Montréal: Théophile-Alajouanine.
Lenneberg, E. (1967). *Biological foundations of language*. New York: Wiley.
McGlone, J. (1980). Sex differences in human brain asymmetry: A critical survey. *Behavioral and Brain Sciences* 3:215–63.
Métellus, J. Cathala, H. P., Issartier, A., & Bodak, A. (1981). Une étude d'aphasie chez une illettrée (analphabète): Réflexions critiques sur les fonctions cérébrales concourant au langage. *Annales médico-psychologiques* 139:992–1001.
Morais, J., Cary, L., Alegria, J., & Bertelson, P. (1979). Does awareness of speech as a sequence of phones arise spontaneously? *Cognition* 7:323–31.
Moutier, F. (1908). *L'aphasie de Broca*. Paris: Steinheil.
Parente, M. A. (1984). *Habilidades construtivas em analfabetos: Um estudo através de desenho e construc; aao do cubo*. Unpublished dissertation. Sao Paulo: Pontificia Universidade Catolica.
Patterson, K., Marshall, J. C., & Coltheart, M. (eds.) (1985). *Surface dyslexia*. Hillsdale, N.J.: Erlbaum.

Scribner, S., & Cole, M. (1981). *The psychology of literacy.* Cambridge, Mass.: Harvard University Press.
Siegel, S. (1956). *Nonparametric statistics for the behavioral sciences.* New York: McGraw-Hill.
Tikofsky, R. (1970). Personal communication to Cameron et al., as quoted in R. F. Cameron, R. D. Currier, & A. F. Haerer (1971). Aphasia and literacy. *British Journal of Disorders of Communication* 6:161–3.
Tzavaras, A., Kaprinis, G., & Gatzoyas, A. (1981). Literacy and hemispheric specialization for language: Digit dichotic listening in illiterates. *Neuropsychologia* 19:565–70.
Weber, E. (1904). Das Schreiben als Ursache der einseitigen Lage des Sprachzentrums. *Zentralblatt fur Physiologie* 18:341–7.
Wechsler, A. F. (1976). Crossed aphasia in an illiterate dextral. *Brain and Language* 3:164–72.

# 15
## Literacy as metalinguistic activity
DAVID R. OLSON

When the "literacy hypothesis" emerged in the early writings of Havelock (1963, 1976), Ong (1982), McLuhan (1962), Goody and Watt (1963) and others, it had some of the properties of a ground-clearing operation, a sort of slash-and-burn quality, and it has fallen to a second generation of scholars to clean up the debris and turn the clearing into arable land.

The central claims made on literacy's behalf were that writing had, historically, been responsible for the evolution of new forms of discourse, prose fiction and essayist prose being two examples, that reflected a new approach or understanding of language and a new, more subjective and reflective frame of mind. Literacy, too, it was argued, had been responsible in part for new forms of social organization, of states rather than tribes, and of reading publics rather than oral contact groups. When these arguments were stated more expansively, literacy was seen as the route to "modernity," a route that was exportable to developing countries that also aspired to that modernity.

Among the debris created in those bold theoretical ventures were some notable limitations and contradictions. First, to celebrate the significance of literacy was, even if inadvertently, to mark nonliteracy or "orality" as inferior, something to be grown or developed out of or, if necessary, eradicated. As Pattanayak puts it (Chapter 6, this volume), to even call nonreaders "illiterates" is to mark over half of the world's population as second class. No use of literacy is so important that it warrants the branding of one-half of humankind as inferior. But in addition to the mislabeling problem, the "general claim," as Feldman (Chapter 3, this volume) has referred to it, is misleading in that it ascribes to literates characteristics that linguists and anthropologists have shown to be present in some form in members of nonliterate, or traditional, societies. Second, it was the case that some cultures were in fact literate, the Vai and the Cree being typical examples, and yet the forms of speech and thought associated with modernity failed to appear. Third, linguists such as Biber (1986) and

Ainsworth-Vaughn (1987) failed to find systematic differences in the lexical, syntactic, or discourse structures of oral and written productions. And finally, students of reasoning (Cole & Scribner, 1974; Scribner & Cole, 1981) reported that while the premises from which members of various cultures drew inferences varied, the logical processes themselves did not, and further that literacy, per se, had no appreciable effect on the solutions offered to such problems. These and other such facts had to be ignored in order to sustain the general view that literacy had historically transformed mind and society and the more particular view that the acquisition of literacy was a major factor in intellectual, linguistic, and social development.

Clearly, it is time either to retreat or to formulate the literacy hypothesis along somewhat more defensible lines. An appropriate formulation is not yet available but will, among other things, first have to put literacy into a functional context as Scribner (1986), Griffin and Cole (1987), Heath (1983), and others have argued. Literacy, like orality, is a means to a variety of ends, not an end in itself. The functions served in various social contexts may make many of the oral–written differences dwindle into insignificance. Second, it will have to examine the forms of literacy relevant to various individuals, social groups, and different cultures (Street, 1984; Wagner, 1987), factors that again limit the generalizability of findings regarding Western literacy. Third, it will have to acknowledge the differences among orthographies and, consequently, their uses (Taylor & Olson, in preparation). And fourth, it will have to spell out more precisely the relations among various means of communication and between these media and the more fundamental properties and uses of human language generally.

My concerns in this chapter are much more limited. I shall discuss four hypotheses relating Western literacy to the forms of thought we value and encourage through schooling. The hypotheses I shall consider are the modality hypothesis, the medium hypothesis, the mental skills hypothesis, and the metalinguistic hypothesis. Before I examine these hypotheses, it is essential to consider the conception of literacy, the intellectual implications of which I am attempting to explain.

### Conditions necessary for the development of literacy

While literacy, strictly speaking, refers to an individual's ability to read and write, the literacy hypothesis is considerably more general, bearing on the general competence required to participate in a literate tradition. The conditions essential for this more general literacy include four factors.

First, there has to be some device for "fixing" and accumulating texts. The primary means for fixing texts is a script but as Narasimhan (Chapter 11, this volume) and Feldman (Chapter 3, this volume) have pointed out, "texts" can also be fixed via oral means. The Vedic tradition is one in which texts are fixed by means of elaborate mnemonic schemes that keep them as invariant as writing does. In the tradition of the oral poets studied by Parry (1971), Lord (1960), Goody (1987), and Finnegan (1977), however (see Havelock, Chapter 1, this volume), the preserved form was not a verbatim form but one that exploited rhythm, meter, and formulaic expressions such as the Homeric "wine red sea" in oral composition. Thus the poem was fixed while the wording was somewhat variable. Yet both types of oral tradition "fix" a text and make it an object of repetition and reflection.

Such texts have an accumulative, archival function. New information can be added and old superseded or abandoned. Writing has an enormous advantage in that it allows the accumulation of texts that go far beyond the storage capacities of any knower. Indeed, Eisenstein (1979) has made an extremely strong case for the view that it is the archival functions of literacy with its provisions for accumulating and updating information that is critical to understanding the social and intellectual implications of literacy. Conversely, the Vai (Scribner & Cole, 1981) and the Cree (Bennett & Berry, Chapter 5, this volume) both possess a script that could "fix" a text, but as those texts were used primarily for records and friendly letters, they did not contribute to the growth of an accumulative archival tradition. A literate tradition requires both fixing and accumulating those texts.

Second, there must be institutions for using texts. As long as texts are of no relevance to social practices such as religion, law, business, justice, science, and literature, they have limited cognitive significance. The growth of literacy, therefore, requires some institutions for using texts: the church, the court, the government, the academy, and the family. Indeed, literacy contributes greatly to the specialization and differentiation of these institutions.

Third, there must be institutions for inducting learners into those institutions. These institutions include the family, the church, and, in literate societies primarily, the school. Not only does the school train children to take the roles as experts in literate institutions, but also, more generally, it trains the majority to use and to trust those institutions, to be what Illich (Chapter 2, this volume) refers to as "lay literates." The lay literate has the broad range of knowledge that people possess about literacy and literate institutions even if they themselves are not readers or writers.

And fourth, the one of most relevance for what follows, there must be the evolution of an oral metalanguage, tied to a "mental language," for talking and thinking about the structures and meanings of those accumulated texts and the intentions of their authors and their interpretation in particular contexts. It is this metalanguage that permits speakers and writers to refer to a text, its properties, its structure, as well as to its meaning and appropriate interpretation. Just what this metalanguage refers to and how it functions are primary concerns of this chapter.

Once we approach literacy in this broader sense, as the ability to participate in a literate tradition, in the science, philosophy, and literature of the tradition, the claim that literacy is a significant social and psychological factor seems to be too obvious to require detailed comment. Yet just how literacy contributes to these social and psychological processes remains obscure. To narrow the range of possible explanations we may return to our four hypotheses.

### Four hypotheses linking literacy and thought

*The modality hypothesis: an eye for an ear*

One of the first hypotheses relating literacy and forms of thought, indeed it was McLuhan's view (1962), was that literacy called into play a highly spatializing sensory modality, the eye, which came to substitute for the ear. The simple fact that language is written and subject to visual scanning was thought to influence its form and its uses.

While the general claim regarding the importance of the eye now seems extravagant, in fact there is some evidence that simple modality differences do alter people's linguistic productions. Chafe (1985) and Chafe and Danielewicz (1987) provided ample evidence that people write differently from the way that they speak. Writers draw on a somewhat more elaborate vocabulary and use more complex clause constructions in writing than do speakers. These differences tended to show up in different "genres" more so than in the use of a different modality per se. That is, the properties of writing are more visible in scientific papers than in friendly letters. Indeed, Tannen (1985) has suggested that a more useful way of classifying language is in terms of such dimensions as involvement versus information – speech often, but not always, emphasizing the former, writing the latter. Yet there is some evidence that, even holding the genre constant, oral and written productions diverge. Hildyard and Hidi (1985) studied the oral and written productions of elementary school children. Until they were twelve years old, there were no differences between their oral and their written texts. From that point on, their oral and written productions diverged, the written ones manifesting a higher degree of structural complexity. This improvement was tied directly to the beginnings of revising texts; it was the revision process that appeared to give rise to more complex texts. They also found that writing their texts led children to recall more of the very words they had used whereas oral production led to a better memory for gist. It seems that writing permitted subjects to devote greater attention to the linguistic properties of the text, both its surface form and its logical structure.

Nystrand (1986) reports a similar effect in college students. In one writing conference group, students read aloud their papers and had them criticized by the group, whereas in a second group, copies of the papers were distributed to the group. He observed that in the first case, revisions tended to be superficial, whereas in the second, the revisions tended to involve the basic structure of the text. The mere presence of the written text enabled critics and writers to improve the basic structure of the text. But even if the written record permits one to look back, to re-read, to revise, and hence to create a public document, those effects are somewhat specialized and tied not merely to the practice of reading and writing but to the entire educational enterprise, these effects not even appearing until well into the school years. Hence, it is not as if it is the simple modality differences that account for differences in discourse and thought but rather the forms of discourse developed around speech and writing, namely, the medium of communication rather than the modality exploited. Moreover, it is not clear that there are particular cognitive effects that are uniquely associated with the visual processes of reading and writing. Dyslexic children cannot read or write, and yet they often perform normally on intelligence tests (Vellutino, 1979). Since they are nonreaders, if reading is what is responsible for visual-spatial forms of thought, they ought to perform poorly on such ability tests whereas, in fact, they perform normally. Hence, the modality of input would not appear to be the decisive factor. McLuhan's (1962) "eye for an ear" formula, a pun on the ancient Jewish law, is a metaphor for the implications of literacy, not an explanation of them.

*The medium hypothesis: speaking and writing as distinctive forms of discourse*

A second hypothesis is that writing as a medium, as opposed to writing as a modality, refers to the fact that writing not only appeals to the eye but serves as an alternative medium of communication. Writing relates individuals and groups in a way quite different from speech. The notion of audience (from the Latin for listening) gives way to the notion of public (the reading public, for example). As a medium of communication, writing leads to the evolution of new forms of discourse, new genres, such as the business letter, the résumé, the encyclopedia article, the list, the table, and many other forms that capitalize on the resources of writing (see Goody, 1987). According to this hypothesis, the cognitive implications of literacy arise not simply from using the eye, the modality, but from learning to exploit the resources of this medium of communication with its specialized genres. These genres are specialized to serve particular purposes: alphabetization for information retrieval, categories and lists for organizing information, fiction for entertaining, essayist prose for examining the implications of a statement, and so on.

And the publics reached by these written texts are no longer the primary oral audiences but the extensive network of readers, united only by their access to these forms of discourse. A reading public in modern society, like the "textual community" in the Middle Ages (Stock, 1983), are new social groups created around texts, their reading, and their interpretation. Indeed, it may be argued that some of the distinctive properties of written texts are a consequence of the peculiarities of dealing with an impersonal audience (Ainsworth-Vaughn, 1987). Godzich and Kittay (1987) cite Boas's suggestion that prose is peculiar in that it is composed to be read rather than listened to.

The linguistic properties of writing as a medium have been examined by Halliday (1987) who suggests that written language tends to be lexically dense but grammatically simple whereas spoken language tends to be grammatically intricate but lexically simple. He suggests that the critical variable is that of consciousness: "Writing is in essence a more conscious process than speaking . . . spontaneous discourse is usually spoken, self-monitored discourse is usually written" (pp. 67–9). What this consciousness permits is a higher level of concern with textual structure. He discusses the phenomenon of "grammatical metaphor" exploited in writing whereby whole propositions are nominalized to become subjects and objects in higher-level propositions. In the sentence "(The current popular concern over the environment) has stimulated (private civil actions)," whole propositions marked with parentheses serve as noun phrases of the higher-order proposition. While such noun phrases tend to become somewhat ambiguous, the gain in textual cohesion – the relations between propositions – more than compensates for the loss. As a result, grammatical metaphor is a device for backgrounding texts, for making them create contexts for themselves. This self-contextualizing property is what makes written texts somewhat "autonomous" relative to most speech (see Olson, 1977).

But what is the cognitive significance of competence with the written medium of communication? The functions that these forms of discourse serve, including describing, explaining, ordering, promising, reminding, and the like, tend to be universal to all human cultures, and the specialized literate forms may simply provide alternative means to the same ends. Further, the uniqueness of the written medium is diminished by Biber's (1986) finding that the particular features usually associated with writing – such as elaboration, explicitness, detachment, decontextualization – when examined in a wide range of orally produced and written texts were overridden by three, more fundamental parameters: interactive versus edited text, abstract versus situated context, and reported versus edited style. It remains possible, however, that even if differences of medium tend to disappear at the lexical and sentence level, they may remain at the discourse level.

The major arguments against both the modality and the medium hypotheses is that people can behave in a "literate" manner in oral as well as in written language and that, worse still for those hypotheses, nonreaders – dyslexics, for example – often manifest the linguistic and conceptual features typical of literates.

*The mental skills hypothesis: learning to think like a reader or writer*

A third hypothesis relating literacy to thought may be constructed through an analysis of the skills involved in becoming a reader and writer. This hypothesis gets around the objections raised to the earlier hypotheses in that it allows that skills transfer across media and modalities. Thus the knowledge acquired in reading and writing may apply in speaking and listening; having learned to analyze written words into letters one may come to divide the spoken words into sounds (Ehri, 1985; Read, Zhang, Nie, & Ding, 1986). Having learned to recognize words in written texts, one may come to recognize the words present in one's speech. And having learned to read a text and analyze its implications, one may come to treat an utterance as if it were a "text" and subject it to a similar sort of analysis, and so on.

Scribner and Cole (1981), in their careful study of the implications of literacy among the Vai of Liberia, found that the specific skills involved in reading and writing Vai script transferred to task implicating these same skills. Thus, those who could read Vai, for example, could also read a novel, rebus form of writing as well as carry out auditory integration tasks that were similar in principle to the reading tasks. Further, formulating a general statement of purpose or intent, a feature important to letter writing, was transferred to the task of orally explaining a game to novices. The generality of these skills, however, was quite limited. There were no major cognitive differences in rationality, abstraction, or logical reasoning between the literate and nonliterate subjects; the relations were between much more specific activities and forms of competence.

But is it the case that literacy skills acquired in learning to read and write are simply transferred to oral activities? It is now reasonably well established that the skills of literacy may be conveyed and acquired, at least in part, orally. Wells (1985a, 1985b) and Hedelin and Hjelmquist (1988) found that the best indication of how well children would do in literate activities in the school was the form and extent of literate activities, primarily book reading, in the home. The skills here, although literate ones, are developed via oral means. Scollon and Scollon (1979), too, noticed that literate skills may be communicated orally: "teachers of children use a style of speaking . . . that is instrumental in developing a literate orientation" (p. 1). Heath (1987) and Olson (1984) have advanced similar arguments. Hence, the directness of the link between actual reading practice and the acquisition of literacy skills is indirect indeed.

It seems clear that there are special skills such as letter and word recognition, comprehension of fixed texts, and of expression of ideas in writing that are acquired in the course of learning to read and write and that do transfer to similar orally presented tasks. But the usefulness of the notion of skill begins to wane when we note that transfer between oral and written competencies can occur even in the absence of reading and writing skills, as is the case, for example, when children and adults acquire some of the competencies usually associated with reading and writing from such oral practices as being read to and talking about texts. In such cases it is not simply that children are applying the skills acquired in one domain to another domain so much as that they have acquired some knowledge *about* language and its uses, knowledge that is peculiar to particular literate traditions. This leads to our fourth hypothesis relating literacy and thought.

*The metalinguistic hypothesis: making language into an object of thought and discourse*

Many writers have commented on the development of the ability to not only use language, but also to "decenter" or "step aside" or "step back" and look at the language being used. If the ability to use language is "linguistic ability," the ability to reflect on the language used is "metalinguistic ability." Mattingly (1972, p. 133), in discussing learning to read, commented that if speaking and listening are primary linguistic abilities, then reading, being a secondary activity, relies upon the reader's awareness of those primary activities. The suggestion is that in order to understand the secondary activity, one must be aware of the primary activity. To mention a specific case, in order to read an alphabetic script, a learner would first have to be able to segment speech into the phonemic constituents represented by the letters of the script. Indeed, there is a burgeoning literature on the role of "metalinguistic awareness" in learning to read (see Tunmer, Pratt, & Herriman, 1984; Bertelson, 1986). However, the notion of metalinguistic knowledge and its relation to reading is not restricted to letter–sound relations, but also to larger units of texts including words, sentences, and texts.

In an earlier paper (Olson, 1977), I had tried to show that literacy had and continues to have an effect on thought through the formulation and comprehension of explicit, "autonomous" texts, texts in which the meaning depended critically on the wording. The argument had much in common with Donaldson's (1978) discussion of the effects of schooling on children's reasoning in which she pointed out that younger, but not older children failed on reasoning tasks that required them to "pay scrupulous attention to the language in its own right" (p. 70). The question was how, precisely, this attention developed. Literacy and schooling were implicated, but it was not clear why.

Herriman (1986) has suggested that there is a conceptual relationship between literacy and metalinguistic awareness. The link arises from the fact that in reading and especially in writing, language can become the object of thought and discussion. He argues:

Metalinguistic awareness may be related to the attainment of literacy, via its emphasis on the kind of attention that can be given to the construction and comprehension of written language. The process of expository prose writing involves constantly attending to the syntax and semantics of language. The choice of words and grammatical constructions, especially in relation to details such as tense, mood, and aspect of the verb, is important to conveying the precise intention of the writer. (p. 167)

That is, the reason that prose reading and writing can be an instrument of metalinguistic reflection is that in those cases, one must assess the particular meanings of terms and of grammatical relations between them in order either to understand such texts or to write them.

This is not to say that such metalinguistic knowledge is a precondition of literacy but rather that it is a product of literacy. It is this hypothesis that I shall pursue here. Before proceeding, however, it is worth noting that the metalinguistic hypothesis is not the only contender in the field. Nystrand (1986) among others offers a rhetorical theory of text formation that is built on the notion that texts have their uses and effects not by virtue of the metalinguistic effects but because of their communicative effects. In writing one learns to address a larger, or a less well known, audience, and so the text tends to become more elaborate. That theory is entirely plausible. It is just different from the one offered here, namely, that texts have their particular form and recruit their particular cognitive processes by virtue of changing the level of discourse from one about the world into one about the text.

### Literacy and metalinguistics

My suggestion is that writing is by its very nature a metalinguistic activity. On this point, if no other, Bloomfield (1933) was right when he claimed that "writing is not language, but merely a way of recording language by means of visible marks" (p. 21). Chafe and Danielewicz (1987) quote this to disagree with it, but their purpose was quite different from mine. Bloomfield made this claim in order to dismiss the notion of "written language"; mine on the other hand is to indicate that writing is intrinsically metalinguistic.

Of course, not everything in the linguistic code is reflected in the metalinguistic code. Among other things, different writing systems select in different ways from the oral language – logographic writing represents word structures, syllabaries represent syllables, alphabets represent phonemes, and so on. In addition to the mapping relations between language and writing there is also an oral metalanguage consisting of such terms as "letters," "words," "sentences," "stories," "essays," and the like for referring to aspects of the written form. It is important to distinguish the metalinguistic form, writing, from the oral metalanguage because writing may have its effects either through representing aspects of oral language in its orthography *or* through marking those aspects in an explicit metalanguage. I would tentatively distinguish four levels of analyses:

1. the world of objects,
2. oral language that takes the world as its object (producing a linguistic form of world awareness),
3. writing that takes oral language as its object (producing linguistic awareness), and
4. an oral metalanguage that takes writing or any other aspect of an utterance or text as its object (producing metalinguistic awareness).

The hypothesis under consideration is that writing is in principle metalinguistic in that it is a representation of language, and an oral metalanguage may be used to refer to aspects of writing. Distinguishing linguistic awareness (level 3) from metalinguistic awareness (level 4) may seem like splitting hairs, but the distinction is necessary for several reasons. First, it is only level 3 that is involved in making language an object of reflection. Thus, at least by hypothesis, one does not need to be conversant with the oral metalanguage to notice subtle properties of the language as long as those properties are represented in the writing system. For a writer to choose "for you and me" over "for you and I," he or she need not be in possession of the oral metalanguage used for describing prepositional phrases. Of course, the oral metalanguage may be useful for formalizing and explicating that understanding, and it will be routinely exploited by teachers. But for the writer it is sufficient that it be represented in the script. Second, the oral metalanguage for referring to letters, words, inflections, tenses, and so on is not essential for such activities as phonemic segmentation, detecting subject–verb agreement for tense and number, and the like. All that is required is that the written form marks the relevant distinctions and the reader become competent with those forms. Similarly in regard to grammatical form, writing permits revision toward standard forms even if the writer does not know the oral metalanguage for talking about the grammar in terms of subject, verbs, objects, complements, and the like. It is in that sense that I refer to writing as metalinguistic; writing makes language into an object.

Consider some implications of that argument. One is that people will reflect on their language in terms of their orthography. If the orthography marks words, they will be aware of words, those represented by the orthography. Thus children's understanding of what a word is (Francis, 1975, 1987) and their ability to segment the stream of speech into words are tied to the acquisition of literacy although the cause–consequence issue remains unresolved. It remains unresolved, I would suggest, because children can acquire this knowledge either through learning to read or through acquiring the oral metalanguage about those forms. In learning to read a segmented script (see Saenger, Chapter 12, this volume) one cannot help learning that units represent spoken words. However, one could also learn about words through oral discourse about language. If that is true, then while there is no answer to the cause–consequence question, it nevertheless remains true that metalinguistic knowledge about language is a consequence, whether directly or indirectly, of literacy.

A similar case may be made of the phonemic awareness controversy. Bradley and Bryant (1983) have shown the intimate connection between the recognition of phonemes as measured by rhyme and alliteration and learning to read while Ehri (1985) and Francis (1984) have provided evidence that learning to read promotes such awareness. This latter view is supported by the impressive studies by Morais, Bertelson, Cary, and Alegria (1986) showing that Portuguese peasants who had received only a minimal introduction to schooling and reading were still, years later, vastly superior in such tasks as phoneme substitution to those who had never had any exposure to reading. Scholes and Willis (Chapter 13, this volume) report a similar finding with adult nonliterates in the United States. Similarly, the studies by Read, Zhang, Nie, and Ding (1986) also provide clear evidence that the consonants a speaker is able to detect in speech depend upon the structures marked in the orthography. Specifically, Chinese readers who had learned to read the Roman-augmented Chinese characters could delete specified consonants whereas those who read ordinary Chinese characters could not. Again, it appears that it is the matter of representing speech in writing that makes speech the object of reflection whether or not the writing is further represented in an oral metalanguage consisting of such terms as letters, words, and the like.

This last point is also supported by the research of Ferreiro (1985), who found that when children invent their own writing systems, those invented scripts may represent and bring into awareness a variety of features whether the child knows oral terms for referring to those features or not. Thus, again, level 3 is critical to the awareness of language quite independently of level 4.

So what is the relation between this linguistic awareness and the metalanguage mentioned earlier as level 4? My own earlier papers on the importance of level 4, the oral metalanguage, I now see as a bit of an oversimplification. I argued that it was the metalanguage that made the language an object of reflection; I would now argue that the primary factor is the orthography. The oral metalanguage may, of course, draw attention to the features of the orthography, making it an object of discourse whereas the orthography in and of itself makes language an object of awareness.

The oral metalanguage has an additional advantage, however. It can be used to represent language and aspects of texts quite independently of the orthography. That is, the oral metalanguage is not restricted to literacy. For example, there is also a more complex metalanguage that is used in referring to language, part of which is shared with speaking and part of which is specialized for writing. This is the metalanguage discussed by Feldman (Chapter 3, this volume) and others for referring to the content of texts. This metalanguage includes such verbal concepts as *tell, say, ask,* and such nominal concepts as *story, talk, song*, and the like. These concepts, in a manner somewhat parallel to writing, make some verbal structures the objects of discourse. Calling a speech act a lie is to comment on an utterance by referring to it with a metalinguistic term. As Feldman shows, devices for referring to talk are not restricted to literate cultures or to literate activities. But as Olson and Astington (1990) have shown, these concepts tend to be very elaborate in a literate culture. Of special importance are the devices for referring to speech acts by means of such terms as *claim, state, assert, explain, demonstrate*, and the like and those for referring to the corresponding mental states by means of such terms as *believe, infer, hypothesize, assume, conclude*, and the like. As Traugott (1987) has suggested, the elaborateness of these distinctions, while associated with literacy, tend to reflect the social practices of government, justice, commerce, and religion, not only the availability of writing.

In our earlier work we have argued that these metalinguistic concepts are of enormous educational significance. To cite a simple case, while the understanding of the difference between an *assumption* and an *inference* is a subtle one, it is one that is extremely important for writing and argumentation; for if a proposition is an assumption, then it should be acknowledged, whereas if it is an inference, then it should be justified. These somewhat subtle concepts form an important part of the higher levels of literacy that we expect from our schools and colleges. We should note that it is not only the terms that are of importance but the patterns in discourse that children are sensitive to; it is possible, if unlikely, that writers are sensitive to just these distinctions even if they do not know the metalanguage for referring to them. Empirical research would be helpful on this point.

I have introduced two levels of metalinguistic structure, the first being the writing system that marks, and thereby represents, aspects of linguistic structure. Included here are distinctions between sounds, as represented by letters; distinctions between words, as represented by spaces; distinctions between clauses, as represented by punctuation; between thematic elements, as represented by topic sentences and paragraphs; and between types of discourse, as represented by genre. Some of these distinctions, as mentioned, are marked in the oral metalanguage by terms such as *letter, word, sentence, clause, topic, paragraph, narrative, exposition, essay, play, poem*, and the like.

The second set is the oral metalanguage for referring to the content of the text. This text may be fixed either orally – through direct quotation, for example – or through writing. Once fixed, a text is subject to an additional set of considerations: Is it true? Is it logical? Is it clear? Is it persuasive? Particular utterances may be characterized by readers as assertions, hypotheses, conclusions, speculations, and the like. All of these considerations are relevant to the formation of particular types of texts and text-based arguments, and they are critical to what we think of as literate or educated thought.

But these latter are not exclusive to literacy. I have argued that literacy, through both writing and oral metalanguage, makes language an object of talk and reflection. But in the light of such arguments as those presented by Feldman (Chapter 3, this volume), it must be acknowledged that writing is not the only means for making language an object of discourse. As Leech (1983) has pointed out, any language contains a metalanguage. All languages have terms for referring to what was said and to forms of discourse, whether stories, prayers, serious talk, or the like. Feldman's discussion of *kiyori*, the political rhetorical genre of the Wana of Indonesia, exemplifies this point.

But while not exclusive to a literate culture, writing in a literate culture tends to exploit metalinguistic concepts much more so than does speech. Tannen (1987) has recently commented on children's use of speech-act verbs in reporting dialogue orally as opposed to in a written form. Whereas in an oral report children used only the verbs "says," "goes," "like," or no speech-act verb at all, the same children when writing their reports resorted to a wide variety of speech-act verbs, including "insisted," "exclaimed," "shrieked," and the like. While available for speech, they tend to be recruited much more extensively in writing and encountered much more frequently in reading.

A similar point could be made about children's phonemic awareness. Certainly, reading and writing with an alphabet competently requires some level of awareness of the mapping between writing and speech, but children's rhymes and verses also play into and require such awareness, not precisely that required for reading an alphabet, but with knowledge that is sufficiently related to produce a high level of transfer (Bradley & Bryant, 1983). The primary, in my view unsolved, problem is just what set of concepts are implicated in which types of activities and, more importantly, just what use speakers make of these concepts in their thought and talk.

**Literacy and thought**

How does this relate to thought? Thought is the activity of making any object the object of reflection. I have indicated how writing makes language into an object of such reflection. It remains to indicate how that reflection on language may be turned to intellectual advantage.

From this point on, the argument takes a by now familiar form. Language is used for representing the world; it makes it possible to reflect on, to become aware of, the world. Writing is used for representing language; it makes it possible to reflect on, to become aware of, language. Here is where reading and writing have their role in thought. In dealing with written language, whether in reading it or writing it, one is simultaneously aware of two things, the world *and the language*.

One need not be aware of both to reject false statements or to make repairs and corrections, an assumption that had blocked earlier hypotheses relating literacy to linguistic awareness (see also Herriman, 1986). In such cases the discourse is about the world. Consider the child who is asked, "Is snow black?" and who replies, "No, it's not [black]." This discourse is about the snow. This is precisely what language is for – discourse about the world. Now consider the question "Is it true that snow is black?" and the answer "No, it's not [true]." In this case, the discourse is no longer simply about the snow but about the sentence. Judgment about truth and falsity are therefore metalinguistic judgments. Writing performs an analogous function. In writing the discourse is both about the world represented and about the language used for representing it. The reader and writer now have the possibility of reflecting on both and revising the latter in order to bring them into agreement. The writer can reflect on the choice of the noun, the verb, the tense, the aspect, on whether the clause should be a subordinate or a main clause, and so on. As Herriman (1986) suggested, this checking process is essentially a metalinguistic one. Knowledge of explicit grammar, an oral metalanguage, may or may not help in these decisions. The decades of research on the teaching of grammar suggest that explicit grammar adds little to the awareness of structure produced by writing per se.

A variety of other tasks may be accounted for in terms of this metalinguistic hypothesis: Donaldson's (1978) finding about children's paying scrupulous attention to wording in problem solving tasks; Luria's (1976) Uzbekis subjects who, when asked to judge if a certain conclusion followed from a pair of premises, refused to talk about the text but insisted upon talking about the bears mentioned in the text; and Torrance and Olson's (1987) finding that four- and five-year-old children typically subordinate what a speaker actually "says" to what the listener takes them to "mean" – all are indicative of the fact that literacy encourages people to be aware of the text as object as well as of the content of the text. That, presumably, is what makes text revision possible in more skilled writers (Bereiter & Scardamalia, 1981; Herriman, 1986). In other places I have suggested that the basic insight in literate discourse is a metalinguistic one, the recognition that sentences have a meaning that may or may not correspond to the meaning intended by the writer (Olson & Torrance, 1987).

While the writing system is responsible for making some features of language the objects of thought, the oral metalanguage may mark other features of language or discourse and turn them into objects of reflection as well. Hence, consciousness of language and reflection on texts are not unique to literacy.

## Conclusion

I have set out four hypotheses that have been offered as explanations of how literacy may be related to thought. I have cast my lot primarily with the fourth one, namely, that writing takes language for its object and just as language is a device for "fixing" the world in such a way as to make it an object of reflection, so writing "fixes" language in such a way as to make it an object of reflection. This "objectification" of language through writing adds to the already existing set of devices for turning speech into an object of discourse that exists in such oral metalinguistic concepts as *tell, say, ask, lie,* and *swear,* which appear to be universal, as well as the more complex ones for referring to forms of discourse that appear to differ widely from culture to culture as they mark a variety of their respective practices. However, it also appears to be the case that by virtue of a fixed written text, suitable for rescanning, comparison, commentary, and analysis, the literate tradition has evolved an elaborate set of speech-act and mental-state verbs useful for legal, scholarly, and literary discourse.

But if what is involved in literacy is the acquisition of a form for representing language and thereby turning it into an object of reflection, the third hypothesis we considered, namely, that the forms of literacy we have been considering have their effects on cognition primarily through the acquisition of generalized skills of reading and writing, is also true. The very act of reading involves not only reading skills but also metalinguistic skills, how property *x* of language is represented in writing. Once represented, that property *x* is available for application to new activities and new tasks. Thus, as we have seen, once the child sees that the written word consists of sound units represented by letters, the child can also think of the spoken word consisting of those same sound units.

But if we accept this hypothesis, we see, in addition, that the second hypothesis, although incomplete, was also correct. In exploiting the structure of writing, we are exploiting the resources of the written medium of communication, with its more specialized audiences addressed through more specialized forms of discourse. It is through the resources of writing as a medium of communication that specialized forms of discourse arose (Godzich & Kittay, 1987), and it is through dealing with these special forms of discourse that that specialized set of intellectual competencies arise.

But if we grant the second hypothesis, we must also grant the first, namely, the particular relevance of the visual modality. It is the visual modality that picks up and processes the orthography, the system for representing language. Granted, one could, as do the Vedics, represent language by means of another oral language and do so with distinctive social and intellectual effects. But it is the representation of language by means of visible marks that, at least in Western culture, turns language into an object of thought and analysis. "Only the phonetic alphabet makes a break between eye and ear, between semantic meaning and visual code; and thus only phonetic writing has the power to translate men from the tribal to the civilized sphere, to give him an eye for an ear" (McLuhan, 1962, p. 27).

### ACKNOWLEDGMENTS

I am grateful to Denese Coulbeck for her editorial and bibliographic assistance and to Nancy Torrance for her critical comments. I am also grateful for the support of the SSHRC, the Spencer Foundation, and the Ontario Ministry of Education through its Block Transfer Grant to OISE.

### REFERENCES

Ainsworth-Vaughn, N. (1987). *Cohesion and coherence in oral and written narratives* (mimeo). East Lansing: Michigan State University.
Bereiter, C., & Scardamalia, M. (1981). From conversation to composition: The role of instruction in a developmental process. In R. Glaser (ed.), *Advances in instructional psychology* (Vol. 2). Hillsdale, N.J.: Erlbaum.
Bertelson, P. (1986). The onset of literacy: Liminal remarks. *Cognition* 24:1–30.
Biber, D. (1986). Spoken and written textual dimensions in English: Resolving the contradictory findings. *Language* 62(2):384–414.
Bloomfield, L. (1933). *Language*. New York: Holt.
Bradley, L., & Bryant, P. E. (1983). Categorizing sounds and learning to read: A causal connection. *Nature* 301:419–21.
Chafe, W. (1985). Linguistic differences produced by differences between speaking and writing. In D. R. Olson, A. Hildyard, & N. Torrance (eds.), *Literacy, language, and learning: The nature and consequences of reading and writing* (pp. 105–23). Cambridge University Press.

Chafe, W., & Danielewicz, J. (1987). Properties of spoken and written language. In R. Horowitz & S. J. Samuels (eds.), *Comprehending oral and written language* (pp. 83–13). New York: Academic Press.
Cole, M., & Scribner, S. (1974). *Culture and thought: A psychological introduction.* New York: Wiley.
Donaldson, M. (1978). *Children's minds.* Glasgow: Fontana/Collins.
Ehri, L. (1985). Effects of printed language acquisition on speech. In D. R. Olson, A. Hildyard, & N. Torrance (eds.), *Literacy, language, and learning: The nature and consequences of reading and writing* (pp. 333–67). Cambridge University Press.
Eisenstein, E. (1979). *The printing press as an agent of change.* Cambridge University Press.
Ferreiro, E. (1985). Literacy development: A psychogenetic perspective. In D. R. Olson, A. Hildyard, & N. Torrance (eds.), *Literacy, language, and learning: The nature and consequences of reading and writing* (pp. 217–28). Cambridge University Press.
Finnegan, R. (1977). *Oral poetry.* Cambridge University Press.
Francis, H. (1975). *Language in childhood: Form and function in language learning.* London: Elek.
  (1984). Children's knowledge of orthography in learning to read. *British Journal of Educational Psychology* 54:8–23.
  (1987). Cognitive implications of learning to read. *Interchange* 18(1 & 2):97–108.
Godzich, W., & Kittay, J. (1987). *The emergence of prose: An essay in prosaics.* Minneapolis: University of Minnesota Press.
Goody, J. (1987). *The interface between the written and the oral.* Cambridge University Press.
Goody, J., & Watt, I. (1963). The consequences of literacy. *Contemporary Studies in Society and History* 5:304–45. Republished in J. Goody (ed.) (1968). *Literacy in traditional societies.* Cambridge University Press.
Griffin, P., & Cole, M. (1987). New technologies, basic skills, and the underside of education: What's to be done? In J. Langer (ed.), *Language, literacy, and culture: Issues of society and schooling* (pp. 199–231). Norwood, N.J.: Ablex.
Halliday, M. A. K. (1987). Spoken and written modes of meaning. In R. Horowitz & S. J. Samuels (eds.), *Comprehending oral and written language* (pp. 55–82). New York: Academic Press.
Havelock, E. (1963). *Preface to Plato.* Cambridge, Mass.: Harvard University Press.
  (1976). *Origins of Western literacy.* Toronto: Ontario Institute for Studies in Education.
Heath, S. (1983). *Ways with words.* Cambridge University Press.
  (1987). The literate essay: Using ethnography to explode myths. In J. Langer (ed.), *Language, literacy, and culture: Issues of society and schooling* (pp. 89–107). Norwood, N.J.: Ablex.
Hedelin, L., & Hjelmquist, E. (1988). Preschool children's mastery of the form/content distinction in spoken language. In K. Ekberg & P. E.

Mjaavatn (eds.), *Growing into a modern world*. The Norwegian Center for Child Research, University of Trondheim.
Herriman, M. (1986). Metalinguistic awareness and the growth of literacy. In S. de Castell, A. Luke, & K. Egan (eds.), *Literacy, society, and schooling: A reader* (pp. 159–74). Cambridge University Press.
Hildyard, A., & Hidi, S. (1985). Oral–written differences in the production and recall of narratives. In D. R. Olson, A. Hildyard, & N. Torrance (eds.), *Literacy, language, and learning: The nature and consequences of reading and writing* (pp. 285–306). Cambridge University Press.
Leech, G. N. (1983). *Principles of pragmatics*. London: Longmans.
Lord, A. (1960). *The singer of tales*. Harvard Studies in Comparative Literature, Vol. 24. Cambridge, Mass.: Harvard University Press.
Luria, A. R. (1976). *Cognitive development: Its cultural and social foundations*. Cambridge, Mass.: Harvard University Press. (Originally published in Russian in 1974.)
Mattingly, I. G. (1972). Reading, the linguistic process, and linguistic awareness. In J. F. Kavanagh & I. G. Mattingly (eds.), *Language by ear and by eye* (pp. 133–47). Cambridge, Mass.: MIT Press.
McLuhan, M. (1962). *The Gutenberg galaxy*. Toronto: University of Toronto Press.
Morais, J., Bertelson, P., Cary, L., & Alegria, J. (1986). Literacy training and speech segmentation. *Cognition* 24:45–64.
Nystrand, M. (1986). *The structure of written communication: Studies in reciprocity between writers and readers*. New York: Academic Press.
Olson, D. R. (1977). From utterance to text: The bias of language in speech and writing. *Harvard Educational Review* 47:257–81.
  (1984). "See! Jumping!" Some oral language antecedents of literacy. In H. Goelman, A. Oberg, & F. Smith (eds.), *Awakening to literacy* (pp. 185–92). Exeter, N.H.: Heinemann.
Olson, D. R., & Astington, J. (1990). Talking about text: How literacy contributes to thought. *Journal of Pragmatics* 14(5):557–73.
Olson, D. R., & Torrance, N. (1987). Language, literacy and mental states. *Discourse Processes* 10(2):157–67.
Ong, W. (1982). *Orality and literacy: The technologizing of the word*. London: Methuen.
Parry, M. (1971). *The collected papers of Milman Parry* (A. Parry, ed.). Oxford University Press.
Read, C., Zhang, Y., Nie, H., & Ding, B. (1986). The ability to manipulate speech sounds depends on knowing alphabetic writing. *Cognition* 24:31–44.
Scollon, R., & Scollon, S. (1979). *Linguistic convergence: An ethnography of speaking at Fort Chipewyan, Alberta*. New York: Academic Press.
Scribner, S. (1986). Thinking in action: Some characteristics of practical thought. In R. J. Sternberg & R. K. Wagner (eds.), *Practical intelligence: Nature and origins of competence in the everyday world* (pp. 13–30). Cambridge University Press.
Scribner, S., & Cole, M. (1981). *The psychology of literacy*. Cambridge University Press.

Stock, B. (1983). *The implications of literacy.* Princeton: N.J.: Princeton University Press.
Street, B. (1984). *Literacy in theory and practice.* Cambridge University Press.
Tannen, D. (1985). Relative focus on involvement in oral and written discourse. In D. R. Olson, A. Hildyard, & N. Torrance (eds.), *Literacy, language, and learning: The nature and consequences of reading and writing* (pp. 124–47). Cambridge University Press.
 (1987). The orality of literature and the literacy of conversation. In J. Langer (ed.), *Language, literacy, and culture: Issues of society and schooling* (pp. 67–88). Norwood, N.J.: Ablex.
Taylor, I., & Olson, D. (in preparation). *Scripts and literacy: East and West.*
Torrance, N., & Olson, D. R. (1987). Development of the metalanguage and the acquisition of literacy. *Interchange* 18(1/2):136–46.
Traugott, E. C. (1987). Literacy and language change: The special case of speech act verbs. In J. Langer (ed.), *Language, literacy, and culture: Issues of society and schooling* (pp. 111–27). Norwood, N.J.: Ablex.
Tunmer, W. E., Pratt, C. J., & Herriman, M. L. (eds.) (1984). *Metalinguistic awareness in children: Theory, research, and implications.* Berlin: Springer.
Vellutino, F. R. (1979). *Dyslexia: Theory and research.* Cambridge, Mass.: MIT Press.
Wagner, D. (1987). Literacy futures: Five common problems from industrialized and developing countries. In D. A. Wagner (ed.), *The future of literacy in a changing world.* New York: Pergamon.
Wells, G. (1985a). *Language development in the pre-school years.* Cambridge University Press.
 (1985b). Preschool literacy-related activities and success in school. In D. R. Olson, A. Hildyard, & N. Torrance (eds.), *Literacy, language, and learning: The nature and consequences of reading and writing* (pp. 229–55). Cambridge University Press.

# Author index

Italic numbers denote pages with bibliographic information.

Aarsleff, H., 154, *161*
Adams, M. J., 207, *212*
Addis, A. B., 203, 205, *213*
Adolf, H., 119, *126*
Ainsworth-Vaughn, N., 251–2, 256, *267*
Akinnaso, F. N., 228, *232*
Alcott, D., 227, *232*
Alegria, J., 246, *249*, 262, *269*
Alleton, V., 199, *212*
Angelicus, R., 125n4
Annis, R. C., *87*
Aquinas, T., 154, *161*
Astington, J. W., 156, 159, 160, *161*, *163*, 263, *269*
Atkinson, J., 53–4, *64*
Au, T.K.-F., 84, *87*
Augustine, Saint, 36, *45*, 113–14, 118, 125n3, 126n8, *126*, 132
Austin, G., 134, *147*
Austin, J. L., 19, *26*, 50, *64*

Bacon, F., 147, 151, 154, 155, 156, *161*
Bahuchet, S., *87*
Balogh, J., 205, *212*
Barnes, J., 195n7, *196*
Balogh, J., 205, *212*
Baron, N. S., 229, *232*
Bartlett, F. C., 50, *64*, 135, *147*
Basham, A. L., 207, *212*
Basso, A., 238, *249*
Bauml, F., 111–12, *126*
Beal, C., 159, *161*
Bede, St., 36, *147*
Begg, I., 200, *212*
Bennett, J. A., 1, 3, 25
Benveniste, E., 132, *147*
Bereiter, C., 265, *267*
Berkowitz, N., 68, *88*
Bernstein, D., 74, *87*
Berry, J. W, 1, 3, 67, 68, 71, *87*, 253
Bertelson, P., 218, *232*, 246, *249*, 259, 262, *267*, *269*
Besner, D., 227, *232*
Bever, T., 231n2, *267*

Biber, D., 251–2, 257
Bishop, A. J., 68, *87*
Black, M., 101, *103*
Bloch, H., 123, *126*
Bloch, M., 53–4
Bloom, A., 84
Bloom, H., 55, *64*
Bloomfield, L., 215, *232*, 260, *267*
Bloomfield, M., 125n2, *126*
Boas, F., 156, 256
Bodak, A., 238, *249*
Bond, G. B., 216, *232*
Boureau, A., 198, *212*
Bowen, B. C., 119, *127*
Bradley, L., 261–2, 264, *267*
Bradshaw, J. L., 236, 246, *248*
Braine, M. D. S., 81, *87*
Bright, W., 52, *64*, 85, *87*
Broca, P., 236, 237, 247n1, *248*
Brodsky, J., 132, *147*
Brown, C. H., 82, *87*
Bruce, D. J., 217, 218, *232*
Brumfield, S., 223, *235*
Bruner, J. S., 2, 3, 4, 133, 134, 137, 141, *147*
Bryant, P. E., 261–2, 264, *267*
Bugarski, R., 229, 230, *232*
Bundy, M. N., 125n2, *127*
Burlin, Robert, 125n6, *127*
Burnell, A. C., 210, *212*
Burwash, N., 92, *102*

Cameron, R. F., 238–9, 245, *248*
Canton, W., 94, *102*
Carpenter, E., 70, *87*
Carter, B., 218, *234*
Cary, L., 246, *249*, 262, *269*
Cassirer, E., 33, *45*
Castro, S. L., 245, *248*
Castro-Caldas, A., 238, 239–40, 246, *248*
Cathala, H. P., 238, *249*
Cavalli-Sforza, L. L., *87*
Cazden, C., 231n1, *232*

Chafe, W. L., 47, 49, *64*, 79, 80–1, *87*, 158, *161*, 229, *232*, 254, 260, *267*, *268*
Chandler, M. J., 159, *161*
Chartier, R., 198, 205, 211n4, *212*
Chaytor, H. J., 18, *26*
Chiarello, R. J., 231n2, *232*
Chomsky, N., 215, 216, 228, 229, *233*
Clanchy, M. T., 38, *45*, 152, *161*, 184, 195n10, 196n14, *196*
Cohen, M., 199, 207, 210, *212*, 223, *235*
Cole, M., 72, *89*, 92, 147, *148*, 149, 177–8, *197*, 202, *213*, 246, *249*, 252, 253, 257, *268*, *269*
Coltheart, M., 237, *249*
Commen, C., 202, *212*
Comrie, B., 73, *88*
Coomaraswamy, A., 105, *108*
Cot, F., 241, *249*
Creider, C. A., 71, 83, *88*
Cressy, D., 195n8, 196n14, *196*
Critchley, M., 237, 245, *248*
Crosby, R., 114, *127*
Culler, J., 131, *147*
Currier, R. D., 238–9, 245, *248*

Damasio, A. R., 238, 239–40, 245, 246, *248*
Damasio, H., 245, 246, *248*
Danielewicz, J., 47, 49, *64*, 80, 254, 260, *268*
Darnell, R., 93, *103*
Das, J. P., 83, *87*
Davelaar, E., 227, *232*
Dax, M., 236, *248*
de Ajuriaguerra, J., 247n2, *249*
De Castell, S., 160, *161*
DeGelder, B., 218, *232*
Dennis, M., 232n2, *233*
Denny, J. P., 1, 2–3, 15, 21, 69, 73, 76, 83, 84, *87–8*
De Renzi, E., 200, 211n2, *212*, 239–40, *248*
De Reuck, A. V. S., 238, 245, *248*
Derrida, J., 14, 17, *26*, 119
Dewey, J., 22, *26*
Ding, B., 218, *234*, 257, 262, *269*
Docreux, M.-E., 198, *212*
Dollard, J., 134, *147*
Donaldson, M., 259, 265, *268*
Douglas, M., 70, 88, 122, *127*, 149, *162*
Downing, J., 204, *212*
Dronke, P., 125n2, 126n12, *127*
Duncan, E. H., 124n1, *127*
Dunn, J., 141, *147*
Duranti, A., 157, *162*

Eakin, P. J., 131, *147*
Ehri, L. C., 199, *212*, 216, *233*, 257, 262, *268*

Eisenson, J., 238, 245
Eisenstein, E. L., 4, 7, 18, *26*, 30, *45*, 149–51, *162*, 195n10, 196n14, *196*, 253, *268*
Ellis, C. D., 99, *103*
Entus, A. K., 236, *248*
Evans-Pritchard, E. E., 75, *88*, 157, *162*

Fairbank, J. K., 199, *213*
Fanshel, D., 167, *173*
Faral, E., *127*
Farmer, L. J., 245, *248*
Febvre, L., 18, *26*
Feitelson, D., 202, 211n3, *212*
Feldman, C. F., 1, 2, 15, 52, 64n3, *64*, 77, 153, 157–8, 251, 253, 262–3, *264*
Ferguson, C. A., 229, *233*
Ferguson, M., 114, *127*
Fernandez, J., 71, 72, 79, 83, *88*
Ferreiro, E., 262, *268*
Ferro, J. M., 238, 239–40, *248*
Ferster, J., 126n7, *127*
Filliozat, J., 207, *212*
Finley, M., 195n7, *196*
Finnegan, R., 15, *26*, 253, *268*
Fischer, W., 218, *234*
Fisher, D. F., 203, 204, *212*, *213*
Flavell, J. H., 159, *161*, 228, *233*
Fletcher, J. M., 216, *233*
Foley, J. M., 114, *127*, 173n3, *173*
Francis, H., 261, *268*
Frank, R., 126n11, *127*
Fromkin, V., 215, 218, 221, *233*
Fry, D. B., 217, *233*

Galaburda, A., 237, *248*
Galilei, Galileo, 154, 155, 156, *161*
Gardner, H., 106, *108*
Garfinkel, H., 167, *173*
Garin, R., 94, *103*
Gatzoyas, A., 245, *249*
Geertz, C., 49, *64*, 134, *147*
Gelb, I. J., 14–15, *27*, 195n9, *196*, 221, 230, *233*
Givon, T., 229, *233*
Godzich, W., 156, *162*, 169, *173*, 256, 267, *268*
Gonda, J., 195nn1, 3, 4, *196*
Goodglass, H., 216, *233*, 239, *249*
Goodnow, J. G., 134, *147*
Goody, J., 2, 12, 15, *27*, 30, *46*, 47, *65*, 72, 79, *88*, 149, 153, *163*, 170, 177, 183, 185, *196*, 251, 253, 256, *268*
Gorlitzer von Mundy, V., 237–8, 245, *249*
Gottwald, N. K., 207, *212*
Gough, K., 178, 182, *196*
Goulet, P., 236, 245, 246, *249*
Gratiolet, L. P., 247n1, *249*

# Author index

Gray, W. S., 200, *212*
Greenbaum, S., 143, *148*
Greenfield, P. M., 69, 76, *88*, 149, *162*
Griffin, B. C., 217, *234*
Griffin, P., 252, *268*
Grosso, J. J., 238, *248*

Haerer, A. F., 238–9, 245, *248*
Haidu, P., 114, *127*
Hall, M. A., 216, *233*
Halle, M., 216, 229, *233*
Halliday, M. A. K., 256, *268*
Hamsher, K. de S., 245, 246, *248*
Hannequin, D., 236, 245, 246, *249*
Harder, R., 207, *212*
Harris, K. S., 217, *234*
Harris, M. B., 125n3, *127*
Harris, P., 159, *161*
Harvey, W., 155, *162*
Hasuike, R., 200, 211n2, *213*
Havelock, E. A., 1, 2, 12, *27*, 30, 34, *46*, 47, *65*, 77–9, 85, 86, *88*, 105, 149, *162*, 158, 160, 177, 178, 181, 188, *196*, 251, 253, *268*
Hawkinson, A. K., 71, 83, *88*
Hayes, J. R., 217, *233*
Heath, S., 158, *162*, 252, 258, *268*
Hecaen, J., 247n2, *249*
Hedelin, L., 258, *268*
Heilman, K.-M., 216, 223, *233*
Helm, D., 159, *161*
Helm, J., 91, *103*
Herriman, M. L., 259, 265, *269*
Hidi, S., 254, *269*
Hildyard, A., 1, 7, 254, *269*
Hjelmquist, E., 258, *268*
Hofmann, H. S., 217, *234*
Honigman, J. J., 91, *103*
Hook, S., 138, *147*
Hooke, R., 155, *162*
Hoskin, K., 160, *162*
Householder, F. W., Jr., 229, *233*
Howard, D., 117, *127*
Howarth, W. L., 132, *147*
Hung, D., 199, 200, 211n2, *213*, *214*
Huot, S., 168, *173*
Hurlich, M. G., 100
Hutchins, E., 69, 77, 81, *88*, 156, *162*
Hyde, Lewis, 126n10, *127*
Hymes, Dell, 61, *65*

Illich, I., 1, 2, 30–2, *46*, 107, 253
Innis, H., 13–14, *27*, 149, *162*
Issartier, A., 238, *249*

Jakobson, R., 50, *65*, 238, 245
Jansen, M., 211n3
Jaynes, J., 17, *27*, 232n2, *233*
Jerman, R. F., 83, *87*

Joanette, Y., 236, 241, 245, 246, *249*
Johnson, M. R., 74, *88*
Jones, W., 57
Jouhaud, C., *212*
Jousse, M., 15, *27*

Kahrl, S., 126n12, *127*
Kalmar, I., 229, *233*
Kaplan, E., 216, *253*, 239, *249*
Kaplan, E. L., 206, *213*
Kaprinis, G., 245, *249*
Kardiner, A., 134, *148*
Karpova, S. N., 218, *234*
Kean, M.-L., 216, *234*
Keenan, E. L., 73, *88*
Kelber, W., 17, *27*
Kermode, F., 130, *148*
Kirby, J. R., 83, *87*
Kittay, J., 3, 4–5, 156, *162*, 169, 170, *173*, 256, 267, *268*
Klepper, B. R., 223, *235*
Kuhn, T., 34, *46*

Labov, W., 167, *173*
Lafond, D., 241, *249*
Lamoureux, M., 236, 246, *249*
Lancy, D. F., 82, *88*
Langer, S., 34, *46*
Lanham, R., 126n9, *127*
Laverloche, R. P., 94, *103*
Leach, E. R., 149, *162*
Lecours, A. R., 5, 6, 238, 240, 241, 243, 244, 246, *249*
Lee, D., 77, *88*
Leech, G. N., 264, *269*
Lehmann, P., 209, *213*
Lejeune, M., 207, *213*
Lemay, A., 241, *249*
Lenneberg, E., 247n2, *249*
Leong, C. K., 204, *212*
Lepage, Y., 236, 246, *249*
Levin, H., 203, 205, 206, *213*
Lévi-Strauss, C., 12, 15, *21*, *27*, 78, 82, *88*
Levy, R. I., 157, *162*
Lewin, R., 147, *148*
Liberman, A. M., 217, *234*
Lieberman, I. Y., 218, *234*
Liu, L. G., 84, *88*
Lomax, A., 68, *88*
Lonner, W. J., 67–8, *89*
Lord, A. B., 2, 15–16, 17, 22, *27*, 30, 34, *46*, 166, 253, *269*
Lucariello, J., 137, *147*
Luke, A., 160, *161*
Luke, C., 160, *161*
Luria, A. R., 16, *27*, 29, *46*, 69, 76, 79, *89*, 157, *163*, 228, *234*, 265, *269*
Lydgate, 125n6
Lyons, J., 76, *89*

Macrobius, 126n12
Mailhot, J., 84, *88*
Makita, K., 200, 201, *213*
Malinowski, B., 15, *27*
Manning, S., 126n9, *127*
Marshall, J. C., 237, *249*
Martin, H.-J., 18, *26*
Mattingly, I. G., 258–9, *269*
Mausse, M., 126n10, *127*
Maxwell, W., 131, *147*
Mayr, Ernst, 23, *27*
Maziotta, J. C., 200, *213*
McCarthy, M., 131, *147*
McCormick, P., 157, *163*
McGlone, J., 247n2, *249*
McIntyre, L. A., 68, *89*
McKellin, W., 157, *163*
McLean, J., 90, *104*
McLuhan, M., 2, 12, 16, 18, 27, 47, 65, 79–80, 81, *89*, 149, 160, *163*, 226–9, 232n2, *234*, 251, 254, 255, 267, *269*
McNeill, D., 73–4, *89*, 217, *234*
Mead, G. H., 42–3, *46*
Mehler, J., 238, 240, 243, 244, *249*
Meillet, A., 13, 198, *213*
Meodell, P., 200, *213*
Merton, R., 149, *163*
Métellus, J., 238, 245, *249*
Mie, H., 218, *234*, 257, *269*
Minnis, A. J., 125n5, *127*
Molfese, D. L., 216, 223, *234*
Monty, R. A., 204, *213*
Morais, J., 245, 246, *248*, 262, *269*
Moraschini, S., 238, *249*
Moutier, F., 237, *249*
Muller, R. W., 210, *213*
Murdoch, J., 92, *104*

Nakamura, H., 83–4, *89*
Narasimhan, R., 5, 77, 107, 195n6, *196*, 253
Needham, J., 83–4, *89*
Neisser, U., 133, 134, *148*
Nelson, K., 137, *147*, *148*
Nespoulous, J. L., 238, 241, *249*
Nettleton, N. C., 236, 246, *248*
Nicholas of Trevisa, 125n5
Nickerson, R. S., 228, *234*
Nicoll, A., 119, *127*
Nie, H., 257, 262, *269*
Notopoulos, J. A., 34, *46*
Nystrand, M., 255, 260, *269*

O'Connor, M., 238, 245, *248*
Ogilvy, J. D. A., 119, *127*
Olson, D. R., 3, 4, 5, 6–7, 47, 52, 65, 77, *89*, 105, 106, *108*, 149, 156, 159, *163*, 177, 180, *197*, 228, *234*, 252, 256, 258, 259, 263, 265, 266, *269*, *270*

Olson, G., 126n9, *128*
Ong, W. J., 2, 12, 15, 16, 27, 30, 34, 46, 47, 65, 77–8, 81, 85, *89*, 105, *108*, 123, 125n3, *128*, 149, 170, 177, 181, 188, 251
Orwell, G., 42–4, *46*

Pacey, A., 183–4, 196n14, *197*
Paivio, A., 200, *213*
Palermo, D. S., 216, 223, *234*
Panofsky, E., 34, *46*
Parente, M. A., 5, 6, 240, 243, 244, 246, *249*
Parry, M., 2, 11, 13, 14, 15–16, 17, 22, 23, *27*, 29–30, 34, *46*, 78, *89*, 253, *269*
Parry, P., 227, *232*
Partee, B. H., 224, *234*
Patel, P. G., 216, 218, *234*
Pattanayak, D. P., 1, 3, 251
Patterson, K., 237, *249*
Patterson, P., 218, *234*
Peabody, B., 34, *46*
Perfetti, C. A., 228, *234*
Perkins, R. V., 73, *89*
Perner, J., 159, *164*
Perry, B. E., 112, *128*
Peters, A. M., 232n2, *234*
Phelps, M. E., 200, *213*
Piaget, J., 22, *27*, 159, 228
Plato, 23, 24, 25, 35, *46*, 72, 79, 113, 121
Polanyi, K., 32, 33, *46*
Polonoff, D., 132, *148*
Postman, N., 151, *163*
Power, D. J., 223, *235*
Pratt, C. J., 259, *270*
Puel, M., 241, *249*
Pugh, T., 205, *213*

Quigley, S. P., 223, *235*
Quine, W. V., 135, *148*
Quirk, R., 143, *148*

Ramig, C. J., 216, *233*
Ranade, A., 188, *197*
Rascol, A., 241, *249*
Read, C. A., 218, 231n1, *234*, 257, 262, *269*
Reich, H., 119, *128*
Reischauer, E. O., 199, *213*
Reuning, H., 68, *89*
Robinson, E., 159, *163*
Robinson, W., 159, *163*
Rodman, R., 215, 218, 221, *233*
Rogers, E. S., 91, 92, 100, *104*
Rosaldo, M. Z., 50–1, 57–61, 65, 134, *148*, 157, *163*
Rosaldo, R., 57, 65, 134, *148*

# Author index

Ross, T., 125n2, *128*
Rousseau, J., 149, *163*
Rubin, D. C., 133, *148*
Ruffman, T., 159, *163*
Russell, W. K., 223, *235*
Rybczynski, W., 143, *148*

Sacks, H., 167, *173*
Saenger, P., 5–6, 7, 25, 36, 46, 156, *163*, 198, 203, *213*, 261
Sakamoto, T., 200, 201, *213*
Salemi, J. S., 120, *128*
Sanders, B., 3–4
Sapir, E., 215, *235*
Scardamalia, M., 265, *267*
Scharfe, H., 195n11, *197*
Schieffelin, B., 158, *164*
Scholes, R. J., 4, 5, 6, 74, 125n3, 216, 218, 219, 222, 223, 224, *233*, *235*, 243, 262
Scollon, R., 258, *269*
Scollon, S., 258, *269*
Scribner, S., 69, 72, 76, 79, *89*, 92, *104*, 147, *148*, 149, *164*, 177–8, *197*, 202, *213*, 246, *250*, 252, 253, 257, *268*, *269*
Searle, J., 58, *65*
Senders, J. W., 204, *213*
Seneca, 209, *214*
Senechal, C., *87*
Shankar, R., 105, *108*
Shankweiler, D. F., 218, *234*
Sharp, D. W., 67–8, *89*
Shikibu, M., 79, *89*
Shirali, K. A., 105, *108*
Shweder, R. A., 134, *148*
Siegel, S., 247nn9, 13, 14, *249*
Skinner, A., 99, *104*
Slobin, D. I., 217, *235*
Smith, M., 92, *104*
Sokolov, A. N., 203, *214*
Spence, D. P., 136, *148*
Sprat, T., 151, 155–6, *164*
Starobinksi, J., 133, *148*
Steegman, A. T., Jr., 100, *104*
Steffens, F., 202, *214*
Stock, B., 4, 5, 149, 152, 153, *164*, 196n14, *197*, 256, *270*
Street, B., 149, *164*, 252, *270*
Strohm, P., 126n12, *128*
Stubbs, M., 105, *108*

Tannen, D., 75, *89*, 254, 264, *270*
Tatlock, J. S. P., 119, *128*
Taylor, G., 91, *104*
Taylor, I., 199, 200, 201, 205, 211n1, *214*, 217, *235*, 252, *270*
Taylor, M. M., 159, *164*, 199, 200, 205, 211n1, *214*
Thomas, K., 126n13, *128*

Thorndike, L., 125n4, *128*
Tikofsky, R., 238, 245, *250*
Tinker, M. A., 206, *214*, 216, *232*
Torrance, N., 1, 7, 158–9, *163*, 265, 266, *269*, *270*
Traugott, E. C., 159, *164*, 263, *270*
Tulving, E., 134, *148*
Tunmer, W. E., 259, *270*
Turner, D. H., 68, *89*
Turner, E. G., 209, *214*
Tzavaras, A., 245, *249*
Tzeng, O., 199, 200, 211n2, *213*, *214*

Ullman, B. L., 202, *214*

Vachek, J., 200, 211n1, *214*
Vallant, A., 210, *214*
Van de Koppel, J. M. H., *87*
Vanek, A. L., 93, *103*
Velay-Vallantin, C., 212
Vellutino, F. R., 255, *270*
Vendryes, J., 198, *214*
Vignolo, L. A., 239–40, *248*
Vogel, 216, *235*
Vygotsky, L., 147, *148*

Wagner, D., 252, *270*
Walker, W., 92, *104*
Wang, W. S.-Y., 201, *214*
Wasson, B. B., 216, *232*
Watt, I., 2, 27, 47, *65*, 149, 177, *196*, 251, *268*
Weber, E., 237, 245, *249*
Weber, M., 149, *164*
Wechsler, A., 238, 245, *249*
Weisser, S., 141, *147*
Wells, G., 258, *270*
Welsford, E., 123, *128*
Whitaker, H. A., 232n2, *235*
White, H., 130, 135, *148*
White, J. K., 92, *104*
Whiting, J., 134, *148*
Whorf, B. L., 229–30, *235*
Wilkes, K. V., 224, *235*
Willis, B. J., 4, 5, 6, 74, 125n3, 216, 218, 219, 222, 223, 224, 228, *235*, 243, 262
Wimmer, H., 159, *164*
Wingo, E. O., 207, 208, *214*
Winterhalder, B., 100, *104*
Witkin, H. A., *87*
Wittgenstein, L., 19, 49–50, 63n2, *65*
Wortley, W., 68, *89*
Wright, T., 119, *128*

Yates, F. A., 196nn13, 14, *197*

Zalta, E. N., 224, *235*
Zang, Y., 218, *234*, 257, 262, *269*

# Subject index

Abelard, Peter, 37, 40
abstract-situational, 78, 79
abstraction, 75, 76, 79, 87–8, 185–6, 258; context bound, 188; decontextualizing, 79; generalizing, 81; model as, 185; representational models for articulated, 186–9, 187t; writing and, 78
Aelfric, King, 119
*Aeneid* (Virgil), 25, 35
affixes, 73, 221,225; inflectional, 216–17, 221
Africa, 16, 73, 74, 86; integrative thought in, 70–2; oral historians of, 106
agency, 133, 146
aggregates, 78–9
agrammatism, 216–17
agricultural societies, 3, 66, 67–70, 71–2, 83, 86; decontextualization, 73–4; integrative/contextualizing thinking in, 72–3
agriculture, 67, 105, 147; and changes in human thought, 70–1, 72
alexias: developmental/acquired, 237; social, 236–50
alphabet(s), 28, 36, 41, 45, 260, 264; and intensionality, 226; and phoneme manipulation, 220; in writing, 30
alphabetic literacy, 5, 177, 181
alphabetic notation, 42
alphabetic recording, 35
alphabetic script, 5, 206–7, 269
alphabetic text, 39
alphabetization, 30, 237, 246, 256
ambicerebrality, 236, 238
ambiguity, 55, 56, 158–9, 167; in ancient languages, 209; in jokes, 118; in reading, 203, 205
Ambrose, 205
analepsis, 133
analogy, 143, 228
analphabetism, 246
analysis: oral/written categories of, 106
analytic-aggregative, 78–9
analytic thought, 75, 78–9

*Animal Species and Evolution* (Mayr), 23
*annales*, 130, 134, 135, 138, 141
*Annals of St. Gall*, 130
anthropologists, 15–16, 33, 251
anthropology, 47, 48, 133–4, 156–7
aphasia, 216–17, 236; illiteracy and, 6, 237–46
aphasia testing, 241–2
aphasiology, 6
Arabic, 208, 210
Aramaic, 208
architectural technology, 183–4
archival tradition, 4, 253
Aristotle, 33, 161, 195n7
"art of memory," 196nn13, 14
artful genre, 52, 53
artful oral genres, 47–8, 50, 52, 53; Ilongot oratory as, 59–61; Wana poetry as, 53–7
articulation, 180–3, 184; representation of, 189–90; uniqueness of post-Homeric Greek, 181, 182
artifacts, 199
Assyria, 20
astronomy, 179, 184
audience(s), 126n7, 255–6; of Chaucer, 111, 114, 115, 116–18, 120, 122, 123; written text and, 181, 256, 267
Australian Aborigines, 68
*Australopithecus*, 147
author, 4, 114, 119, 126n7; Chaucer as, 111–28; denial of, 106; of fiction, 118–19; God as, 111, 113–14
authority: to elucidate, 173n9; of text, 115
autobiography, 4, 135; act of, 136; function of, 133; and its forms, 129–48; as locational activity, 133, 140–1; as representation of memory, 133–4; as rhetorical strategy, 131–2
autonomous texts, 259
autonomy, 143, 145

Babylon, 20
Bantu, 71
bard(s), 30, 34–5, 114

276

bedtime soliloquies, 129, 137–40, 146
behavior, human, 136, 185–6
beliefs, 159
Bentham, Jeremy, 32
Berkeley, Bishop, 156
Bernhard, 37
Biaka (people), 68
*Bias of Communication, The* (Innis), 13–14
Bible, 7, 48, 56, 78, 98, 107, 152, 156; interpretation of, 154, 161; levels of meaning in, 154; Old Testament, 17, 24, 112; printing press and, 150
binary opposites, 78, 82–3
biology of language, 246
Boccacio, Giovanni, 117, 118
Bol (oral notational scheme), 188, 191–4
book (the), 18, 28, 190
Book of Nature, 111, 154–5, 161, 177
book production, 184
Boyle, Robert, 155
Bracciolini, Poggio, 119–20
Brahmi syllabary alphabet, 207
braille, 211n2
brain, specialization of, 20, 24; *see also* left-brain specialization
brain cybernetics, 237
brain damage, and aphasia in illiteracy, 240–6
brain function, left–right asymmetry, 246
brain size, 20
Browne, Sir Thomas, 154
Buddhism, Tibetan, 106–7
Bushmen, 68

Canfield, Cass, 30
canonicality, 138, 139, 140, 146
*Canterbury Tales* (Chaucer), 3–4, 114–18; "Miller's Tale," 3–4, 112, 118–19, 120–2; "Reeve's Tale," 121–2; "Tale of Sir Thopas," 118
Catholicism, 15
causal thinking, 81
causality, 140, 146, 261
cerebral dominance for language, 6; *see also* brain, specialization of; left-brain specialization; left cerebral dominance
cerebral functions: in music, 231–2n2; in reading, 199–200, 204, 211n2
cerebral lesions, unilateral, effects on illiterates, 240–6
Charlemagne, 119, 124
Chaucer, Geoffrey, 3–4, 111–28
children, 158–60
China, Chinese, 21, 178; writing system, 227
Chinese language, 199–200, 201, 262
Chinese tradition, 84, 182, 191

Chinook myths, 61–2
*chroniques,* 130, 135
Church: disestablishment of, 30–1; and literacy development, 253
Cicero, 119
civilization, literacy and, 105
classification, 78, 81, 82–3
clerical literacy, 30, 37–8, 40, 41, 44–5; in education, 28–9
codes, 165–6, 207; elaborated, 74; notational, 170
cognition: effect of changes in communication on, 149, 150; language in, 19; and literacy, 2–3, 165–6, 171–2, 184, 185–90, 230, 256, 258, 266; orality in, 16–17, *see also* cross-cultural cognition
cognitive change: book in, 18; literacy and, 106, 178
cognitive development, in Indian tradition, 179
*Cognitive Development* (Luria), 16
cognitive evolution, 206
cognitive process, 83, 149; writing systems and, 6–7
cognitive skills, in reading, 198, 200–1, 203–4, 205, 206
cognitive styles, 83
communication, 4–5, 19, 36, 80, 100, 252; changes in, and cultural change, 149–52, 165–6; electronic media and, 18; and literacy–thought relationship, 255–7; through ordinary language, 185–6; speech as, 43–4, 168; writing and kinds of, 106, 165–72, 267; *see also* oral communication; written communication
communication technology, 12; Cree use of, 100–1, 102–3; social/cultural effects of, 13–14
*communitas,* 122
community, 133; shared recognition in, 143–4
composition, Homeric oralist theory of, 13, 14; *see also* oral composition
comprehension: split by writing, 160
computer(s), 28, 32, 42–3, 44, 182, 183, 185
computer-as-metaphor, 29, 42, 44–5
conceptualization, 136
confession, 39; under torture, 40, 113
*Confessions* (Augustine), 36
conjunct mode, 85–6
conscience, lay, 39–41
consciousness, 18, 149, 156, 256; abstract literate, 26; of language, 266; in orality, 11, 78; origin of, 132, 232n2; of unconscious processes, 81; writing necessary to Western, 2, 47–8

"Consequences of Literacy, The" (Goody and Watt), 12
consequences of literacy, 180, 189, 190
consonantal transcription, 208
context, 167, 207; fixed, 78; shared, 73, 74, 81, 86
contextualization, 3, 70, 72, in agricultural societies, 71; case of, 84–6; cultural variation in, 66–70, 67–8, 75, 76–7, 82, 86–7; as empathetic and participatory, 79; types of, 78–9
continuity theory, 7
conventions, in autobiography, 129, 133
conversation, everyday, 48–9, 50–1, 56, 63n1; genres different from, 51–2
coordinating conjunctions, 81
Coptic (dialect), 207
counterfactual conditional, 84
counterfactual situations, 181
Counter-Reformation, 153–4
craft literacy, 72, 79
craft techniques, 182, 183
creativity, 26
Cree, 76, 83, 84; example of contextualized thought, 84–6; text fixing, 253
Cree literacy, 3, 251; English language, 3, 94–5; in syllabic script, 3, 90–104, 107
Cree syllabarium, 92–4, 93t, 97, 99
crooked speech, 51, 57
cross-cultural cognition, 82–4; theory of, 66–70
cross-cultural comparisons: in differentiation, 47–8, 66–70, 75, 82, 86–7; literacy, 190–1; in reading, 199–200
cultural anthropologists, 15–16
cultural attitudes, and Cree literacy, 99, 101–2, 103
cultural change: and changes in communication, 149–52, 165–6; literacy and, 184
cultural development, evolution and, 23
cultural differences: in aphasia testing, 243; and literacy, 166, 168–9, 170, 171–2; in text–interpretation distinction, 157–8
cultural information, stored in literature, 23–4
cultural transmission, 133–4
culture(s), 2, 5; self-location in, 133
Cyrillic (dialect), 207

Dante, 117
Darwin, Charles, 111
*De la grammatologie* (Derrida), 14
decoding, 165, 166–7, 170, 200, 203, 204, 244; cognitive skills in, 198

deconstructionism, 17–18
decontextualization, 3, 167, 257; defined, 66; as distinctive property of Western thought, 66, 70, 72–82, 86–7; literate, 66–89; as objectively distanced, 79; preliterate/literate, 73–5; table(s), 79, 170; types of, 78–9
deductive reasoning, 68–9, 183
democracy, 18, 177
Descartes, 34, 156
*De-schooling Society* (Illich), 30–2
diary writing, 129
dictionary, 211n6
differentiation, 3, 70, 72, 83; cross-cultural variation in, 66–70, 67t, 75, 82, 86–7; functional basis of, 74
discourse: direct, 172; evolution of specialized forms of, 3–5; forms of, 255; free indirect, 168, 170, 172; language as object of, 258–60, 264, 265–6; literate/nonliterate, 105; referring to, 263; speaking and writing as distinctive forms of, 255–7, 267
discourse strategy, in self-report, 132–3
discourse structures, 251, 252
dispute resolution, 49, 58–9
*Divine Comedy, The* (Dante) 25
Dogons, 33
Donne, John, 106
Dumont, René, 32
duplicity, 112–13
Dürer, Albrecht, 34
dyslexia, 237, 255, 257

Early Modern period, 3
ecclesiology, 31
economics, 32–3
education, 7, 15, 26, 186, 190, 196n14, 255; adult, 107–8; among Cree, 94–6; epistemological break in oral–literate existence and, 42–6; and functional lateralization, 246; Greek, 23, 25, 35; lay literacy and, 28–32; and literacy, 253, 263; and mental space, 34–5; need for, 32–5; reading and writing in, 21–2
egocentrism, 159
Egypt, Egyptians, 20, 21
electronic media, 18; among Cree, 103
elucidation, 173n9
embedded figures test, 67–8
encoding, 165, 166
engineering techniques, 182, 183–4, 190
environment, and left-brain specialization for language, 236, 237
epic, 30, 79, 106
episodic memory, 134, 135, 136
*Epithète traditionelle dans Homère, L'* (Parry), 13, 14

## Subject index

Eskimos, 69–70
ethnocentrism, 7
ethnolinguists, 33
ethnomethodologists, 63n1, 167
etymology, 179
Euclidean space, 33–4
European culture, prose in, 25–6; see also Western European culture
European literacy, as world of fiction, 114
Evans, James, 92–4, 99
evidentials, 158
evolution, 20, 23, 41–2
excellence, literacy as strategy for, 105–6
explanation, 81, 183, 257
explanatory theories, myths as, 78
explicitness, 56, 167, 173n4
expression, 98; fixing in forms, 50, 51–2
extensional competence, 230, 232n2
extensional elements, 224, 225, 226, 227
extensional grammar, 226, 228, 229
extensionality, 224
externalization, 181, 182
eye–ear substitution, 254–5, 267
eye movements (reading), 203–4
eye–voice span, 203, 206

fable, 111, 118, 126n12
*facetiae*, 119, 120
family, 144, 253; autobiography and, 133, 146; self-location in, 141–5
Fang (people), 71
feedback, 5; to oral mode, 183–4, 190, 191
fiction, 41, 112, 114, 126n7, 132, 256; Chaucer and, 4, 111, 117, 126nn6, 12; storytelling and joking in, 118–19, 123; use of memory in, 117
*Fictions in Autobiography* (Eakin), 131
forgetting, 116, 118
form–meaning distinction, 160
Fourth Lateran Council, 39
Freud, Sigmund, 41–2, 132
*From Memory to Written Record in England, 1066–1307* (Clanchy), 38
function words, 216–17, 221

*Gargantua and Pantagruel* (Rabelais), 123
"general claim," 2, 47, 48, 251; and text–interpretation distinction, 48–53, 56–7, 60–1
genetics, 133; and left-brain specialization for language, 236, 237, 246, 248n23
genre(s), 254, 263; choices imposed by, 132–3, 136; new, 256; and text, 131

genre patterns, 56–7
genre rules, in self-report, 129, 131, 132–3, 136–45, 146
gift exchange, 122, 126n10
given (the), 4, 151, 152, 153, 154–5, 156; compilations of, 160
given–interpretation distinction, 160–1
Glagolitic (dialect), 207
God, 151; as author, 111, 113–14, 177
Gower, John, 117
Graeco-Latin alphabetical scripts, 206–7
grammar(s), 6, 40–1, 74, 179, 205, 207, 224; explicit, 265; extensional, 226, 228, 229; Indian, 178, 187; intensional, 226; of linguistic knowledge, 215–16, 221, 222, 223, 229; of nonliterate speakers, 223–4; vernacular, 41; writing system(s) as, 230, 261
grammatical metaphor, 256
grapheme(s), 165, 166
graphic conventions, 198–9, 200–2
graphic symbols, 183, 226; graphic signs, intensional, 227
graphic systems, 207, 208, 209; see also writing system(s)
great-divide theory, 7
Greece, Greeks, 12, 17, 19, 22–6, 30, 52, 67; alphabetic literacy, 177, 178; duplicity, 112–13; literacy, 24–6, 72, 79, 181
Greek alphabet, 2, 14, 17, 19, 177; superior technology of, 24–5, 26
Greek culture: divide in, 23–4
Greek language, 5; reading, 202–3, 204, 205; word separation, 24, 207, 208–10
Greek texts, 204, 205
Guibert de Nogent, 40
*Gutenberg Galaxy, The* (McLuhan), 12
Gutenberg, Johannes, 18

habit mechanisms, 134
Harry Frank Guggenheim Foundation, 240–6
Harvard Studies in Classical Philology, 13
Hebrew composition, 17, 20
Hebrew language, 5, 202, 207, 208, 210
Hebrews, 21
Heidegger, Martin, 18
hemispheric specialization, 199–200, 231–2n2; see also left-brain specialization
Heraclitus, 22
hermeneutics, 18–19, 156, 177, 186; and scientific epistemology, 152, 154–60, 161, 180
Hermes, 113, 122

# Subject index

hero, as a device, 134
Hindi, 202
Hindus, 106–7
*Hippias Minor* (Plato), 113
*histoires*, 130, 135
history, 130, 177
home, and real world, 143, 144, 146
Homer, 35, 79, 117
Homeric composition, 13, 14, 17, 22–4, 34–5
Hopis, 33
hunter-gatherer societies, 3, 66–70, 83, 86; and decontextualization, 73–4; integrative thought in, 71, 72
hypothetical thinking, 83–4, 155

identification, 136
ideographic writing, 211n2, 227
*Iliad*, 30
illiteracy, illiterates, 29, 105, 230, 237, 251; agrammatic, 216–17; and aphasia, 237–46; in Chaucer's audience, 115; effects of left-brain damage on, 238, 239–46; and second-class status, 105
illocution, 51, 63n1
Ilongot, 134, 146, 157; oral genres, 50–1
Ilongot oratory (*purung*), 47, 53, 57–61
imagination, 29, 112, 181
implicitness, 167
improvisation, 22, 23
*In Vain I Tried to Tell You* (Hymes), 61
India, 5, 30, 83, 84; Vedic tradition in, 106
Indian languages, 202, 210
Indian myths, 47
Indian tradition: literacy hypothesis and, 177–89; literacy practices in, 179, 190–1; nonliterate characteristics of, 179–80; representational modalities in, 190
Indians, 21, 52
individualism, 107; Cree, 101
individuation, 133, 136
Indo-European languages, 206–7, 209, 210, 211
industrial societies, 1, 3, 86; decontextualization as habit of thought in, 80; differential/integrative thinking in, 68–70
inference(s), 29, 134, 136, 252, 263; observation and, 155, 156, 160, 161
Institut de recherche et d'histoire des textes (Paris), 199
institutions, 3; for using texts, 253
instruction, 180; *see also* education; pedagogy

integrative thought, 66–70, 71–2, 83, 86, 188; in service of social integration, 71–5
intensional–extensional dichotomy (linguistic knowledge), 6
intensional grammar, 226
intensionality, 61, 158–9, 224–6, 227, 228–30, 232n2; caveats and heuristics, 229–30; literate–illiterate distinction in, 228–30
intentionality, 81, 157
interpretation, 47, 48, 77, 86, 185, 186; ambiguities in, 15; as analysis, 61; and denial of author, 106; forced by autobiography, 132, 133, 135–45, 146; of lives, 129, 130; in oral artful genres, 54–7, 59–62; in oral cultures, 52, 53, oral genres and, 2, 50, 52; self-consciousness as primitive form of, 137; source of, 156–60; text and, 47; word separation and, 211; *see also* text–interpretation distinction
interpretation assignment process, 190, 191
interpreted (the), 151, 152, 154–5, 156
*Investigations* (Wittgenstein), 63n2

*Jacob's Well*, 122
Japanese language, 200, 201–2, 206
John of Salisbury, 173
joke *kiyori* (poetry), 55, 56
joke *purung*, 59
joking, jokes, 114, 118–21; in Chaucer, 3–4, 111, 112, 118, 120–2, 123–4; collections of, 119–20; invention of modern, 120
Judaism, 17–18
juggler-raconteurs, 119
justice, 2, 7, 152

Kpelle (people), 76–7

language, 6, 11, 19, 23, 182; consciousness of, 266; event-making forms of, 49–50; formal, 53–4; identified with speech, 215; 229; learning of, 25; literate/nonliterate, 108; in nonliterate societies, 16; as object of thought and discourse, 258–60, 264, 266, 267; ordinary, 185–6; in prehistoric societies, 21; in representation of world, 265; science of, 215, 230; and self-accounts, 146; storage function of, 26; writing representation of, 261; *see also* written language
language acquisition, 216, 217, 227; and phoneme manipulation, 220

language behavior, 236; and reflective behavior, 180–1
language impairments, 216
language representation, ambicerebrality of, 236
language structure, 4, 107; and reading, 198–9
Latin language, 5, 173n9, 200, 202–3, 204, 205, 209–10
laughter, 119, 120, 122, 124; analysis of, 121
law, 24, 39; *see also* legal system
lay literacy, 38–9, 44, 107, 184; defined, 2, 28, 41; evolution of, 40–1; history of, 28–35; plea for research on, 28–46
lay literates, 253
learning-imitation mechanisms, 134
learning theory, 134
left-brain damage, 236, 237, 240; differences between illiterates and readers in effects of, 238, 239–40
left-brain specialization, 6, 236, 240; and acquisition of reading/writing skills, 237, 238
left cerebral dominance, 231n2, 236, 237, 244–6; genetically constrained, 236, 246, 248n23
legal system, 49, 152
letter writing, among Cree, 3, 102
letters, 227, 263; *see also* alphabet(s)
lexical access, 203, 207, 208, 209, 244
lexical analysis, 226
lexical devices, 85–6
Liberia, 202–3
libraries, 37, 199
*Life of St. Kentigern*, 123
linguistic abilities, 258–9
linguistic awareness, 260, 261, 265; and metalanguage, 260, 262–3
linguistic behavior, 216, 231n1; right hemisphere in, 246
linguistic changes, literacy and, 106
linguistic competence, 216, 231n1; and illiteracy, 230; and literacy, 229; of nonliterates, 224
linguistic description, 216
linguistic elements, in self-accounting, 143
linguistic knowledge: levels of, 6, 226; of literate/nonliterate speakers of English, 215–26, 228–30
linguistic production, modality hypothesis regarding, 254–5
linguistic relativity hypothesis, 229–30
linguistic theory, 13, 231n1
linguistic usage, in autobiography, 136
linguistics, linguists, 16, 215–17, 223, 229–30, 251–2

lip movement (reading), 25, 206
listening, 131, 258–9
literacy, 1, 2, 18, 77, 116, 189, 217–24, 227; and acquisition of language, 216; adult, 107–8; in aphasiological analysis, 217; archival function of, 253; in *Canterbury Tales*, 126n6; characterization and implications of, 177–97; cognitive implications of, 1, 178, 185–90, 256; and community, 107–8; conditions necessary for development of, 252–4; among Cree, 90–104; and culture change, 149–52; and decontextualization, 67, 72, 80, 81, 86; diffusion of, 208; early writing systems and, 20; education and, 263; effects of, 2–3, 66, 106, 190; and evolution, 23, 24; general considerations in characterization of, 180–4; and grammar, 223–4; as instrument of oppression, 105–8; intellectual advantages of, 6–7; and intensionality, 229–30; jokes and, 122; in language acquisition, 217; levels of, 184; and linguistic competence, 215; as metalinguistic activity, 251–70; and modernity, 146–7, 152, 251; morphology and, 222; and objectivity, 149–64; and orality, 1–2, 123, 166–72, 258; polyglot quality of, 169; properties of, independent of writing, 165; psychological effects of, 77–82; role of technology in, 183–4, 185, 189, 190; and self-consciousness, 146–7; and semiliteracy, 29; as signifying practice, 4–5; as social condition/state of mind, 11; social group acquisition of, 50; and social/psychological change, 1, 160; syntax and, 223; teaching of, 21–2; textual, 5, 107, 180; thinking through, 165–73; vernacular, 111–12
literacy hypothesis, 5, 251–2; criticisms of, 177–8, 180, 189; factors in, 252–4; and Indian tradition, 177–89; issues underlying, 180–4
literacy–lateralization issue, 238–46
literacy–thought relationships, 264–6; hypothesis regarding, 254–60
literary criticism, 17, 55
literary inventions, 111
literate ideas/practices: institutionalization/technologization of, 183–4
literate mind: exile of, 41–5; self and society in, 39–41
literate/nonliterate speakers of English: linguistic skills of, 215–26, 228–30
literate space, 42, 44, 45
literate tradition/society, 1, 2; ability to

## Subject index

participate in, 254; evolution of, 160; written text in, 266
literateness, 107; levels of, 185, 186; reflection in, 185, 189
literature, 7, 35, 98, 116, 123; in ancient world, 208–9; clerical literacy and, 38; Greek literacy and, 24; Indian, 178–80
liturgy, of schooling, 30–2
lives: possible, 134; as texts, 129–30, 136
locatives, 144
Locke, John, 156
locution, 51–2, 54–5, 56; in oral artful genres, 59, 60, 61–2
logic, 40–1, 81, 86, 258; alphabetic literacy and, 177; formal, 227
logicality, 75–7
logograms (Chinese), 199, 200
logographs, 201, 260
*Logopoeia*, 123
lying, 112–13; in Chaucer, 112, 117, 123; origin of consciousness in, 132

Mandeville, Bernhard, 32
marked (the), or new, 50
marked forms, 56, 58
Marx, Karl, 32
mass-communication technologies, and Cree literacy, 94–5
matching data (aphasia), 241–2, 243, 244–5
mathematical notation, 195n12
Mayans, 147
meaning, 52, 200, 266; in oral artful genres, 59, 61
media, 14, 168
medium hypothesis, 6–7, 252, 255–7, 266–7
*Memories of a Catholic Girlhood* (McCarthy), 131
memorization, 3, 26, 50; in Greek education, 23, 25; of oral texts, 17, 178, 179, 191; rote, 201, 202
memory, 24, 26, 39, 78, 134; autobiography as representation of, 130, 132, 133–4; Chaucer's use of, 116–18; episodic, 134, 135, 136; lay, 39–41; limitations of, 50, 56; literate, 112; in oral cultures, 34–5; reconstruction of, 50, 136; as text, 112, 131; transmission systems in, 134–5
mental (the), priority of, 156
mental language, 254
mental modeling, 83, 87
mental processing, 29, 108
mental skills, 5–6
mental skills hypothesis, 6–7, 252, 257–8, 266–7

mental space, 29, 32–5, 40; new, 35, 42
mental-state terms, 61, 158, 159–60, 263, 266
mentalism, 153, 160
Merlin, 122–3
metalanguage, 106; oral, 47–65, 254, 260–4, 265, 266
metalinguistic (term), 230–1n1
metalinguistic awareness, 259, 260, 261
metalinguistic hypothesis, 6–7, 252, 258–60, 264–7
metalinguistic structure, levels of, 263–4
metalinguistics, 231n1; literacy as, 6, 251–70
metaphor, 51, 53–4, 55, 57, 59; in visualization of self, 28, 29
method, 190, 196n14
metrics, 179
Middle Ages, 2, 4, 39, 111, 152, 160, 210; codex of, 36–7; French, 169–70; narration in, 112; nature as God's book in, 154; shift from verse to prose in, 169–70; textual community in, 256; truth in, 113
mind: cybernetic, 29, 44, 45; formed by act of inventing self, 133, 145–6; literate, 29–30, 34, 36, 37; *see also* modern mind
mind-set: and acquisition of clerical literacy, 28, 29, 45; schooling and, 31–2
minimal pairs test, 219
Mishnah, 56
mnemonics, 116–17, 188, 201, 209, 253
*Mnemosyne* (Homer), 117, 118
mnemotechnics, *Rigveda*, 178, 179, 186–7, 196n13
modality hypothesis, 6–7, 252, 254–5, 257, 266–7
model(s), 185, 186, 187t
modern mind, 4; oral–literate equation and, 11–27; self-consciousness determinant of, 146
modern thought, 1, 4; written prose in, 2
modernity, 2, 106, 146–7; literacy and, 1, 7, 105, 146–7, 152, 251
morphemes, 221–2; intensional/extensional, 224, 228
morphemic analysis, 221–2, 226
morphemic knowledge, 217–24
morphological analysis, 225
morphology, 215, 217, 221–2, 229
music, 231–2n2; Indian tradition, 179, 187–8, 191–4
musical notation, 212n8
myth(s), 12, 26, 77, 78; Chinook, 61–2
myth making, education and, 31, 32

naming data (aphasia), 242, 244–5
*narratio*, 123
narration: and autobiography, 136; in Chaucer, 116–17, 120; in Middle Ages, 112, 119
narrative, 111–12, 118; about self, 136–45, 146; verisimilitude in, 132
narrativization, 24, 25
natural language, 5, 182, 183, 189
nature, 177, 181; as book of God, 161, 177; interpretation of, 151, 152; objectivity of, 154–60
Near East, 15; craft literacy in, 72, 79
Newton, Sir Isaac, 155
*1984* (Orwell), 42–4
nonliterate cultures, 50
nonliterates: and given–interpretation distinction, 156–60; grammar of, 223–4; linguistic knowledge of, 217–24; and morphological analysis, 221–2; sentence comprehension of, 222–3
nonreaders, 257
Northern Ojibway, 91–2, 101
notation, 170, 182, 198–9; alphabetic, 42; musical, 212n8; nonalphabetic, 39, 45; oral, in Indian tradition, 187–8, 191–4
Nuer (people), 75–6

oath (the), 38, 39–40, 113
object, made in language by writing, 260, 261, 262, 264, 265
objectivity, 4, 75, 149–64; of nature, 154–60; and rise of modern science, 161; of texts, 153–4
observation, 155, 156, 160, 161
Odysseus, 113
*On the Lie* (Augustine), 113
ontogenetic development, 227
oppression, literacy as instrument of, 105–8
*Oral and the Written Gospel, The* (Kelber), 17
oral artful genres, *see* artful oral genres
oral communication, 21, 29; rules of, 17–18
oral composition, 13, 78, 178, 253
oral consciousness, 17
oral culture(s), 2, 48; features characterizing, 3; oral genres in, 2, 62; rational thought in, 66–89; text fixing in, 157–8; word in, 34–5, 39–40
oral devices, in poetry, 116
oral discourse, 1, 2
oral forms, 1–2
oral genres, 48, 57, 62; anthropological literature on, 47–8; comparable to written, 48–53, 56–7; of Ilongot, 57; *see also* artful oral genres
oral inheritance, 20–2, 26; and education, 21–2
oral language, 267; form/meaning in, 153; *see also* speech
oral memory, 22; rhythms in, 25–6
oral metalanguage, 47–65, 254, 260–4, 265, 266
oral mode, 185–6; articulation in, 182, 183; in Cree communication, 100–1; interaction context-bound in, 181; literacy and, 180, 183
oral production, different from written, 254–5
oral reading, 201; in ancient world, 208–9; by syllables, 205, 206
oral tradition: in Indian literature, 178–80; literate underpinnings of, 179; in text fixing, 253
oral utterance, decoding of, 166–7
oral word, 16
oralism (term), 11, 12
orality, 1, 2, 12, 251; in *Canterbury Tales*, 117; and community, 107; as distinct system, 107; effects of, 106; historical dimension of, 16–17, 20–1, 26; jokes in, 120; language behavior underpinning, 181; lie in, 113; and literacy, 5, 123, 166–72, 185; precedents of, 13–17; primary, 16; schools of, 106; term, 11
*Orality and Literacy* (Ong), 12
orality–literacy hypothesis, 2; *see also* literacy hypothesis
oral–literate equation, 11–27, 107, 168; epistemological break in, 12, 29–30, 34–5, 42–5; Greek inheritance in, 22–6; inheritors of, 17–19; precedents of, 13–17; in representations and their uses, 182; spatial representations in, 188, 189; theoretic order on, 19–26
oralization, 202, 206; in ancient reading, 209
oratory, 2, 47, 64n4; Ilongot, 57–61
organization (concepts), cross-cultural variations in, 82–3
originality, 78, 81, 111; in Chaucer, 112
orthography, 215, 229, 230, 252, 260, 262, 267; alphabetic, 232n2; and intensionality, 227–8; and language as object of reflection, 262–3; linguistic function of, 230; and metalinguistics, 261; as representation of linguistic intuitions, 230

Pacific Islanders, 68, 73
pagination, 209

*paideia*, 33
Palestine, 17, 20
Papua-New Guinea, 68, 69, 82
*Paradise Lost* (Milton), 25
pedagogical space, 35
pedagogy, 42, 107; in teaching reading, 198, 200–2, 203, 205; *see also* education
penmanship, 37–8
*Pensée sauvage, La* (Lévi-Strauss), 12
perception, 26, 29, 134
perceptually based utterances, 172
perlocution, 50, 63n1
perspectivalism, 138, 139, 140, 146
perspective, 34, 184
perspectively based utterances, 172
Petrarch, Francesco, 119
*Phaedrus* (Plato), 35
*Philebus* (Plato), 121
philosophers, 22–3, 34
philology, comparative, 16
philosophy, 2, 7, 18, 24; oral–literate question in, 18–19
Phoenicians, 21; alphabet, 206, 207; writing system, 14–15
phoneme, 16, 165, 166, 205; intensional, 226, 227
phoneme deletion, 218–20
phonemic awareness controversy, 261–2, 264
phonemic knowledge, 217–24, 226
phonetic alphabet, 267
phonetics, 16, 179, 201, 203, 217
phonology, 215, 217, 218–20, 228
phylogeny, 227
physiological process, in reading, 198, 199–200, 203, 204, 211
picture writing, 195n9
poet, 35, 114, 253
poetry, 34–5, 48, 85; oral devices in, 115–16
*Politics* (Aristotle), 33
Polynesia, 15, 16
population size, 3; and decontextualization, 72–3, 74, 86
postliteracy, 29
Pound, Ezra, 123
*Preface to Plato* (Havelock), 12
preliterate stage, 106
printing, 14, 184, 190; and modern science, 149, 150–1; and utterance–text distinction, 177
printing press, 4, 18, 30, 37, 41, 42; as agent of change, 149–50
*Printing Press as an Agent of Change, The* (Eisenstein), 18
propositional thinking, 83, 87
prose, 25–6, 156, 251, 256, 259; Platonic, 23, as product of literacy, 2; shift to, from verse, 169
Protestant Reformation, 149–51, 152, 153–4, 160
Protocole MT-86 d'Examen Linguistique de l'Aphasie, 241
proton emission tomography scanners, 200
psychoanalysis, 134, 135–6
psychobiology, 236
psycholinguistics, 217
psychological change, 7, 149, 160, 254
psychology of literacy, 5–7
public, 256
punctuation, 210, 229, 263

Quechua (language), 157

Rabelais, François, 123
radio, 12; and Cree literacy, 95, 100, 101
*Ramus: Method and Decay of Dialogue* (Ong), 15
ratiocination, 189
Rashi, 56
rational thought, in oral culture, 66–89
rationality, 75–7, 81, 258; of illiterates/nonliterates, 105
reader(s), 41, 115, 206, 217, 256; as audience, 4; professional, 209; skills involved in becoming, 257–8; and word separation, 210–11
reading, 36, 166, 169, 255, 264; ambiguities in, 15; in antiquity, 208–10; development of, 198, 199, 200; in education, 21–2; genres as modes of, 131; in lay literacy, 29; metalinguistic awareness in, 259; and thought, 265–6; transcultural comparative, 199–200; word separation and physiology of, 198–214; and writing, 5–6, 170; *see also* silent reading
reading aloud, 203, 211n4; *see also* oralization
reading skills, 206, 216, 230, 257–8; acquisition of, 237, 238; and intensional competence, 227–8
reality, 112, 133
reasoning, 29, 30, 183, 259
recitation, 21–2, 202, 203
record keeping, 38, 184
reference concepts, 158
reference reading, 201, 208
reflection, 5, 47, 48, 50, 52, 56, 75, 156; and articulation, 181; language and, 180–1, 261, 266; and literateness, 107, 185, 189; metalinguistic, 258–60, 262; reflecting on, 57; text fixing and,

52; on texts, 266; writing and, 189
reflective process, 185, 186
reinterpretation, of life accounts, 129, 146
relative clause formation, 73–4
religion, 153; printing and, 149–51
remembering, 116–18; *see also* memory
*Remembering* (Bartlett), 135
Renaissance, 30, 160
repetition, 86; as oratorical device, 120
repetition data (aphasia), 242, 243–5
representation, 29, 149, 183, 184; in autobiography, 136; modalities of, 186–90, 187t; of Greeks, 182; of reflective process, 185; techniques relating to, 186
*Rerum Memorandum Libri* (Petrarch), 119
research tradition, 150, 160
rhetoric, 15, 120, 177, 209
rhythm(s), 24, 25–6
right hemisphere (brain), 246, 247n2
Riemann, Georg Friedrich Bernhard, 33
*Rigveda*, 77; textual tradition relating to, 178–9, 186–7
ritual, 2, 179
role theory, 42–3
Roman Empire, 208, 209
rote memorization, in learning to read, 201, 202
Royal Society of London, 155–6
rubrics, 168, 170

Samoans, 157
Sanskrit, 207, 210
say–mean distinction, 2
scaling, 188
scarcity, 32–3
schematizing systems, 134, 135, 136
schooling, 253, 259; liturgy of, 30–2; *see also* education
science, 2, 5, 18, 35, 38, 182; Greek literacy and, 24; in Indian tradition, 179; rise of modern, 4, 149–64
scientific epistemology, and hermeneutics, 152, 154–60, 177
scientific hypothetical thought, 83–4
scribal literacy, 107; defined, 2
scribes, 208, 210
script(s), 40, 253; Graeco-Latin, 206–7; *see also* syllabic scripts
script literacy, 5, 180, 183, 184, 187, 189; absence of, in Indian tradition, 191; technology underpinning literateness, 185
*scriptura continua*, 202, 206–8, 209
self, 1, 157; concepts of, 2, 134, 181; invention of, 4, 52, 129–48; lay, 39–41; metaphors in visualization of, 28,

29; mind formed by act of inventing, 145–6; as narrator/as subject, 132, 133, 146; thinking, 112
self-accounting, 136, 146; beginning with language, 146; in family cuture, 142–5; generic, 138–40; textualization in, 137; *see also* self-report
self-articulation, 182, 183, 184, 189
self-consciousness, 29, 47, 48, 137; as determinant of modern mind, 146; family and management of, 146; historical transformation of, 4; literacy and, 146–7
self-expression, articulated, 180–1
self–I distinction, 44, 132
self-location, 133, 136, 140; in family, 141–5
self-report, 4, 129, 130–1; act of, 132; false, 132; interpretation in, 135–6
semantic memory, 134–5, 136
Semitic languages, 208
sentences, complex, 115, 125nn3, 4
sentence comprehension, 222–3
sequence(ing), 78, 138, 139, 146; and adjacency, 224, 225
silent reading, 5–6, 36, 37, 200, 201, 203; by ancients, 205; and comprehension, 206
*Singer of Tales, The* (Lord), 13
Slavic languages, 210
social alexia, 237; neurological point of view in, 236–50
social change: book in, 18; literacy and, 7, 106, 160, 190
social communication, orality in, 16–17
social dyslexia, 237
social institutions, thought in maintenance of, 70, 71, 86
social groups, created around texts, 256
social integration, integrative thought in service of, 71–5
social organization, and literacy, 7, 251, 252, 254
social reality: education and, 31, 32; lay literacy and, 28
social relations, contextualized by jokes, 122
socialization, 33, 145
society, 1; concepts of, 2, 181; prehistoric, 20–1
sound(s), 263; intensional, 227; linguistic, 24–5; and spelling, 107; *see also* speech sound(s)
sound mechanisms, 16
space, 181
spatial deictics, 73, 144
spatial modality, 186, 188–9, 190
spatiotemporal modality, 186, 188

speaking, 258–9; as distinctive form of discourse, 255–7; formal/informal, 80–1; genres as modes of, 131
specification, 180
speech, 7, 24–5, 45, 229; as communication, 43–4; dividing continuum of, 226; identification of language with, 215, 229; segmentation of, 232n2; transmogrified into thought, 112
speech-act terms, 158, 159–60
speech acts, referring to, 263, 264, 266
speech community, size of, 72–4
speech sound(s), 42, 207, 232n2; specialization of organs articulating, 20, 24
spelling, 107; see also orthography(ies)
spells, language of, 51, 52, 57
spoken language; differences from written, 256; exposure to and functional lateralization, 236, 237; see also oral language
spoken word, in Cree communication, 100–1
Steiner, George, 112
stories, 51, 118, 130, 134
storytelling, 49, 114, 118, 123
straight speech, 51, 57
*Study of Writing, A* (Gelb), 14–15
style, in autobiography, 133, 138, 139, 146
subjectivity, 4, 156
subordinating conjunctions, 81
subordinative-additive, 78
suffixes, 225
Sumer, Sumerians, 20, 21
*Summa Theologia* (Aquinas), 154
Swahili, 71
syllabary method, 201, 207
syllabic literacy (Cree): history of, 94; invention of, 92–4; spread of, 94–6, 97, 102–3; transmission of, 96–7, 98–103
syllabic scripts, 5; of Cree, 90–104, 107
syllable, as minimal unit of analysis, 232n2
syllable recognition, 205, 206–7
syntactic devices, 85–6
syntactic knowledge, 217–24
syntactic rules, 223, 224, 226
syntax, 24, 132, 207, 215, 217, 222–3; activist, 25; and intensionality, 225, 229; of performative speech, 19; reflective, 25
Syriac, 208

*tabla* (percussion instrument), 187–8, 191–4
Tabla Bols, 107

*Tale of Genji, The*, 79
talk: reference to, 158; about talk, 60, 61–2; see also discourse; speaking
Talmudic scholarship, 17–18
teaching process; see pedagogy
technology(ies), 179, 196n14; and literateness, 107, 190; supporting reflective process, 183–4, 185, 189
telephone, Cree use of, 3, 100, 101
television, 12, 95, 101
temporal modality, 186, 188, 189–90
text(s), 16, 185, 186, 207, 265; accumulation of, 98, 106, 253; assigning meaning to, 190; authoritative, 160; autonomous, 259; backgrounding, 256; in Chaucer, 115; cognitive value of written, 170–2; as constitutive metaphor for existence, 38; contingent on author, 114; creation of, 50, 107; deconstruction of, 17–18; form of, 198; and genre, 131; Greek, 210; hidden realities in, 18–19; ideal, 160; institutions for using, 253; and interpretation, 47; lives as, 129–30, 136; memory as, 112; metalanguage and, 254, 262–4, 265; objectivity of, 153–4; observation–inference distinction in, 156; ontological status of, 111–12; in oral cultures, 2, 52, 53; oral delivery of, 209; printed, 18; religious, 97–8; *Rigveda* as, 178–9; story of, 28, 35–41; in study of reading, 199; visible, 39, 40, 41, 42; written, 106–7, 152, 170–2
text–context relationship, 165–6
text fixing, 50, 51–2, 77, 86, 263–4; devices for, 253; oral, 106–7, 263; in artful oral genres, 54–6, 60–1; in oral cultures, 3, 157–8; through writing, 151, 263
text–interpretation distinction, 2, 177; in autobiography, 132; lacking in preliterate cultures, 106; and objectivity of nature, 154–60; in oral genres, 48–53, 56–7, 59–61; and rise of modern science, 152, 153–4, 160–1
text making, 106, 260; in motivated memory, 131
text revision, 255, 265
textual communities, 115, 256
textual literacy, 5, 107, 180
textual tradition, 179–80, 186, 190–1; of *Rigveda*, 178–9
textualization, in self-accounting, 137, 146
theme, 133, 143, 144, 146
theology, 7, 152, 154
theories, 81, 147

## Subject index

thinking/thought, 4, 83, 112, 134; critical, 170; differentiated/integrated, 66–70, 71–2; functional basis of, 70–5; hypothetical, 83–4, 155; language as object of, 258–60, 264, 266, 267; linear, 18, 42; literacy and, 264–6; modern, 1, 2, 4; rational, in oral culture, 66–89; *see also* literacy–thought relationship; Western thought
Thoth (god of writing), 119
time, 125nn3, 4, 181; *see also* temporal modality
timelessness, 139–40, 140t, 146
torture, 40, 43, 113
trail signs (Cree), 99–100, 107
transcription, 198–202, 206–7, 208, 211n2
transmission: oral, cultural, 133–4; in Indian literature, 178, 179, 191; and the past, 133–4
trial by ordeal, 40, 152
tribal encyclopedia, 23
tribal societies, 16
Trobriand Islanders, 77
truth/falsity, 113–14, 118, 265
*Turing Machine*, 29, 42
*tuydek*, 57–8, 63n1
Twain, Mark, 118

uncial script, 209
universals, 1–2, 5, 52–3, 64n2
unmarked, genre as, 50
untruth, fictive, 118
utterance–situation relationship, 165–6, 168, 170–2
utterance–text distinction, 177
utterances, manipulation of, 170

Vai (people), 72, 147, 202–3, 246, 251; literacy of, 257–8; text fixing by, 253
Vai script, 92
values, communal, 79
Vedas, 52, 178–9; *see also Rigveda*
Vedic tradition, 106, 253, 267
verbs: metalinguistic/metacognitive, 158–60; stative/action, 132
verisimilitude, 117, 132, 167
verse, 2, 169; *see also* poetry
Vietnamese language, 199
Virgil, 35
*vis imaginativa*, 112
*vis phantastica*, 112
visual field, 203–4, 206
visual–graphic techniques, 182, 183
vocalic writing, 208
vocalization, 203, 205
*voluntas fallendi*, 113

vowels, 206–8

Walras, Léon, 32
Wana (Indonesia), 2, 264
Wana poetry (*kiyori*), 47, 53–7, 264
Western European culture, 5, 182, 189; effect of Greek alphabet on, 177, 178; literacy in changes in, 184, 190; outrage in, 41–2; representational modalities in, 189–90
Western man: of McLuhan, 226–8
Western thought, 2–3, 66, 67; decontextualization in, 68–70, 72–82, 86–7
whole-word method, 202
word (the): lack of, in oral culture, 34–5, 39–40; poetic, 25–6; technologies of, 14, 30; *see also* oral word; written word
word order, 205, 207
word recognition, 199, 201, 202, 205, 206, 208, 258
word separation, 5–6, 36–7, 201, 203–5, 208–10, 263; and division between antique cultures and those of modern Occident, 210–11; and physiology of reading, 198–214
words, 51; Cree, 98–9, 99t; function, 216–17, 221; marked, 50; morphemic constituents of, 221–2
world(s): conceptualization of, 232n2; modeled, 185, 186; new, 184; real, 185, 186
world articulation, 182–3, 184, 189
writer, 167–8, 170, 254; and context, 169; skills involved in becoming, 257–8
writing, 11, 35, 50, 106, 153, 166, 184; and abstract thought, 78; and adult literacy, 107; advantage of, in text fixing, 253; ancient, 208; cognitive effects of, 189, 255; comprehension split by, 160; as decontextualized, 5; as distinctive form of discourse, 255–7; in education, 21–2; effects of, 251; to elaborate different kind of representation of reality, 168–9; in emergence of autonomous psyche, 177; in enforcing articulation, 181–2; in fixing locution, 51, 52; formal/informal, 80–1; genres as modes of, 131; inadequate for engineered world, 182; in Indian tradition, 179, 191; language as object of, 265, 266, 267; in lay literacy, 29; and literacy, 165–72, 264; in low culture, 52; as memory and composition aid, 78–9; as metalinguistic activity, 7, 260–6; necessity of, 47–8, 53, 183; in permitting revi-

sion, 261; playful, 123, 126n9; and reading, 170; and reflection, 189; role of, in thought, 265–6; technologies for, in Cree syllabic script, 97; as technology of literacy, 189; text fixing through, 56–7, 151; in twelfth- and thirteenth-century England, 38; uniqueness of, 170, 257; vocalic, 208; as way of recording language, 215, 266, 267

writing materials, 167; Cree, 97

writing skills: acquisition of, 237, 238, 245

writing systems, 14–15, 147, 206–7, 227, 260; and cognitive processes, 6–7; as grammars, 230; and mental skills relevant to reading, 5–6; and oral metalanguage, 260, 261, 262, 263; pre-Greek, 20, 21; representation of language in, 215, 266, 267

written communication, 29

written discourse, forms of, 155–6

written genres, comparable to oral genres, 48–53, 56–7

written language, 2, 215, 260, 265; cognitive significance of, 257; differences of, from oral, 254–5, 256

written prose, 2

written texts, 1, 106–7, 152, 211, 266; in administration of justice, 152; cognitive value of, 170–2; decoding of, 160–8; distinctive properties of, 256

written word, 18; communication through, 106; distrust of, 17; use of, among Cree, 109

Yugoslavia, 17, 22